Teacher's Book

Anita Warwick

Series editor: John Jackman

Text © Anita Warwick, 2003
Illustrations © Nelson Thornes 2003

The right of Anita Warwick to be identified as author of this work has been asserted by her in accordance with the Copyright, Designs and Patents Act 1988.

All rights reserved. No part of this publication may be reproduced or transmitted in any form or by any means, electronic or mechanical, including photocopy, recording or any information storage and retrieval system, without permission in writing from the publisher or under licence from the Copyright Licensing Agency Limited, of Saffron House, 6–10 Kirby Street, London EC1N 8TS.

Any person who commits any unauthorised act in relation to this publication may be liable to criminal prosecution and civil claims for damages.

Published in 2003 by:
Nelson Thornes Ltd
Delta Place
27 Bath Road
CHELTENHAM
GL53 7TH
United Kingdom

10 / 10 9 8 7

A catalogue record for this book is available from the British Library

ISBN 978 0 7487 6997 1

Cover illustration by Lisa Smith
Logo by Woody Fox
Page make-up by Green House Design and IFA Design

Printed by Multivista Global Ltd

CONTENTS

1 INTRODUCTION

Like it or not, the quality and fluency of a child's handwriting is often the basis on which performance judgements are made. But of greater importance, the ability to write legibly and appropriately is a skill without which children will not be able to reach and demonstrate their true potential throughout their school careers. Historically, handwriting models have been prescriptive and inflexible. *Nelson Handwriting's* enormous popularity has arisen from its underlying principle and approach; leading through carefully structured stages to the encouragement and development of an individual style in each child, rather than an inflexible 'one model fits all' approach to handwriting.

Nelson Handwriting is the definitive course for developing a fluent and legible handwriting style. Nelson Handwriting has established a national reputation based on its fluent, legible script and its careful progression from pre-writing patterns to the development of an individual style. The new edition builds on this firm foundation but takes into account the current demands of the statutory curricula and of practising teachers.

Nelson Handwriting provides a clearly structured programme with full coverage of the technical aspects of writing (including letter formation, basic joins, printing, speedwriting and slope). These are taught in meaningful and curriculum-relevant contexts, particularly in the areas of punctuation, spelling and vocabulary.

Increased provision has been made in this edition for the Foundation stage with Workbooks 1–4. Exit flicks are used from the beginning of the programme, and joined writing is now taught in Red level.

The page design is clear and accessible, using full colour in the Developing Skills books and two colours in the Workbooks. Each unit of work in the Developing Skills books has a clear focus which is followed by opportunities for extra practice and extension for the more able pupils. The Developing Skills books may be used for whole class teaching and support and extension resource sheets are provided to cater for individual needs.

There is provision for both group and individual assessment, with an emphasis on self-assessment throughout the programme.

NELSON HANDWRITING AT A GLANCE

Handwriting Skills											
Work books						Developing Skills					
1	2	3	4	5	6	Red	Yellow	1	2	3	4
Handwriting patterns Pencil control Hand-eye co-ordination Presentation											
	Letter formation (lower case) Overwriting										
		Numerals									
			Capitals Underwriting Word spacing Full stops Sentences Letter spacing								
				Copywriting from a model							
				The four joins and the break letters						Fluency	
							Printing				
								Writing with a slope Decorated capitals Punctuation			
									Speedwriting		
										Presentation Paragraphs Individual style Difficult joins	
											Hand-writing for different purposes
Spelling											
Initial letter sounds											
		cvc words									
				Vowels/consonants Magic e Alphabetical order	Vowel + consonant modifier	Rhyming words	Consonant digraphs Consonant blends				
							Double consonants		Vowel digraphs		
									Triple consonants blends		Silent letters
										Word endings	Suffixes
											Difficult spellings Prefixes

Genres
The materials make use of many different writing contexts including poetry and rhyme, environmental print, labelling, recipes, plays, letters, form filling and report writing as well as narrative. Children are also asked to draft, edit, revise and present their ideas.

HANDWRITING AND THE STATUTORY REQUIREMEN

Aims

Nelson Handwriting has been developed in response to the aims of the statutory curricula for handwriting:

- Children should be taught joined up writing 'as soon as possible once children are secure in the movements of each letter.' (England Wales: *Developing early writing*)
- Children should be taught handwriting that culminates in a joined script that is a 'neat, fluent, legible style of handwriting'. (Scotland: *English 5–14 Guidelines*)
- This should be achieved through 'purposeful, guided practice'. (Northern Ireland: *English Programmes of Study and Attainment Targets*)
- Children should be taught a style of handwriting that follows the conventions of English, including: 'writing from left to right and from top to bottom of the page; starting and finishing letters correctly; regularity of size and shape of letter; regularity of spacing letters and words'. (England and Wales: *English in the National Curriculum*)
- Children should develop 'an awareness of the importance of clear, neat presentation' (England and Wales: English in the National Curriculum) and to 'set out work, giving attention to presentation and layout'. (Scotland: *English 5–14 Guidelines*)
- Children should be 'taught to use different forms of handwriting for different purposes, e.g. print for labelling maps or diagrams; a clear, neat hand for finished, presented work; a faster script for notes'. (England and Wales: *English in the National Curriculum*)

England and Wales

Age	4–5	Workbooks 1–4		Level 1
	5–6	Workbooks 5–6		Levels 2/3
	5–6	Developing skills	Red	Levels 2/3
	6–7		Yellow	Level 3
	7–8		1	Level 3
	8–9		2	Level 4
	9-10		3	Levels 4/5
	10-11		4	Levels 4/5

These extracts from the key documents and programmes of study provide a backdrop to *Nelson Handwriting*.

Guidance from the Foundation Stage

Early Learning Goals for handwriting. Use a pencil and hold it effectively to form recognisable letters, most of which are correctly formed.

- Give children extensive practice in writing letters, for example labelling their work, making cards, writing notices.
- Continue writing practice in imaginative contexts, joining some letters if appropriate, for example 'at', 'it', 'on'.
- Intervene to help children hold a pencil effectively.
- Use opportunities to help children form letters correctly, for example when they label their paintings.

English in the National Curriculum

Programmes of study - KS1

In order to develop a legible style, pupils should be taught:

- how to hold a pencil/pen
- to write from left to right and top to bottom of a page
- to start and finish letters correctly
- to form letters of regular size and shape.
- to put regular spaces between letters and words
- how to form lower-case and upper-case letters
- the importance of clear and neat presentation in order to communicate their meaning effectively.

Programmes of Study – KS2

Pupils should be taught to:

- write legibly in both joined and printed styles with increasing fluency and speed
- use different forms of handwriting for different purposes (for example, print for labelling maps, or diagrams, a clear, neat hand for finished presented work, a faster script for notes.

Scotland

Age 4–5	Workbooks 1–4		Level A
5–6	Workbooks 5–6		Levels A/B
5–6	Developing Skills	Red	Levels A/B
6–7		Yellow	Level B
7–8		1	Level B/C
8–9		2	Level C
9-10		3	Levels C/D
10-11		4	Levels C/D

A Curriculum Framework for Children 3-5

Children should learn to:

- Experiment with symbols, letters, and in some cases, words in writing.

English 5-14 Guidelines

Programmes of study for Handwriting and Presentation

Level A Pupils will spend much of their time drawing and using material to develop hand-eye co-ordination. Pupils will be introduced systematically to letter formation and word spacing. . . At an appropriate stage, linkage of letters will be taught.

Levels B/C The process of development will continue, with the aim being to help pupils build up an easy flow which will not hamper the train of thought. The teacher will take time to ensure pupils lay out and present their writing in a neat, legible form which aids the reader. The eventual outcome will be that the pupil can consistently employ a fluent, legible style of handwriting.

Levels D/E As pupils gain experience across a wide variety of forms, from verse to scripts, from prose to diagrams, the teacher will point out the positive effects of careful, imaginative layout and presentation. This will be more significant if pupils are given regular opportunities to publish and display completed work both in and out of the classroom.

Northern Ireland

Age 4–5	Workbooks 1–4		Level 1
5–6	Workbooks 5–6		Levels 1/2
5–6	Developing Skills	Red	Levels 1/2
6–7		Yellow	Levels 2/3
7–8		1	Level 3
8–9		2	Levels 3/4
9-10		3	Levels 4/5
10-11		4	Levels 4/5

English Programmes of Study and Attainment Targets

Programmes of study – KS1
Teachers should take account of the attainment of pupils in writing when they begin school and provide opportunities for them to progress in the manipulative, creative and secretarial aspects of writing. Pupils should progress from having some control over size and shape of letters towards handwriting that is accurately formed and consistent in size. Pupils should develop the ability to use the conventional ways of forming letters in upper and lower case.

Programmes of study – KS2
Pupils should progress from using upper and lower case letters towards handwriting which is well-formed, swift and legible. Pupils should develop the ability to use a swift and legible style of handwriting.

HOW *NELSON HANDWRITING* WORKS

The **Developing Skills** books provide structured progression throughout the course. Each unit opens with a Focus in which the main objective of the lessons is clearly stated; this is then followed by Extra and Extension activities which increase in difficulty.

UNIT 1

Practising the first join.

un

Run, Mum. Run.

FOCUS

A Copy this pattern into your book.

B Copy these letters into your book.

un un un un un

um um um um um

Be careful! Make sure you take your pencil back up to the top before you start your next letter.

EXTRA

Make these words. Copy them into your book.

b + un = bun bun bun

m + um = mum mum mum

EXTENSION

Match a caption to each holiday snap and write them into your book.

Tip mum in.

Fun in a bun.

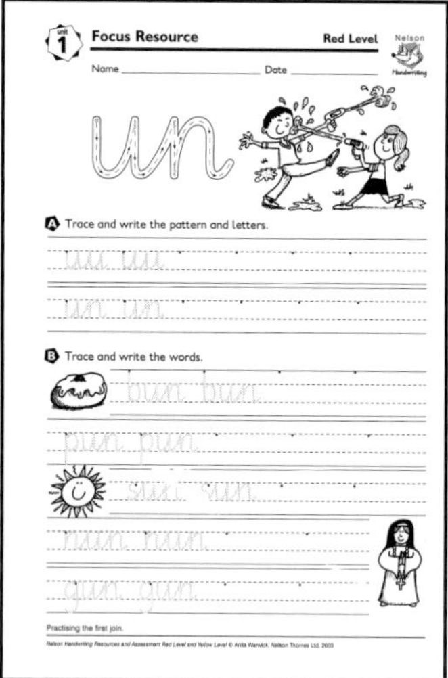

Focus Resource Red Level

Name Date

un

A Trace and write the pattern and letters.

B Trace and write the words.

Practising the first join.

The **Focus** Resource sheets provide consolidation and reinforcement of the basic teaching point.

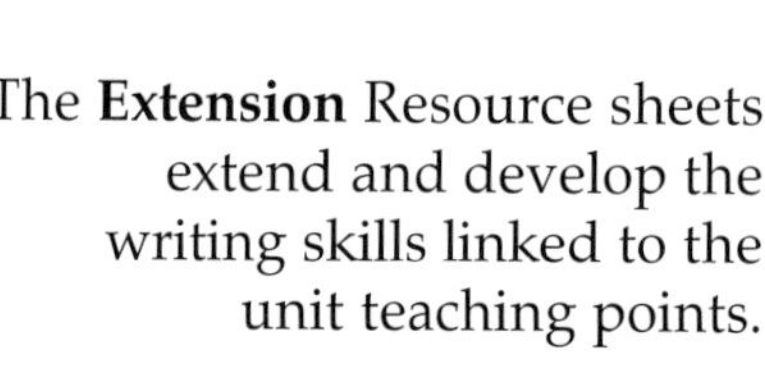

The **Extension** Resource sheets extend and develop the writing skills linked to the unit teaching points.

Extension Resource Red Level

Name Date

A Trace and write the letters and words.

B Trace and write the sentence.

Practising the first join.

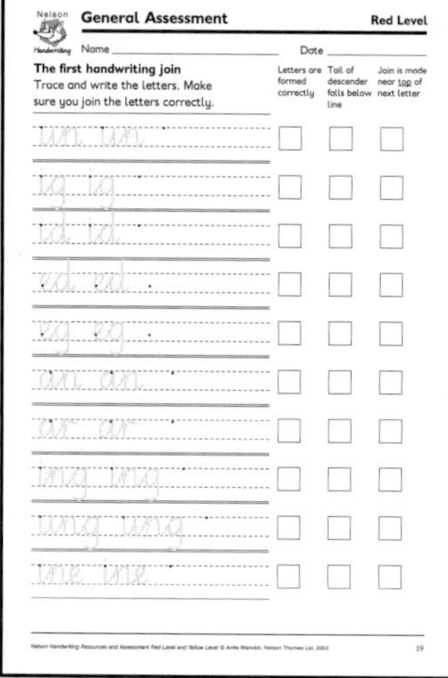

General Assessment Red Level

Name Date

The first handwriting join

Trace and write the letters. Make sure you join the letters correctly.

Letters are formed correctly | Tail of descender falls below line | Join is made near top of next letter

The **Resources and Assessment** books also contain an assessment section designed to monitor the children's handwriting progress.

The **Teacher's Book** fully supports all the components of *Nelson Handwriting*. It contains full lesson plans, references to separate Focus and Extension resources, as well as useful tips on how to develop and assess handwriting skills.

READY REFERENCE GUIDE

The letter forms

The lower-case alphabet for Workbooks 1–4

a b c d e f g h i j k l m
n o p q r s t u v w x y z

The lower-case alphabet for Developing Skills books, Resources and Assessment books Red, Yellow, 1, 2, 3, 4 and Workbooks 5 and 6.

a b c d e f g h i j k l m
n o p q r s t u v w x y z

A letter slope of 8° from the vertical to the right is introduced in *Developing Skills Book 1*.

a b c d e f g h i j k l m
n o p q r s t u v w x y z

The lower-case print alphabet

a b c d e f g h i j k l m
n o p q r s t u v w x y z

The capital letters

A B C D E F G H I J K L M N
O P Q R S T U V W X Y Z

These are the same throughout the scheme.

The numerals

1 2 3 4 5 6 7 8 9 0

The joining sets

Set 1

a c d e h i k l m
n s t u

Twelve letters with exit flicks plus **s**.

Set 2

a c d e g i j m n o
p q r s u v w x y

Nineteen letters which start at the top of the x-height

Set 3

b f h k l t

Six letters which start at the top of the ascender

Set 4

f o r v w

Five letters which finish at the top of the x-height

The break letters

b g j p q x y z

Eight letters after which no join is made. Joins are not made to or from the letter z.

The joins

	Set		Set		
The first join	1	→	2	in	am
The second join	1	→	3	ab	ch
The third join	4	→	2	oa	wo
The fourth join	4	→	3	wh	ob

The break letters bigger

The joined style

The quick brown fox jumps over the lazy dog.

Letter size

Book	*height of letter (mm)*
Workbooks 1–3	12 (reducing to 10 in Workbook 3)
Workbooks 4–6	10 (reducing to 8 in Workbook 6)
Developing Skills, Red Level	8
Developing Skills Yellow Level	7
Developing Skills Book 1	6
Developing Skills Book 2	5
Developing Skills Book 3	4
Developing Skills Book 4	4 (reducing to 3)

Guidelines are provided in the Resources and Assessment books.

The Resources and Assessment sheets for *Developing Skills Books 1* and 2 have plain ruled lines 10mm apart, and those for Developing Skills Books 3 and 4 are 8mm apart to reflect the lined paper that children are likely to be using.

Changes from the previous edition

- In accordance with best practice, joining is now introduced at Red level. Those schools not wishing to join letters from Red Level can use the Workbooks in the initial stages.

WHY USE JOINED HANDWRITING IN YEAR 1/P2?

From Developing Early Writing:

> *Skills for handwriting can be introduced from a very early stage.*
> *When should I introduce joined up writing?*
> *As soon as possible once children are secure in the movements of each letter.*

Many educationalists have put forward a variety of arguments to support the introduction of a cursive style of writing much earlier than is still current practice in many schools, although for many, up until now, these arguments have gone largely unheard.

The introduction of the National Curriculum, however, has caused many to reflect seriously upon the growing wealth of research evidence which supports the early introduction of a cursive style of writing. Not only is it now recognised as 'good practice', but it enables children to achieve well, at age 7, in the end-of-key-stage assessments.

The National Curriculum English orders state that:

> *Pupils should be taught the conventional ways of forming letters, both lower case and capitals. They should build on their knowledge of letter formation to join letters in words.*

We need to ensure that there is a smooth progression from young children's early graphic attempts to the fast, efficient hand that students need. Children need to be equipped with the skill to get their ideas down on paper. It is not a natural skill and must be taught carefully.

The influence of print script still remains today in the initial teaching of handwriting in many schools. Some say that it is the cause of many handwriting problems which are currently evident.

Benefits of teaching joined writing

1. *Letter formation*
   When a child is taught to join his or her writing, the ligatures (the small exit strokes used to join letters together) lead to the correct starting point for the next letter. As all letters start at the top, except 'd' and 'e', a cursive script aids correct letter formation right from the start.
2. *Letter spacing*
   When children are taught to join letters they also learn how to space letters. In cursive writing the joining stroke makes a natural space between letters and between words.
3. *Progression*
   Cursive writing follows on from the free scribble movements that children make when they first hold a pencil. If children are introduced to joined writing from the beginning, this natural sequence of developments is not broken. When children are taught print script they begin with scribbles and pattern-making but then learn disconnected forms and cramped movements. Later they learn joined writing. Moreover, many find it hard to progress from a print style of writing and therefore revert back to the disconnected letters they first learned at school. Others often produce a mixture of joins and print script. If joined writing is taught from the beginning it is no longer necessary to change from print to cursive in the junior years. Many teachers now recognise that we have been asking children to change their style of writing just at the stage when they are becoming increasingly creative. Changing from print to cursive understandably slows them down as they concentrate far more on the formation of the letters and the joins rather than the actual content of what they are writing. In many junior classrooms we often hear, 'How do I join this letter?' rather than, 'What shall I write?'
4. *Spelling*
   Charles Cripps (*Joining the ABC*, 1989) argues that when both handwriting and spelling are taught together it is clear that children become more confident and more aware of the structure of the words. With print script the writer concentrates on letter formation rather than seeing the word as a whole. As adults we can sometimes produce, for example, wall charts with misspellings because we are simply concentrating on the formation of the printed letters, rather than seeing the word as a whole.

   Peters (1986), in her book, *Spelling, Caught or Taught*? concludes that 'speed of writing is clearly basic to spelling progress'. She observed children writing very slowly as though they were drawing unrelated symbols rather than producing blocks of letters as whole words. With joined writing, children are able to see words as a whole. Since the English spelling system can often have more than one spelling for any sound (e.g. cup, done) spelling cannot be taught merely through listening. For spelling it is vital that children are taught to focus closely on the words they are learning to write. Early practice of writing from memory helps the children to meet the challenge of writing whole words. Most observers now recognise that spelling practice which is linked to phonics/letter strings and handwriting practices will help children improve their spelling.

5. *Speed of writing*
   Printing involves writing series of individual letters. Each letter requires the pencil to be put on the paper in the correct place to allow the correct letter formation. After each letter the pencil is lifted off the page. The child then has to decide where to start the next letter. Furthermore, letters and words often appear the same to young children. It can be difficult for them to know where to put the spaces. Joining, however, allows a flowing movement to develop. Words tend to be seen as a whole rather than as separate letters. It is not necessary to decide how and where to begin each letter as the writing flow aids letter formation. The ligatures automatically lead up to the correct starting place for the next letter.

6. *Development of motor-control skills*
   Introducing children to joined writing at an early age helps the development of their fine motor-control skills. Early pattern practice, followed by the writing of two- and then three-letter words, enables the child to practice basic handwriting movements.

7 TEACHING METHODS AND ORGANISATION

The role of the teacher

There is no single formula for success in the teaching of handwriting, but some basic principles are identifiable:

- Handwriting lessons should be in line with school policy and should build on what has gone before.
- As handwriting is a movement skill, demonstration by a competent teacher is essential.
- When children practice using models from the *Nelson Handwriting* materials, teachers should observe them carefully and be ready to intervene with support and encouragement.
- In the early stages of learning to write, the process is more important than the product. Irregular letter forms starting in the correct place with movement in the correct direction are to be preferred to uniformly regular letters achieved through wrong movements.
- Every effort should be made to prevent significant faults becoming ingrained habits that will be difficult to break.
  Common faults include:
  - faulty pencil/pen grip,
  - incorrect letter formation,
  - reversals and inversions,
  - poor posture and paper positioning.

Raising children's awareness of key points

The teacher's role in raising children's awareness of the technical aspects of handwriting is essential. *Nelson Handwriting* provides a clear development structure for teachers to refer to through demonstration and discussion. The fox boxes remind children of key points. Each Developing Skills book has a flap. On the flap there is a 'Getting ready to write' section, and on the reverse a 'Checklist'. These features encourage children to review their writing methods.

Terminology

As teachers demonstrate the skills of handwriting, it is important to describe the movements involved. Many teachers have developed their own user-friendly descriptors which are age-appropriate and which may involve mnemonics. However, there are some technical terms which are so useful in discussion about handwriting that it is important for pupils to understand them.

These include:

Clockwise, anticlockwise, vertical, horizontal, diagonal, parallel, ascender, descender, consonant, vowel, joined, sloped, x-height.

Whole-class and group teaching

To some extent the decision whether to take handwriting lessons with individuals, groups or whole classes is a matter of personal preference. However, the varied developmental stages of pupils and the need for sensible economy of time and effort also influence practice. The following suggestions should be considered:

- In the early stages, it seems appropriate to give handwriting lesson to small groups of children with similar levels of readiness and motor control. Individuals within each group may require specific help.
- Later on, as children come to understand the concept of written language and show evidence of developing control, it may be economical to work with large groups and whole classes.

Regular practice

In primary schools where class teachers are generally responsible for teaching handwriting to their own classes, there are many opportunities to practice the skills of handwriting in the course of writing across the curriculum. However, it is also necessary to provide regular lessons for the teaching and/or revision of handwriting skills.

The frequency and length of handwriting lessons is likely to vary according to the age and competence of the pupils. With young children it is appropriate to have short, daily lessons, while older pupils may benefit from one or two longer sessions each week.

The amount of time devoted to handwriting may also depend on the point reached in the programme. For example, it may be helpful to provide extra lessons when joins are being introduced.

8 THE WRITING PROCESS

Writing materials

Tools

Throughout the school, children should be encouraged to experience writing with different tools. Pens, pencils, chalks and crayons should be available for them to experiment with. In the early stages a soft pencil with a thick stem may be most appropriate. Too thin a pencil, offered too soon, may result in a tight grip. The standard pencil should be introduced as a child's motor skills begin to improve. At the beginning of the junior school a child's main writing tool will probably be a standard pencil, although some schools allow the use of ballpoint pens.

At some point, schools will encourage children to write in ink, using a fountain pen or something similar. It is best to avoid the use of fine-pointed nibs.

Paper

In the early stages, children should be encouraged to make free-flowing movements and to produce large patterns, letters and words on large sheets of plain paper. As their motor skills increase, the size of the writing should decrease and exercise books can then be used for handwriting practice. The *Nelson Handwriting* Workbooks provide a structured introduction to letter formation, giving guidance on shape and directional flow. Guidelines are provided in the Workbooks and in the Resource sheets accompanying *Developing Skills Red* and *Yellow Level* and *Book 1*. These help children to appreciate the relative proportions of letters and to understand how to position them.

These guidelines are useful for handwriting practice as children, even aged 11, still find forming letters which are the correct size, height and shape difficult.

In the Resource Sheets for *Developing Skills Books 2, 3* and *4*, guidelines are replaced by single ruled lines.

Throughout their schooling, all children should be encouraged to use unlined paper from time to time. This allows them to determine letter size, spacing and the arrangement of the page, and to consider other issues of aesthetics and presentation.

Getting ready to write

Atmosphere

Try to create a relaxed atmosphere. Wrist-shaking exercises, scribbling and practising writing patterns all help to loosen up muscles ready for writing.

Seating and posture

The child's chair and table should be at a comfortable height. The table should support the forearm so that it rests lightly on the surface and is parallel to the floor. Children should be encouraged to sit up straight and not to slouch. The height of the chair should be such that the thighs are horizontal and the feet flat on the floor. Tables should be free of clutter and there should be adequate light to allow children to see what they are doing. Ideally, left-handed pupils should sit on the left of their partners so that their movements are not restricted.

Pencil and pen grip

'Pupils should be taught to hold a pencil comfortably.' (England and Wales: *English in the National Curriculum*)

For all children, especially left-handers, a pen or pencil with a rounded nib or point is best for writing.

For right-handers a tripod grip is generally accepted as the most efficient way of holding a pen or pencil. It should be held lightly between the thumb and forefinger about 3cm from the point. The middle finger provides additional support. The book or writing paper should be placed to the right, tilted slightly to the left. The left hand should be used to steady the paper.

Left-handers are in a minority, and our writing system favours the right-hander. Left-handers therefore need plenty of encouragement and support. When a left-hander makes joining strokes they are pushed, not pulled as they are by a right-hander. Encourage them to hold their pencils far enough away from the point to allow them to see what they are writing. The tripod grip should be much the same as for a right-hander. The book or paper should be positioned to the left and tilted slightly to the right.

Encourage children to refer to the checklist on the back of the flap at the front of each Developing Skills book to help them to prepare for writing. A left-hand version of the flap is available in the accompanying Resources and Assessment books.

Handwriting patterns

Pupils should use material 'to develop hand-eye co-ordination'. (Scotland: *English 5–14 Guidelines)*

Writing patterns that reinforce basic handwriting movements will help to develop fluency, control and confidence. Patterns are provided throughout *Nelson Handwriting*, and children should be encouraged to use a variety of writing implements to complete them. Patterns may be used purely for practice, or to decorate pieces of written work.

Focus

Each handwriting lesson should have a clear focus. This should be discussed, and demonstrations given to emphasise key teaching points. Each unit in the Developing Skills books begins with a Focus section.

Practice

Pupils should have opportunities for 'purposeful, guided practice'. (Northern Ireland: *English Programmes of Study and Attainment Targets*)

Motivated and directed handwriting practice is essential. The focus of each unit of work in the Developing Skills books is followed by purposeful practice of a specific handwriting skill. Focus and Extension Resource sheets allow for further practice at the pupil's own level.

Writing for a purpose

'Pupils should gain experience across a wide variety of forms.' (Scotland: *English 5–14 Guidelines*)

Pupils should be taught 'to use different forms of writing for different purposes'. (England and Wales: *English in the National Curriculum*)

All the exercises in *Nelson Handwriting* are designed to be interesting and enjoyable, and are relevant to the curriculum wherever possible. The activities are designed to reinforce key English skills in spelling, grammar, vocabulary and punctuation and care has been taken to complement the work in *Nelson English* and *Nelson Spelling*.

Children should be taught to adapt their writing according to the requirements of the task. In *Nelson Handwriting*, they are taught a print script in *Developing Skills Yellow Level* and are encouraged to use it in a variety of situations, e.g. for labelling maps and diagrams. They are also taught to write quickly, without losing legibility, for making notes. The writing activities span a range of genres, including real-life writing situations.

Fluency and rhythm

Pupils should be expected to 'develop greater control and fluency'. (England and Wales: *English in the National Curriculum*)

Fluent handwriting is writing in which the pencil literally flows from letter to letter in a smooth and almost continuous process. Children should be encouraged to write at a reasonable speed in order to develop this skill. Handwriting patterns are a useful aid in this respect.

Speed

The essential qualities of good writing are fluency, neatness and speed. Fluency is best achieved at speed, but writing done too quickly often suffers from loss of form, regularity and legibility. The *Nelson Handwriting* style and joining methods have been designed to stand up to demands for speedy, efficient handwriting. Activities to develop speed writing are provided from *Developing Skills Book 1*, together with tests enabling children to work out their own writing speed.

Individuality

Children should not be expected to make exact reproductions of the letter forms presented as models in Nelson Handwriting. In due course it is likely that many children will develop individual variations on this style. These variations will give their writing character, and, provided that the writing is legible, are to be encouraged. In Developing Skills Book 3 and 4 children are actively encouraged to explore different styles of handwriting.

Presentation

Pupils should develop an awareness of the 'importance of clear, neat presentation, in order to communicate their meaning effectively'. (England and Wales: *English in the National Curriculum*)

Children need to learn to consider the visual impact of their writing as well as its accuracy. Aspects of presentation (including spacing, margins, borders, illustration and calligraphic effects) are focused on throughout the course.

Not every occasion warrants 'best' writing. It is more helpful for children to write with a degree of care, at an appropriate speed, for most normal purposes, so that their writing is legible and fluent and not too painstakingly produced. 'Best' writing can be reserved for those occasions when attention can be concentrated on the mechanical skills of writing and when there is seen to be a clear purpose for producing aesthetically pleasing work. Older children should be helped to realise that some writing tasks require a draft version to be written first. Then, after revision and editing, the draft can be re-written in 'best' writing.

Some suggestions for encouraging aesthetic presentation of written work are as follows:

- Hold an annual or termly handwriting competition.
- Have a notice board on which frequently changed displays of good work are pinned.
- Write out work for wall displays in connection with other work being undertaken, after rough drafts have been corrected.
- Encourage children to compile individual anthologies of favourite poems and extracts which may be illustrated appropriately.
- Produce a class magazine in which individual contributions are handwritten.
- Produce handwritten, decorated programmes for bazaars, concerts and parents' evenings.
- Ask children to decorate their work with writing patterns.
- Encourage children to experiment with different ways of presenting writing:
    - ♦ a poem or narrative which forms a shape relating to its subject,
    - ♦ curved or spiral writing,
    - ♦ decorated capitals,
    - ♦ writing in coloured ink,
    - ♦ writing over illustrations which have been lightly coloured,
    - ♦ experimenting with the relationship between writing and illustration.

Handwriting across the curriculum

There are many opportunities to practice the skills of handwriting during the course of lessons in other subjects. In the same way, *Nelson Handwriting* pays attention to other aspects of the English curriculum – grammar, punctuation, spelling and vocabulary – and to other subjects such as History and Geography.

Research has confirmed the natural link between spelling and handwriting. The examples used in *Nelson Handwriting* consolidate pupils' mastery of common spelling rules and develop both a visual and a motor memory of spelling patterns.

Computers and word processors are now a common feature in all schools and offer exciting possibilities for the writing process and for the presentation of written work. Children should be encouraged to experiment with the range of fonts available and with different sizes of print.

9 ASSESSMENT

It is important to establish ways of assessing handwriting at several levels:

- whole school assessment,
- class assessment,
- individual assessment,
- self-assessment.

Whole school and class assessment

From time to time it is useful to confirm that the school or class handwriting policy is effective. A regular survey of children's writing allows for a general, impressionistic assessment and may indicate the need for a more detailed investigation. This kind of monitoring of school-wide standards is most likely to occur if one member of staff is responsible for starting the process at regular intervals and ensuring that any weaknesses or problems are followed up. Criteria might include:

- Is the writing generally legible and pleasant?
- Are the letters correctly shaped and proportioned?
- Are the joins made correctly?
- Are the spaces between letters, words and lines appropriate?
- Is the size of the writing appropriate?
- Is the writing properly aligned?
- Are the writing standards achieved by the majority of pupils in line with the Level Descriptors of the statutory curricula? (See page 18)

Appropriate assessment materials are provided in the Resources and Assessment books which accompany the Developing Skills books.

Individual assessment

To assess the progress of individual children it is necessary to observe them as they write, as well as studying their finished writing. Criteria for individual assessments include:

- Does the child adopt the correct posture?
- Does the child hold the pen/pencil correctly?
- Does the child use the correct movement when forming and/or joining letters?
- Does the child reverse or invert any letters?
- Does the child write fluently and rhythmically?
- Is the writing easily legible?
- Is the writing appropriate?
- Is the pupil's handwriting development in line with the Level Descriptors of the statutory curricula? (See page 18)

Each Developing Skills book contains Check-ups to assess the individual progress of each child. Each Resources and Assessment book contains an assessment section with resource sheets designed to be used as placement tests, general assessment and self-assessment.

The 'Getting ready to write' flap at the front of each Developing Skills book is intended to remind pupils about how to prepare themselves for writing. The checklist on the reverse of this gives a list of criteria to help pupils focus on, and check critically, particular aspects of the writing they have done. Throughout the Developing Skills books, children are frequently reminded to assess their own writing and this checklist will help them. The checklist may also be used as a basis for pairs of pupils to discuss each other's writing, or as a basis for a handwriting conference between teacher and child.

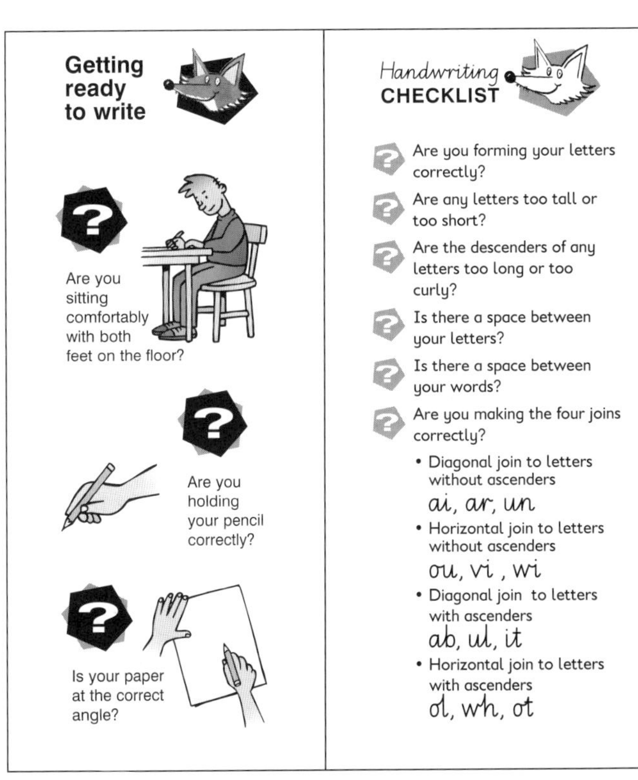

Level Descriptors in the statutory curricula

England and Wales

Level 1 'Letters are usually clearly shaped and correctly oriented.'

Level 2 'In handwriting, letters are accurately formed and consistent in size.'

Level 3 'Handwriting is joined and legible.'

Level 4 'Handwriting style is fluent, joined and legible.'

Level 5 'Handwriting is joined clear and fluent and, where appropriate, is adapted to a range of tasks.'

Scotland

Level A In writing tasks pupils 'form letters and space words legibly for the most part. At an appropriate stage, linkage of letters will be taught.'

Level B In writing tasks pupils 'form letters and space words legibly in linked script'.

Level C In writing tasks pupils 'employ a fluent, legible style of handwriting'.

Level D In writing tasks pupils 'employ a fluent, legible style of handwriting and set out completed work giving attention to presentation and layout'.

Level E In writing tasks pupils 'employ a fluent, legible style of handwriting, and set out completed work clearly and attractively'.

Northern Ireland

Level 1 'Pupils should show some control over the size, shape and orientation of letters.'

Level 2 'There is evidence of the use of upper and lower case letters.'

Level 3 'Handwriting is accurately formed and consistant in size.'

Level 4 'Handwriting is swift and legible.'

Level 5 'Handwriting is swift and legible.'

Specific handwriting difficulties

The assessment sections of the Resources and Assessment books are designed to be used throughout the course as appropriate, specifically with those few pupils who are experiencing major problems in learning to write. The sheets can indicate starting points for remedial treatment, and should be updated as progress is achieved.

Some problems and possible solutions

Faulty pencil grip
An over-tight pencil grip is the most common fault. Crooking of the forefinger and pressing too hard are common indications of this. Encourage the pupil to relax and to hold the pencil lightly between the thumb and the middle finger, while the forefinger rests lightly on the pencil.

Incorrect letter formation
Children are often able to write letters which are correctly shaped but which have been produced by incorrect movements. If bad habits of this kind are allowed to become ingrained, the child will be seriously hampered when he or she progresses to joined writing. It is important, in the early stages of development, to ensure that:

- all letters are started in the correct place,
- in general, movements start at the top and go down,
- ovals are made with an anticlockwise movement.

Reversal, inversions and mirror writing
Common problems include:

- reversal: b for d and p for q,
- inversions: w for m,
- mirror writing: was for saw.

Causes include:

- confusion between left and right,
- a lack of commitment to one hand,
- a natural tendency for left-handers to pull the hand across the body from right to left, thus causing confusion,
- a general lack of maturity or confidence.

Children with these problems can be helped by increased emphasis on the writing direction and the consistent use of one hand for writing.

10 HELPING THE LEFT-HANDER

Pen hold

The left-handed, like the right-handed child, needs to be shown as early as possible how to hold a writing implement correctly. Please note that there is a photocopiable version of the Developing Skills flap in each of the Resources and Assessment books. This can be copied and used with the left-handed children. Bad habits are easily learnt and many left-handers adopt a hooked pencil hold which can result in a tired grip and affect the quality of their writing. When they begin to use a pen their hand can easily smudge the ink as they write.

If a child already has a 'hooked' pencil hold, do not force them to change. It is very difficult to alter the way you have learnt to hold a pencil, and confidence can easily be destroyed. Encourage them *instead* to angle their paper 20–30° to the left, i.e. the same angle used for a right-handed child. If possible, demonstrate how to hold a pen and how to form and join letters with your left hand.

The left-hander should hold the pencil in the left hand in the same way as a right-handed person holds theirs. The pencil is held between thumb and forefinger, resting on the first knuckle of the middle finger. The pencil should be held about 3cm from the tip.

The hand should be kept below the writing line. This enables the children to see what they are writing and encourages correct pen hold.

The grip the left-hander uses means the pencil is pushed as the child writes, whereas the right-hander pulls their pencil across the page as they write. It is important therefore that the left-hander's pencil is not too sharp, so that it will run smoothly across the page.

Paper position

The left-hander will find it easier if the paper is tilted slightly to the right, at about 20–30°. The higher the angle the harder it is for most children to write efficiently. The right hand is used to steady the paper, above the writing line.

Crossing letters

The left-hander often crosses the 'f' and 't' from right to left. Many left-handers therefore will find it easier to leave the 'f' unjoined.

Teachers need to be aware of left-handers in the classroom as they do have different needs. It is very important that a right-handed child is not seated on the left-hand side of a left-handed child as their elbows will collide!

?
Are you sitting comfortably with both feet on the floor?
?
Are you holding your pen correctly?
?
Is your paper at the correct angle?

11 LINKING HANDWRITING AND SPELLING

The English National Curriculum includes the requirement that:

> *In spelling, pupils should be taught to: write each letter of the alphabet; use their knowledge of sound–symbol relationships and phonological patterns; recognise and use simple spelling patterns; write common letter strings within familiar and common words;*

Indeed, a balanced spelling programme would be incomplete without techniques for stimulating visual memory and, as has been recognised for generations, the classic way of achieving this is to integrate the learning of spelling with the development of handwriting; one of the most powerful methods of stimulating the visual memory.

Remembering the feeling of tracing the shapes of letters is important in the early stages of handwriting. This too can be part of the early spelling programme, as has been described with some of the pre-writing activities.

Nelson Handwriting provides a progressive, carefully graded programme of activities, based around phonically regular words, ensuring that in parallel with the important regular handwriting practice, the children are undertaking meaningful spelling tasks. If handwriting is practised using letters in regular combinations, be they blends, strings or digraphs, then young writers will begin to internalise the patterns and increase both their handwriting and spelling ability and confidence.

Given the pressures and time constraints in the average modern classroom, it has to make good classroom management sense to integrate handwriting and spelling whenever possible.

Look – Say – Cover – Write – Check

The child:

Looks at the word very carefully, including how the letters join.

Says the word.

Covers the word so that it can't be seen.

Writes the whole word from memory, saying it softly as they write, taking care both to spell the word correctly and to join the letters correctly.

Checks what has been written. If they have not written the word correctly, or have not joined the letters correctly, they go back and repeat all these steps again.

Once the child has learnt to spell a new word correctly, they write it into their wordbooks. Even if they get the spelling and the joins right first time, it is useful to practice both again.

Some children can struggle with Look Say Cover Write Check if left on their own, or in a small group. Initially the words they practice will be two-letter words, but later the Look Say Cover Write Check process can be used to correct two or three spellings from a child's piece of creative writing. Look Say Cover Write Check can also be linked to the school's phonic programme.

Don't forget:

- To praise and encourage the child for what they have already written. This builds confidence – confidence builds success – success builds confidence.
- To ask the child if you can show them how to write what they have written in joined-up writing.
- The child watches as the teacher writes.

Nelson Handwriting Links to NLS Spelling Objectives (Spelling Bank)

The spelling link in each unit of work in the Developing Skills books is also highlighted in the corresponding teaching notes for that unit.

Unit	Book 1	Book2	Book 3	Book 4
1	Y3 T1 W8	Y4 T1 W5	Y5 T2 W4 (2 of 3)	Y6 T1 W5
2	N/A	Y4 T1 W9	Y5 T3 W11	Y6 T1 W5
3	Y3 T1 W8	Y4 T1 W9 (1 of 2)	Y5 T1 W4	Y6 T1/2/3 W4
4	Y3 T3 W13	Y4 T1 W14	Y5 T2 W4 (3 of 3)	N/A
5	Y3 T3 W8	Y4 T1 W8	Y5 T1 W6	N/A
6	Y3 T2 W8 (1 of 2)	Y4 T1 W7	Y5 T2 W8 (Y5 T1 W6)	N/A
7	Y3 T2 W8 (2 of 2)	Y4 T3 W6	Y5 T1 W5 (1 of 2)	Y5 T3 W5 (1 of 3)
8	Y3 T1 W10	Y4 T3 W9	N/A	N/A
9	Y3 T2 W9	Y4 T1 W6	N/A	N/A
10	Y3 T2 W9	Y4 T3 W8	Y5 T2 W5	N/A
11	Y3 T3 W8 and 11	Y4 T1 W5	Y5 T2 W5	Y6 T1 W6
12	Y3 T2 W13	Y4 T1 W7	N/A	N/A
13	Y3 T1 W10	Y4 T3 W11	N/A	N/A
14	Y3 T1 W9	Y4 T3 W5 (2 of 2)	Y5 T2 W4 (2 of 3)	N/A
15	N/A	Y4 T3 W11 (recap)	Y5 T1 W4	N/A
16	Y3 T2 W13	Y4 T3 W5 (1 of 2)	Y5 T3 W4	N/A
17	Y3 T2 W12	Y5 T1 W5 (1 of 2)	N/A	N/A
18	Y3 T3 W8	Y4 T3 W11	N/A	N/A
19	Y3 T3 W8	Y4 T3 W10	Y5 T2 W4 (2 of 3)	Recap Y5 T2 W4 (2 of 3)
20	Y3 T3 W9	N/A	N/A	N/A

12 A HANDWRITNG POLICY

School policy

An aim of every school should be to teach each child to write legibly, fluently and at reasonable speed. To achieve this schools should consider the following recommendations:

- One member of staff should have responsibility for handwriting. This responsibility should be written into that person's job description.
- This member of staff should be given time and resources to help other staff.
- The school should develop a 'whole school approach' so that teaching is consistent and all teachers are giving the same advice to parents, visiting teachers and supply teachers.
- School policy ought to be consistent between linking key stages.
- The staff need to agree on a common approach to such things as timetabling handwriting activities, style to be adopted, implements to be allowed, involvement of parents and policy on correcting work.

The success of whole school policies depends upon the level of ownership and understanding felt by all people whose behaviour and thinking they seek to influence. This applies equally to creating, implementing and managing a policy for handwriting. In the author's experience, a sequence of five stages may be helpful in establishing a handwriting policy.

Stage 1: Identify current practice

Ask staff to bring some examples of handwriting from their class. The examples should illustrate a range of ability levels.

- In small groups, discuss current practice.
- How is handwriting currently taught in your class?
- Discuss examples of work.
- Share any difficulties, concerns, successes or issues.
- What might be the advantages of introducing joined handwriting earlier?
- What might be the disadvantages?

Report back to main group. Discuss the issues and record the results of discussion. Unresolved issues will need to be discussed at another time.

Stage 2: Review current practice

In groups discuss the following questions:

Does the school's current approach ensure that every child achieves their full potential?

- Would more children achieve Levels 2/3 in English at the end of Key Stage 1 (or equivalent) if the school's handwriting policy was different?
- Would more children be able to write legibly, fluently and neatly with speed if they were introduced to joined writing earlier?
- Discuss and try to resolve any concerns.
- What resources do you have or need?
- Can handwriting practice be linked to spelling/phonic progression?

Feed back to main group.

Stage 3: Agree an approach

- Decide on a model to use, for example the one provided by *Nelson Handwriting*.
- Agree the time allocation to be given to handwriting.
- Decide on materials that will be used, and when.

Some teachers will never agree on handwriting. It is an emotive subject and many hold strong views and opinions. It may help if one person or the senior management team makes the final decision. Remind staff that the new policy can be trialled, evidence collected and a review carried out in twelve months time.

Stage 4: Draw up the policy

It helps if one person or group draws up a draft policy which can be brought to the staff and discussed.

Include in your handwriting policy:

- The model used,

  lower case letters,

  capital letters,

  numerals.
- The break letters.
- The four joins.

- The order of teaching, i.e. it is useful to group letters together based on similar movements, followed by phonic progression.
- The three 'P's,

  posture,

  pen hold,

  paper position.
- Advice for left-handers.
- Use of lined or unlined paper.
- Equipment used.
- Assessment and record keeping procedures.
- A small information booklet could be provided and given to parents before their child starts school (and given to supply teachers). Such a booklet should include:
- an illustration of the three 'P's,
- lower case letters showing correct entry point and direction of movement,
- an example to show how letters join, e.g. a poem,
- handy hints on appropriate writing tools and paper.

A well-thought-out and consistently applied policy will benefit all the teachers and the children at your school. Continuity throughout the school enables children to build on what they have already been taught and know. It also helps eradicate confusion and avoids difficulties and problems later on.

Stage 5: review and evaluation of policy

Review and evaluation of any policy is important. It keeps both policy and guidelines alive and informs both old and new staff.

Evaluate and review your policy annually if you can. The model or style of writing you choose to adopt is not as important as the fact that you are encouraging joined handwriting with all the positive benefits it entails. Teachers need encouragement too. We don't always get the model and style correct all the time, but both pupils and staff can perfect style at a later stage.

Finally recognise, celebrate and advertise your successes!

13 THE WORKBOOKS

Introduction

The Workbooks are the foundation of the *Nelson Handwriting* programme. Statutory requirements in England and Wales, Scotland and Northern Ireland have highlighted the need for earlier teaching of handwriting skills, and in this context teachers have expressed the importance of the following features:

- a simple, clear, fluent style of lettering with exit flicks taught from the outset to lead naturally into joined handwriting,
- materials which teach joined writing during the infant years,
- accessible, pupil-friendly resources which balance the teaching of technical skills with their application in a range of curriculum-relevant contexts.

The *Nelson Handwriting* Workbooks are developed in response to these demands.

There are four Workbooks intended for children aged 4–5, and Workbooks 5–6 for children aged 5–6. They provide material suitable for class, group or individual teaching styles. Workbooks 5 and 6 are specifically designed for pupils who are ready to move onto a joined script but have not yet developed the necessary transferring skills to work from the Red Level Developing Skills book. The content of the Red Level Developing Skills book has been translated into a workbook format and split over two books for children who need the extra support of working on the page.

The clear, logical approach is designed to help children develop the fine motor-control and hand-eye co-ordination skills necessary for forming letters. Letter shapes are introduced in groups, according to the way they are formed. Most letters are written in one continuous smooth movement, encouraging fluency.

Links are made with the corresponding letter sounds, and the letters are used in meaningful writing activities in a range of contexts. This gives children the ideal preparation for beginning joined writing at Red Level.

Each Workbook page has a self-assessment feature which allows children to reflect on the standard of their work on a page by page basis. The clear developmental sequence of skills makes lesson planning straightforward. The Workbooks contain 22–26 teaching pages, and each page features concise teacher's notes discreetly located at the foot of the page. These notes summarise the skills being taught and suggest practical ideas on how to teach them.

The page layouts are clear, consistent and accessible, encouraging independent use by children. The instructions are brief and readable. Large starting dots and directional arrows are used to indicate where to begin and the correct direction to follow when making handwriting patterns or forming letters or numerals. Large model letters introduce each letter form, allowing for ample tactile reinforcement using finger tracing and over-writing in different colours. Plenty of guided opportunities are provided for over-writing, under-writing and copying practice. Guidelines are used throughout to provide additional guidance on letter size and positioning.

Every effort has been made to contextualise the action in a relevant and meaningful way, making links with other areas of the curriculum where possible. These contexts include labelling, rhyming, vocabulary development, sequencing, writing names, matching and writing birthday cards. Frequent links are made with phonics and spelling. Letters are linked to their source which leads to simple word-building activities. Focus letters are written in the context of words, phrases and sentences.

Learning objectives taught through Workbooks 1-4

	Blue Level			
	Workbook 1	Workbook 2	Workbook 3	Workbook 4
2	Left to right hand movement	Pre-letter pattern for forming i, l, t	Pre-letter pattern for forming h, b, p	Letter c
3	Use a comfortable pencil grip	Pre-letter pattern for forming i, l, t	Pre-letter pattern for forming h, b, p	Letter a
4	Hand–eye co-ordination	Letter i	Letter h	Letter d
5	Hand–eye co-ordination	Letter i	Letter h	Letter g
6	Produce a controlled line	Letter l	Letter b	Letter q
7	Pre-letter patterns for forming c, a, d, g, q, o	Letter l	Letter b	Letter o
8	Pre-letter patterns for forming c, a, d, g, q, o	Letter t	Letter p	Letter e
9	Letter c	Letter t	Letter p	Letter s
10	Letter c	Pre-letter pattern for forming u, y ,j, k	Pre-letter pattern for forming v, w, x, z	Letter f
11	Letter a	Pre-letter pattern for forming u, y, j, k	Pre-letter pattern for forming v, w, x, z	Letter i
12	Letter a	Letter u	Letter v	Letter l
13	Letter d	Letter u	Letter v	Letter t
14	Letter d	Letter y	Letter w	Letter u
15	Letter g	Letter y	Letter w	Letter y
16	Letter g	Letter j	Letter x	Letter j
17	Letter q	Letter j	Letter x	Letter k
18	Letter q	Letter k	Letter x	Letter r
19	Letter o	Letter k	Letter z	Letter n
20	Letter o	Pre-letter pattern for forming r, n, m	Pre-numeral patterns	Letter m
21	Pre-letter pattern for forming e, s, f	Pre-letter pattern for forming r, n, m	Numerals 0, 1, 2, 3, 4	Letter h
22	Letter e	Letter r	Numerals 5, 6, 7, 8, 9	Letter b
23	Letter e	Letter r	Numerals and number words 1, 2, 3, 4, 5	Letter p
24	Letter s	Letter n	Numerals and number words 6, 7, 8, 9, 10	Letter v
25	Letter s	Letter n	Animals	Letter w
26	Letter f	Letter m	Parts of the body	Letter x
27	Letter f	Letter m	Question mark formation	Letter z

Techniques for teaching letter formation

- Provide demonstrations when introducing and teaching letter shapes. Chalkboards and OHPs are useful for this.
- Observe individuals as much as possible while they practice. This enables the teacher to recognise and correct bad habits as they arise.
- Talk the children through the process using appropriate language.
- Encourage children to verbalise what they are doing from time to time. This gives a window into the thought processes they are using as they write.
- Writing involves visual and motor skills. Use the following ideas to reinforce the teaching of letter shapes:
  - Encourage children to form letters by drawing them in the air.
  - Finger trace over tactile letters, on desk or table tops.
  - Write over dotted or 'shadow' writing.
  - Draw round templates.
  - Write in sand with a finger or stick.
  - Write with chalk on a chalkboard.
  - Write letters boldly with a wax candle and then apply a colour wash.
  - Form letters with pegs on a pegboard or with beads in plasticine.
  - Finger trace the outline of a letter on the back of the person in front of you.
  - Form letters with fingers and/or bodies, individually and in groups.
- Draw attention to the connection between letters and the related writing patterns. Encouraging children to use the basic handwriting patterns both for practice and for decorative purposes is a valuable technique for fostering fluency and rhythmic movement.

14 THE JOINS

Joins between letters increase the speed, rhythm and ease of writing without reducing legibility.

In *Nelson Handwriting*, the 26 lower case letters have been divided into five sets according to the nature of the joins they require. There are four types of join and a set of 'break' letters after which joins are never made. (See page 9 for details of these sets of letters.)

The joins are taught in Red Level and practice is provided in all subsequent books.

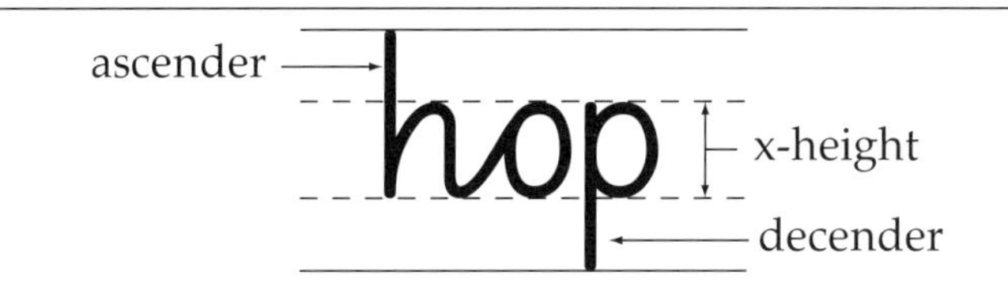

The first join

The join from any member of Set 1 to any member of Set 2 is made with exactly the same movement as the upswing in the swings pattern.

in

The second join

The join from any member of Set 1 to any member of Set 3 is the same as the first join except that the join meets the ascender halfway up the letter and then continues to the top of the ascender.

il

The third join

The join from any member of Set 4 to any member of Set 2 is a shallow horizontal curve because the join is from x-height of one letter to the x-height of the next.

og

The fourth join

The join from any member of Set 4 to any member of Set 3 is the same as the first join except that it goes from the x-height of one letter to the top of the ascender of the next.

ob

The break letters

Joins are never made after the letters in this set. No join is ever made to or from the letter z. A small space should be left after each break letter so that it is spaced as evenly as the joined letters.

The letters e and s have slightly varying forms because their shapes depend on the nature of the preceding join. Attention is drawn to these special cases in the *Developing Skills Red* and *Yellow Levels*.

As the size of writing decreases, children should be encouraged to decrease the space between words. By the time children are using *Developing Skills* this space should be the width of a lower case letter **a**, and the space between two lines of writing should be about twice the height of this letter.

Teaching the joined style

- In the early stages the correct movements are more important than the appearance of the writing. Children should be discouraged from forming writing with incorrect movements, even if they manage to achieve results that appear satisfactory. However, in later stages a more individual style based around *Nelson Handwriting* is encouraged
- As joined handwriting is a movement skill, it is essential for teachers to provide demonstrations. Chalkboards and OHPs are useful for this.
- Observe individuals as much as possible while they practice. This enables the teacher to recognise and correct bad habits as they arise.
- Talk the children through the process, using appropriate language.
- Encourage children to verbalise what they are doing from time to time. This gives a window into the thought processes they are using as they write.
- Most children will need extra practice with making the joins. The Developing Skills and Resources and Assessment books provide ample material for this.
- Encouraging children to use the basic handwriting patterns both for practice and for decorative purposes is a valuable technique for fostering fluency and rhythmic movement.

Teacher's Notes

SCOPE AND SEQUENCE
DEVELOPING SKILLS RED LEVEL

Introduction and practice of the four handwriting joins.

Page	Focus	Extra	Extension	Focus resource	Extension resource
4-5 Unit 1 Holidays	practise the first join: un, um	bun, mum	match and copy captions	un, bun, gun, sun, nun trace and copy pattern and copy words	un, um, buns, nuns, hums, mums, sums trace and copy the first join, words and sentence
6-7 Unit 2 Holidays	practise the first join: ig, id	lid, dig	choose words and copy sentences	ig, big, pig, dig trace and copy pattern and copy words	ig, big, id, did, kid, lid, hid trace and copy the first join, words and sentence
8-9 Unit 3 Birthdays	practise the first join: ed, eg	bed, leg	punctuate and copy sentences	ed, bed, ted, led trace and copy pattern and copy words	Jed, eg, beg, peg, leg trace and copy the first join, words and sentence
10-11 Unit 4 Birthdays	practise the first join: an, ar	nan, car	choose words and copy sentences	an, can, man, nan, pan, tan trace and copy pattern and words	an, Nan, ar, car, tar, star trace and copy the first join, words and sentence
12-13 Unit 5 Food	practise the first join: ing, ung	rhyming ing, ung and ang words	copy sentence	ng, ing, ding, sing, ping, king trace and copy pattern and words	ung, lung, sung, ang, gang, sang trace and copy the first join, words and sentence
14-15 Unit 6 Food	practise the second join: ch, sh	chip, ship	write out menu order	ch, chip, child, chew, sh, ship, shed, shell trace and copy pattern and words	ch, chips, chimps, cheeky trace and copy second join, words and sentence
16-17 Unit 7 Foxes	practise the second join: th, tl	the, them	choose words and copy sentences	th, them, then, this, that, thank trace and copy pattern and words	the, think trace and copy second join, words and sentence
18-19 Unit 8 Foxes	practise the second join: ll, ill	ill, pill	choose words and copy sentences	ill, hill, mill, pill, bill, till trace and copy pattern and words	hill, Bill, Jill trace and copy second join, words and sentence
20-21 Unit 9 Beans	practise the second join: sli, slu	slid, slug	choose words and copy sentences	sl, slid, slide, slip, slippy, slipper trace and copy pattern and words	sl, slug, slugs, slush trace and copy second join, words and sentence
22-23 Unit 10 Beans	practise the second join: ck, ack	sack, back	choose words and copy sentences	ack, pack, ick, kick, eck, peck trace and copy pattern and words	ck, back, mack, sack trace and copy second join, words and sentence
24-25 Check-up 1	*Check-up*	*Check-up*	*Check-up*	*Check-up*	*Check-up*

Page	Focus	Extra	Extension	Focus resource	Extension resource
26-27 Unit 11 Toys	practise the second join: st, sti	still, stilts	choose words and copy sentences	st, stick, sticky, sticker, sting, stitch trace and copy pattern and words	st, still, stile, step, steep, stay, stall trace and copy words and sentence
28-29 Unit 12 Toys	practise the second join: ink, unk	pink, junk	choose words and copy sentences	nk, ink, pink, sink, link, blink trace and copy pattern and words	unk, bunk, punk, dunk, sunk trace and copy second join, words and sentence
30-31 Unit 13 Homes	practise the third join: od, og	dog, frog	choose words and copy sentences	og, cog, dog, log, fog, frog trace and copy pattern and words	nod, rod, log, frogs trace and copy words and sentence
32-33 Unit 14 Homes	practise the third join: re, ve	are, there	copy poem	re, read, reed, reel, real trace and copy pattern and words	re, red, ve, very, we, went trace and copy third join, words and sentence
34-35 Unit 15 Tigers	practise the third join: oon, oom	moon, room	choose words and copy sentences	oo, soon, spoon, moon, room, broom, groom trace and copy pattern and words	oo, zoo, zoom, soon trace and copy third join, words and sentence
36-37 Unit 16 Tigers	practise the fourth join: wl, vl	growl, prowl	copy acrostic poem	wl, bowl, slowly, crawl, trawl, trawler trace and copy pattern and words	howl, growl, prowl trace and copy words and sentence
38-39 Unit 17 Myself	practise the fourth join: of, ff	of, off	choose words and copy sentences	of, ff, uff, huff, puff, cuff, stuff trace and copy pattern and words	ff, of, off trace and copy pattern and words choose word and copy sentence
40-41 Unit 18 Myself	practise the fourth join: fl, flo	floor, flood	copy poem	fl, flo, float, flood, floor, flower trace and copy pattern and words	copy poem
42-43 Unit 19 Unjoined letters	practise the break letters: b, p, g, q, y, j, z	be, poke	copy poem and underline break letters	practise the break letters	copy phrases
44-45 Unit 20 Unjoined letters	practise capital letters	alphabetical ordering: children's names	alphabetical ordering: children's names	finish the patterns	copy classroom captions using capital letters
46-48 Check-up 2	*Check-up*	*Check-up*	*Check-up*	*Check-up*	*Check-up*

UNIT 1

Objectives

- To introduce the first handwriting join.
- To practise the correct formation of the first join.

UNIT 1

Practising the first join.

un

Run, Mum. Run.

FOCUS

A Copy this pattern into your book.

uuu uuu uuu uuu

B Copy these letters into your book.

un un un un un

um um um um um

Be careful! Make sure you take your pencil back up to the top before you start your next letter.

EXTRA

Make these words. Copy them into your book.

b + un = bun bun bun

m + um = mum mum mum

EXTENSION

Match a caption to each holiday snap and write them into your book.

Tip mum in.

Fun in a bun.

1 2

Spelling links

- CVC words with the short **u** sound in a medial position

Nelson theme – holidays

Developing Skills

Focus

- Before the lesson, draw four lines on the board (two rows of dotted lines in the middle) and write the whole class phrase between them.
- Demonstrate on the board how to write the letter **u** and the letter **n**.
- Join the two letters using the first join (using a different coloured pen to show the join can be helpful).
- Point out that the join is a diagonal line. It begins at the bottom of the first letter and goes to the top of the next letter.
- Show how to form and join the two letters **un**, using one continuous movement.
- Ask the children to:
  - trace their fingers or the blunt end of a pencil over the large **un** in the book
  - write the letters in the air
  - trace the letters with their fingers on the back of the person in front
- Draw the pattern from the book on the board. Explain that the pattern should help with joining.
- Demonstrate the letters **u** and **m** in the same way.
- Ask the children to practise the pattern and the letters on their whiteboards, before copying them into their books.

Extra

- Ask the children if they can think of a letter to put before **un** to make a word, e.g. **b**. Write it on the board.
- Ask the children to compile a list of **un** words.
- Model writing the words on the board.
- Do the same for **um**.
- Explain the exercise in the book. Explain to the children about the tramlines and demonstrate writing **bun** and **mum** between the lines.
- Ask the children to copy these words into a lined handwriting book.

Extension

- Ask the children to read the captions.
- The children should try to match the captions to the holiday snaps.
- Tell the children to copy the captions into their handwriting books.

Resources and Assessment

Focus

Further practice of the swings pattern and the first join, using rhyming words all ending in **un**.

1 Focus Resource Red Level

Name Date

un

A Trace and write the pattern and letters.

B Trace and write the words.

Practising the first join.

Extension

Practice with plurals, i.e. words ending **uns** and **ums**. Sentence provides both a tracing opportunity and a chance for higher attainers to write a sentence on their own.

1 Extension Resource Red Level

Name Date

A Trace and write the letters and words.

B Trace and write the sentence.

Practising the first join.

Assessment

- The join is made from the bottom of the letter **u** to the top of the letter **n** or **m**, not the bottom.

NIT 2

Objectives

- To practise the correct formation of the first join using letter patterns **ig** and **id**.

Spelling links

- CVC words with the short **i** sound in a medial position

Nelson theme – holidays

Developing Skills

Focus

- Before the lesson, draw four lines on the board (two rows of dotted lines in the middle) and write the whole class sentence between them.
- Demonstrate how to write the individual letters **i** and **g**.
- Next add the joining line. Point out that the join is a diagonal line and it goes up and round to the top of the letter **g**.
- Show the class how to form and join the two letters without lifting the pencil. The tramlines are useful because you can discuss how the descender of the **g** goes below the baseline.
- Model the joining of the letters **id** in one continuous movement.
- Draw the pattern on the board. Explain that the pattern should help with joining.
- Explain that the join to the letters **g** and **d** means the pencil must come back round.
- Tell the children to trace their fingers over the large **ig** in their books to get the feel of the join.
- Ask the children to practise the pattern and the letters on their whiteboards, before copying them into their books.

Extra

- Tell the children that they are going to make three-letter words.
- Write **l** and **id** on the board to make the word **lid**. If time, ask the children if they can think of more words ending with **id**. Do the same for **ig**.
- Explain the exercise in the pupil book.
- Ask the children to copy the words into a lined handwriting book.

Extension

- Ask the children to look at and read the words in the box.
- Ask the children to read the sentences.
- Tell them to copy the sentences carefully, filling in the missing words.
- Remind them to use a capital letter and a full stop.
- Show the children where the capital letter sits on the line – draw lines on the board to show how the first two words fit on the lines.

Resources and Assessment

Focus

Further pattern practice. Practising the first join in **ig**. Tracing and copying the patterns and words.

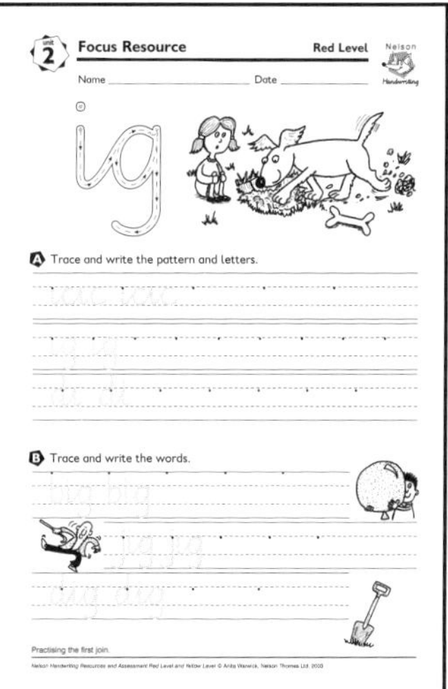

Extension

This extends the practice by introducing further CVC words with **i** as the medial vowel. The sentence provides both a tracing opportunity and a chance for higher attainers to write a sentence on their own.

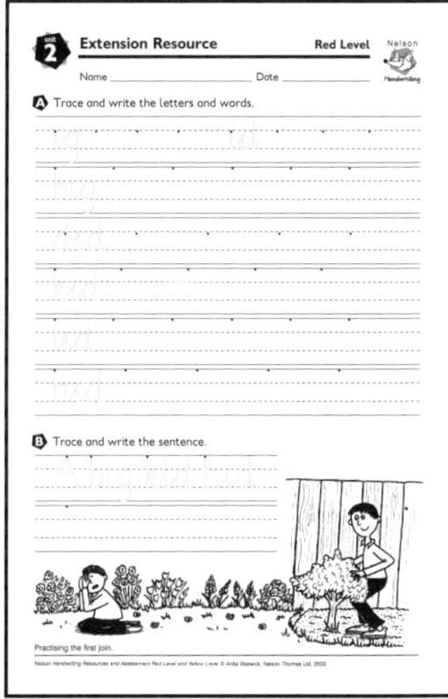

Tip! For those who find it difficult to copy under the sentence, write the beginning of the sentence to start them off (you could use a highlighter pen).

Assessment

- The letters **g** and **d** are formed correctly, i.e. check pencil is brought back round.
- The descender of the letter **g** falls below the line.
- The diagonal join is made to *the top* of the next letter.

UNIT 3

Objectives

- To practise the correct formation of the first join.

Spelling links

- CVC words with the short **e** sound in a medial position

Nelson theme – birthdays

UNIT 3 Practising the first join.

ed

Jed has a bed.

FOCUS

A Copy this pattern into your book.

eee eee eee eee

B Copy these letters into your book.

ed ed ed ed ed

eg eg eg eg eg

EXTRA

Make these words. Copy them into your book.

b + ed = bed bed bed

l + eg = leg leg leg

EXTENSION

Copy these sentences into your book.
Put in the missing capital letters and full stops.

1 ed has a new bed

2 ben has a bad leg

Be careful! Capital letters do not join.

Developing Skills

Focus

- Before the lesson, draw four lines on the board (two rows of dotted lines in the middle) and write the whole class sentence between them.
- Look at, model and discuss the formation of the letters **ed**.
- Explain that these two letters are also joined using the first join.
- Point out that the formation of the letter **e** begins near the bottom.
- Demonstrate how these two letters are formed in one continuous movement.
- Children can trace over the large **ed** in their books, to get the feel of the join.
- Draw the pattern on the board. Explain that the pattern should help with joining.
- Show the class how to form and join the letters **e** and **g** in the same way.
- Explain that the join to the letters **d** and **g** means the pencil must go up to the top of the x-height of the body of the letter and then come back round.

Extra

- Demonstrate on the board that joining **b** and **ed** makes the word **bed**.
- Ask the children if they can think of more words ending **ed**. They could practise writing their own list on their whiteboards.
- If time, repeat for **eg**.
- Explain the exercise. Tell the children to copy the words into a lined handwriting book.
- It may be useful to show how to write the words **bed** and **leg** on the four lines in front of the group – this will help children to see the correct size of letters.

Extension

- Write the first sentence on the board as it is.
- Ask the children to tell you what is wrong with it.
- Discuss use of capital letters and full stops.
- Remind the children capital letters should be the same height as ascenders and about twice the height of small letters.
- Children should then copy the corrected sentences carefully into their books.

Resources and Assessment

Focus

Further pattern practice. More practice of the first join, joining to and from the letter **e**. Children trace and copy letters and words.

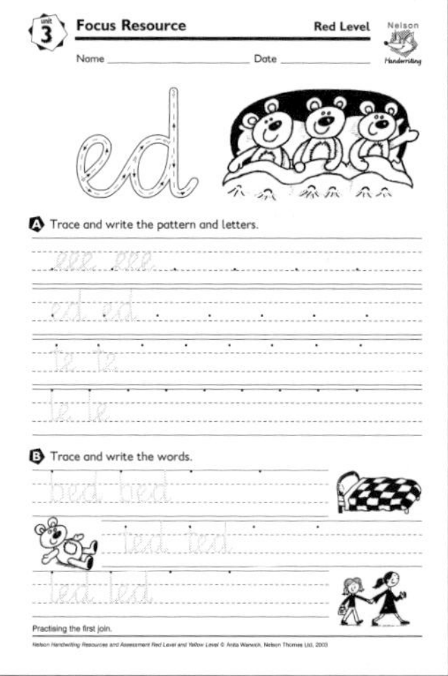

3 Focus Resource Red Level

Name Date

ed

A Trace and write the pattern and letters.

B Trace and write the words.

Practising the first join.

Extension

This extends the practice by introducing more CVC words with **e** as the medial vowel. This exercise also practises forming capitals at the start of a name. Higher attainers can trace and copy the sentence. Trace and copy each word underneath – one word at a time.

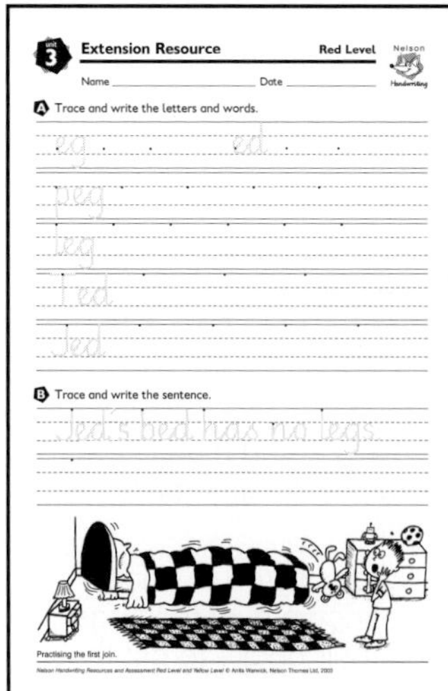

3 Extension Resource Red Level

Name Date

A Trace and write the letters and words.

B Trace and write the sentence.

Practising the first join.

Assessment

- The letter **e** begins near the bottom of the line.
- The joining line curves up to the start of the letter **d** (and **g**) to ensure letter can be formed correctly.
- The letters **d** and **g** are formed correctly, i.e. the pencil is brought back round from the top of the x-height.

NIT 4

Objectives

- To practise the correct formation of the first join using letter patterns **an** and **ar**.

UNIT 4

Practising the first join.

an

I can go in my car.

FOCUS

A Copy this pattern into your book.

B Copy these letters into your book.

an an an an an

ar ar ar ar ar

EXTRA

Make these words. Copy them into your book.

n + an = nan nan nan

c + ar = car car car

Take care! Make sure all these letters are the same height and size.

EXTENSION

Look at the words in the box.

Nan car

Copy the sentences into your book. Write in the missing words.

1 ____ has a nap.

2 Dad is in Ben's new ____

10

11

Spelling links

- CVC words with the short **a** sound in a medial position

Nelson theme – birthdays

Developing Skills

Focus

- Show the class how to write the individual letters **a** and **n**.
- Then join the two letters using the first join. Use a different coloured pen to show the join.
- Point out that the join is a diagonal line and it starts at the bottom of the first letter and goes to the top of the next letter, which is not an ascender.
- Write the two letters **an** on the board. Point out that the join is formed without lifting the pencil off the paper.
- Draw the letters in the air.
- Ask the children to copy you, drawing in the air or with their fingers on the back of the person in front, or finger tracing the large **an** in their books.
- Repeat with **ar**.
- Draw the pattern on the board. Explain that the pattern should help with joining.
- Ask the children to practise the pattern and the letters on their whiteboards, before copying them into their books.

Extra

- Tell the children they are going to make three-letter words.
- Demonstrate on the board that joining **n** and **an** makes the word **nan**.
- Ask the children what **c** and **ar** spells. They could list words with the same ending.
- The children should copy the words into a lined handwriting book to practise forming letters of the correct height and size.

Extension

- Ask the children to read the words in the box.
- Copy the first sentence on the board in front of the group. Leave a line for the missing word.
- Ask a child to come up and write the missing word in the gap.
- The group should copy the sentences carefully into their books.
- Remind them to use a capital letter and a full stop.

Resources and Assessment

Focus

Further practice of the swings pattern and the first join. Tracing and copying CVC words with **a** as medial vowel.

4 Focus Resource Red Level

Name Date

an

A Trace and write the pattern and letters.

B Trace and write the words.

Practising the first join

Extension

This extends the practice by introducing further CVC words and a capital letter. The sentence provides both a tracing opportunity and a chance for higher attainers to write a sentence on their own.

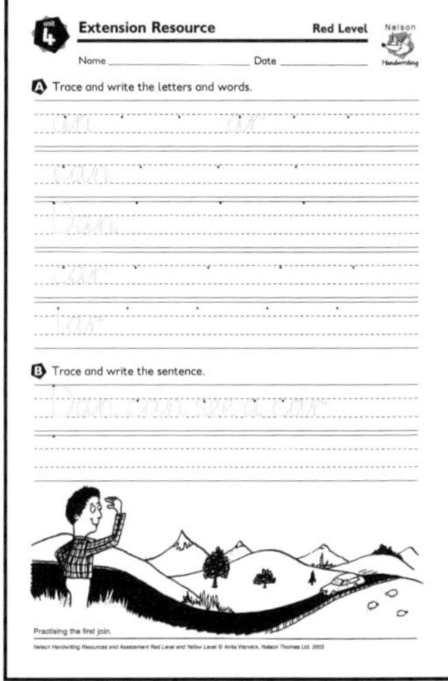

4 Extension Resource Red Level

Name Date

A Trace and write the letters and words.

B Trace and write the sentence.

Practising the first join.

Assessment

- The letters from the Focus and Extra sections are all the same height.
- The joining line is a diagonal join to the top of the next letter.
- Capital letters are almost twice the height of small letters.

UNIT 5

Objectives

- To practise the correct formation of the first join using letter patterns **ing**, **ung** and **ang**.

UNIT 5

Practising the first join.

ng

Sing, sing, sing.

FOCUS

A Copy this pattern into your book.

B Copy these letters into your book.

ing ing ing ing ing

ung ung ung ung ung

EXTRA

Copy the words below.
Write two words that rhyme.

ing	ung	ang
sing	hung	bang
ding		
king		

Be careful! The letter g has a **descender**. Its tail goes below the line.

EXTENSION

Copy this sentence into your book.

Ten sausages in a pan go bang.

12 13

Spelling links

- CVCC words
- rhyming words

Nelson theme – food

Developing Skills

Focus

- Before the lesson, draw four lines on the board (two rows of dotted lines in the middle) and write the whole class sentence between them.
- Read the sentence, or ask a child or the whole class to read the sentence.
- Look at, model and discuss the letters **ng**.
- Underline the letters **ng** in the words of the sentence on the board.
- Show the class how to form and join the letters **ng** in one movement.
- Draw the pattern on the board. Say that the pattern should help with joining.
- Tell the children to practise the pattern on their whiteboards.
- Show the children how to form and join the letters **ing**.
- Children then do this on their whiteboards.
- Repeat for **ung**.
- Explain that the join to the letter **g** means the pencil must come back round from the top of the x-height.
- Remind the children that the descender of the letter **g** goes below the line.

Extra

- Ask the children for words that end with **ing**.
- Write them on the board. (Use four lines on the board to help children see how to write on the lines.)
- Repeat for **ung**.
- Ask the children to complete the exercise in their books.
- They should copy all the **ing** words. Then they should copy **hung** and **bang**, and find two words that rhyme with each.

Extension

- Ask the group to read the caption. This sentence contains words using only the first join.
- Demonstrate by writing the sentence on the board.
- Emphasise how important it is that there is a space between each word and that the bodies of the letters are the same height, and that the ascenders and capitals are the same height.
- Children should copy the caption into their books.

Resources and Assessment

Focus

Further pattern practice and more practice of the first join. Tracing and copying more words ending **ing**.

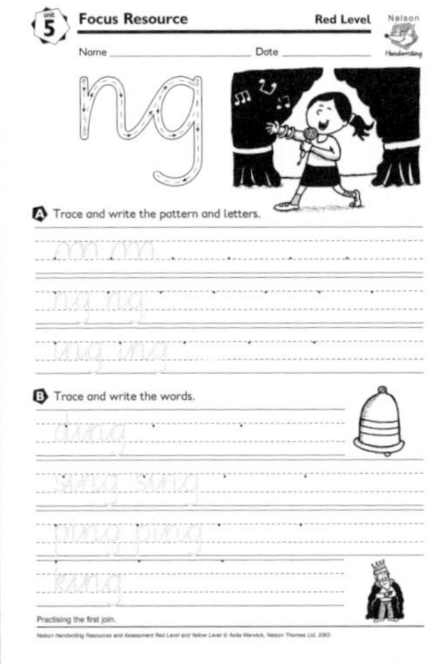

5 Focus Resource Red Level

Name Date

ng

A Trace and write the pattern and letters.

B Trace and write the words.

Practising the first join.

Extension

This extends the practice by tracing and copying more words ending **ung** and **ang**. The sentence puts the words the children have practised into context.

5 Extension Resource Red Level

Name Date

A Trace and write the letters and words.

B Trace and write the sentence.

Practising the first join.

Assessment

- The diagonal joining line curves up and round, to the start of the letter **g**.
- The letter **g** is formed correctly
- The descender of the letter **g** falls below the baseline.

UNIT 6

Objectives

- To practise the correct formation of the second join using letter patterns **ch** and **sh**.

Spelling links

- consonant digraphs **ch** and **sh**

Nelson theme – food

Developing Skills

Focus

- Before the lesson, draw four lines on the board (two rows of dotted lines in the middle) and write the whole class sentence between them.
- Introduce the lesson. Read the phrase. Point out the letters **ch** and **sh**.
- Write **c** and then **h** on the board.
- With a different coloured pen, show the joining line.
- Explain that the second join is similar to the first. It too is a diagonal join, but it is used when joining a small letter to a letter with an ascender.
- Explain that the joining line meets the ascender of the letter **h** at x-height and then continues to the top of the ascender.
- Show how to write and join the letters **ch** (and then **sh**) in one continuous movement.
- Draw the letters in the air.
- Children can trace over the letters at the top of the page.
- Ask the children to practise the pattern and the letters on their whiteboards, before copying them into their books.

Extra

- Demonstrate on the board that **ch** and **ip** make **chip**. Repeat for **ship**.
- Ask the children to copy these words into a lined handwriting book.
- Emphasise that it is important that the ascender of the letter **h** reaches the top line. Also explain that **p** has a descender which goes below the baseline.

Extension

- Ask the group to read the menu. What would they choose to eat?
- Tell them to copy their choice carefully into their handwriting books. Model one order on the board.
- Talk about the capital letters.
- Remind the group that the tail of the **p** goes below the line.

Resources and Assessment

Focus

Further pattern practice. More practice of the second join, tracing and copying words beginning with **ch** and **sh**.

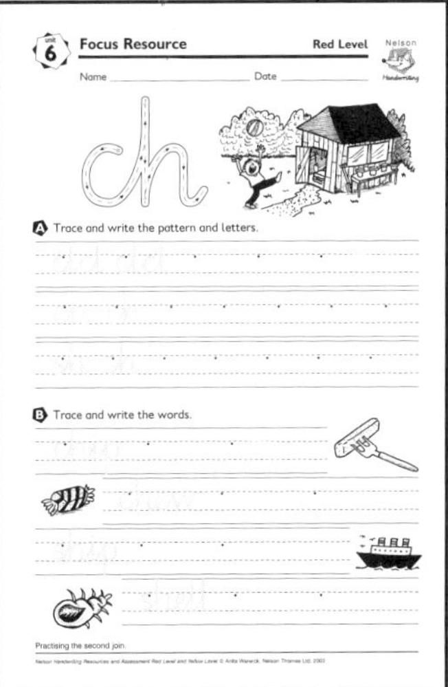

Extension

Further practice of the **ch** join. The sentence puts the join in context and provides both a tracing opportunity and a chance for higher attainers to write a sentence on their own.

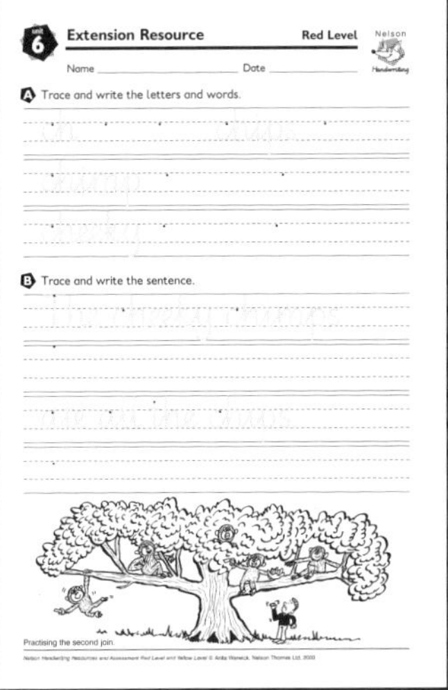

Assessment

- The ascender of the letter **h** is almost twice the height of the letters **c** and **s**.
- The join is made to the letter **h** at x-height.
- The body of the letter **h** is same height as letter **c** and **s**.

NIT 7

Objectives

- To practise the correct formation of the second join using letter patterns **th** and **tl**.

Unit 7
Practising the second join.
th
The cub and the cat hid.
Focus
A Copy this pattern into your book.
B Copy these letters into your book.
th th th th th
tl tl tl tl tl
Xtra
Copy these words into your book.
the the the the
them them them them
Be careful! The letter t is not as tall as the letter h.
Extension
Choose the right word. Write the sentences into your book.
1 I can see (the/them).
2 A little cub is eating all (the/them) cakes.

Spelling links

- letter pattern **th**

Nelson theme – foxes

Developing Skills

Focus

- Before the lesson, draw four lines on the board (two rows of dotted lines in the middle) and write the whole class sentence between them.
- Look at, model and discuss the letters **th**.
- Point out that although the letter **t** has an ascender it is not as tall as the letter **h**. It starts halfway between the top line and the x-height.
- The join comes from the bottom of the **t** and meets the ascender of the **h** about halfway up and then continues to the top.
- Point out that these two letters are joined in one continuous movement. Show this by writing them on the board or drawing in the air.
- Children should trace over the **th** at the top of the page to get the feel of the second join.
- Draw the pattern on the board.
- Illustrate the joining of **tl** on the board.
- Ask the children to practise the pattern and the letters on their whiteboards, before copying them into their books.

Extra

- Tell the group they are going to make three- and four-letter words beginning with **th**.
- Ask for examples. Write the suggestions on the board.
- Explain the exercise. Children should copy the words into a lined handwriting book.
- Emphasise that the ascender of the letter **t** does not reach the top line.

Extension

- Ask the group to read the sentences and to decide which word in the brackets makes sense.
- Model the first sentence on the board to illustrate.
- Discuss the height of the capital letter.
- Children copy the sentences into their books.

Resources and Assessment

Focus

Further pattern practice and more practice of the second join, using words beginning **th**. Tracing and copying the words.

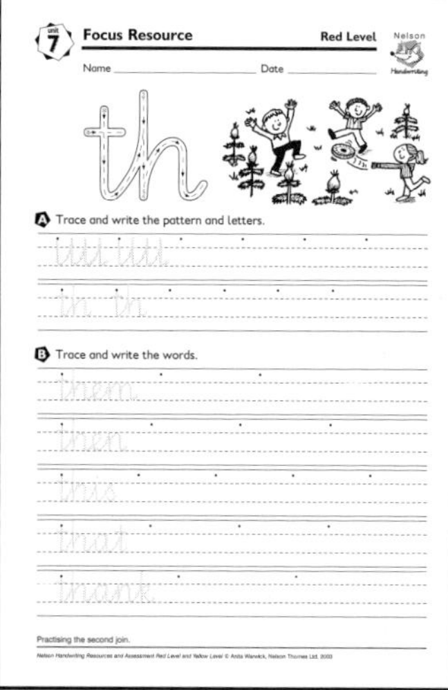

Extension

Further practice of the **th** join. The sentence puts the pattern in context and provides both a tracing opportunity and a chance for higher attainers to write a sentence on their own. Encourage those who need more practice to trace over the word and then copy the word underneath. You can also use a highlighter pen to help those children who are unsure where to begin on the lines. Writing the first two words will help some children complete the sentence correctly on their own.

Assessment

- The letter **t** begins about halfway between the top line and the top of the x-height.
- The **t** is crossed *just above* the x-height.
- The join, to the letter **h** and **l**, is made at x-height.

NIT 8

Objectives

- To practise the correct formation of the second join using letter patterns **ll** and **ill**.

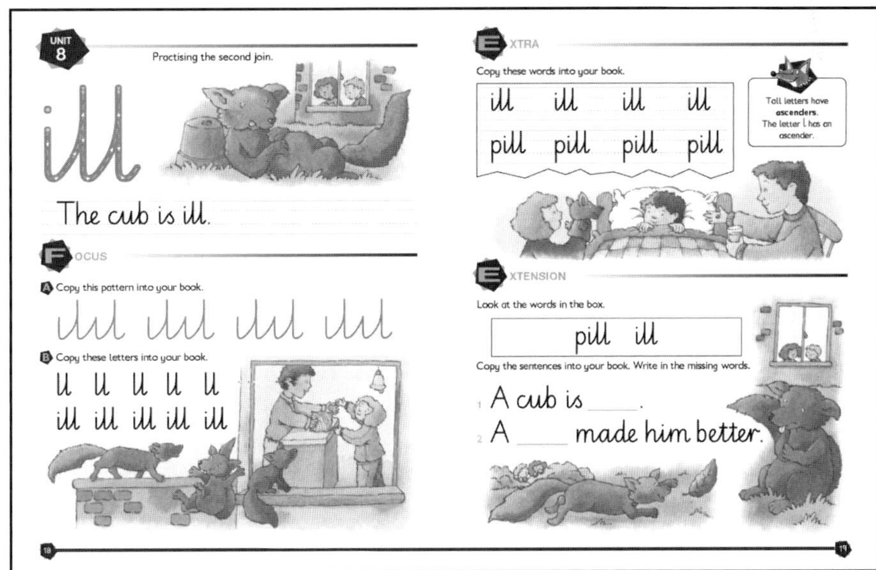

Spelling links

- letter pattern **ill**

Nelson theme – foxes

Developing Skills

Focus

- Before the lesson, draw four lines on the board (two rows of dotted lines in the middle) and write the whole class sentence between them.
- Look at, model and discuss the letters **ill**.
- Remind the children that the second join is the same as the first, except that it meets the ascender halfway up the letter and then continues to the top.
- The first and second joins should both slant at about 45 degrees.
- Point out that these three letters are joined with one continuous movement.
- Draw the letters in the air to illustrate.
- Children should trace over the large **ill** to get the feel of the join.
- Remind the children to dot the **i** after they have finished writing the rest of the word.
- Draw the pattern on the board. Explain that the pattern should help with joining.
- Ask the children to practise the pattern and the letters on their whiteboards, before copying them into their books.

Extra

- Ask the children to think of more words that rhyme with **ill**.
- Write the suggestions on the board.
- Emphasise that the ascenders of tall letters must reach the top line.
- The children should copy the words into their handwriting books.

Extension

- Ask the children to read the words in the box.
- Then they should read the sentences underneath and choose a word from the box to complete the sentences.
- Model the first sentence on the board.

Resources and Assessment

Focus

Further pattern practice and more practice of the second join using words that rhyme with **ill**.

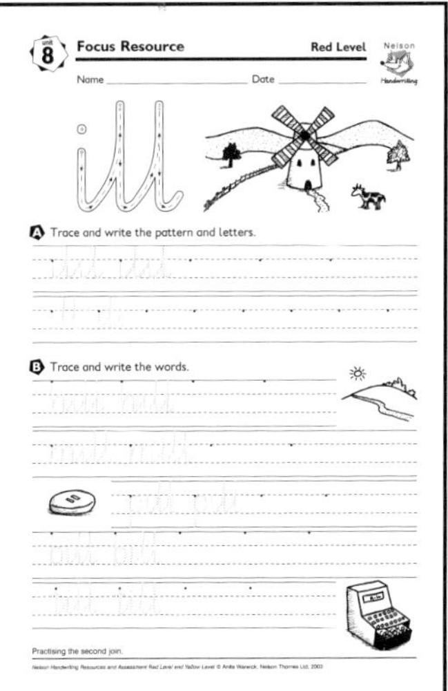

Extension

Further practice of the **ill** letter pattern. The sentence puts the pattern in context and provides both a tracing opportunity and a chance for higher attainers to write a sentence on their own.

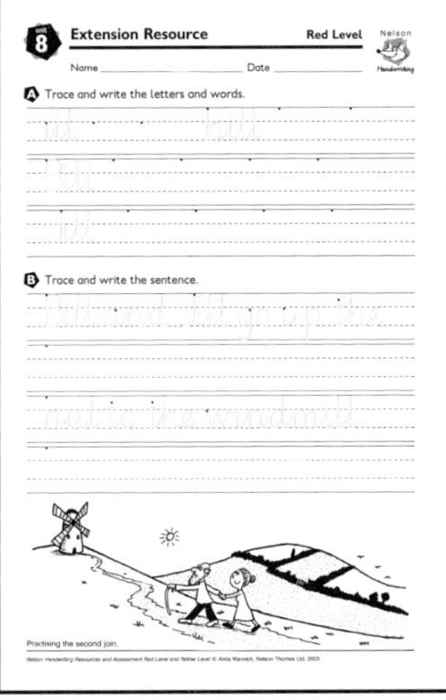

Assessment

- The letter **l** has an ascender which reaches the top line. It is almost twice the height of the small letters.
- The join to the letter **l** is made at approximately x-height (not at the bottom of the letter).
- The dot is placed above the letter **i** when the child has finished writing the word.

NIT 9

Objectives

- To practise the correct formation of the first and second joins using the letter patterns **sli** and **slu**.

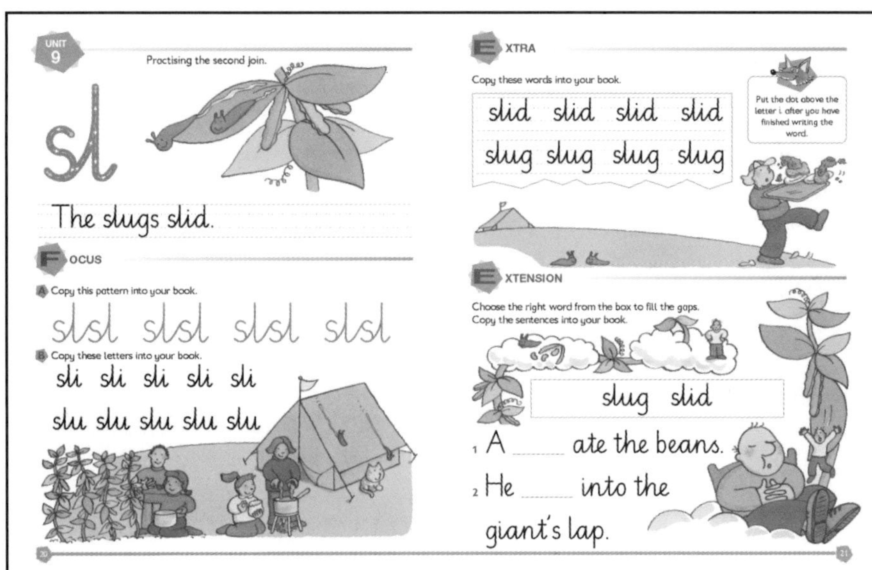

Spelling links

- letter pattern **sl**
- CCVC words

Nelson theme – beans

Developing Skills

Focus

- Before the lesson, draw four lines on the board (two rows of dotted lines in the middle) and write the whole class sentence between them.
- Look at, model and discuss the letters **sl**.
- Remind the children how the second join is formed.
- Point out how the letters are parallel and all letters are equidistant.
- Demonstrate by drawing in the air.
- Children should trace over the large **sl** to get the feel of the join.
- Draw the pattern on the board. Explain that the pattern should help with joining.
- Point out the formation of the **s**. Tell the children how the letter starts at the top and comes back round.
- Remind them that **l** is a tall letter: it has an ascender which touches the top line.
- Ask the children to practise the pattern and the letters on their whiteboards, before copying them into their books.

Extra

- The children should practise writing the words **slid** and **slug** in their books. Point out that these words contain both the first and second joins.
- Ask children to think of more words beginning with **sl**.
- Write these suggestions on the board.
- Emphasise that the ascenders of the tall letters must reach the top line.
- Discuss how the descender of the letter **g** goes below the baseline.

Extension

- Discuss the pictures.
- Ask the children to read the words in the box.
- Then they should read the sentences underneath and choose a word from the box to complete the sentences.
- Model the first sentence on the board.

Resources and Assessment

Focus

Further practice of the letter pattern and more practice of the first and second join, using the **sl** letter pattern. Tracing and copying words.

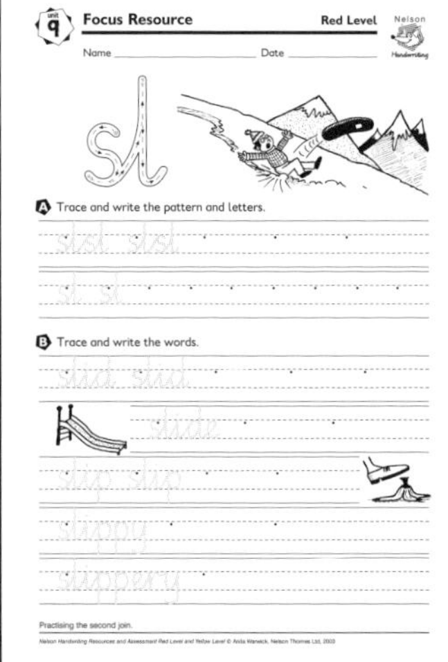

Extension

Further practice of the **sl** letter pattern. The sentence puts the pattern in context and provides both a tracing opportunity and a chance for higher attainers to write a sentence on their own.

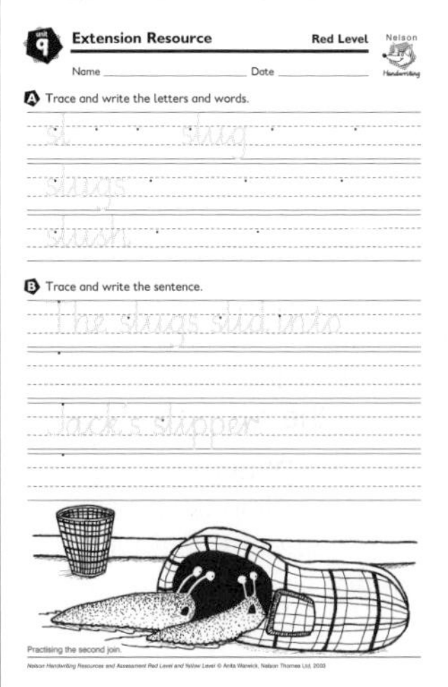

Assessment

- The letters are the correct height and size, e.g. the letter **l** is almost twice the height of the letter **s**, **i**, and **u**.
- The join is made at approximately x-height to the letter **l**.
- The join is made at or near the top of the letters **u** and **i**.

NIT 10

Objectives

- To practise the correct formation of the second join using letter patterns **ck** and **ack**.

UNIT 10 Practising the second join.

ck

Quick, Jack. Get the sack.

FOCUS

A Copy this pattern into your book.

ckck ckck ckck ckck

B Copy these letters into your book.

ck ck ck ck ck

ack ack ack ack ack

XTRA

Make these words. Copy them into your book.

sa + ck = sack sack sack

ba + ck = back back back

b is a break letter. It does not join to the next letter.

XTENSION

Copy these sentences into your books. Choose the right word to fill the gaps.

1 back / sack — Jack had a .... on his ....

2 packed / sack — Jack made it. He .... all the gems in his ....

22 23

Spelling links

- letter pattern words ending in **ck**
- CVCC words

Nelson theme – beans

Developing Skills

Focus

- Before the lesson, draw four lines on the board (two rows of dotted lines in the middle) and write the whole class sentence between them.
- Look at, model and discuss the letters **ck**.
- Remind the children how the second join is formed.
- Demonstrate by drawing in the air.
- Children should trace over the large **ck** to get the feel of the join.
- Draw the pattern on the board.
- Point out the letter formation of **ck** and **ack**.
- Ask the children to practise the pattern and the letters on their whiteboards, before copying them into their books.

Extra

- The children should practise writing the words ending in **ck**.
- Ask them to think of more rhyming words.
- Write their suggestions on the board.
- Emphasise correct formation of the letter **k**: the pencil comes back over at the same height as the **c**.
- Tell children that **b** is a break letter: it does not join to the next letter.

Extension

- Ask the children to read the words in the tinted boxes.
- They should then read the sentences and choose the correct words to fill the gaps.
- Model the first sentence on the board.

Resources and Assessment

Focus

Further pattern practice and more practice of the second join, using **ack**, **ick** and **eck** letter patterns.

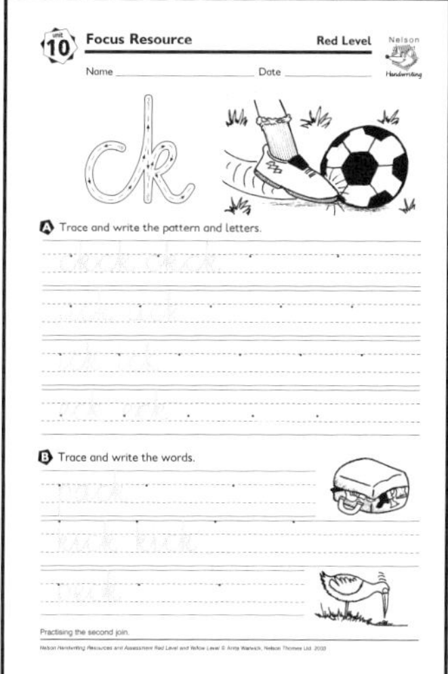

10 Focus Resource — Red Level

Name .... Date ....

ck

A Trace and write the pattern and letters.

B Trace and write the words.

Practising the second join.

Extension

Further practice of the **ack** letter pattern. The sentence puts the pattern in context and provides both a tracing opportunity and a chance for higher attainers to write a sentence on their own.

10 Extension Resource — Red Level

Name .... Date ....

A Trace and write the letters and words.

B Trace and write the sentence.

Practising the second join.

Assessment

- The letter **k** is formed correctly: the body of the letter is same height as letter **c**.
- The join to the letter **k** is made at approximately x-height.
- The letters **b**, **k** and **d** have ascenders which reach the top line.

CHECK-UP 1

Objectives

Explain to the pupils that this exercise is an assessment activity. The objective of the check-up is to assess what the pupils can do and where they need extra practice. This exercise will help assess each pupil's ability to form and use the first two handwriting joins.

CHECK-UP 1

FOCUS

Copy these patterns into your book.

EXTRA

Copy these words into your book.

bun	mum	leg	bed
sing	chips	nan	car
slug	sack	back	ill

EXTENSION

Copy this sentence into your book.

Jack and Jill go up the hill.

24

25

Focus

Ask the pupils to copy the patterns into their books. Pattern one, two and three help with the formation of the first handwriting join. The last two patterns help with the formation of the second join.

Extra

Ask the pupils to copy these words into their books. The words in the first line contain letters linked with the first handwriting join. The words on the second and third line contain the first join and some contain both the first and second join.

Extension

Ask the pupils to copy this sentence into their books. It contains both first and second handwriting joins.

Assessment

- Are the first and second joins formed correctly?
- Is the join made from the bottom of one letter to the top of the x-height of the next?
- Are similar letters the same height?

- For more Assessment see *Resources and Assessment Book Red and Yellow Level*

UNIT 11

Objectives

- To practise the second join to the letter **t**.

Spelling links

- letter pattern **st**
- CCVC and CCVCC

Nelson theme – toys

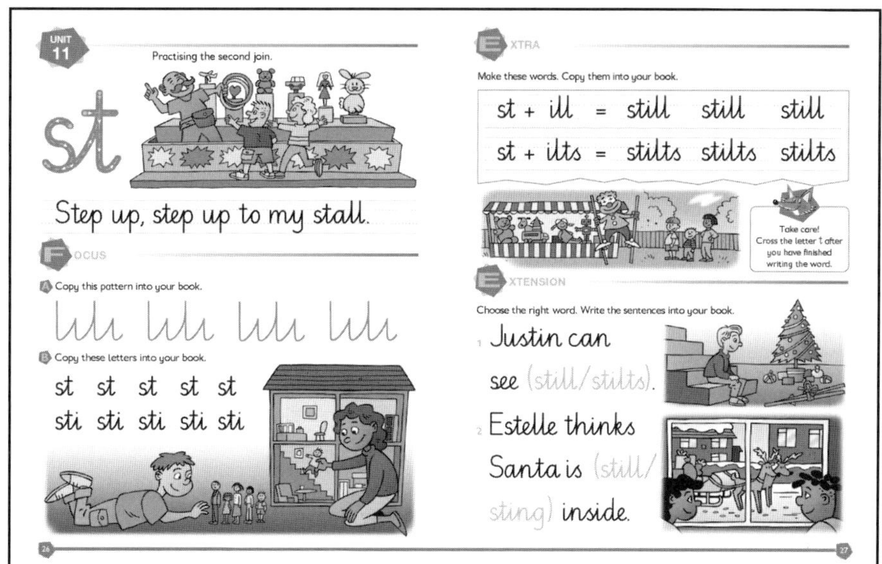

UNIT 11
Practising the second join.
st
Step up, step up to my stall.
FOCUS
A Copy this pattern into your book.
B Copy these letters into your book.
st st st st st
sti sti sti sti sti
EXTRA
Make these words. Copy them into your book.
st + ill = still still still
st + ilts = stilts stilts stilts
Take care! Cross the letter t after you have finished writing the word.
EXTENSION
Choose the right word. Write the sentences into your book.
1 Justin can see (still/stilts).
2 Estelle thinks Santa is (still/sting) inside.
26
27

Developing Skills

Focus

- Before the lesson, draw four lines on the board (two rows of dotted lines in the middle) and write the whole class sentence between them.
- Look at, model and discuss the letters **st**.
- Some children find joining letters to **t** difficult. When demonstrating the join, remind the class that the ascender of the letter **t** is not as tall as other ascenders, and the crossbar is added after the join or joins have been made.
- The join should still be made at the crossbar height of the **t**.
- Demonstrate by drawing in the air.
- Children should trace with their fingers over the large **st** in their books to get the feel of the join.
- Draw the pattern on the board.
- Ask the children to practise the pattern and the letters on their whiteboards, before copying them into their books.

Extra

- The children should copy the **st** words which use both the first and the second join. Ask the children to think of other words beginning **st**.
- Write these suggestions on the board.
- Point out the difference in the height of the **t** compared with the **l**.

Extension

- Read the first sentence together.
- Ask the group to decide which word they should choose.
- Model the first sentence on the board.

Resources and Assessment

Focus

Further pattern practice and more practice of the first and second joins using **sti** at the beginning of words. Tracing and copying words.

Extension

Further practice of the **st** consonant digraph at the beginning of words. The sentence puts the pattern in context and provides both a tracing opportunity and a chance for higher attainers to write a sentence on their own.

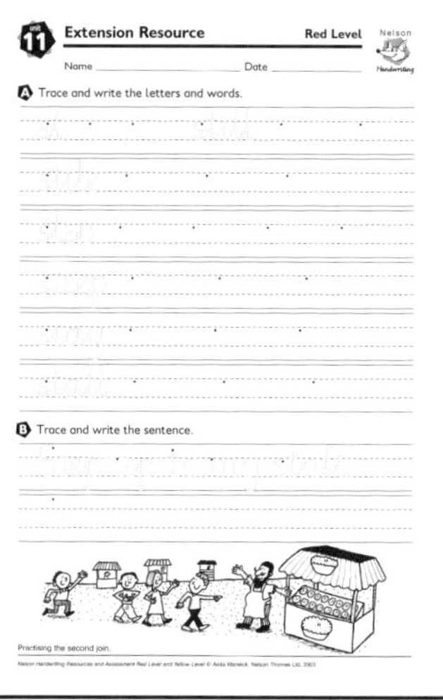

Assessment

- The ascender of the letter **t** is not as tall as the other ascenders.
- The cross, on the letter **t**, is made just above the top of the x-height.
- The join to the letter **t**, is made at approximately x-height.

NIT 12

Objectives

- To practise the second join to the letter **k**.

Spelling links

- letter pattern **nk**
- CVCC words

Nelson theme – toys

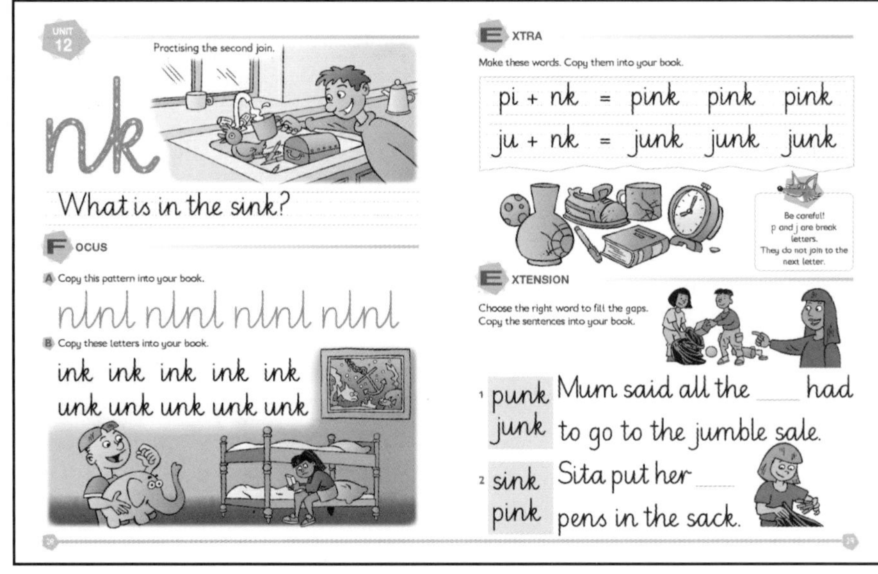

UNIT 12

Practising the second join.

nk

What is in the sink?

FOCUS

A Copy this pattern into your book.

nlnl nlnl nlnl nlnl

B Copy these letters into your book.

ink ink ink ink ink

unk unk unk unk unk

EXTRA

Make these words. Copy them into your book.

pi + nk = pink pink pink

ju + nk = junk junk junk

Be careful! p and j are break letters. They do not join to the next letter.

EXTENSION

Choose the right word to fill the gaps. Copy the sentences into your book.

1 punk junk Mum said all the ____ had to go to the jumble sale.

2 sink pink Sita put her ____ pens in the sack.

Developing Skills

Focus

- Before the lesson, draw four lines on the board (two rows of dotted lines in the middle) and write the whole class sentence between them.
- Look at, model and discuss the letters **nk**.
- Some children find joining letters to **k** difficult. When demonstrating the join, point out that when the letter **k** is formed the main body of the letter is the same height as letters without ascenders, e.g. **n**.
- Draw the letter **k** in the air.
- Children should trace over the large **nk** in the book with their fingers to get the feel of the join.
- Ask children to suggest words ending **ink**. Repeat for **unk**.
- Draw the pattern on the board.
- Ask the children to practise the pattern and the letters on their whiteboards, before copying them into their books.

Extra

- Ask the children to copy the words ending with **nk** which use both the first and the second join.
- Write a list of words that rhyme with **pink** and **junk**. Children could write their own words on their whiteboards.

Extension

- Read the sentences together.
- Ask the group to decide which word they would choose to fill the gaps.
- Help the children by writing the first sentence on the board.

Resources and Assessment

Focus

Further pattern practice and more practice of the first and second joins using words ending **ink**.

12 Focus Resource Red Level

Name Date

nk

A Trace and write the pattern and letters.

B Trace and write the words.

Practising the second join

Extension

An opportunity for further practice of the **nk** letter pattern using words ending with **unk**. The sentence puts the pattern in context and provides both a tracing opportunity and a chance for higher attainers to write a sentence on their own.

12 Extension Resource Red Level

Name Date

A Trace and write the letters and words.

B Trace and write the sentence.

Practising the second join

Assessment

- The body of the letter **k** is same height as letter **n**.
- The diagonal join is made to the top of the letter **n** and at x-height on the letter **k**.
- The letters **p** and **j** have descenders which fall below the baseline.

NIT 13

Objectives

- To introduce and practise the third join.

Spelling links

- CVC words with **o** as the medial vowel

Nelson theme – homes

UNIT 13 Practising the third join.

og

The frog is on a log.

Focus

A Copy this pattern into your book.

ooo ooo ooo ooo

B Copy these letters into your book.

od od od od od

og og og og og

Remember to keep your letters spaced correctly like this: od

Extra

Make these words. Copy them into your book.

d + og = dog dog dog

fr + og = frog frog frog

Extension

Choose the right word. Copy the sentences into your book.

1 A (cat/dog) lives in a kennel.

2 A (bird/frog) lives in a pond.

30 31

Developing Skills

Focus

- Before the lesson, draw four lines on the board (two rows of dotted lines in the middle) and write the whole class sentence between them.
- Look at, model and discuss the letters **og**. Stress the shallow horizontal curve of the join.
- Some children find this join tricky. Stress that the distance between the two letters should be the same as between letters using the first or second join.
- Encouraging and practising this join now will prevent bad habits forming later on.
- Demonstrate the third join made to the letters **o**, **r**, **m** and **i**.
- Emphasise again the distance between the letters. The fox box reminds the children to keep the letters well spaced.
- Draw the letters in the air.
- Children should trace over the large **og** to get the feel of the join.
- Ask the children to practise the pattern and the letters on their whiteboards, before copying them into their books.

Extra

- The children should practise writing the words containing a medial **o**.
- Ask children to think of other words that rhyme with **dog**.
- Write these on the board.

Extension

- Read the first sentence together.
- Ask the group to decide which word they should choose to complete the sentences.
- Model the first sentence on the board.

Resources and Assessment

Focus

Further practice of the **og** letter pattern and the first and third join using medial **o**. Words are practised to put the joins into context.

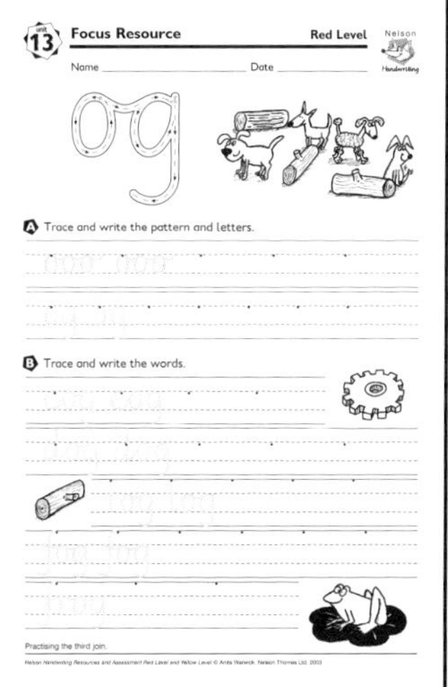

13 Focus Resource Red Level

Name Date

og

A Trace and write the pattern and letters.

B Trace and write the words.

Practising the third join.

Extension

Further practice of the **og** letter pattern and introduction of words ending **od**. The sentence puts the pattern in context and provides both a tracing opportunity and a chance for higher attainers to write a sentence on their own.

13 Extension Resource Red Level

Name Date

A Trace and write the letters and words.

B Trace and write the sentence.

Practising the third join.

Assessment

- The letters **o** and **d**, and **o** and **g** are joined using a horizontal joining line.
- There is a space between the letters **o** and **g**, and **o** and **d**.
- The letter **f** has a full-height ascender, and its descender almost touches the bottom line.

NIT 14

Objectives

- To introduce and practise the horizontal join to the letter **e**.

Spelling links

- CCVV words

Nelson theme – homes

UNIT 14

Practising the third join.

re

There are people moving in.

FOCUS

A Copy this pattern into your book.

rere rere rere rere

B Copy these letters into your book.

re re re re re

ve ve ve ve ve

Take care! Bring your pencil down to write the letter e, like this: re

EXTRA

Copy these words in to your book.

are are are are

there there there there

EXTENSION

Copy this poem into your book.

Are there any apples
On your apple tree?
Do you think your mother
Will ask me in to tea?

from 'The New Neighbour' by Rose Fyleman

Developing Skills

Focus

- Before the lesson, draw four lines on the board (two rows of dotted lines in the middle) and write the whole class sentence between them.
- Look at, model and discuss the letters **re**. Stress the horizontal curve of the join.
- Most children find this join tricky. Stress that the joining line from letters that finish at the top, e.g. **w**, **r** and **v**, comes down quite low to join to the letter **e**.
- Children should trace over the large **re** to get the feel of the join.
- Contrast and compare the two different joins to **e** using the words **we** and **me**. The distance between the two letters should be the same as that between letters joined using the first or second join.
- Time spent encouraging and practising this join to the letter **e** will prevent bad habits forming later on.
- Demonstrate by drawing in the air.
- Ask the children to practise the pattern and the letters on their whiteboards, before copying them into their books

Extra

- The children should practise writing the words which end in **re**.
- The word **there** enables the children to practise both joins to the letter **e**.

Extension

- Read the poem together.
- Ask children to point out words which contain the third join, i.e. **there**, **tree**.
- It helps children to see the handwriting expected of them modelled. Demonstrate by copying this poem on the board.

Resources and Assessment

Focus

Further practice of the third join using **re**. Words put the pattern in context.

14 Focus Resource Red Level

Name Date

re

A Trace and write the pattern and letters.

rere rere

re re

B Trace and write the words.

read

read read

read read

read read

Practising the third join.

Extension

Further practice of the third join to **e**, adding **ve** and **we**. The sentence puts the pattern in context and provides both a tracing opportunity and a chance for higher attainers to write a sentence on their own.

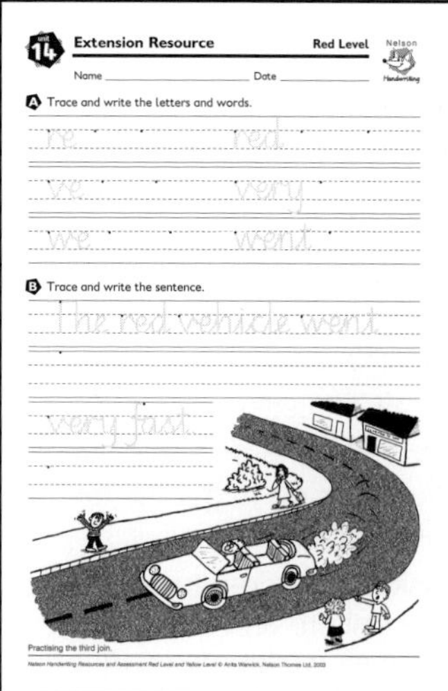

14 Extension Resource Red Level

Name Date

A Trace and write the letters and words.

re red

ve very

we went

B Trace and write the sentence.

The red vehicle went

very fast.

Practising the third join.

Assessment

- The letter **e** is formed correctly.
- The pencil is brought down, after the letter **r** and **v**, to enable the letter **e** to be formed correctly.
- There is a space between the letters **v** and **e**.

UNIT 15

Objectives

- To practise the third join.

UNIT 15 Practising the third join.

oo

I can see the moon.

FOCUS

A Copy this pattern into your book.

roro roro roro roro

B Copy these letters into your book.

oon oon oon oon oon

oom oom oom oom oom

Remember to keep your letters spaced correctly, like this: oom

EXTRA

Copy these words in to your book.

moon moon moon moon

room room room room

EXTENSION

Choose the correct word to finish the sentence. Copy the sentences into your book.

1 The tiger crept into the (broom/room).

2 The (moon/soon) was shining through the window.

Spelling links

- letter pattern **oo**
- long **oo** sound

Nelson theme – tigers

Developing Skills

Focus

- Before the lesson, draw four lines on the board (two rows of dotted lines in the middle) and write the whole class sentence between them.
- Look at, model and discuss the letters **oo**. Stress the horizontal curve of the join.
- Most children find this join tricky. Children should trace over the large **oo** to get the feel of the join.
- Children often write these letters too close together. Point out that the distance between the two letters should be the same as between letters using the first or second join.
- Time spent encouraging and practising this join will prevent bad habits forming later on.
- Demonstrate by drawing in the air.
- Ask the children to practise the pattern and the letters on their whiteboards, before copying them into their books.

Extra

- The children should copy the simple **oo** words carefully.
- These words enable the children to practise the first and third joins.

Extension

- Read the sentences together.
- Ask the group to decide which word makes sense in each sentence.
- Model the first sentence on the board.
- Children copy the correct sentences into their lined books.

Resources and Assessment

Focus

Further practice of the third join. Words put the **oo** pattern in context.

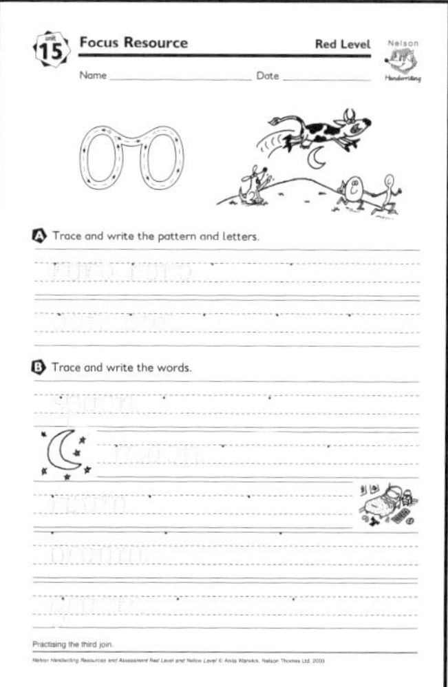

15 Focus Resource Red Level

A Trace and write the pattern and letters.

B Trace and write the words.

Extension

An opportunity for further practice of the **oom** and **oon** patterns. The sentence puts the patterns in context and provides both a tracing opportunity and a chance for higher attainers to write a sentence on their own.

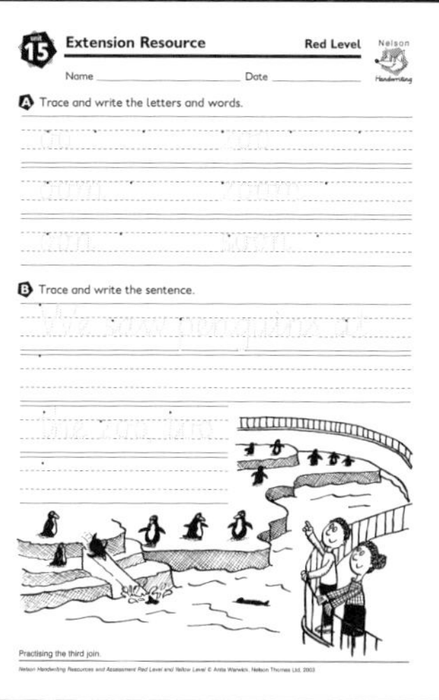

15 Extension Resource Red Level

A Trace and write the letters and words.

B Trace and write the sentence.

Assessment

- There is a space between the letters **o** and **o**, and **o** and **m** or **n**.
- There is a consistent space between the letters.

UNIT 16

Objectives

- To introduce and practise the fourth join.

Spelling links

- words ending **wl**
- rhyming words

Nelson theme – tigers

Developing Skills

Focus

- Before the lesson, draw four lines on the board (two rows of dotted lines in the middle) and write the whole class sentence between them.
- The fourth join joins letters from set 4 to letters from set 3 (see page 10).
- Look at, model and discuss the letters **wl** and **vl**.
- It should be noted that the fourth join is the same as the first join except that it is made from the x-height to the top of an ascender. Encourage the join to be made towards the top of the ascender rather than at the very top.
- Children should trace over the large **wl** to get the feel of the join.
- Point out that the distance between the two letters should be the same as between letters using the first, second or third joins.
- Draw the letters in the air. Use the correct vocabulary as you demonstrate.
- Ask the children to practise the pattern and the letters on their whiteboards, before copying them into their books.

Extra

- The children should copy the words containing the **wl** letter pattern. These words enable the children to practise the third and the fourth join.
- Point out that the letters **g** and **p** are break letters: they do not join to the letters which follow them.

Extension

- Discuss what an acrostic poem is.
- Read the poem together.
- Point out the word which contains the fourth join, i.e. **prowl**.
- It helps children to see the handwriting expected of them modelled.
- Demonstrate by copying this poem on the board.

Resources and Assessment

Focus

Further practice of the fourth join using letter pattern **wl**. Words are used to put the pattern into context.

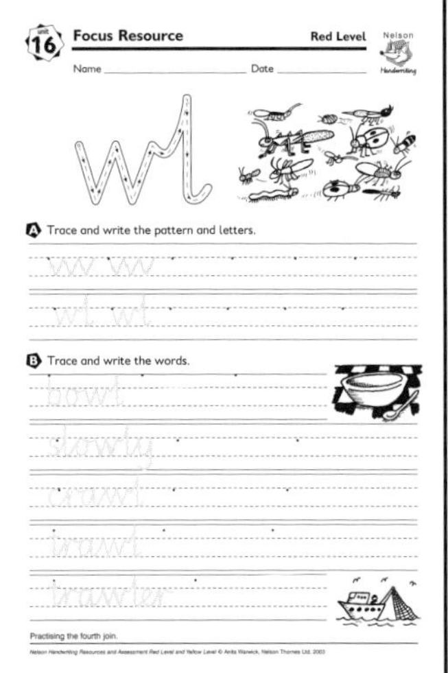

Extension

An opportunity for further practice. The sentence puts the **wl** pattern into context and allows higher attainers to write a sentence on their own.

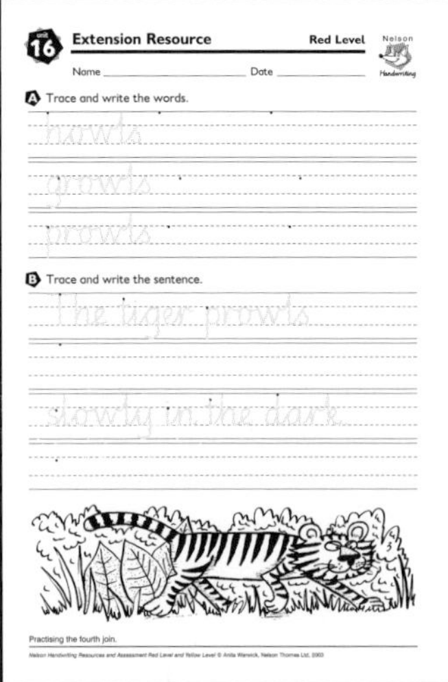

Assessment

- The joining line, from the letter **w**, dips down then goes up almost to the top of the letter **l**.
- The join creates a space between the letters **w** and **l**, **vl** and **rk**.

NIT 17

Objectives

- To practise the fourth join.

Spelling links

- **of** and **off**

Nelson theme – myself

UNIT 17 Practising the fourth join.

of

I like soft coffee toffees.

FOCUS

A Copy this pattern into your book.

fff fff fff fff

B Copy these letters into your book.

of of of of of
ff ff ff ff ff

Be careful! The join to the second f starts when you cross the first f, like this: ff

EXTRA

Copy these words into your book.

of of of of
off off off off

EXTENSION

Choose of or off to finish these sentences. Copy the sentences into your book.

1 I love the smell ___ daffodils.

2 Fluff falls ___ my jumper.

Developing Skills

Focus

- Before the lesson, draw four lines on the board (two rows of dotted lines in the middle) and write the whole class sentence between them.
- Look at, model and discuss the letters **of** and **ff**.
- Many children find **f** a difficult letter to form and join correctly. It should be noted that the **f** begins *just below* the top line and finishes *just above* the bottom line. It has a straight back.
- Encourage the join to the **f** to be made towards the top of the letter rather than at the very top.
- Children should trace over the large **of** to get the feel of the join.
- Point out that the distance between the two letters should be the same as between letters using the first, second or third joins.
- Demonstrate by drawing in the air.
- Point out that when **f** is joined to another letter, e.g. **ft**, the join is made from the crossbar of the **f** to a point near the top of the **t**.
- Ask the children to practise the pattern and the letters on their whiteboards, before copying them into their books

Extra

- The children should practise writing **of** and **off**.
- These words enable the children to practise the fourth join.

Extension

- Read the sentences together.
- Discuss which word **of** or **off** fits the context of the sentence.
- Model the writing of the first sentence on the board.
- The children should copy the sentences into their book.

Resources and Assessment

Focus

Further practice of the fourth join using the letter patterns **of**, **ff** and **uff**.

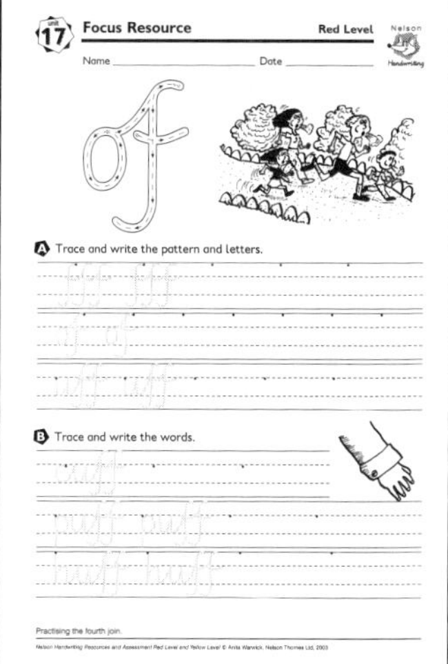

17 Focus Resource Red Level

Name ______ Date ______

of

A Trace and write the pattern and letters.

B Trace and write the words.

Practising the fourth join.

Extension

Practising correct formation of the **ff** letter pattern. Choosing the right word to fit the sense of a sentence and copying sentences into lined handwriting books.

17 Extension Resource Red Level

Name ______ Date ______

A Trace and write the letters and words.

B Choose the correct word. Write the sentences.

Practising the fourth join.

Assessment

- The letter **f** begins near the top line and finishes just above the bottom line.
- The letter **f** has a straight back.
- The join is made from the top of the letter **o** and past the cross on the letter **f**, up and round to the start of the letter **f**.

NIT 18

Objectives

- To practise the fourth join.

Spelling links

- consonant digraph **fl**

Nelson theme – myself

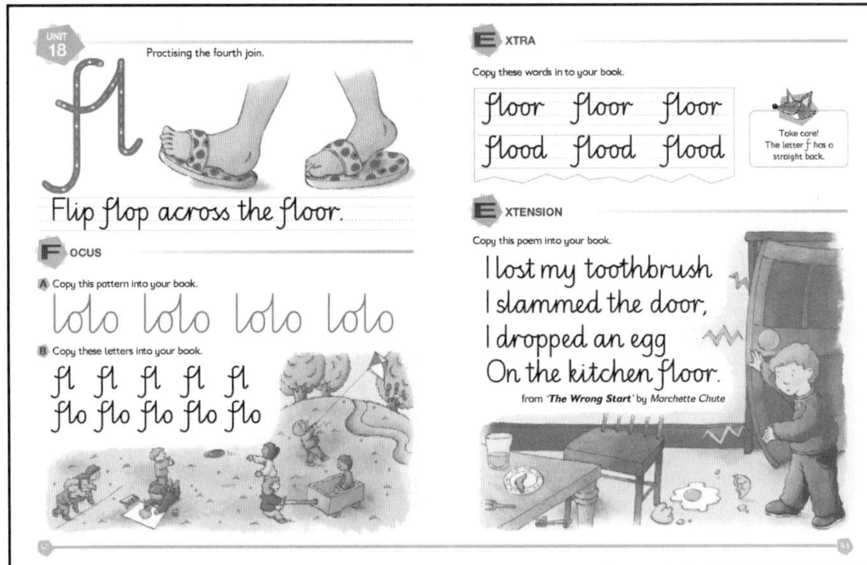

UNIT 18

Practising the fourth join.

fl

Flip flop across the floor.

FOCUS

A Copy this pattern into your book.

lolo lolo lolo lolo

B Copy these letters into your book.

fl fl fl fl fl

flo flo flo flo flo

EXTRA

Copy these words in to your book.

floor floor floor

flood flood flood

Take care! The letter f has a straight back.

EXTENSION

Copy this poem into your book.

I lost my toothbrush
I slammed the door,
I dropped an egg
On the kitchen floor.

from '*The Wrong Start*' by Marchette Chute

Developing Skills

Focus

- Before the lesson, draw four lines on the board (two rows of dotted lines in the middle) and write the whole class sentence between them.
- Look at, model and discuss the letters **fl**.
- Many children find **f** a difficult letter to form and join correctly. It should be noted that the **f** begins *just below* the top line and finishes *just above* the bottom line. The letter **f** has a straight back.
- Encourage the join from the crossbar of the **f** to be made towards the top of the letter **l**.
- Children should trace over the large **fl** to get the feel of the join.
- Point out that the distance between the two letters should be the same as between letters using the first, second or third joins.
- Demonstrate by drawing in the air.
- Point out that when **f** is joined to another letter, e.g. **fl**, the join is made from the crossbar of the **f** to somewhere near the top of the **l**.
- Ask the children to practise the pattern and the letters on their whiteboards, before copying them into their books.

Extra

- The children should copy the **fl** words to practise the fourth join.

Extension

- Read the sentences together, decide which spelling fits the context of the sentence.
- The children should copy the sentences into their books.

Resources and Assessment

Focus

Further practice of the fourth join using the consonant digraph **fl**. Ensure any errors are noticed and corrected.

18 Focus Resource — Red Level

Name ______ Date ______

fl

A Trace and write the pattern and letters.

lolo lolo

fl fl

flo flo

B Trace and write the words.

Practising the fourth join.

Extension

More practice of the fourth join by writing a neat copy of a poem.

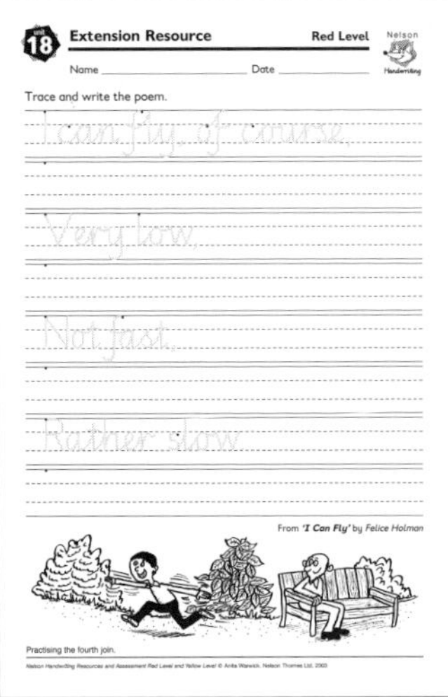

18 Extension Resource — Red Level

Name ______ Date ______

Trace and write the poem.

I can fly, of course,

Very low,

Not fast,

Rather slow.

From '*I Can Fly*' by Felice Holman

Practising the fourth join.

Assessment

- The letter **f** begins near the top line and finishes just above the bottom line.
- The letter **f** has a straight back.
- The join is made from the cross on the letter **f** up to near the top of the letter **l**.

UNIT 19

Objectives

- To introduce and practise the break letters **b**, **g**, **j**, **p**, **q**, **y** and **z**.

It is not easy to make joins from these letters. Some schools do teach children to join from some, or all, of these letters. At this stage it is easiest to encourage children ***not*** *to join these letters. Later on (Year 5 P6 onwards) as children begin to develop their own style of writing, many will begin to join all letters to aid speed and fluency.*

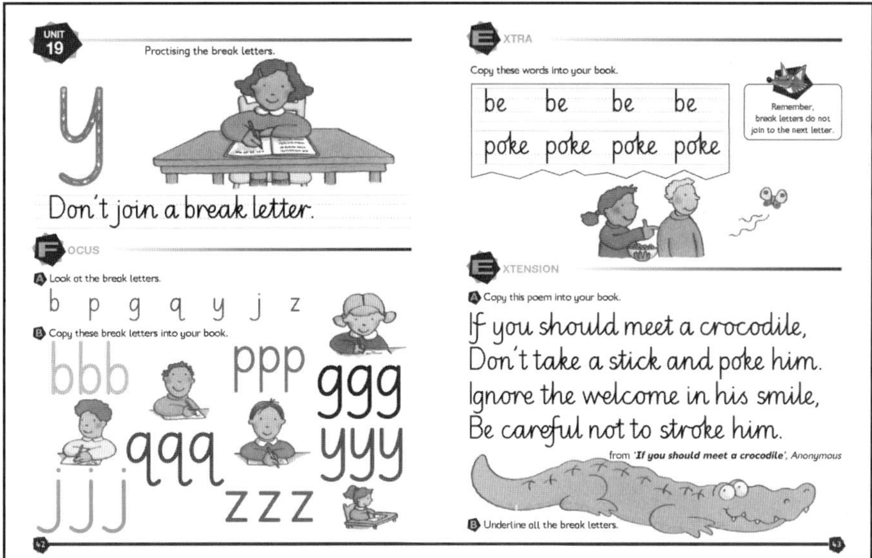

UNIT 19 Practising the break letters.

y

Don't join a break letter.

FOCUS

A Look at the break letters.

b p g q y j z

B Copy these break letters into your book.

bbb ppp ggg qqq yyy jjj zzz

EXTRA

Copy these words into your book.

be be be be

poke poke poke poke

Remember, break letters do not join to the next letter.

EXTENSION

A Copy this poem into your book.

If you should meet a crocodile,
Don't take a stick and poke him.
Ignore the welcome in his smile,
Be careful not to stroke him.

from *'If you should meet a crocodile'*, Anonymous

B Underline all the break letters.

Developing Skills

Focus

- Before the lesson, draw four lines on the board (two rows of dotted lines in the middle) and write the whole class sentence between them.
- Look at, model and discuss the break letters.
- Point out that joins are not made from these letters.
- Write the letters on the board. Stress that when we write these letters they all begin at the top.
- Demonstrate by drawing in the air.
- Ask children to write the letters on their own individual whiteboards.
- Point out that the letters **g**, **j**, **p**, **q** and **y** all have descenders – their tails go below the line.

Extra

- The children should copy the words which contain the break letters **b** and **p**.
- Encourage children to ensure the **p** sits on the baseline and its descender goes below it.

Extension

- Read the poem together.
- Ask the children to identify the break letters.
- Demonstrate good handwriting by copying some of the poem onto the board.
- Underline the break letters.

Resources and Assessment

Focus

Children trace over break letters and then practise on their own. Do watch to ensure any errors are noticed.

19 Focus Resource Red Level

Name Date

Trace and write the break letters.

Practising the break letters

Extension

Phrases featuring words containing the break letters provide further practice for higher attainers.

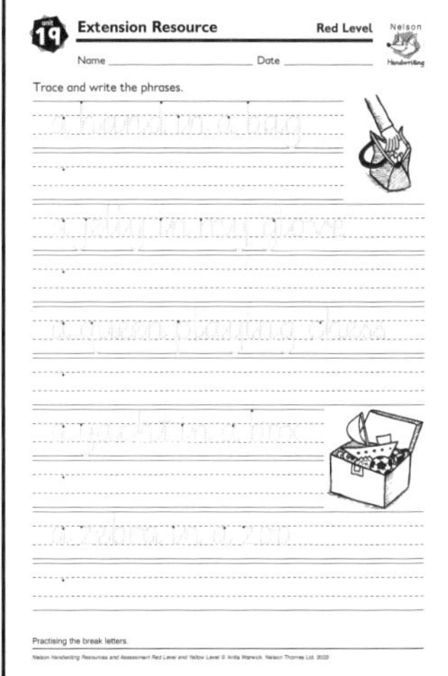

19 Extension Resource Red Level

Name Date

Trace and write the phrases.

Practising the break letters

Assessment

- No joins are made from the break letters.
- The descenders of the letters **p**, **g**, **q**, **y** and **j** fall below the line.
- The break letter and the letter following it do not touch.

NIT 20

Objectives

- Revising capital letters.

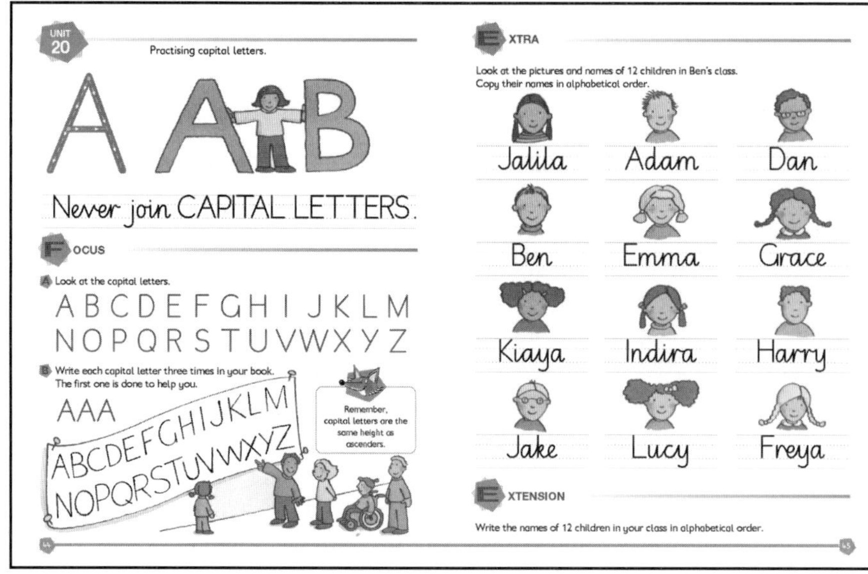

UNIT 20 Practising capital letters.

Never join CAPITAL LETTERS.

FOCUS

A Look at the capital letters.

A B C D E F G H I J K L M
N O P Q R S T U V W X Y Z

B Write each capital letter three times in your book. The first one is done to help you.

AAA

Remember, capital letters are the same height as ascenders.

EXTRA

Look at the pictures and names of 12 children in Ben's class. Copy their names in alphabetical order.

Jalila Adam Dan
Ben Emma Grace
Kiaya Indira Harry
Jake Lucy Freya

EXTENSION

Write the names of 12 children in your class in alphabetical order.

Spelling links

- punctuation – capital letters
- vocabulary – dictionary skills

Nelson theme – myself

Developing Skills

Focus

- Before the lesson, draw four lines on the board (two rows of dotted lines in the middle) and write the whole class sentence between them.
- Stress that a capital letter is never joined to another letter.
- Point out that these letters all begin at the top.
- Remind children that capital letters are always used to begin a sentence and a person's name.
- Demonstrate good handwriting by copying some of the capital letters onto the board.
- Ask the children to practise writing some of the letters on their own individual whiteboards and then copy them into their books.

Extra

- Read the names of the children together.
- Ensure that the children understand the concept of ordering the names.

Extension

- Try to make sure that the group choose 12 names starting with as many different letters as possible.

Resources and Assessment

Focus

This provides further practice in forming capital letters. Children need to finish the rows of two-letter patterns. Watch to make sure they start each letter at the top.

20 Focus Resource Red Level

Name Date

Trace and write these capital letters.

AM BD
CG EF
HI JK
LN OQ
PR ST
UV WX
YZ

Practising capital letters.

Extension

This provides an opportunity to write sentences including people's names. Remind the group about the capital letter at the start of the sentence too, and point out the full stop at the end. It might be helpful for the teacher's name to be written on the board.

20 Extension Resource Red Level

Name Date

A Trace and write these classroom words.

BOOKS
RULERS
PAPER
APRONS
PAINT
BRUSHES
GLUE
PENCILS
CRAYONS

B Now write some classroom words of your own on a sheet of paper.

Practising capital letters.

Assessment

- Capital letters start at the top line.
- Capital letters are almost twice the height of small letters.
- Capital letters do not touch the letters following.

HECK-UP 2

Objectives

Explain to the pupils that this exercise is an assessment activity. The objective of the check-up is to assess what the pupils can do and where they need extra practice. This exercise will help assess each pupil's ability to form and use the four handwriting joins.

CHECK-UP 2

FOCUS

Copy these patterns into your book.

lili lili lili lili
nlnl nlnl nlnl nlnl
ooo ooo ooo ooo
rere rere rere rere
vvv vvv vvv vvv
lolo lolo lolo lolo

EXTRA

Copy these words into your book.

lid	dig	sing	ding
the	them	still	stilts
are	there	moon	room
growl	prowl	off	flood

EXTENSION

A Copy these sentences into your book.

A quick brown fox jumps over the lazy dog.

The five boxing lizards jumped quickly into the water.

B What do you notice about the sentences in **A** above?

Focus

Ask the pupils to copy the patterns into their books. Pattern one and two help with the formation of the first and second handwriting joins. The next three patterns help with the formation of the third join and the last pattern, with the fourth join.

Extra

Ask the pupils to copy these words into their books. The words in the first line contain letters linked with the first handwriting join. The words on the second line contain letters joined with the first and second join. The third line letters join using the first, second and third join. The fourth line contains letters within each of the words that are joined using the fourth join.

Extension

Ask the pupils to copy the sentences into their books. The sentences contain all the letters of the alphabet.

Assessment

- Are all the letters formed correctly?
- Is each of the four handwriting joins made correctly?
- Is the join made from the bottom of one letter to the top of the x-height of the next for first and second joins?
- In the case of the third and fourth joins, is the join made from the top of one letter to the top of the next?
- Are similar letters the same height?

- For more Assessment see *Resources and Assessment Book Red and Yellow Level*

SCOPE AND SEQUENCE
DEVELOPING SKILLS YELLOW LEVEL

Further practice of the four handwriting joins.

Page	Focus	Extra	Extension	Focus resource	Extension resource
4-5 Unit 1 First join revision	revising the first join: in, ine	pine, dine	choose words and copy sentences	in, bin, din, pin trace and copy pattern and words, trace and copy sentence	(magic e words) pin, pine, din, dine, hid, hide, pip, pipe, shin, shine, slim, slime trace and copy words
6-7 Unit 2 Second join revision	revising the second join: ut, ute	tube, cube, cute	choose words and copy sentences	ub, tub, cub, ut, but, put, hut, cut trace and copy pattern and words	(magic e words) tub, tube, cub, cube, cut, cute trace and copy words and sentence
8-9 Unit 3 Third join revision	revising the third join: ve, vi	cave, caving, save, saving, wave, waving	choose words and copy sentences	ve, very, over, we, were, went, re, tree, three trace and copy letters and words	we, were, ve, very, fe, feet, trace and copy letters, words and sentence
10-11 Unit 4 Fourth join revision	revising the fourth join: ok, oh	choke, choking, smoke, smoking, joke, joking	choose words and copy sentences	oke, joke, ole, hole, ort, fort, irt, skirt, dirt trace and copy letters and words	poked, poking trace and copy words and sentence
12-13 Unit 5 Secrets	practising the two ways of joining the letter s: sh, as, es	code, codes, ship, ships, message, messages	choose words and copy sentences	sh, es, shines, shoes, shapes, shaves, shoves, shares trace and copy pattern, letters and words	us, house, as, has, ds, dads, es, gates trace and copy letters, words and sentence
14-15 Unit 6 Secrets	practising joining from the letter r: ri, ru, ry	trick, trust, try	choose words and copy sentences	ri, trip, triangle, ru, true, truth, ry, cry trace and copy pattern, letters and words	ru, trunk, ry, carry, ri, carries trace and copy letters, words and sentence
16-17 Unit 7 Roads	practising the join to and from the letter a: oa, ad, as	load, road, toad, boat, goat, coat, toast, roast, boast	copy poem	oa, soap, ad, had, as, has, gas, last trace and copy pattern, letters and words	goat, coat, boat, afloat trace and copy words and sentence
18-19 Unit 8 Roads	practising the join from the letter e: ee, ea, ed	see, bee, fee, seed, need feed, sea, pea, flea	copy poem	ee, bee, tree, three, ea, beach, peach, teach trace and copy patten, letters and words	ea, ear, eat, meat, eals, meals, eas, peas trace and copy, letters, words and sentence
20-21 Unit 9 Animals	practising the join from the letter o: ow, ov, ox	bow, cow, how, now, frown, brown, crown, drown ox, pox, box, fox	match questions to answer and copy jokes	ow, cow, now, how, bow, ox, boxes, foxes trace and copy pattern, letters and words	trace and copy poem
22-23 Unit 10 Animals	practising joining to the letter y: ky, hy, ly	sly, fly ply sky, spy, shy high, higher, highest	copy poem	ky, milky, silky, hy healthy, wealthy, ly, jolly, dolly trace and copy pattern, letters and words	ay, Monday, Tuesday, Wednesday, Thursday, Friday, Saturday, Sunday, January, February, May, July
24-25 Check-up 1	*Check-up*	*Check-up*	*Check-up*	*Check-up*	*Check-up*

Page	Focus	Extra	Extension	Focus resource	Extension resource
26-27 Unit 11 Woods	practising joining to the letter a: ha, ta, fa	hair, hare, fair, fare stair, stare, pair, pare	choose words and copy sentences	ha, hail, hailstorm ta, tail, tailor, fa, fail trace and copy pattern, letters and words	trace and copy sentences
28-29 Unit 12 Woods	practising joining from the letter o: od, oo, og	good, hood, wood book, took, look dog, hog, log	choose words and copy sentences	od, nod, rod, og, bog, frog, oo, cook trace and copy pattern, letters and words	trace and copy poem
30-31 Unit 13 Reptiles	practising joining to the letter r: er, ir, ur	sister, mister, blister, bird, dirt, shirt hurt, hurtle, turtle	copy poem	er, her, ir, stir, third, ur, burn, turn trace and copy pattern, letters and words	trace and copy poem
32-33 Unit 14 Reptiles	practising the first and second join: ai, al, ay	tail, sail, pail tale, sale, pale, tray, stray, play	choose words and copy sentences	ai, rain, again, al, ball, call, ay, may, stay trace and copy pattern, letters and words	copy poem
34-35 Unit 15 Bridges	practising joining from the letter o: oy, ou, oi	speech marks and apostrophes	copy sentences	oi, oil, soil, spoil, oy, joy, coy, boy	speech marks and apostrophes, copy words and sentences
36-37 Unit 16 Transport	practising the horizontal join to the letter e: re, oe, fe	toe, foe, woe fear, dear, year dream, cream, stream	copy poem	re, there, where, oe, Zoe, Chloe, fe, feet, feed trace and copy pattern, letters and words	trace and copy letters, words and sentence
38-39 Unit 17 People	practising the horizontal join to the letter u: fu, wu, vu	care, careful, carefully, help, helpful, helpfully, wonder, wonderful, wonderfully	choose word and copy sentences	fu, fun, funny, wu, swum, swung, vu, vulture trace and copy pattern, letters and words	copy poem
40-41 Unit 18 People	practising print: copy print letters	arm, hair, hand, knee, thumb, eye, fingers, foot, shoulder, leg, wrist, mouth	draw and label picture	copy print letters	copy print words, label parts of dog
42-43 Unit 19 Weather	practising joining to ascenders: ot, ol, ok	not, hot, rot, blot, got, cot, dot, spot	copy poem	ot, soot, foot, ol, fool, cool, ok, hook, book trace and copy pattern, letters and words	make and add 'ing' to words copy sentence
44-45 Unit 20 Weather	practising all the joins: ai, al, ow, ol	raindrop, rainbow, rainfall	make and copy compound words	ai, hail, al, fall, ow, snow, ol, cold trace and copy pattern, letters and words	copy poem
46-48 Check-up 2	*Check-up*	*Check-up*	*Check-up*	*Check-up*	*Check-up*

UNIT 1

Objectives

- To revise the first join: a diagonal join to letters without ascenders.

Spelling links

- **i-e**
- 'magic **e**' words

Developing Skills

Focus

- Before the lesson, draw four lines on the board (two rows of dotted lines in the middle) and write the whole class sentence between them.
- Remind children that in joined-up writing there are four joins to learn. See if they can remember the four joins and then demonstrate them on the board.
- Discuss the first join. Point out that the letters **i** and **n** both begin at the top. The join is made from the bottom of the letter **i** to the top of the letter **n**.
- A diagonal joining line is used to join these two letters together. The diagonal join can be modelled with a different coloured pen. Point out that the join is made in one continuous movement.
- Ask the children to practise the pattern, and joining **in** and **ine**, on their individual whiteboards.

Extra

- Discuss the 'magic **e**'. Read the words in the box to ensure the concept is understood.
- Draw four lines on the board and model writing these words.
- Ask a child to come up and show the class how to write **dine**.
- Tell the children to copy the words into their books.

Extension

- Explain the extension activity.
- Tell children to look at the picture for clues.
- Ask the group to copy the sentences and fill in the missing words.
- Model the first sentence on the board.

Resources and Assessment

Focus

Further practice of the swings pattern and of the first join using the words **in**, **bin**, **din** and **pin**.

The sentence provides extra practice of the first join. Children can trace and copy or just copy the sentence. Some children find it helpful if the first word is done for them – this shows them where to write the letters on the line. For lower attainers, use a highlighter pen and write the sentence for them to trace.

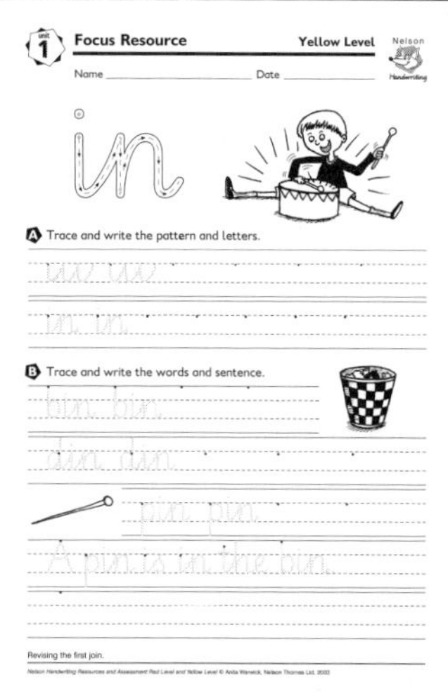

Extension

Further practice of the first join and 'magic **e**'. Children change the words by adding **e**. Each word is written three times. Remind children that the letter **p** has a descender, which goes below the line.

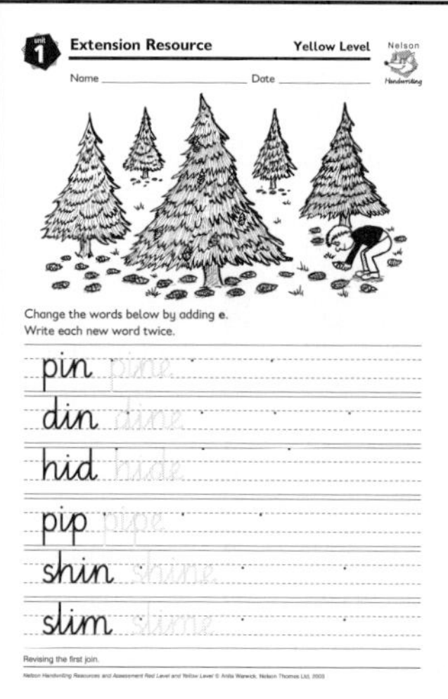

Assessment

- The joining line is diagonal.
- The letters are the correct height.
- The join to **n** is made at or near the top, *not* at the bottom of the letter.

UNIT 2

Objectives

- To revise the second join: a diagonal join to letters with ascenders.

Spelling links

- **u-e**
- 'magic **e**' words

UNIT 2
Revising the second join.
ut
Ruby has a cut.
FOCUS
A Copy this pattern into your book.
B Copy these letters into your book.
ut ut ut ut ut
ute ute ute ute ute
Remember, the second join is made by taking your pencil from the bottom of one letter up to the top of the next, like this:
u + t = ut
EXTRA
Make these words.
Copy them into your book.
tub + e = tube tube tube
cub + e = cube cube cube
cut + e = cute cute cute
EXTENSION
Choose the correct words to finish these sentences.
Copy the sentences into your book.
1 Ruby (cut/cute) her knee.
2 Her mum used a (tub/tube).
3 Ruby held her (cub/cube).

Developing Skills

Focus

- Before the lesson, draw four lines on the board (two rows of dotted lines in the middle) and write the whole class sentence between them.
- Ask the children if they can tell which letters in the sentence on the board are joined using the second join. Underline **ub** and **ut**.
- Point out that the letters **u**, **b** and **t** all begin at the top.
- Note how the **u** is joined from the baseline to the x-height of the **t**. A diagonal joining line is used to join these two letters together. Point out that the join is made in one continuous movement.
- Model the joining line with a different coloured pen.
- Ask children to practise the pattern, and joining **ut** and **ute**, on their individual whiteboards.

Extra

- Discuss the 'magic **e**'. Read the words in the box to ensure the concept is understood.
- Model the handwriting using the words **tube** and **cube**.
- Remind children that **t** is slightly shorter than the other tall letters. It is helpful for children to see this. Remind them, too, that all the other letters with ascenders go up to the top line.
- Ask the children to copy the words into their books.

Extension

- Use the picture for clues.
- Remind the group that capital letters are the same height as ascenders and that they start at the top line.
- Model the first sentence on the board.
- Ask the group to copy the sentences and fill in the missing words.

Resources and Assessment

Focus

Further pattern practice and more practice of the second join in the context of words with **u** as the medial vowel. Tracing and copying pattern, letters and words.

2 Focus Resource — Yellow Level

Name ______ Date ______

ut

A Trace and write the pattern and letters.

B Trace and write the words.

Revising the second join.

Extension

Further practice of the second join and 'magic **e**'. The sentence offers tracing and copying practice.

2 Extension Resource — Yellow Level

Name ______ Date ______

A Change the words below by adding **e**. Write each new word twice.

tub

cub

cut

B Trace and write the sentence.

Revising the second join.

Assessment

- There are diagonal joins to the ascenders.
- There is equal space between letters.
- The first and second joins are formed correctly.

UNIT 3

Objectives

- To revise the third join: a horizontal join to letters without ascenders.

Spelling links

- **a-e**
- 'magic **e**' words.

UNIT 3 Revising the third join.

ve

They waved and waved.

Focus

A Copy this pattern into your book.

B Copy these letters into your book.

ve ve ve ve ve

vi vi vi vi vi

Remember, the third join is a horizontal join between two letters, like this: v + e = ve

Extra

Make these words. Copy them into your book. Remember to drop the letter e when adding ing.

cave + ing = caving caving

save + ing = saving saving

wave + ing = waving waving

Extension

Choose the correct word from the **Extra** above to finish these sentences. Copy the sentences into your book.

1 The family went ______.

2 They saw a man in the sea ______.

3 They saw the lifeguard ______ him.

Developing Skills

Focus

- Before the lesson, draw four lines on the board (two rows of dotted lines in the middle) and write the whole class sentence between them.
- Ask the children to look at the sentence on the board and identify letter patterns using the third join, i.e. **wa** and **ve**.
- Discuss the third join. Point out that it is made in one continuous movement.
- Show the class how the join from **v** to **e** uses a deeper curve than the joins **vi** and **wa**. This is because the starting point for forming the letter **e** is nearer the bottom of the line. Tell the children that this is one of the most difficult joins to master. Draw attention to the fox box, which reinforces the correct join.
- It is helpful for children to see this join demonstrated on the board – both in its correct and incorrect version.
- The children should practise the **ve** and **vi** joins on their whiteboards.

Extra

- Talk about adding **ing** to words ending in **e**.
- Read the words and model the correct handwriting on the board.
- Point out that the letter **g** has a descender – its tail goes below the line.
- Children should copy the **ing** words into their books.

Extension

- Talk about the picture and the sentences.
- Ask three children to read a sentence each and tell you the missing word.
- Remind the group that capital letters begin at the top line.
- Model the first sentence on the board.
- Remind the children too that the letters **f**, **g** and **y** have descenders – their tails go below the line.
- Children should copy the sentences into their books.

Resources and Assessment

Focus

Further pattern practice and more practice of the third join, including the tricky **re** join, using high frequency words.

3 Focus Resource Yellow Level

Name Date

ve

A Trace and write the pattern and letters.

B Trace and write the words.

Revising the third join.

Extension

Further practice of the third join. The sentence provides tracing and copying practice – putting the words into context.

3 Extension Resource Yellow Level

Name Date

A Trace and write the letters and words.

B Trace and write the sentence.

Revising the third join.

Assessment

- The correct formation of the letter **e** when joined to **v**.
- Check **v** and **e** are the same height.
- The correct space between letters. Look at the joins between the **v** and **e**, **v** and **i**: the letters must not be touching.

NIT 4

Objectives

- To revise the fourth join: a diagonal join to letters with ascenders.

Spelling links

- **o-e**
- adding **ing** to 'magic **e**' words

UNIT 4

Revising the fourth join.

ok

Stoke the fire to make it smoke.

FOCUS

A Copy this pattern into your book.

olol olol olol olol

B Copy these letters into your book.

ok ok ok ok ok

oh oh oh oh oh

Remember, the fourth join is made by joining the top of one letter to the top of another, like this:

o + k = ok

EXTRA

Make these words. Copy them into your book.
Remember to drop the letter e when adding ing.

choke + ing = choking choking

smoke + ing = smoking smoking

joke + ing = joking joking

EXTENSION

Choose the correct words to finish these sentences. Copy the sentences into your book.

1 Sita said she could see (smoke/smoking).

2 They thought Sita was (joke/joking).

3 People were (choke/choking).

10

11

Developing Skills

Focus

- Before the lesson, draw four lines on the board (two rows of dotted lines in the middle) and write the whole class sentence between them.
- Underline **ok** in **stoke** and **smoke**. Discuss the fourth join. Point out that the fourth join is the same as the first join except that it is made from the x-height to the top of an ascender.
- Draw attention to the fox box, which reinforces the fourth join.
- Remind children that forming, and joining to, the letter **k** is tricky. Tell them that although **k** has an ascender, the body of the letter is the same height as small letters, e.g. **o** and **e**. Demonstrate on the board the joins **ok** and **oh**.
- Ask children to come to the board and demonstrate joining **ok** and **oh**. Watch and praise those who form and join the letters correctly.
- Ask children to practise the pattern and the **ok** and **oh** joins on their individual whiteboards before they copy them into their books.

Extra

- Discuss adding **ing** to words ending in **e**.
- Read the words in the box to ensure the concept is understood.
- Model the first line on the board.
- Explain the importance of letters being the correct height and size. Point out that **h** and **k** have ascenders: they are tall letters and they start at the top line. Mention too that **g** and **j** have descenders which go below the line. (Using handwriting lines helps to teach this point.)
- Ask the children to copy the **ing** words into their books.

Extension

- Tell the children to copy the sentences, choosing the correct word for the sense.
- Model the first sentence on the board.

Resources and Assessment

Focus

Further pattern practice and more practice of the fourth join using **ok**, **ol** and **rt**. Tracing and copying words puts the joins into context.

4 Focus Resource Yellow Level

Name Date

ok

A Trace and write the pattern and letters.

B Trace and write the words.

Revising the fourth join.

Extension

Further practice of the fourth join linked to the **o-e** sound and of dropping the **e** when adding **ing**.

The sentence provides tracing and copying practice, putting the words into context and using the connective and high frequency word **because**.

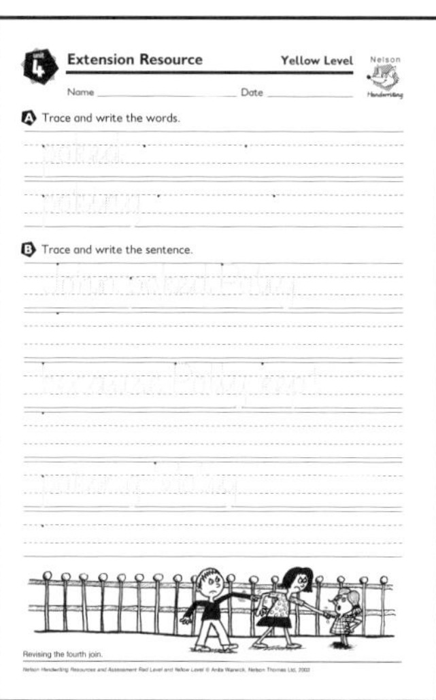

Extension Resource Yellow Level

Name Date

A Trace and write the words.

B Trace and write the sentence.

Revising the fourth join.

Assessment

- The correct formation of the diagonal join to letters with ascenders.
- The correct formation of the letter **k**.
- The same space is allowed between letters linked with the fourth join as between letters linked with other joins.

NIT 5

Objectives

- To introduce the two ways of joining to and from the letter **s**.
- To practise the first and second joins to the letter **s**.

Spelling links

- plurals – adding **s**

Nelson theme – secrets

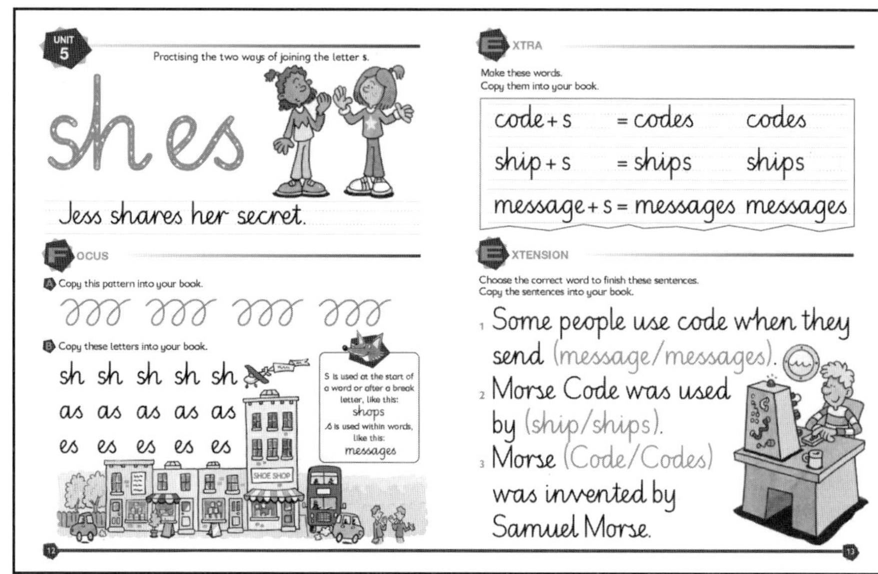

UNIT 5 Practising the two ways of joining the letter s.

sh es

Jess shares her secret.

FOCUS

A Copy this pattern into your book.

B Copy these letters into your book.

sh sh sh sh sh

as as as as as

es es es es es

s is used at the start of a word or after a break letter, like this: shops

s is used within words, like this: messages

EXTRA

Make these words. Copy them into your book.

code + s	= codes	codes
ship + s	= ships	ships
message + s	= messages	messages

EXTENSION

Choose the correct word to finish these sentences. Copy the sentences into your book.

1 Some people use code when they send (message/messages).

2 Morse Code was used by (ship/ships).

3 Morse (Code/Codes) was invented by Samuel Morse.

12 13

Developing Skills

Focus

- Before the lesson, draw four lines on the board (two rows of dotted lines in the middle) and write the whole class sentence between them.
- Ask the children what difference they can see between the two ways of joining **s**. Discuss the two different joins to the letter **s**.
- Point out that **s** changes its shape in the middle and at the end of words as this helps us to write more quickly and fluently.
- If the letter **s** comes at the start of a word we use the 'normal' **s**.
- Draw attention to the fox box, which reinforces the two shapes for **s**.
- Point out that **es** uses the first join and **sh** uses the second. When we join a Set 1 letter (see page 9) to **s**, we use the first join and when we join a Set 4 letter to **s**, we use the second join.
- Model the pattern and ask the children to practise it.

Extra

- Discuss plurals. Tell the group that words ending in **e** usually just add **s** (**code/codes**).
- Draw four lines on the board. Model writing the words **codes**, **ships** and **messages**.
- Ask the class why **s**, after the letter **p**, is not joined. Remind them that **p** is a break letter, and that the letter following a break letter does not join to it.
- Tell the children to copy the words into their books. Point out that the descenders of the letters **p** and **g** go below the baseline. (Using handwriting lines helps to teach this point.)

Extension

- Tell the group that at the start of a sentence we use the normal **s**, but it is a capital. Capital letters like break letters do not join.
- Read the sentences and ask the children to choose the correct word.
- Model writing the first sentence on the board.
- Ask the children to copy the sentences, checking that they make sense.

Resources and Assessment

Focus

Further pattern practice and more practice of the joins to and from the letter **s**. Practice of: the first, second and third joins; writing letters the correct height and size; writing plurals. Tracing and copying words.

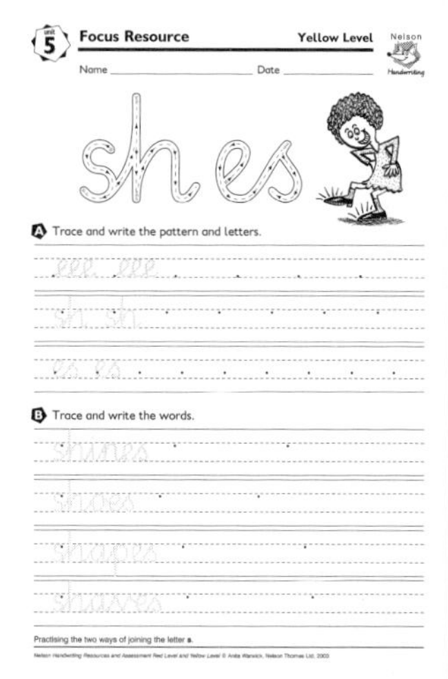

5 Focus Resource Yellow Level

Name Date

sh es

A Trace and write the pattern and letters.

B Trace and write the words.

Extension

Further practice of the first join to the letter **s**. The sentence provides tracing and copying practice –putting the words into context.

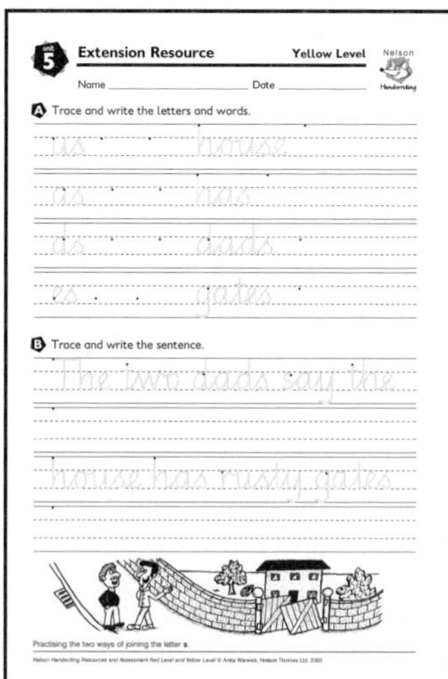

5 Extension Resource Yellow Level

Name Date

A Trace and write the letters and words.

B Trace and write the sentence.

The two lads say the house has rusty gates

Assessment

- The correct form of the letter **s** is used.
- The use of capital **S** at the start of a sentence with no join following.
- The descenders of the letters **g** and **p** fall below the line.

UNIT 6

Objectives

- To practise the third join from the letter **r**.

Spelling links

- consonant digraph **tr**

Nelson theme – secrets

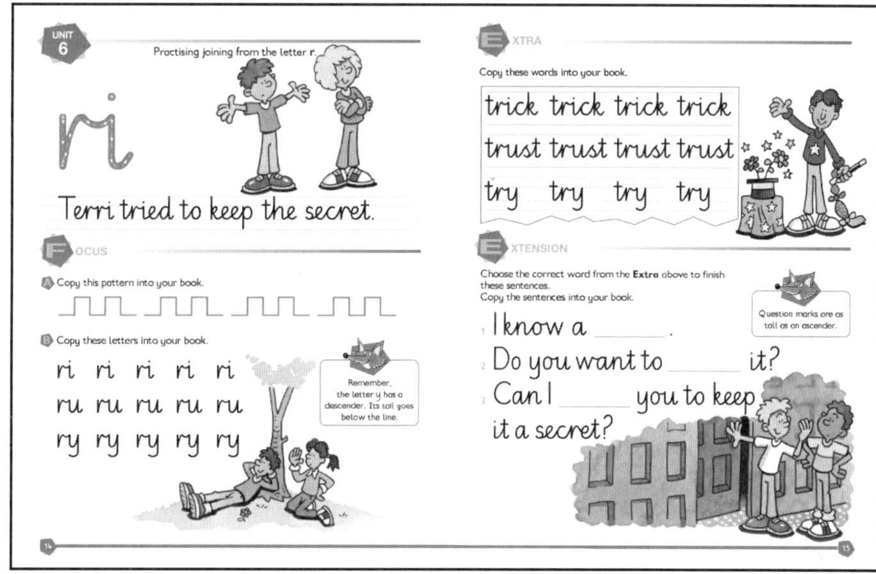

Developing Skills

Focus

- Before the lesson, draw four lines on the board (two rows of dotted lines in the middle) and write the whole class sentence between them.
- Underline the letters joined from the letter **r** (**rr**, **ri**).
- Discuss the **rr** join. The join is quite easy to make. Why? *(Because it is a short join from the end of the formation of the letter **r**.)*
- The join from **r** to **i** is harder. Why? *(Because you must remember the **r** dips and there is a space between the letters.* Children often write these letters too close together.)
- Model the correct formation of this join and ask the children to practise the pattern.
- Remind the children that the letter **y** has a descender which goes below the baseline.

Extra

- Discuss words beginning **tr**. If you have time, write a list of **tr** words on the board.
- Model writing the words from the box between four lines.
- Remind the children that the letter **t** is not as tall as the other letters with ascenders. Mention that the letter **t** is crossed on the line. Remind them that they should cross the letter **t** and dot the letter **i** only after they have finished writing the whole word.
- Tell the children the joining line helps them to leave the correct space between their letters.
- Ask the class to copy the **tr** words into their books.

Extension

- Read the sentences.
- Ask three children to read a sentence each and choose a word from the Extra section to fill the gap.
- Demonstrate writing the first sentence on the board.
- Point out that a question mark is as tall as an ascender. Model the formation and writing of a question mark between the four lines on the board.
- Tell the children to copy the completed sentences into their books.

Resources and Assessment

Focus

Further pattern practice and more practice of the join from the letter **r**. Tracing and copying pattern and words.

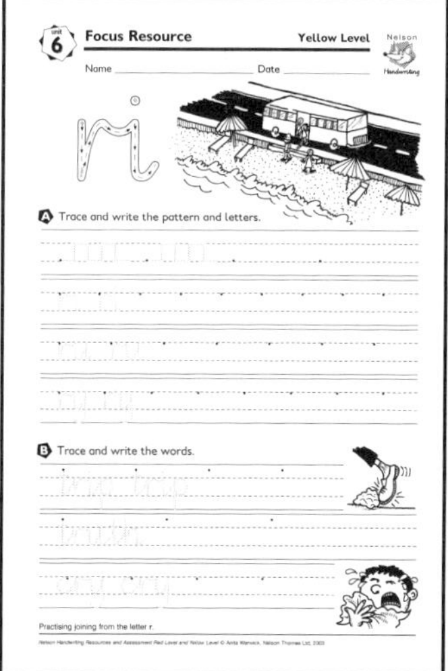

Extension

Further practice of the third join from the letter **r**. The sentence provides tracing and copying practice – putting the words into context.

Assessment

- Correct **ri**, **ru** and **ry** joins.
- The same space is allowed between letters joined to **r** as between letters linked with other joins.
- The letter **t** is begun half way between the top line and the x-height.

NIT 7

Objectives

- To practise the horizontal join to letters without ascenders.

Spelling links

- Medial sound oa

Nelson theme – roads

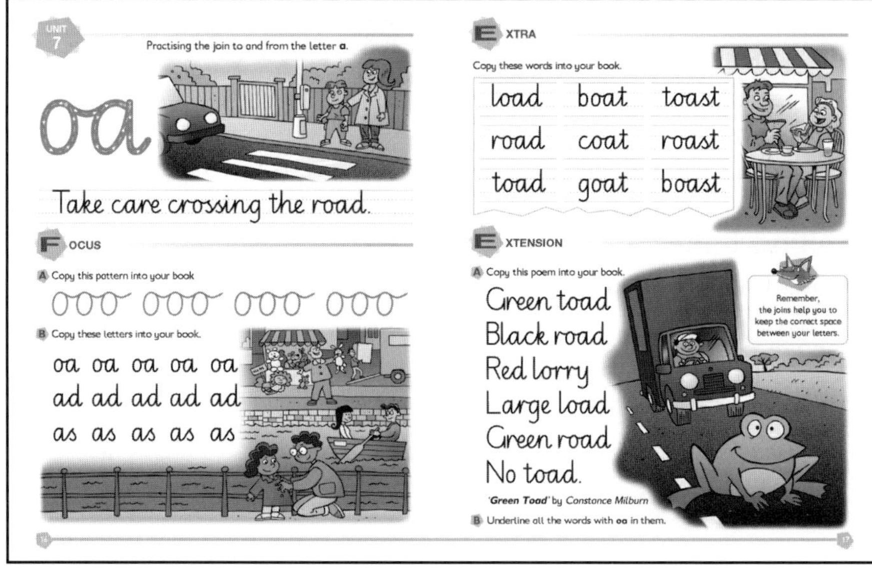

UNIT 7

Practising the join to and from the letter **a**.

oa

Take care crossing the road.

FOCUS

A Copy this pattern into your book

ooo ooo ooo ooo

B Copy these letters into your book.

oa oa oa oa oa
ad ad ad ad ad
as as as as as

EXTRA

Copy these words into your book.

load	boat	toast
road	coat	roast
toad	goat	boast

EXTENSION

A Copy this poem into your book.

Green toad
Black road
Red lorry
Large load
Green road
No toad.

'Green Toad' by Constance Milburn

B Underline all the words with **oa** in them.

Remember, the joins help you to keep the correct space between your letters.

Developing Skills

Focus

- Before the lesson, draw four lines on the board (two rows of dotted lines in the middle) and write the whole class sentence between them.
- Discuss the horizontal join, from the top of the letter **o** to the starting point of the letter **a**.
- Underline **oa** in **coas**t and **road** to show the horizontal joins.
- Then underline the other joins made to and from the letter **a** – **ha**, **al**, **ta**, **ak**, **as** and **ad**.
- Point out that a space must be made between the letters. Demonstrate what happens when the correct join is not made between these letters, e.g. **oa** (*they touch each other*).
- Ask the children to finger trace over the letters **oa** in the book, and then practise the pattern and the joining of **oa**, **ad** and **as** on their whiteboards. Emphasise the importance of forming and joining the letters correctly. Have they left a space between their letters?

Extra

- Discuss the **oa** sound. Which words rhyme with **load**? Then, which words rhyme with **boat/toast**?
- Model writing the words that rhyme with load on the board between four lines. Point out the **oa** and the **ad** joins.
- Remind children that they must leave equal space between their letters.
- Children should copy the nine words into their books. Remind them that letters should be the correct height and size. Re-stress that the letter **t** is not as tall as the other letters with ascenders **l**, **d** and **b**.

Extension

- Read the poem together.
- Model writing the poem on the board.
- Point out that all capital letters are the same height as ascenders.

Resources and Assessment

Focus

Further pattern practice and more practice of the first and third joins – joining to and from the letter **a**.

Tracing and copying the joins **oa**, **ad** and **as** and words putting the joins into context.

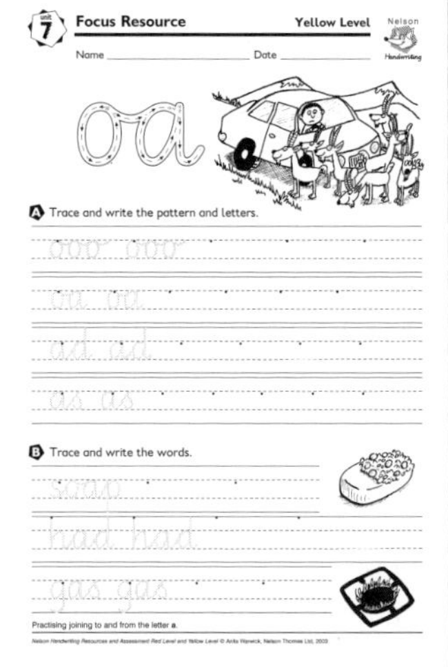

7 Focus Resource Yellow Level

Name Date

oa

A Trace and write the pattern and letters.

B Trace and write the words.

Practising joining to and from the letter a.

Extension

Further practice of the third join – from the letter **o** to the letter **a**. Children practise the join in the context of words with medial **oa** sound. The sentence provides tracing and copying practice – putting the words into context.

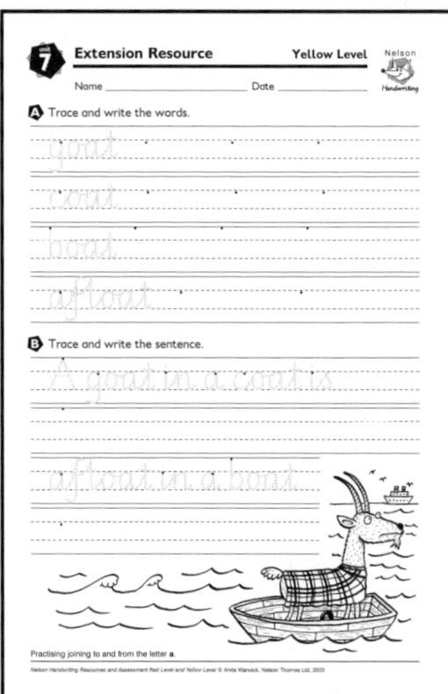

7 Extension Resource Yellow Level

Name Date

A Trace and write the words.

B Trace and write the sentence.

Practising joining to and from the letter a.

Assessment

- There is space between the **oa**, **ad** and **as** joins, so the letters do not touch.
- The capital letters the same height as ascenders.
- The same space is allowed between letters joined to and from the **a** as between letters linked with other joins.

NIT 8

Objectives

- To practise the first join from the letter **e**.

Spelling links

- medial sound **ee** and **ea**

Nelson theme – roads

UNIT 8 Practising the join from the letter e.

ee ea

Hear the beat of feet on the street.

FOCUS

A Copy this pattern into your book.

eee eee eee eee

B Copy these letters into your book.

ee ee ee ee ee
ea ea ea ea ea
ed ed ed ed ed

Be careful! In handwriting, all the letters start at the top except for d and e.

EXTRA

Copy these words into your book.

see	seed	sea
bee	need	pea
fee	feed	flea

EXTENSION

Copy this poem into your book.

Hurry, scurry: lock that door –
this poor car will take no more!
Hurry scurry; turn the key,
We're off at last to see the sea.

from *'All Aboard'* by Judith Nicholls

18 19

Developing Skills

Focus

- Before the lesson, draw four lines on the board (two rows of dotted lines in the middle) and write the whole class sentence between them.
- Ask the children if they know which letters of the alphabet do not start at the top when we write them – there are only two (**e** and **d**). This is mentioned in the fox box.
- Joining to **e** is fairly easy. Remind the class that the letter **e** must be the same size as the other small letters.
- Talk about the **ea** join. The join goes to the top, to the point where the letter **a** is begun, and the pencil comes back round.
- Underline the **ee** and **ea** joins in the sentence.
- Point out that a space must be made between the letters, and that the joining line helps you to leave the correct space between your letters.
- Ask the children to finger trace over the large letters **ee** and **ea**.
- Tell them to practise the pattern and the **ee**, **ea** and **ed** joins on individual whiteboards.

Extra

- Discuss words that rhyme with **see**.
- Model writing **see**, **bee** and **fee** between four lines on the board.
- Point out that these **ee** words rhyme with the **ea** words in the third column. Demonstrate this by writing **sea**, **pea** and **flea**.
- Talk about the formation of the letter **f**. It has a straight back and is the only letter with both an ascender and a descender.
- Ask the children to copy the nine words carefully into their handwriting books.

Extension

- Read the poem together.
- Model writing some or all of the poem on the board.
- Point out that the tall letters are about twice the height of the small letters.
- Remind the group that they practised the **ry** join in the last lesson.
- Point out the words **see** and **sea** at the end of the poem.
- The children could copy this poem onto plain paper – using guidelines underneath.

Resources and Assessment

Focus

Further pattern practice and more practice of the first join from the letter **e**. Words contain the joins **ee** and **ea**. Remind children about the tricky **re** join (see Unit 3 copymasters) in **tree** and **three**.

Extension

Further practice with **ea** words. Remind children that letters should be the correct height, e.g. **t** in **eat** and **l** in **meals** are different sized tall letters. The sentence provides tracing and copying practice – putting the words into context.

Assessment

- Equal space is allowed between the letters (the letters do not touch).
- The joins between **ee**, **ea** and **ed** are formed correctly.
- Ascenders are approximately twice the height of small letters.

NIT 9

Objectives

- To practise the horizontal join from the letter **o**.

Spelling links

- the **ou** and **ow** sound

Nelson theme – animals

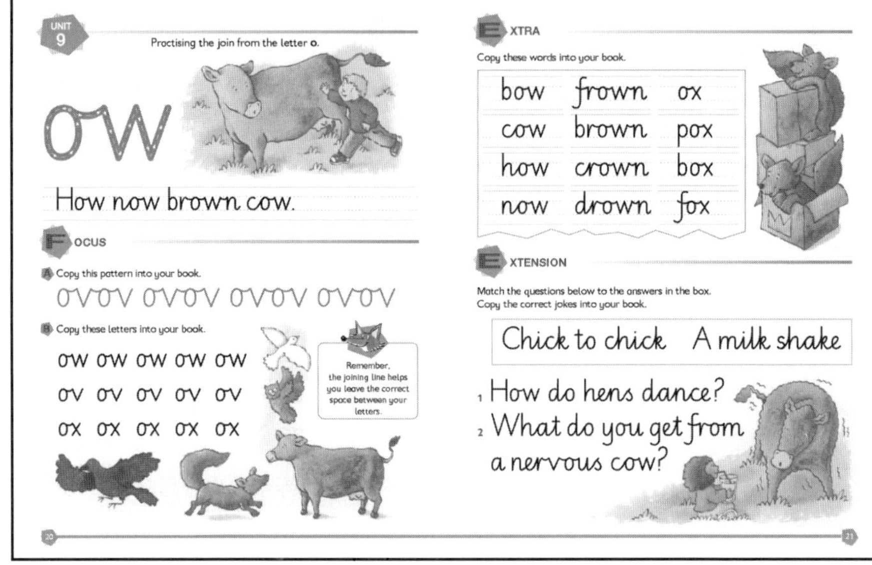

UNIT 9

Practising the join from the letter **o**.

ow

How now brown cow.

FOCUS

A Copy this pattern into your book.

ovov ovov ovov ovov

B Copy these letters into your book.

ow ow ow ow ow
ov ov ov ov ov
ox ox ox ox ox

Remember, the joining line helps you leave the correct space between your letters.

EXTRA

Copy these words into your book.

bow	frown	ox
cow	brown	pox
how	crown	box
now	drown	fox

EXTENSION

Match the questions below to the answers in the box. Copy the correct jokes into your book.

Chick to chick A milk shake

1 How do hens dance?
2 What do you get from a nervous cow?

20 21

Developing Skills

Focus

- Before the lesson, draw four lines on the board (two rows of dotted lines in the middle) and write the whole class sentence between them.
- Remind the class that there is a space between the **o** and the **w** in **ow**. This space is created by the use of the third join.
- Point out that these letters are small letters and they are the same height.
- Encourage the children to finger trace over the large letters at the top of the page.
- Underline all the **ow** blends in the whole class sentence. Ask the class if they can see any other letters that are joined using the horizontal join (***ro** and **wn***).
- Make a list of words containing the **ow** join. Begin with words that rhyme with **bow**.
- Model the **ov** and **ox** joins on the board. Ask the children to come up and demonstrate these joins.
- Tell the class to practise the pattern and the joins on their own whiteboards. Then they can copy the letters into their books.

Extra

- Discuss words that rhyme with **frown** and then words that rhyme with **ox**.
- Make a list of the rhyming words by writing them between the four lines on the board.
- Again point out the space between the letters **ro**, **ow**, **ox** and **wn**.
- Tell the children to copy the words into their books.

Extension

- Read the jokes together; match the questions to the answers in the box.
- Model writing the first joke on the board.
- Remind the group about the height of the letters. The capital **H** is the same height as the ascenders of the other letters in the sentence, **d** and **h**.
- Also point out that the question mark begins at the top line and is the same height as the ascenders.
- Children could copy the jokes onto plain paper, with guidelines underneath, and decorate with pictures or a border.

Resources and Assessment

Focus

Further pattern practice and more practice of the third join using rhyming words with the strings **ow** and **ox**. Encourage children to join **ow** and **ox** using the horizontal join.

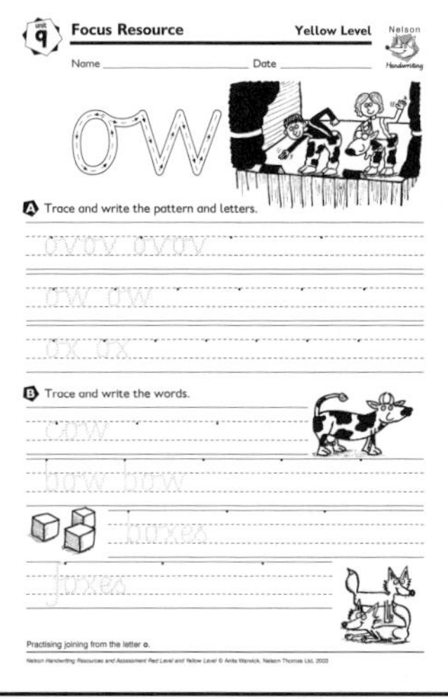

9 Focus Resource Yellow Level

Name ____ Date ____

ow

A Trace and write the pattern and letters.

B Trace and write the words.

Practising joining from the letter o.

Extension

Poem giving more practice of the third join. Copying practice – putting the join into context.

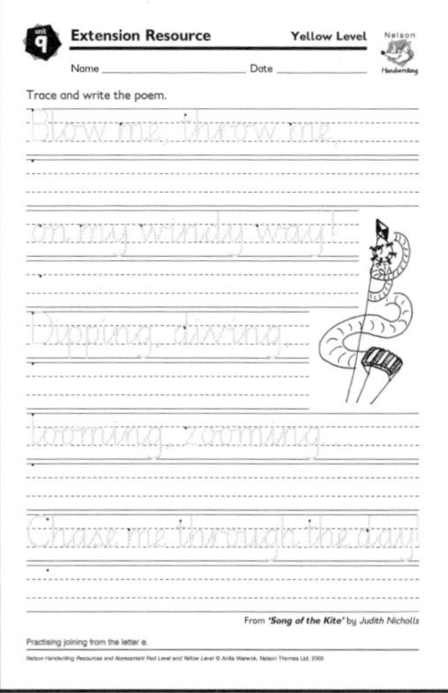

9 Extension Resource Yellow Level

Name ____ Date ____

Trace and write the poem.

Blow me, throw me,
on my windy way!
Dipping, diving,
looping, zooming,
Chase me through the day!

From *'Song of the Kite'* by Judith Nicholls

Practising joining from the letter o.

Assessment

- Equal space is allowed between the letters – look at the **ow** and **ox** joins (letters should not touch).
- Ascenders are approximately twice the height of small letters.
- The small letters all the same height.

UNIT 10

Objectives

- To practise forming and joining the letter **y** correctly.

Spelling links

- the **y** and **igh** sound

Nelson theme – animals

Developing Skills

Focus

- Before the lesson, draw four lines on the board (two rows of dotted lines in the middle) and write the whole class sentence between them.
- Point out the letter **y** in the sentence. It has a descender which goes below the line. Ask the class if they can find other letters in the sentence that have descenders (***g***, ***j***, ***p***). Discuss the formation of the letters **g**, **j** and **p** and how their descenders also go below the baseline.
- Encourage the children to finger trace over the large **ky**.
- Point out the sound these letters make in words, e.g. the letter **y** in **sky** makes same sound as **igh** in **high**.
- Model joining to **y**, using the **ky**, **hy** and **ly**. Explain that all these joins are the first diagonal join.
- Ask the class to draw a line on their whiteboards and practise the pattern and the joins.
- Tell them to copy the pattern and the letters into their books.

Extra

- Discuss words that rhyme with **sly**.
- Put children in pairs and ask them to make a list of these words on their whiteboards.
- Make a list on the board.
- Tell the children to copy the words from the pupil book into their handwriting books.

Extension

- Read the poem together.
- Model writing the poem on the board.
- Remind children about the formation of the letters **g**, **y** and **p** and the height of capital letters.
- Point out that the letter **f** also has a descender which goes below the baseline.
- Discuss the **fl** join. Make a list of words beginning **fl**.

Resources and Assessment

Focus

Further pattern practice and more practice joining words containing **ky**, **hy** and **ly** endings, using rhyming words. Tracing and copying pattern, letters and words.

Extension

Further practice joining to and forming the letter **y**. Days of the week/four months of the year (linked to NLS) provide spelling practice and joining to the letter **y**, using the joins **ay**, **ly** and **ry**.

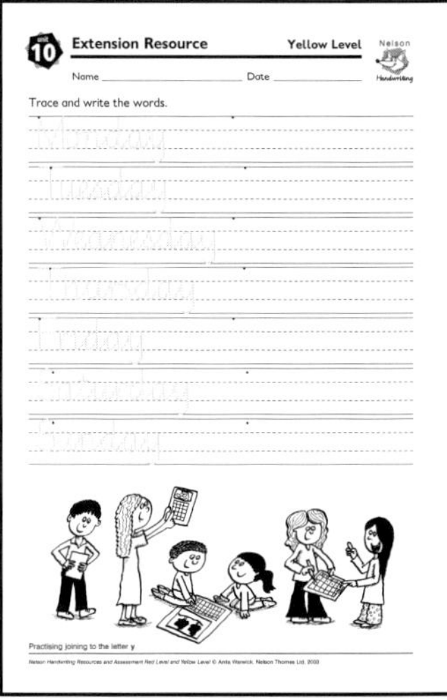

Assessment

- The descenders of the letters **g**, **y** and **p** fall below the line.
- The descenders on the letters **g** and **y** are formed correctly.
- The letter **f** has a straight back and its descender goes below the baseline.

CHECK-UP 1

Objectives

Explain to the pupils that this exercise is an assessment activity. The objective is to assess what the pupils can do and where they need extra practice.

This exercise will help assess each pupil's ability to form and join all four handwriting joins.

CHECK-UP 1

FOCUS

Copy these patterns into your book.

EXTRA

Copy these words into your book.

dine pine see seed
cube tube ship ships
caving waving code codes
joke joking choke choking

EXTENSION

Copy the poem below into your book.

As I was walking up the stair
I met a man who wasn't there;
He wasn't there again today.
I wish, I wish he'd stay away.

'The Little Man'
by Hughes Mearns

24

25

Focus

Ask the pupils to copy the patterns into their books. The patterns are an important part of helping pupils to learn to join letters. The patterns need to be made smoothly with the letter shapes at the correct height.

Extra

Ask the pupils to copy these words into their books. The words in the first line contain letters linked with the first handwriting join. The words in the second line contain letters joined using the first and second join. The third line contains words which join letters using the first and third join. The last line uses the first, second and fourth joins.

Extension

Ask the pupils to copy the poem into their books.

Assessment

- Are the letters formed correctly?
- Are ascenders taller than the small letters?
- Are the letters joined? Is the join made from the bottom of one letter to the top of the x-height of the next, or in the case of the third and fourth joins, from the top of one letter to the top of the next?

- For more Assessment see *Resources and Assessment Book Red and Yellow Level*

UNIT 11

Objectives

- To practise joining to the letter **a**.

Spelling links

- homophones ending with **ir** and **re**

Nelson theme – woods

Developing Skills

Focus

- Before the lesson, draw four lines on the board (two rows of dotted lines in the middle) and write the whole class sentence between them.
- Discuss the join to the letter **a**. Encourage the children to finger trace over the large letters **ha** in their books.
- Point out that the join is a diagonal line and it joins the letter **a** about halfway up. Remind the class that the pencil goes up to the top, ready to form the letter **a**, *and must come back round.*
- Underline the letters joined to **a** in the whole class sentence, i.e. **ha** and **da**.
- Model writing **ha**, **ta** and **fa** on the board.
- Talk about the **fa** join. It is a horizontal join unlike **ha** and **ta**, which are diagonal joins. The join from **f** is made from the crossbar. Point out that these letters must not touch.
- Children should practise the pattern and the joins on their whiteboards before they copy the pattern and letters into their books.

Extra

- Discuss the **re** join (see Unit 3 Resources and Assessment). Remind the class that it is a tricky join – the pencil must come down after the letter **r** to enable the **e** to be formed correctly.
- Write the words **hare** and **stare** on the board, modelling writing between four lines. Ask the group for alternative spellings for these sounds, i.e. **hair** and **stair**.
- Remind them that these words are called homophones. If you have time, ask the children if they can think of any more homophones. Make a list on the board.
- Underline the letters **ha**, **ta** and **fa** in the Extra section words. Tell the group to copy the words into their books.

Extension

- Read the sentences together.
- Ask the children to suggest the correct spelling of the missing word in each case.
- Model writing the first sentence on the board.
- Tell the group to complete the task.

Resources and Assessment

Focus

Further pattern practice and more practice of the joins **ha**, **ta** and **fa**. Tracing and copying words – practising the join and ensuring letters are the correct size and height.

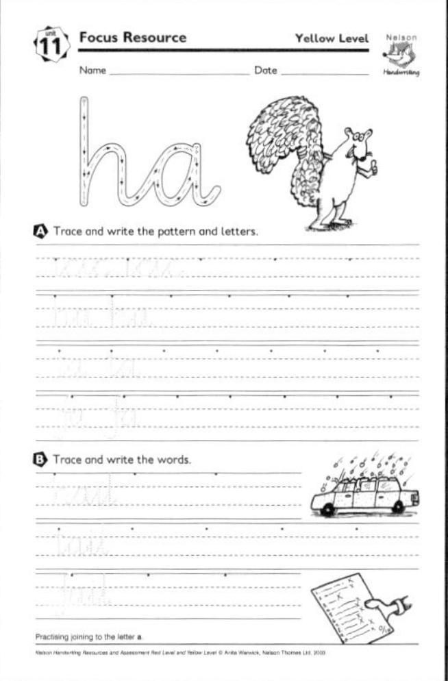

Extension

Further practice joining to the letter **a** using **ha** words. The sentences require children to choose the correct homophone. Copying sentences, putting the words into context.

Assessment

- The correct space is allowed between the letters **ha**, **ta** and **fa**.
- The letter **a** is the right size and has been formed correctly.
- The letter **f** has a straight back, a tall ascender and its descender goes down to the bottom line.

UNIT 12

Objectives

- To practise forming, and joining from, the letter **o**.

Spelling links

- the **oo** short vowel sound
- the medial **o** sound

Nelson theme – woods

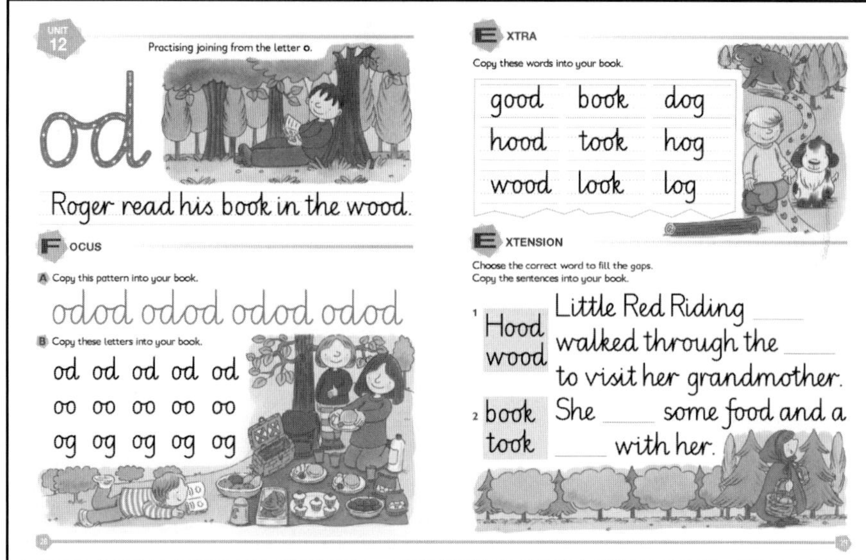

UNIT 12 Practising joining from the letter o.

od

Roger read his book in the wood.

FOCUS

A Copy this pattern into your book.

odod odod odod odod

B Copy these letters into your book.

od od od od od

oo oo oo oo oo

og og og og og

EXTRA

Copy these words into your book.

good	book	dog
hood	took	hog
wood	look	log

EXTENSION

Choose the correct word to fill the gaps. Copy the sentences into your book.

1 Hood / wood — Little Red Riding ____ walked through the ____ to visit her grandmother.

2 book / took — She ____ some food and a ____ with her.

Developing Skills

Focus

- Before the lesson, draw four lines on the board (two rows of dotted lines in the middle) and write the whole class sentence between them.
- Encourage the children to finger trace over the **od** in their books.
- Draw their attention to how the horizontal join dips down as it goes across to join the next letter.
- Point out, and underline, the letters joined from the letter **o** in the sentence, i.e. **og**, **oo**.
- Say the corresponding words out loud so children can hear the short **o** (**Roger**) and **oo** (**book**, **wood**) sounds.
- Model joining from the letter **o** on the board using the letter patterns **od**, **oo** and **og**.
- Point out that the third join is a horizontal join made from the top of the letter **o** to the middle of the letter **d**, and to the top of the letters **o** and **g**.
- The join leaves the correct amount of space between letters. Remind the class that letters must not touch each other.
- Demonstrate the pattern and ask the children to practise the pattern and joins on their whiteboards.
- Ask some children to come to the board and demonstrate the **od** and **og** joins.
- Tell the class to copy the pattern and letters into their books.

Extra

- Discuss words that rhyme with **good** (then with **book** and **dog**).
- Model writing these words on the board, using four lines. Comment on the height and size of the letters as you write them.
- Ask the children to copy the words into their books.

Extension

- Read the sentences.
- Ask the group to supply the correct words to fill the gaps.
- Model writing the first sentence on the board. Point out the capital letters as well as all the words containing the letter **o**.
- Remind children that the join enables a space to be made between the letters.

Resources and Assessment

Focus

Further pattern practice and more practice writing words containing **od**, **og** and **oo** joins. Tracing and copying pattern, letters and words.

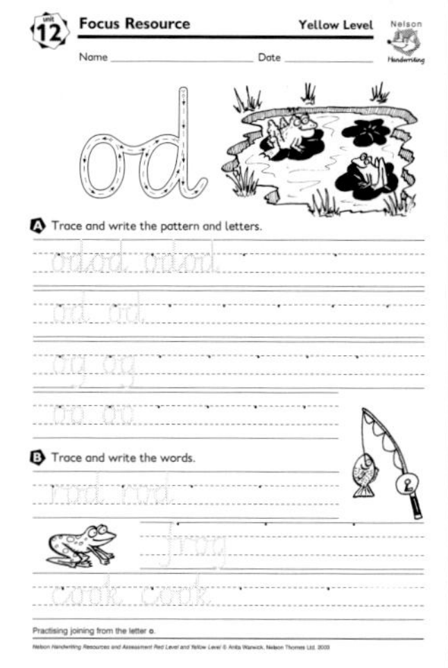

12 Focus Resource — Yellow Level

Name ____ Date ____

od

A Trace and write the pattern and letters.

B Trace and write the words.

Extension

Copying poem, providing further practice joining from the letter **o** (contains **oo** and **ou** joins). Putting the joins learned and practised into context.

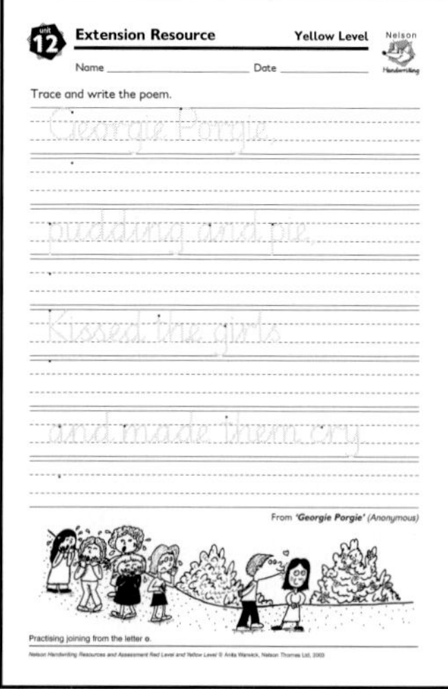

12 Extension Resource — Yellow Level

Name ____ Date ____

Trace and write the poem.

Georgie Porgie
pudding and pie,
Kissed the girls
and made them cry.

From 'Georgie Porgie' (Anonymous)

Assessment

- The correct formation of the letters **o**, **d** and **g**.
- The join from the letter **o** dips down slightly.
- The correct space is allowed between the letters **o** and **d**, **o** and **o**, and **o** and **g**.

NIT 13

Objectives

- To practise forming, and joining to, the letter **r**.

Spelling links

- the **er**, **ir** and **ur** sound

Nelson theme – reptiles

UNIT 13 Practising joining to the letter r.

er

Slippery, slithery, sliding snake.

FOCUS

A Copy this pattern into your book.

erer erer erer erer

B Copy these letters into your book.

er er er er er

ir ir ir ir ir

ur ur ur ur ur

Be careful! These letters should all be the same height.

EXTRA

Copy these words into your book.

er	ir	ur
sister	bird	hurt
mister	dirt	hurtle
blister	shirt	turtle

EXTENSION

Copy this poem into your book.

A rabbit raced a turtle,
You know the turtle won;
And Mister Bunny came in late
A little hot cross bun!

Anonymous

30 31

Developing Skills

Focus

- Before the lesson, draw four lines on the board (two rows of dotted lines in the middle) and write the whole class sentence between them.
- Underline the letters **er** in the sentence.
- Encourage the children to finger trace over the large **er**.
- Point out the sound these letters make, e.g. in **slippery** and **slithery**.
- Discuss how **er**, **ir** and **ur** make a similar sound, but are different letter combinations.
- Demonstrate joining to **r**, using the **er**, **ir** and **ur** joins.
- All these joins are the first diagonal join.
- Ask the class to practise the pattern, then copy the pattern and letters into their books.

Extra

- Talk about words that end in **er**, e.g. **sister**, **mister**. Can the children think of any more?
- Model writing these words on the board.
- Repeat for words containing **ir** and **ur**.
- Ask the children to copy the **er**, **ir** and **ur** words into their books.

Extension

- Read the poem together.
- Model writing the first line of the poem on the board. Remind children about the formation of the letters **er** and **ur**.
- Ask the group to identify words in the poem that contain these two letters joined together (***Mister** and **turtle***).
- Point out that **Mister** has a capital **M** because it is part of the rabbit's name (***Mister Bunny***).
- Ask the group to note the punctuation marks (*comma, semi-colon and exclamation mark*) and position them correctly on the lines when they copy the poem.
- This is a good poem to use as an assessment activity. Children could copy the poem onto plain paper, with guidelines underneath. Emphasise the importance of letters of the correct size and height and all letters joined except capital letters and break letters.

Resources and Assessment

Focus

Further pattern practice and more practice joining **er**, **ir** and **ur** in words. Tracing and copying pattern, letters and words.

Extension

Further practice joining to and forming the letter **r**. The poem provides handwriting practice using words containing the **er** joins in context.

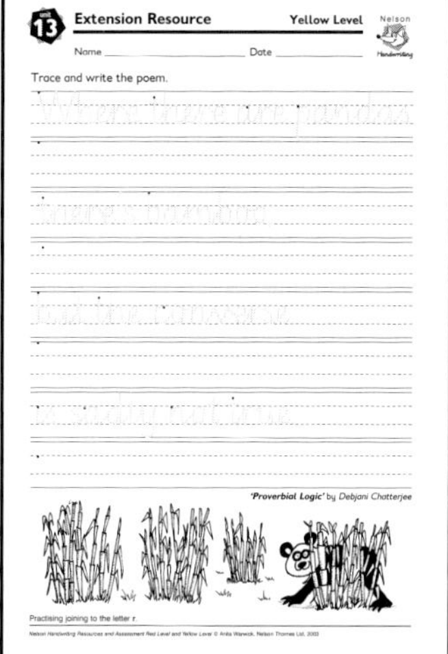

Assessment

- Correct formation and joining of **er**, **ir** and **ur**.
- Use of the first diagonal join, *not* joining to the bottom of the letter.
- Consistent space between letters.

NIT 14

Objectives

- To practise the first and second joins, from the letter **a**.

UNIT 14

Practising the first and second join.

ai

Jake the snake. Gail the snail.

FOCUS

A Copy this pattern into your book.

aiai aiai aiai aiai

B Copy these letters into your book.

ai ai ai ai ai

al al al al al

ay ay ay ay ay

Remember to leave the correct space between your letters.

EXTRA

Copy these words into your book.

tail tale tray

sail sale stray

pail pale play

EXTENSION

Use your dictionary to decide which is the correct homophone for each sentence. Copy the sentences into your book.

1 The gecko had a long (tail/tale).

2 Hayley asked if the tortoise was for (sail/sale).

3 The man turned (pail/pale) as the snake slid towards him.

Spelling links

- the **a** sound (**a**, **ai**, **ay**)

Nelson theme – reptiles

Developing Skills

Focus

- Before the lesson, draw four lines on the board (two rows of dotted lines in the middle) and write the whole class sentence between them.
- Encourage the children to finger trace over the large **ai** in the book.
- Point out that the join is made from the bottom of the letter **a** to the top of the letter **i** (and not to the bottom of the letter **i**, as this can result in poor letter formation and can hamper the development of sloped writing later on).
- Identify the words containing **a** and **ai** in the sentence. Discuss the similar sounds these letters make in these words
- Demonstrate joining from the letter **a**, to make **ai**, **al** and **ay**. Stress that these are all diagonal joins. The join to the letters **i** and **y** is the first join: a diagonal join to a small letter. The join to the letter **l** is the second join: a diagonal join to a letter with an ascender.
- Ask the children to practise the pattern and the joins on their whiteboards.
- Tell the class to copy the pattern and letters into their books.

Extra

- Discuss words that rhyme with **tail**. Model writing these words on the board.
- Point out that **tail** and **tale** are homophones.
- Model writing the word **tale** on the board.
- Point out the sound that **ai** makes in words – it sounds the same as **ay** in **tray**.
- Tell the children to copy the words into their books.

Extension

- Read the sentences together.
- Model writing the first sentence on the board.
- Remind children about the formation and the join from **a** to **i** as well as the height of these letters. Point out that the letter **t** is slightly shorter than the letter **l**.
- Children may use a dictionary to help them decide which is the correct word to complete the sentence.
- They should then copy the sentences into their books, remembering to form and join their letters correctly.

Resources and Assessment

Focus

Further pattern practice and more practice writing words containing **ai**, **al** and **ay**. Tracing and copying pattern, letters and words.

14 Focus Resource Yellow Level

Name Date

A Trace and write the pattern and letters.

B Trace and write the words.

Practising the first and second joins.

Extension

Further practice joining from the letter **a** to the letters **i** and **l**. Copying poem onto a photocopied set of guidelines or onto a piece of plain paper with guidelines underneath, or lined paper.

14 Extension Resource Yellow Level

Name Date

A Trace and write the words.

B Trace and write the poem.

'Policeman Haiku' by Roger Stevens

Practising the first and second joins.

Assessment

- Diagonal joins from the letter **a** are formed correctly.
- The first join is made from the bottom of the letter to the top of the following small letter.
- Second join is made to around the x-height of a letter with an ascender.

UNIT 15

Objectives

- To practise forming, and joining from, the letter **o**.

Spelling links

- **oi**, **ou** and **oy** sounds
- apostrophe of omission

Nelson theme – bridges

Developing Skills

Focus

- Before the lesson, draw four lines on the board (two rows of dotted lines in the middle) and write the whole class sentence between them.
- Point out that the joining line from the letter **o** enables you to leave a space between letters.
- Encourage the children to finger trace over the large **oy**.
- Ask the children to identify the words in the whole class sentence containing a join from the letter **o**, i.e. **boys**, **point**, **coin**.
- Discuss the **oi** and **oy** sound. Illustrate by writing some words containing the letters **oi** and **oy**.
- Draw the pattern in the air and on the board.
- Model joining from the letter **o**, using the **oi**, **ou** and **oy** joins.
- Explain that all these joins are the third horizontal join.
- Ask the class to practise the pattern and the joins on their whiteboards, then copy the pattern and the letters into their books.

Extra

- Talk about speech marks.

Explain that speech marks are used to show words which are being spoken. Model writing speech marks. Some people refer to them as '66' and '99' to help children form them correctly. Show the class that speech marks are written just under the top line.

- Next illustrate the use of the apostrophe. Explain that apostrophes are used when a letter is missed out. Model the writing of an apostrophe on the board, e.g., **who is**/**who's**. The apostrophe is written just below the top line, in the same position as speech marks. Point out that the letters either side of an apostrophe are not joined.

Extension

- Model writing the first sentence on the board. Remind children about the formation of speech marks.
- Point out that this sentence is a question, so it ends with a question mark, inside the speech marks. Remind children that a question mark is the same height as an ascender.
- Discuss the use of the comma inside the speech marks.

Resources and Assessment

Focus

Further pattern practice and more practice joining from the letter **o**. The **oi** and **oy** joins are put into context in words. Tracing and copying pattern, letters and words.

Extension

Further practice joining from the letter **o**. Further practice writing speech marks and apostrophes. Copying words and sentences.

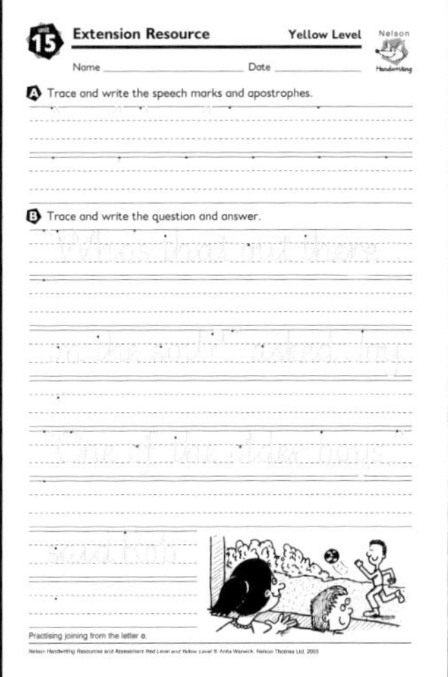

Assessment

- The letter **o** is formed correctly.
- The horizontal join from the letter **o** dips down slightly.
- Adequate space is allowed between the letter **o** and letters joined from it.

UNIT 16

Objectives

- To join, using the third join, to the letter **e**.

Spelling links

- the **ea** sound

Nelson theme – transport

Developing Skills

Focus

- Before the lesson, draw four lines on the board (two rows of dotted lines in the middle) and write the whole class sentence between them.
- Point out the letters **re** in the whole class sentence.
- Mention that the horizontal join to the letter **e** is tricky. Model joining to **e**, using **re**, **oe** and **fe** as examples.
- Explain that all these joins are the third join: a horizontal join from and to a small letter.
- Point out that the pencil must dip down after finishing the letter **r**, ready to form the letter **e**. It is important to stress that the joining line from the letter **r** comes halfway down before writing the letter **e**. Demonstrate on the board what happens if you do not bring the pencil halfway down.
- Ask the children to practise the pattern and the joins on their whiteboards.
- Note that the joins from the letter **o** and from the letter **f** dip down too.
- Tell the class to copy the pattern and letters into their books.

Extra

- Talk about words that rhyme with **toe**. Model writing these words between four lines on the board. Point out the difference between the join from the letter **f** to **o** and the join from the letter **o** to **e**. Notice again how the join to the letter **e** *must* dip down.
- Repeat for words rhyming with **fear**, and then **dream**. Comment on the sound **ea** makes in these words.
- Emphasise the difference between the **fe** and **fo** joins.
- Ask the class to copy the words into their books.

Extension

Read the poem together.

- Ask the children if they can identify the letters which are joined using the horizontal join to the letter **e** *(**oe** in **toes**, **re** in **streams**)*.
- Model writing the first verse on the board. Remind children about the formation and writing of commas and full stops. Demonstrate the correct writing of a semi-colon.

Resources and Assessment

Focus

Further pattern practice and more practice of words containing **re**, **oe** and **fe** joins. Tracing and copying pattern, letters and words.

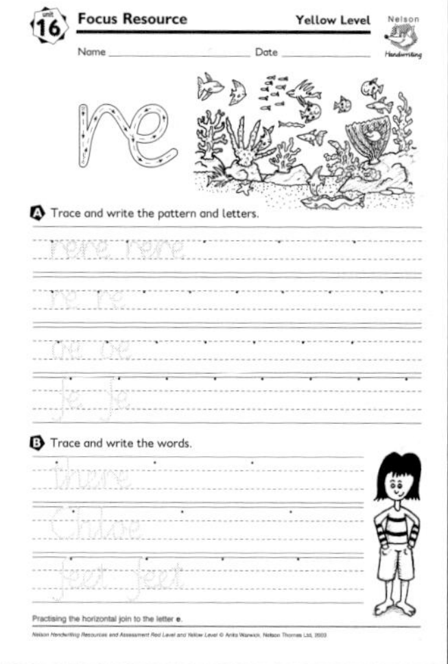

Extension

Further practice joining to the letter **e** (**fe**, **re** and **oe**). The sentence practises the new words in context.

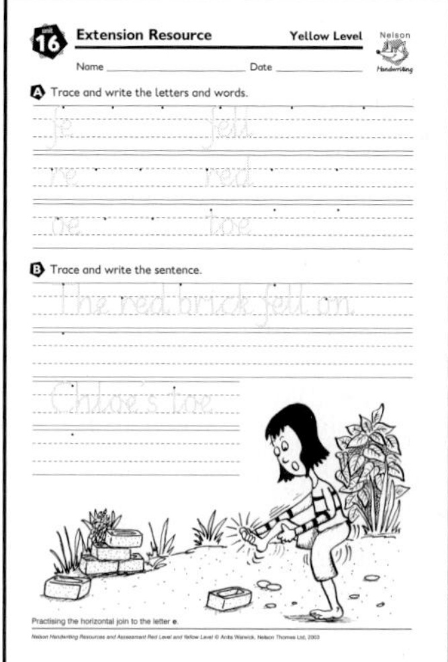

Assessment

- The correct join from the letter **r** to the letter **e** – it dips down to enable the proper formation of the letter **e**.
- The correct join from the letter **o** to the letter **e**.
- The correct join from the letter **f** to the letter **e** – the crossbar on the **f** dips so the **e** can be formed correctly.

UNIT 17

Objectives

- To form, and join from, the letter **f**.
- To form, and join to, the letter **u**.

Spelling links

- adding suffixes **ful** and **fully** to words

Nelson theme – people

UNIT 17 Practising the horizontal join to the letter u.

fu

My friends are full of fun.

FOCUS

A Copy this pattern into your book.

vwu vwu vwu vwu

B Copy these letters into your book.

fu fu fu fu fu

wu wu wu wu wu

vu vu vu vu vu

Be careful! f is a tall letter. It has a straight back.

EXTRA

Copy these words into your book.

care	careful	carefully
help	helpful	helpfully
wonder	wonderful	wonderfully

EXTENSION

Choose the correct word to finish these sentences. Copy the sentences into your book.

1 Trisha's mum (care/careful/carefully) helped the children cross the road.

2 The dinner lady told Alison's teacher she had been a big (help/helpful/helpfully) at lunchtime.

Developing Skills

Focus

- Before the lesson, draw four lines on the board (two rows of dotted lines in the middle) and write the whole class sentence between them.
- Encourage the children to finger trace over the large **fu** in the book.
- Remind the children that the letter **f** has an ascender. It has a straight back and its descender goes below the baseline.
- Discuss the join from **f** to the letter **u**. Identify words in the whole class sentence which contain the **fu** join (***full*** *and* ***fun***).
- Explain that this join is the third horizontal join to letters without ascenders.
- The join from **f** to **u** is made from the crossbar of the **f** to the top of the letter **u**. The join ensures a space is maintained between these letters.
- Demonstrate joining to **u**, using the **fu**, **wu** and **vu** joins as examples.
- Ask the children to practise the pattern and the joins, and then copy them into their books.

Extra

- Talk about adding the suffixes **ful** and **fully** to words, e.g. **care/careful/carefully**.
- Ask the class if they can think of a sentence containing one of these words. Repeat for **help/helpful/helpfully** and **wonder/wonderful/ wonderfully**.
- Model writing the words **care**, **careful** and **carefully** on the board between four lines.
- Tell the children to copy the words into their books.

Extension

- Read the sentences together.
- Ask the children to choose the correct word in each case.
- Model writing the first sentence on the board.
- Remind children about the formation of the letters **f**, **y** and **p**. These letters have descenders which go below the baseline.
- Children should also remember to check capital letters are the correct height as they copy the sentences into their books.

Resources and Assessment

Focus

Further pattern practice and practice of words containing **fu**, **wu** and **vu** joins. Tracing and copying pattern, letters and words.

Extension

Further practice joining to the letter **u**.

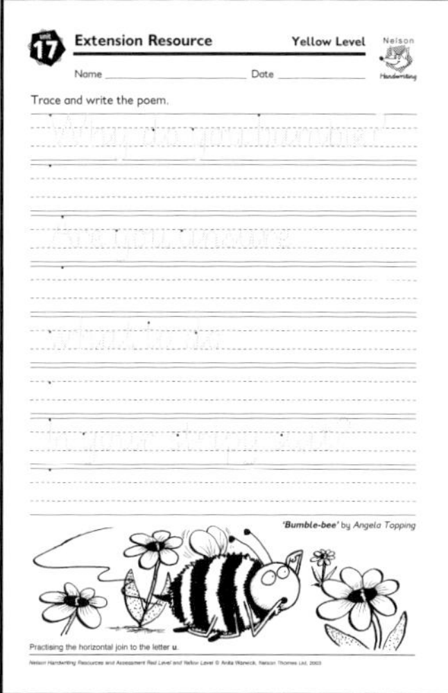

Assessment

- Correct formation of the letter **f** with a straight back, an ascender and a descender.
- Correct horizontal third join from the letter **f** to the letter **u**.
- Descenders of the letters **f**, **y** and **p** all fall below the line.

NIT 18

Objectives

- To practise forming the print letters correctly.

Spelling links

- match and spell words related to parts of the body

Nelson theme – people

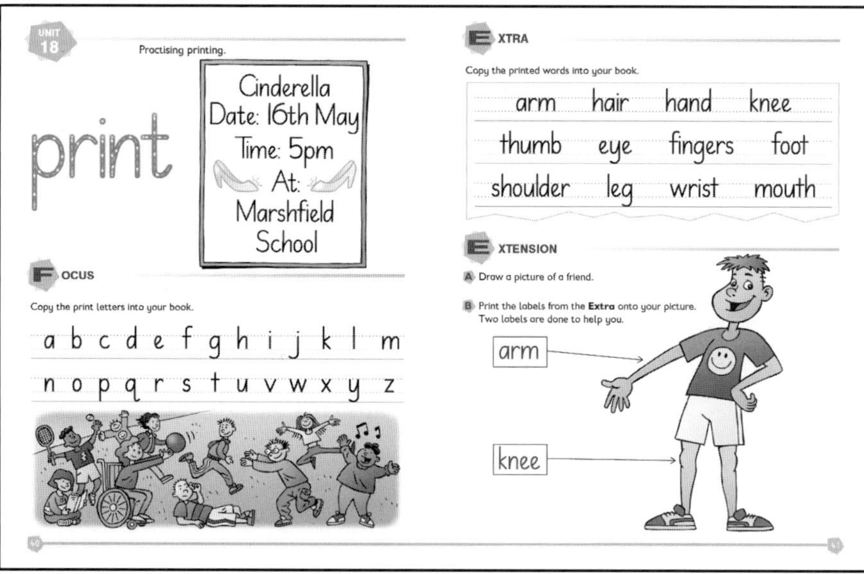

Developing Skills

Focus

- Encourage the children to finger trace over the printed word **print**.
- Stress that printed letters do not join – they do not have flicks (exit strokes).
- Ask children when they think print letters might be used (*e.g. on labels, captions, posters, in titles/headings*).
- Model the print alphabet on the board. Ask the class if they can tell you what the differences are between letters in the print alphabet and letters in joined script. (*There aren't any exit strokes/flicks; the letters **f** and **k** are formed differently – **f** does not have a tail.*)
- Ask the children to practise writing the print letters on their whiteboards, and then copy them into their books.

Extra

- Read the printed words.
- Model writing the first line. Point out that the letters do not have flicks at the end.
- Tell the children to copy the words into their books.

Extension

- Draw a person on the board.
- Model writing a couple of body parts, using print letters.
- Draw an arrow to label the drawing.
- Ask individual children to come up to the board and write a printed label for a body part. The rest of the class can help with spelling as a child demonstrates printing.

Resources and Assessment

Focus

More practice printing letters.

Extension

Further practice printing letters. Labelling the dog picture puts print letters into context.

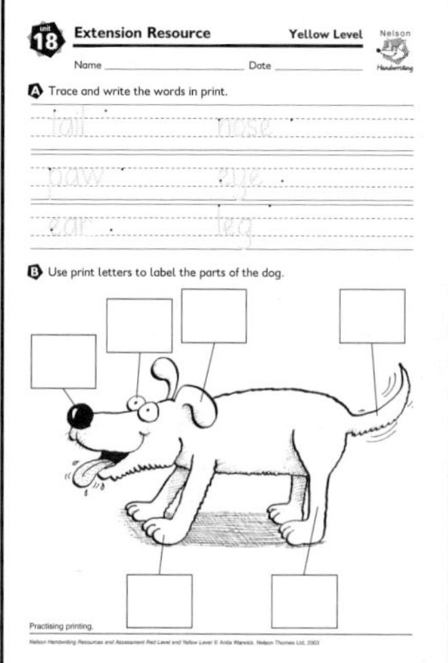

Assessment

- Printed letters are the correct height.
- Print letters do not have an exit flick.
- The letters **f** and **k** are formed correctly.

UNIT 19

Objectives

- To practise the fourth join – joining to ascenders.

Spelling links

- the **o** sound

Nelson theme –weather

Developing Skills

Focus

- Before the lesson, draw four lines on the board (two rows of dotted lines in the middle) and write the whole class sentence between them.
- Encourage the children to finger trace over the large **ot** in the book.
- Say aloud the sound these letters make in words. Underline the letters **ot** in the whole class sentence.
- Demonstrate joining to **t** from the letter **o**. Remind children this join is a horizontal join, like the third join, but it joins to an ascender.
- Model the joins **ot**, **ol** and **ok**. Point out that the join is made towards the top of the ascender. Stress that the join is *not* made at the very top of the letter.
- Ask the children to come to the board and write and join the letters **ot**, **ol** and **ok**. Praise those who form and join the letters correctly – particularly the **ok** join. The body of the letter **k** should be the same size as a small letter, e.g. the same height as the letter **o**.
- Tell the class to practise the pattern, then copy the pattern and the letters into their books.

Extra

- Discuss words that rhyme with **hot**.
- Model correct writing of these words on the board, between four lines to allow children to see the relative height and size of these letters.
- Remind the children that the letter **t** is not as tall as other letters with ascenders.
- Ask the children to copy the words into their books.

Extension

- Read the poem together.
- Model writing the first two lines on the board.
- Point out that an apostrophe is used in the contraction **I'm**. The apostrophe shows where the letter a has been missed out. (See Unit 15.)
- Point out that **wh** in the word **what** is also a fourth join. Remind the group that **ok** in **looking** and **ot** in **hot** and **spot** also use the fourth join.
- Ask the children to copy the poem into their books, or onto a piece of plain or lined paper.

Resources and Assessment

Focus

Further practice of joining from the letter **o** to ascenders.

Tracing and copying words.

Extension

Adding **ing** to make new words while practising joining to ascenders. Tracing and writing a sentence using words from above gives a context for joining to ascenders.

Assessment

- The correct use of the fourth join for letters **ot** and **ok**.
- The correct space is allowed between the letters **o** and **t**, and **o** and **k**.
- The letter **t** is not as tall as the ascenders of other letters.

UNIT 20

Objectives

- To revise joins and check all four joins are being made correctly.

Spelling links

- compound words

Nelson theme – weather

Developing Skills

Focus

- Before the lesson, draw four lines on the board (two rows of dotted lines in the middle) and write the whole class sentence between them.
- Explain that this unit is a revision of all four joins learned in the Red and Yellow Level books.
- Ask the children if they can tell you what all the four joins are. Higher attaining children might be able to give some examples of letters using the joins.
- Demonstrate the joins – **ai**, **al**, **ow** and **ol**.
- Ask the class to practise these joins and the pattern on their whiteboards, then copy them into their books.

Extra

- Discuss compound words: words made from two smaller words added together, e.g. **rain** + **drop** = **raindrop**.
- Ask the children to work in pairs to think of examples of compound words.
- Make a list on the board. Model the handwriting.
- Tell the children to copy the compound words from the pupil book into their books. Remind them that the joins need to be made correctly.

Extension

- Read the words in the box.
- Ask the group if they can put sets of two words together to make compound words.
- Model writing two or three of these words on the board.
- Tell the children to complete the exercise making compound words from the word 'snow'.

Resources and Assessment

Focus

Further practice of the four joins.

Tracing and copying words.

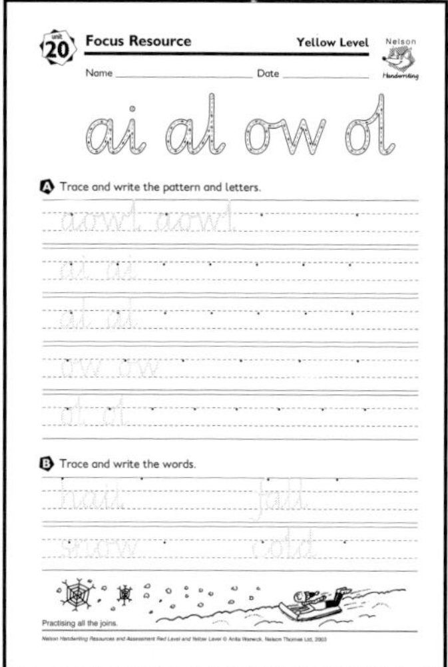

Extension

Practising all four joins and break letters in the context of a poem.

Assessment

- The correct use of all four joins.
- All letters are the correct height and size.
- The correct space is allowed between letters and words.

CHECK-UP 2

Objectives

Explain to the pupils that this exercise is an assessment activity. The objective is to assess what the pupils can do and where they need extra practice. This exercise will help assess each pupil's ability to form and use the four handwriting joins. Ask pupils to look at the checklist on the back of the flap to remind themselves of the important points.

CHECK-UP 2

FOCUS

Copy these patterns into your book.

icic icic icic icic
odod odod odod odod
erer erer erer erer
oioy oioy oioy oioy
vwu vwu vwu vwu
aowl aowl aowl aowl

EXTRA

Copy the words into your book.

dear hear help helpful
tail tale sail sale
fare fair foe woe
look took dirt shirt

46 47

EXTENSION

Copy the poem into your book.

Today I saw a little worm,
Wriggling on his belly.
Perhaps he'd like to come inside,
And see what's on the telly?

'The Worm' by Spike Milligan

48

Focus

Ask the pupils to copy the patterns into their books. The patterns are an important part of helping pupils to learn to join letters. The patterns need to be made smoothly, with the letter shapes the correct height and spaces between the letters and between pattern blocks.

Extra

Ask the pupils to copy these words into their books. The words contain all four handwriting joins.

Extension

Ask the pupils to copy the poem into their books. It practises all the joins and writing fluency.

Assessment

- Are the letters formed correctly?
- Are any letters too tall or too short?
- Do the descenders fall below the line?
- Is there a space between letters?
- Is there a space between words?
- Are the four handwriting joins made correctly?

- For more Assessment see *Resources and Assessment Book Red and Yellow Level*

SCOPE AND SEQUENCE
DEVELOPING SKILLS BOOK ONE

Page	Focus	Extra	Extension	Focus resource	Extension resource
4-5 Flashback	*Flashback*	*Flashback*	*Flashback*	*Flashback*	*Flashback*
6-7 Unit 1 Fairy stories	practising writing descenders: ning, ping, ting	double final letter before adding ing: sit, sitting, hop, hopping, shop, shopping	choose words and copy sentences	practise writing p and g, trace and copy pattern and words, trace and copy sentence	trace and copy words ending in ning, ping and ting and sentence containing descenders
8-9 Unit 2 Fairy stories	practising joining from the letter o: oc, od, oo	copy sentences containing a comma, a question mark and speech marks	copy poem	trace and copy pattern, letters and words: oc, lock, clock, od, nod, rod, oo, moon, spoon	practise speech marks and question marks copy questions, choose and copy the correct answer
10-11 Unit 3 Homes	practising joining to the letter e: ake, ome, are	drop e when adding ing: care, caring, dare, daring, stare, staring, take, taking, make, making, bake, baking	copy poem	trace and copy pattern, letters and words: ake, cake, lake, ome, dome, home, are, hare, share	change words by adding ing make and copy words
12-13 Unit 4 Homes	practising joining to the letter l: fla, flo, fle	copy words: flame, flap, flat, flag, flock, float, floor, flow, flee, fleet, flew, flex	choose words and copy sentences	trace and copy pattern, letters and words: fla, flan, flannel, flo, flower, flowerpot, fle, flee, fleece	copy homonyms choose words and copy sentences
14-15 Unit 5 Weather	practising joining from the letter w: who, wha, whe	copy words: who, what, whatever, when, where, wherever, while, which, whichever	copy poem	trace and copy pattern, letters and words: who, whoever, whose, wha, whale, what, whe, wheel, when, where	copy words choose the correct word to complete sentences copy sentences
16-17 Unit 6 Weather	practising joining from the letter i: ie, in, il	copy words: muddy, muddier, muddiest, chilly, chillier, chilliest, rainy, rainier, rainiest	choose words and copy sentences	trace and copy pattern, letters and words: ie, sunnier, funnier, il, silly, hilly, in, thin, thinner	copy words ending in suffixes ier, iest copy words and sentence
18-19 Unit 7 Animals and homes	practising diagonal joins to the letter y: ly, ky, ny	make words by adding y and copy: twirl, twirly, swirl, swirly, whirl, whirly, cheek, cheeky	copy poem	trace and copy pattern, letters and words ly, bully, fully, ky, smoky, cheeky, ny, sunny, funny	add suffix ly or ny to words copy sentence
20-21 Unit 8 Animals and homes	practising joining from the letter a: ap, ar, an	make words and copy: dis+appear, dis+appearance, re+appear, re+appearance	choose words and copy sentences	trace and copy pattern, letters and words ap, approve, disapprove, ar, arm, disarm, al. allow, disallow	add the prefix un copy sentences choosing correct word
22-23 Unit 9 Magic and parties	practising joining to the letter k: ick, uck, ack	add s to make plural and copy words: trick, tricks, truck, trucks, track, tracks	choose word and copy sentences	trace and copy pattern, letters and words: ick, tick, chick, uck, buckle, chuckle, ack, black, crack	write an informal letter
24-25 Unit 10 Magic and parties	practising writing with a slope	copy words, remember to slope to the right: cake, bake, make, dress, mess, guess, locket, pocket, rocket	choose word and copy sentences, slope writing to right	trace and copy pattern, letters and words: add s, es and ies: tools, stools, schools, es, dishes, wishes, fishes, ies, jellies, wellies, pennies	copy sloping verse of a poem and check slope is even

Page	Focus	Extra	Extension	Focus resource	Extension resource
26-27 Unit 11 Mazes	practising joining to the letter e: he, we, re	make words with apostrophes: here is = here's, where is = where's, there is = there's, he will = he'll, we will = we'll, they will = they'll	copy poem	trace and copy pattern, letters and words: he, heavy, heavier, we, weaken, weakest, re, strength, strengthen	copy words and choose the correct contractions
28-29 Unit 12 Mazes	practising joining from the letter f: fte, fir, fin	copy words and phrases associated with time: after, after a while, afterwards, first, firstly, finally, then, suddenly, once	choose words and copy sentences	trace and copy pattern, letters and words: aft, after, afterwards, after all, fin, finish, final, finally	copy poem
30-31 Unit 13 Hands	practising writing silent letters: wra, wri, kni	copy words: wrap, wrapping, wrapper, write, writing, writer, knit, knitting, knitter	copy tongue-twister	choose word to match picture write word and silent letter	copy words in the correct column
32-33 Unit 14 Hands	practising forming double letters: ii, ll, tt, rr, nn, mm, cc, oo, dd, ss, ff, ee	copy words: ball, call, fall, guess, dress, press, off, offer, cliff	copy poem	trace and copy letters and words: dd, saddle, paddle, oo, noodle, poodle, rr, horrible, terrible, tt, kettle, nettle	practise lists
34-35 Unit 15 Storms	practising spacing letters consistently: ew, ev, ex	copy words: new, blew, flew, even, ever, every, flex, next, text	copy poem	trace and copy pattern, letters and words: ew, view, preview, ev, event, prevent, ex, exchange, exit	copy poem
36-37 Unit 16 Storms	practising writing letters with ascenders in proportion: th, ht, fl	make and copy words, remember to slope to the right: light + ly = lightly, tight + ly = tightly, bright + ly = brightly, light + er = lighter, tight +er = tighter, bright +er = brighter	copy poem, focus on leaving spaces between letters and words	copy words and add suffixes: ly, er, en and ing	practise adjectives and adverbs, add suffix ly to adjectives to make adverbs choose an adverb to complete sentence
38-39 Unit 17 Tea	practising joining from the letter a: ac, ag, af	make and copy compound words: teaspoon, teacup, teatime, teapot	put instructions into correct order and copy	trace and copy pattern, letters and words: ac, back, pack, ag, cage, page, af, raft, daft	practise sequencing
40-41 Unit 18 Tea	practising forming capital letters	copy names of countries: Indonesia, Georgia, India, China, Sri Lanka, Japan	copy sentences and use commas to separate words in a list	copy patterns write own name and address	copy shape poem
42-43 Unit 19 Books	practising writing decorated capital letters: letters of the alphabet	write names of famous buildings in decorated capital letters: Buckingham Palace, Cardiff Castle, Holyroodhouse, York Minster	write own name with initial illuminated letters	trace and copy decorated alphabet	copy poem
44-45 Unit 20 Books	practising with punctuation: ! ? – " " , '	copy words: Explosive! Fantastic! Nonsense! Great! Super! Wow! Terrible! Awful! Miserable!	choose words and copy sentences	copy questions and complete the answers	copy sentences and put in the speech marks
46-48 Check-up	*Check-up*	*Check-up*	*Check-up*	*Check-up*	*Check-up*

FLASHBACK

Objectives

Explain to the pupils that this exercise is an assessment activity. The objective is to assess what the pupils can do from the Yellow level and where they need extra practice. This exercise will help assess each pupil's ability to form and use the four handwriting joins. Ask pupils to look at the checklist on the back of the flap to remind themselves of the important points.

FLASHBACK

FOCUS

Copy these patterns into your book.

uu uu uu uu
olol olol olol olol
ooo ooo ooo ooo
lili lili lili lili
aiai aiai aiai aiai
aowl aowl aowl aowl

EXTRA

Copy these words into your book.

to	no	an	and
it	little	the	tail
care	coat	you	spout
of	off	joking	choking

EXTENSION

Copy this poem into your book.

How doth the little crocodile
Improve his shining tail,
And pour the waters of the Nile,
On every golden scale!

From *'The Crocodile'* by Lewis Carroll

Focus

Ask the pupils to copy the patterns into their books. The patterns are an important part of helping pupils to learn to join letters. The patterns need to be made smoothly, with the letter shapes the correct height and spaces between the letters and between pattern blocks.

Extra

Ask the pupils to copy these words into their books. The words contain all four handwriting joins.

Extension

Ask the pupils to copy the poem into their books.

Assessment

- Are the letters formed correctly?
- Are any letters too tall or too short?
- Do the descenders fall below the line?
- Is there a space between letters?
- Is there a space between words?
- Are the four handwriting joins made correctly?

- For more Assessment see *Resources and Assessment Book 1 and Book 2*

UNIT 1

Objectives

- To form and write letters with descenders correctly.

Spelling links

- doubling a final consonant before adding **ing**

Nelson theme – fairy stories

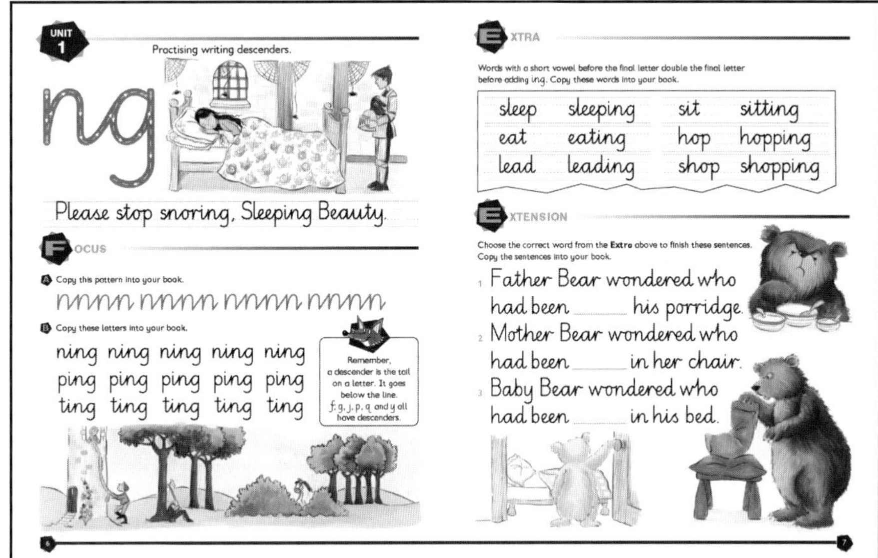

UNIT 1 Practising writing descenders.

ng

Please stop snoring, Sleeping Beauty.

FOCUS

A Copy this pattern into your book.

nnnn nnnn nnnn nnnn

B Copy these letters into your book.

ning ning ning ning ning
ping ping ping ping ping
ting ting ting ting ting

Remember, a descender is the tail on a letter. It goes below the line. f, g, j, p, q and y all have descenders.

EXTRA

Words with a short vowel before the final letter double the final letter before adding ing. Copy these words into your book.

sleep	sleeping	sit	sitting
eat	eating	hop	hopping
lead	leading	shop	shopping

EXTENSION

Choose the correct word from the Extra above to finish these sentences. Copy the sentences into your book.

1 Father Bear wondered who had been ______ his porridge.
2 Mother Bear wondered who had been ______ in her chair.
3 Baby Bear wondered who had been ______ in his bed.

6 7

Developing Skills

Focus

- Before the lesson, draw four lines and write the whole class sentence on the board.
- Tell the class that this lesson will focus on letters with descenders and words ending in **ing**.
- Ask the children if they can tell you all the letters with descenders. Write each letter on the board as it is suggested.
- Refer to the fox box, which lists the letters with descenders in alphabetical order and reminds us that when we write letters with descenders, the tail goes below the baseline.
- Look at the large **ng** join. The join is made from the bottom of the letter **n** to the top of the letter **g** using a diagonal joining line – the body of the letter **g** sits on the baseline, and the descender goes below it. Point out that the descender finishes neatly (not with a curl or a join) on the bottom line.
- Ask the children to practise the pattern and the **ning**, **ping** and **ting** joins on their individual whiteboards.

Extra

- Discuss adding **ing** to words: for most words we just add **ing** to the word, e.g. **sleep** + **ing** = **sleeping**. But for words with a short vowel before the final consonant we have to double the final letter before adding **ing**, e.g. **sit** + **ing** = **sitting**.
- Model the six examples on the board.
- Point out where we begin writing the letters **p** and **g**. These letters are the same height as small letters, e.g. **i** and **n**. The body of the letter sits on the baseline and the tail goes below it.
- Ask the children to copy the words into their books.

Extension

- Read the sentences.
- Ask the children to choose the correct word from the Extra section to finish the sentences.
- Model writing the first sentence on the board.
- Tell the children to copy the sentences and fill in the missing words.
- Remind them that sentences begin with a capital letter and end with a full stop.

Resources and Assessment

Focus

Further practice forming and joining to letters with descenders. Tracing and copying pattern, words and sentence. Remind children that the letters **p** and **g** have descenders which go below the baseline.

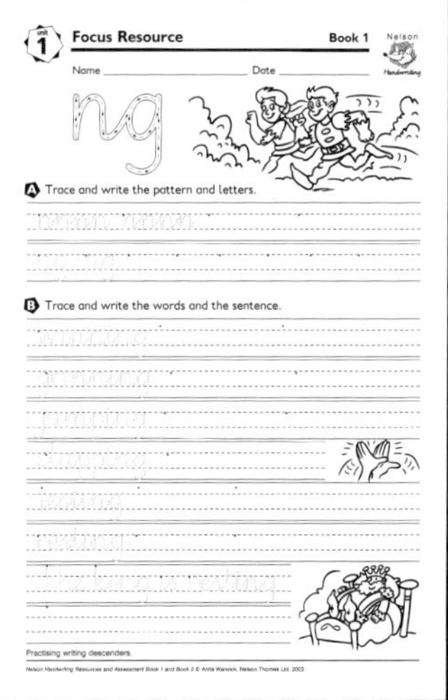

Extension

Further practice forming and joining to letters with descenders.

Extension Resource Book 1

Name Date

A Trace and write the letters and words.

B Trace and write the sentence.

Practising writing descenders.

Assessment

- The descenders of **g**, **p** and **y** fall below the baseline.
- The body of the letters **g**, **p** and **y** sit on the baseline.
- The descenders of **g** and **y** sit neatly on the bottom line.

NIT 2

Objectives

- To join from the letter **o** using the third join.

Spelling links

- question marks
- speech marks

Nelson theme– fairy stories

UNIT 2

Practising joining from the letter o.

oc

Tick tock, watch the clock.

FOCUS

Copy this pattern into your book.

ococ ococ ococ ococ

Copy these letters into your book.

oc oc oc oc oc
od od od od od
oo oo oo oo oo

Remember to leave a space between your letters, like this: knocked

EXTRA

If there is more text after the speech marks have ended, we put a **comma** inside the speech marks at the end of the words spoken. Copy this sentence into your book.

"The wolf is going to eat grandma," cried Little Red Riding Hood.

If someone is asking a question, we put the **question mark** inside the speech marks. Copy this question into your book.

"Who is knocking at my door?"

EXTENSION

Copy this poem into your book.

As soon as Wolf began to feel
That he would like a decent meal,
He went and knocked on Grandma's door.

Poor Grandmamma was terrified,
"He's going to eat me up," she cried.
And she was absolutely right.
He ate her up in one big bite.

From *'Little Red Riding Hood and the Wolf'* by Roald Dahl

Developing Skills

Focus

- Before the lesson, draw four lines and write the whole class sentence on the board.
- Tell the class that the lesson will focus on the third (horizontal) join from the letter **o**.
- Point out that when we write the letter **o** we begin at the top and bring the pen or pencil all the way round. Remind the children that the letter **o** is the same height as other small letters, e.g. **i**, **c**, **a**, **e**.
- Explain that the join from the letter **o** dips down and across to the starting point for the next letter.
- Tell the children to finger trace over the large **oc** join.
- Ask them which words in the whole class sentence contain the **oc** join (***tock***, ***clock***). Are there any other letters in the sentence which are joined using the horizontal join? (***w*** *and* ***a*** *in* ***watch***)
- Ask the children to practise the pattern and the **oc**, **od** and **oo** joins on their individual whiteboards.
- Remind the class that **d** and **e** are the only two letters that do not start at the top – so the **od** join goes across to the start of the letter **d** and back round (the same movement as the join to **c** or **o**).

Extra

- Explain the use of the comma in spoken text: if more text follows the speech, we put a comma inside the speech marks after the words spoken. Show how to write the sentence.
- Model writing a spoken question. Ask the children where to put the speech marks and the question mark. Remind them of the position and shape of these punctuation marks.
- Tell the children to copy the sentences into their books.

Extension

- Read the poem. Point out the commas and speech marks.
- Ask the children to copy the poem. If time is short, they should copy just the second verse.

Resources and Assessment

Focus

Further practice joining from the letter **o**. Tracing and copying pattern, joins and words. Remind children that the joining line from the letter **o** ensures a space is left between the letters.

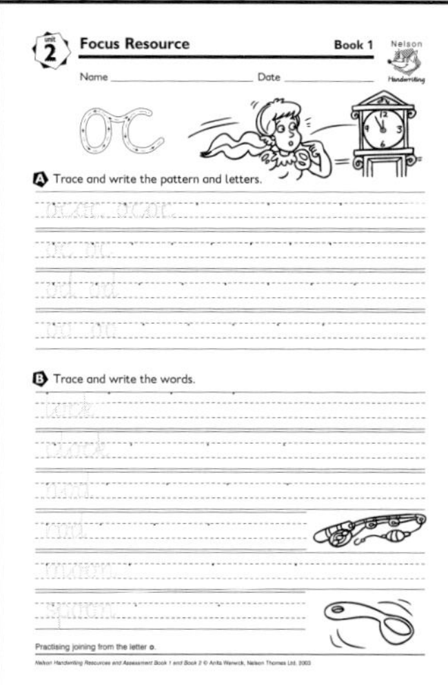

2 Focus Resource Book 1

Name Date

Trace and write the pattern and letters.

Trace and write the words.

Practising joining from the letter o.

Extension

More practice writing questions and answers with speech marks.

2 Extension Resource Book 1

Name Date

Trace and write the question.

What did the wolf do?

Choose the answer from the box and write it under the question.

"The wolf knocked at Grandma's door," sobbed Little Red Riding Hood.

Practising joining from the letter o.

Assessment

- The correct space between the letters **oc**, **od** and **oo**.
- Speech marks are written correctly just below the top line.
- The comma is inside speech marks and written on the line.

NIT 3

Objectives

- To join to the letter **e** using the first join.
- To join to the letter **e** using the third join.

Spelling links

- dropping **e** when adding **ing**

Nelson theme – homes

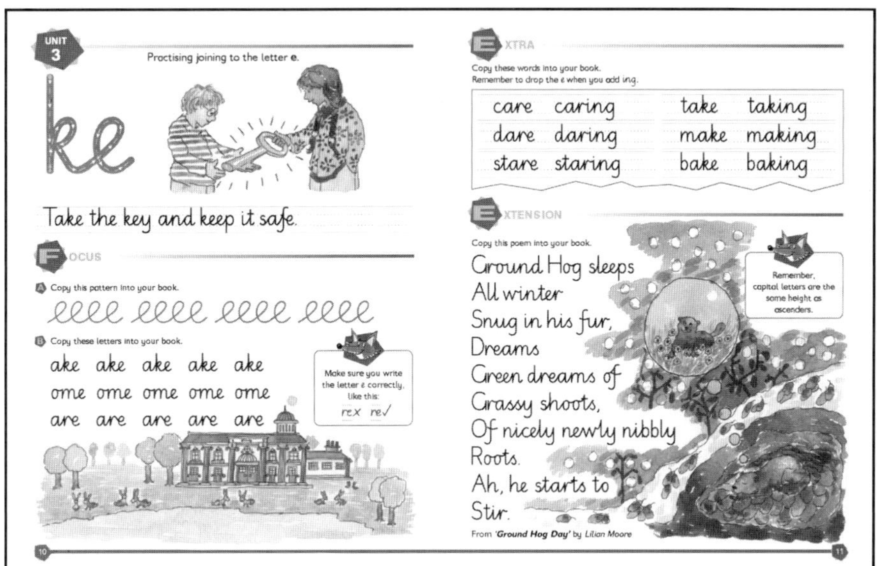

Developing Skills

Focus

- Before the lesson, draw four lines and write the whole class sentence on the board.
- Explain that the lesson will look at both types of join to the letter **e**. Start by talking about the **ke** join.
- Point out that the letter **k** is a tall letter so it has an ascender, but the body of the letter is the same height as a small letter, e.g. **e**.
- Tell the class to finger trace over the large **ke** join.
- Ask the children which words in the whole class sentence contain the **ke** join (***take, key, keep***).
- Look at the other examples of joins to **e**. Are there any other words in the sentence containing joins to the letter **e**? (***the, safe***) Point out that the **fe** and **re** joins are horizontal (third) joins, whereas **he**, **ke** and **me** are diagonal (first) joins.
- Ask the children to practise the pattern and the **ake**, **ome** and **are** joins on their individual whiteboards.
- Refer to the fox box, which reminds children of the correct formation of the letter **e**.

Extra

- Talk about how words ending with the letter **e** drop the **e** when they add **ing**.
- Model writing **care** and **caring**.
- Tell the children to copy the words into their books.

Extension

- Read the poem.
- Point out words containing joins to the letter **e**: **sleeps**, **winter**, **green**, **dreams**, **nicely**, **newly**, **he**.
- Underline the joins in these words. Discuss whether the join in each word, e.g. **te** in **winter**, is a first (diagonal) join or a third (horizontal) join.
- Model writing the words with joins to **e**.
- Ask the group to copy the poem.

Resources and Assessment

Focus

Further practice joining to the letter **e**. Tracing and copying pattern, joins and words.

Extension

More practice writing words that drop the letter **e** when **ing** is added.

Assessment

- The letters **k** and **e** are the correct height and size.
- The correct use of the first join to letter **e**, e.g. the **ke** join.
- The correct use of the third join to letter **e**, e.g. the **re** join.

NIT 4

Objectives

- To form the letter **f** correctly.
- To join from the crossbar of the letter **f**.

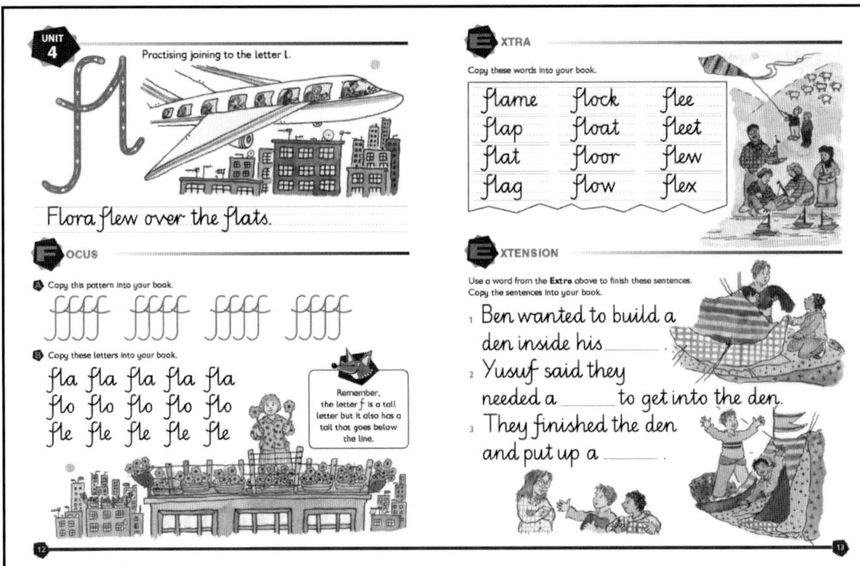

UNIT 4 Practising joining to the letter f.

fl

Flora flew over the flats.

FOCUS

A Copy this pattern into your book.

ffff ffff ffff ffff

B Copy these letters into your book.

fla fla fla fla fla
flo flo flo flo flo
fle fle fle fle fle

Remember, the letter f is a tall letter but it also has a tail that goes below the line.

EXTRA

Copy these words into your book.

flame	flock	flee
flap	float	fleet
flat	floor	flew
flag	flow	flex

EXTENSION

Use a word from the **Extra** above to finish these sentences. Copy the sentences into your book.

1 Ben wanted to build a den inside his ______.
2 Yusuf said they needed a ______ to get into the den.
3 They finished the den and put up a ______.

12 13

Spelling links

- homonyms

Nelson theme – homes

Developing Skills

Focus

- Before the lesson, draw four lines and write the whole class sentence on the board.
- Tell the class that this lesson will focus on the letter **f**.
- Model writing the letter **f** on the board. Explain where it begins and where it finishes.
- Point out that the letter **f** has an ascender, but it also has a descender, which goes below the baseline.
- Mention also that the letter **f** has a straight back and is *not* shaped like an **s**.
- Show the children that we cross the **f** just below the dotted line; the cross is made at the x-height.
- Talk about the **fl** join. Point out that it is a fourth join and goes from the crossbar on the **f** to the top of the letter **l**.
- Ask the class to finger trace over the large **fl** join.
- Underline the **fl** joins in the whole class sentence.
- Point out the capital **F**, and demonstrate its formation. Remind the children that capital letters do not join.
- Model the joins **fla**, **flo** and **fle**. Point out that the cross on the letter **f** should be made at approximately the same height as the letters **a**, **o** and **e**.
- Demonstrate the pattern. It is a tricky pattern. Children can practise in the air, with their fingers on the back of the person in front, on their whiteboards or on the board in front of the class.

Extra

- Model writing the words **flame**, **flap**, **flat** and **flag**.
- Tell the children to copy these and the rest of the words into their books, concentrating on the **fl** joins.

Extension

- Tell the group to finish the sentences using a word from the Extra section above.
- Model writing the first sentence on the board.
- Remind the children to focus on correct formation of and joining from the letter **f**.

Resources and Assessment

Focus

Further practice joining from the letter **f**. Practice joining **fla**, **flo** and **fle** in words. Tracing and copying pattern, joins and words.

4 Focus Resource Book 1 Nelson Handwriting

Name ______ Date ______

A Trace and write the pattern and letters.

B Trace and write the words.

Practising joining to the letter f.

Extension

Practice in writing homonyms. Copying words. Copying sentences into books.

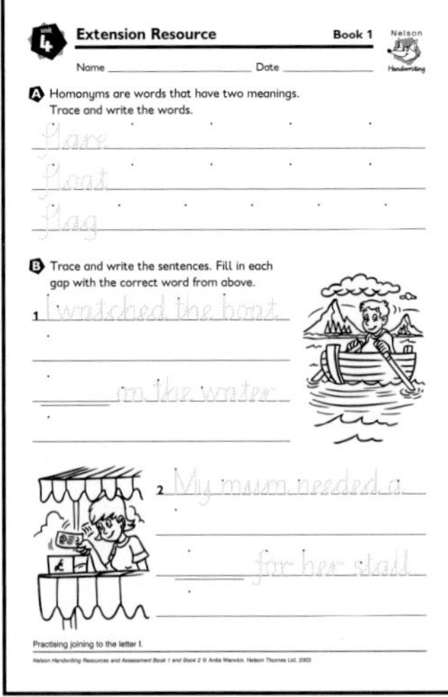

4 Extension Resource Book 1 Nelson Handwriting

Name ______ Date ______

A Homonyms are words that have two meanings. Trace and write the words.

flare
float
flag

B Trace and write the sentences. Fill in each gap with the correct word from above.

1 I watched the boat ______ on the water.

2 My mum needed a ______ for her stall.

Practising joining to the letter f.

Assessment

- The letter **f** is the correct height and size.
- The letter **f** has a straight back.
- The **fl** join is made from the x-height on the letter **f** to the top of the letter **l**.

NIT 5

Objectives

- To form the letter **w** correctly.
- To join from the letter **w** correctly.

Spelling links

- short words within longer words

Nelson theme – weather

UNIT 5 Practising joining from the letter w.

wh

Who knows what the weather will be?

FOCUS

A Copy this pattern into your book.

ww ww ww ww

B Copy these letters into your book.

who who who who who
wha wha wha wha wha
whe whe whe whe whe

Take care! The letter w is not a break letter, unless it is a capital letter.

EXTRA

Copy these words into your book.

who	when	while
what	where	which
whatever	wherever	whichever

EXTENSION

Copy this poem into your book.

Whether the weather be fine
Or whether the weather be not,
Whether the weather be cold
Or whether the weather be hot,
We'll weather the weather
Whatever the weather,
Whether we like it or not.
(Anonymous)

Developing Skills

Focus

- Before the lesson, draw four lines and write the whole class sentence on the board.
- Explain that the lesson will focus on the letter **w**. Write it on the board. Emphasise that all its lines are straight lines. Comment on where it begins and where it finishes.
- Point out that the letter **w** is a small letter. It is the same height as the letters **a**, **e** and **o**.
- Show the children that the **wh** join is the fourth join. It goes from the x-height of the letter **w** to the top of the letter **h**. Stress that the join goes *across* and then up. Some children will try to go straight up from the last line of the letter **w**.
- Tell the class to finger trace over the join at the top of the page.
- Underline the **wh** join in the whole class sentence.
- Point out the capital **W** and demonstrate its formation. Remind children that capital letters do not join.
- Discuss how the words **what** and **weather** start with different letters but the same sound.
- Model the joins **who**, **whe** and **wha**. Point out that the letters **w** and **a** are the same height. They are also the same height as the body of the letter **h**.
- Demonstrate the pattern. Tell the children to practise on their whiteboards before copying the pattern and joins into their books.

Extra

- Model writing the words **whatever**, **wherever** and **whichever**.
- Ask the children if they can identify the short words within these words.
- Write the words **what, where** and **which** on the board.
- Tell the group to copy the words into their books.

Extension

- Read the poem.
- Model writing the first two lines.
- Remind the group to use the correct join from the **w** to the **h** as they copy the poem. They may use plain paper with guidelines, their lined books or lined paper.

Resources and Assessment

Focus

Further practice joining from the letter **w**. Practice of **who**, **wha** and **whe** joins in words. Tracing and copying pattern, joins and words.

5 Focus Resource Book 1 Nelson Handwriting

Name Date

wh

A Trace and write the pattern and letters.

B Trace and write the words.

Practising joining from the letter w.

Extension

More practice writing words and sentences containing the **wh** join.

5 Extension Resource Book 1 Nelson Handwriting

Name Date

A Trace and write the letters and words.

B Trace and write the sentences. Fill in each gap with the correct word from above.

Practising joining from the letter w.

Assessment

- The letter **w** is the correct height and size.
- The letter **w** has straight lines.
- The join is made at the x-height on the letter **w**, across and up to the top of the letter **h**.

UNIT 6

Objectives

- To form the letter **i** correctly.
- To join from the letter **i** using the first join.

Spelling links

- endings **er** and **est**

Nelson theme – weather

UNIT 6

Practising joining from the letter i.

ie

The sunnier it is, the happier I am.

FOCUS

A Copy this pattern into your book.

ieie ieie ieie ieie

B Copy these letters into your book.

ie ie ie ie ie
in in in in in
il il il il il

EXTRA

Copy these words into your book.

muddy	chilly	rainy
muddier	chillier	rainier
muddiest	chilliest	rainiest

EXTENSION

Copy these sentences into your book. Choose the correct word.

1 Annie thought Patch was muddier/muddiest than all the other dogs.

2 After the snowball fight Dad was chillier/chilliest than the snowman.

3 Mum said our town is the rainier/rainiest place on the planet.

Remember to check all your letters are the correct height.

Developing Skills

Focus

- Before the lesson, draw four lines and write the whole class sentence on the board.
- Tell the class that this lesson will concentrate on the letter **i**.
- Point out that a main objective is to ensure that we join from the bottom of the letter **i** to the top of the next letter, rather than to the bottom of the next letter. Joining at the base can result in incorrect letter formation and hampers later development of sloped and therefore speedwriting.
- Show the children that the **ie** join is a diagonal join.
- Demonstrate the complete join from **i** to **e** in one continuous movement.
- Stress that we dot the **i** only when we have finished writing the word.
- Underline the joins from the letter **i** in the whole class sentence, i.e. **ie**, **it**, **is**, **ie**.
- Ask the class to finger trace over the large **ie** join.
- Model the joins **ie**, **in**, **il**. Point out that the letters **i**, **n** and **e** are the same height but **l** has an ascender.
- Demonstrate the pattern. Encourage the children to practise on their white-boards before copying the pattern and joins into their books.

Extra

- Model writing the first column of words on the board.
- Point out how words ending in **y** change the **y** to **i** to add the suffix **er** or **est**.
- Discuss how changing the suffix changes the meaning of the word.
- Remind the children to pay special attention to the diagonal join from the letter **i** as they copy the words into their books.

Extension

- Read the sentences.
- Model writing the first sentence on the board, choosing the correct alternative.
- Tell the group to write the completed sentences into their books.

Resources and Assessment

Focus

Further practice joining from the letter **i**. More practice joining **ie**, **il** and **in** on their own and in words. Tracing and copying pattern, joins and words.

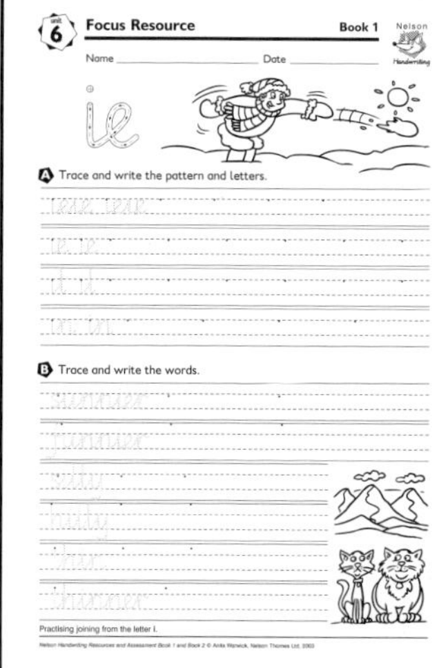

6 Focus Resource Book 1

Name Date

A Trace and write the pattern and letters.

B Trace and write the words.

Practising joining from the letter i.

Extension

Further practice joining from the letter **i**. Copying words and sentence.

6 Extension Resource Book 1

Name Date

A Trace and write the words.

B Trace and write the sentence. Fill in the gap with the correct word from above.

Practising joining from the letter i.

Assessment

- The letter **i** is the correct height and size.
- The correct diagonal join from the letter **i** to the top or start of the next letter.
- The letter **i** is dotted after the rest of the word has been written.

UNIT 7

Objectives

- To form the letter **y** correctly.
- To use the first handwriting join to join to the letter **y**.

Spelling links

- words adding **y**

Nelson theme – animals and homes

UNIT 7

Practising diagonal joins to the letter y

ly

The baby bird will fly slowly.

FOCUS

A Copy this pattern into your book.

uuu uuu uuu uuu

B Copy these letters into your book.

ly ly ly ly ly
ky ky ky ky ky
ny ny ny ny ny

Remember, the letter y has a descender that goes below the line.

EXTRA

Make these words. Copy them into your book.

twirl + y = twirly
swirl + y = swirly
whirl + y = whirly
cheek + y = cheeky

Remember to leave a space between each of your letters, like this: whirly

EXTENSION

Copy this poem into your book.

Whirly, twirly,
Hipperty hop,
Up he goes
To the tree top!

Whirly, twirly,
Round and round,
Down he scampers
To the ground.

From *'Whisky Frisky'* (Anonymous)

Developing Skills

Focus

- Explain that the lesson will focus on joining to the letter **y**.
- Demonstrate joining **l** to **y**. Point out the diagonal join from the bottom of the **l** to the top of the **y**.
- Underline the joins to the letter **y** in the whole class sentence, i.e. **ly** in **fly** and **slowly**. Point out that the letters **b** and **y** in the word **baby** do not join, as **b** is a break letter.
- Point out that the body of the letter **y** sits on the baseline and it is the same height as the small letters. Its descender falls below the baseline. Emphasise that the descender is finished neatly. Discourage children from putting a curl on the end of the tail.
- Ask the class to finger trace over the large **ly** join.
- Model the joins **ly**, **ky** and **ny**. Point out that the letters **l** and **k** have ascenders and start at the top line. The letter **n** is a small letter so it is the same height as the body of the **y**.
- Demonstrate the pattern. Encourage the children to practise on their whiteboards before copying the pattern and joins into their books.

Extra

- Model writing two of the words on the board.
- Point out how the words change from nouns to adjectives when **y** is added. Most nouns just add **y**. Extend the discussion to words which double the final consonant if it is preceded by a short vowel, e.g. **fun**, **funny**; **sun**, **sunny**.
- Discuss how changing the suffix changes the meaning of the word.
- Remind the children to concentrate on the **ly** join as they copy the words.

Extension

- Read the poem.
- Model writing the first part on the board.
- Discuss the capital letters at the start of each line. Remind the group that capitals do not join.
- Tell the children to copy the poem on to plain or lined paper. They could decorate the border with the pattern in the Focus section.

Resources and Assessment

Focus

Further practice joining to the letter **y**. More practice joining **ly**, **ky** and **ny** on their own and in words. Discuss adding **y** to words ending with **e**, e.g. **smoke** – **smoky**. Tracing and copying pattern, joins and words.

7 Focus Resource Book 1

Name Date

ly

A Trace and write the pattern and letters.

B Trace and write the words.

Practising diagonal joins to the letter y

Extension

Further practice using **ly** and **ny** in adverbs and adjectives. Copying words and sentence.

7 Extension Resource Book 1

Name Date

A Add ly or ny to these words. Trace and write the words.

B Trace and write the sentence.

Practising diagonal joins to the letter y

Assessment

- The letter **y** is the correct height and size.
- The diagonal join is made to the start of the letter **y**.
- The descender of the letter **y** falls neatly below the baseline.

UNIT 8

Objectives

- To form the letter **a** correctly.
- To use the first join to join from the letter **a**.

Spelling links

- common prefixes

Nelson theme – animals and homes

UNIT 8

Practising joining from the letter **a**.

ap

Tap, tap, tap! Is Big Bear at home?

FOCUS

A Copy this pattern into your book.

B Copy these letters into your book.

ap ap ap ap ap

ar ar ar ar ar

an an an an an

Remember, the letter p has a descender that goes below the line.

EXTRA

Make these words. Copy them into your book.

dis + appear = disappear

dis + appearance = disappearance

re + appear = reappear

re + appearance = reappearance

EXTENSION

Choose the correct word to finish these sentences. Copy the sentences into your book.

1 Ali said he had seen a tiger appear/disappear into the wood behind his house.

2 Ali's dad told him wild tigers live in Asia. But Ali felt sure the tiger would make a reappearance/disappearance.

20

21

Developing Skills

Focus

- Before the lesson, draw four lines and write the whole class sentence on the board.
- Tell the class that the lesson will focus on joining from the letter **a**.
- Demonstrate the join from **a** to **p**. Point out that the join is a diagonal joining line from the bottom of the letter **a** to the start of the letter **p**.
- Underline the join from **a** to **p** in the whole class sentence, i.e. in the word **tap**.
- Remind the class that the letter **p** has a descender which goes below the baseline.
- Point out that the body of the letter **p** sits on the baseline; it is the same height as the x-height of the small letters, e.g. **a**.
- Ask the children to finger trace over the large **ap** join.
- Model the joins **ap**, **ar** and **an**.
- Demonstrate the pattern. Tell the children to practise on their own whiteboards before copying the pattern and joins into their books.

Extra

- Discuss what a prefix means. The word **prefix** begins with the prefix **pre**, which may help in your definition. Talk about how adding a prefix changes the meaning of the word.
- Ask if the children can tell you what the prefix **dis** might mean *(i.e. 'not', 'the opposite of')*. Write the words **dis** + **appear** = **disappear** on the board.
- Repeat for the prefix **re** *(i.e. 'again')*.
- Remind the class that the join from the letter **a** is a diagonal join to the top of the next letter. Remind the children that all small letters are the same height.
- Ask the children to copy the words into their books.

Extension

- Read the sentences together. Ask for suggestions for the correct word to go in each sentence.
- Model writing the first sentence on the board.
- Talk about sentences starting with capital letters and remind the group that capitals do not join.
- Ask the children to copy the completed sentences into their books.

Resources and Assessment

Focus

Further practice joining from the letter **a**. More practice joining **ap** and **ar**. Practice with **al**. Examples adding prefix **dis**. Tracing and copying pattern, joins and words.

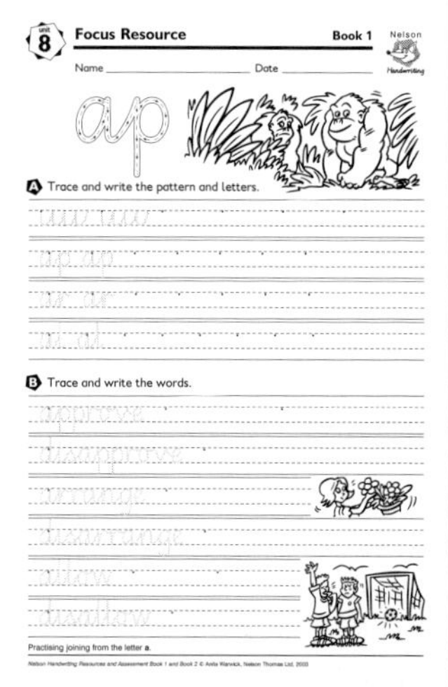

8 Focus Resource Book 1

Name ________ Date ________

A Trace and write the pattern and letters.

B Trace and write the words.

Practising joining from the letter a.

Extension

Further practice joining from the letter **a**. Examples adding prefix **un**. Completing and copying sentences.

8 Extension Resource Book 1

Name ________ Date ________

A Add the prefix un to these words. Write the words.

happy unhappy

popular

usual

B Trace and write the sentences. Fill in each gap with the correct word from above.

1 Yusuf was ________ and had many friends.

2 It was ________ for Wayne to be late.

Practising joining from the letter a.

Assessment

- The letter **a** is the correct height and size.
- The diagonal join is made from the letter **a** to the top/start of the letter **p**.
- The descender of the letter **p** falls below the line.

UNIT 9

Objectives

- To form the letter **k** correctly.
- To practise the correct formation of the second join.

Spelling links

- plurals adding **s**

Nelson theme – magic and parties

UNIT 9

Practising joining to the letter k.

ck

Vicki loves magic tricks!

FOCUS

A Copy this pattern into your book.

ckck ckck ckck ckck

B Copy these letters into your book.

ick ick ick ick ick
uck uck uck uck uck
ack ack ack ack ack

Be careful! The curve of the letter k should not be too tall, like this: k ✗ k ✓

EXTRA

Most words just add s to make the plural.
Copy these words into your book.

trick	tricks
truck	trucks
track	tracks

EXTENSION

Use a word from the Extra above to finish these sentences.
Copy the sentences into your book.

1 I went along the ______ to Nicki's birthday party.

2 The magician showed us lots of ______.

3 At the end of the show, he gave Nicki a ______.

22 23

Developing Skills

Focus

- Before the lesson, draw four lines and write the whole class sentence on the board.
- Explain that this lesson will focus on joining to the letter **k** using the second join.
- Demonstrate the join from **c** to **k**. Point out that the join is a diagonal joining line made to the x-height of the letter **k**, not to the very top.
- Underline the joins to the letter **k** in the whole class sentence, i.e. **ck** in **Vicki** and in **tricks**.
- Point out that the letter **k** has an ascender. It is a tall letter, but the body of the **k** is the same height as the letter **c**. Point out the reminder in the fox box.
- Ask the class to finger trace over the large **ck** join.
- Model the joins **ick**, **uck** and **ack** and demonstrate the pattern. Suggest children practise on their whiteboards before copying the pattern and joins into their books.

Extra

- Discuss plurals. Most words add **s**.
- Model writing the words on the board.
- Remind the group to take special care with the **ck** join.
- Ask the children to copy the words into their books.

Extension

- Read the sentences.
- Ask the children to choose the correct word from the Extra section.
- Model writing the first sentence on the board.
- Ask the children to copy the completed sentences into their books.

Resources and Assessment

Focus

Further practice joining to the letter **k**. More practice joining **ick**, **uck** and **ack**. Tracing and copying words.

9 Focus Resource Book 1

Name ______ Date ______

A Trace and write the pattern and letters.

B Trace and write the words.

Practising joining to the letter k.

Extension

Write an informal letter.

9 Extension Resource Book 1

Name ______ Date ______

A Trace and write this informal letter.

B Now sign the letter.

Practising joining to the letter k.

Assessment

- The letter **k** is the correct height and size.
- The diagonal (second) join is made from the letter **c** to the x-height of the letter **k**.
- The body of the letter **k** is same height as the letter **c**.

NIT 10

Objectives

- To slope letters forward slightly.
- To make the pattern and joins smoothly and quickly.

Spelling links

- plurals adding **s**

Nelson theme – magic and parties

UNIT 10 Practising writing with a slope.

it it

Sloped writing is quick.

FOCUS

Sloping your joined writing slightly to the right will help you build up handwriting speed. To slope your writing correctly you need to position the paper like this:

left-handed right-handed

Copy these patterns into your book.

EXTRA

Copy these words into your book.
Remember to slope your writing slightly to the right.

cake	dress	locket
bake	mess	pocket
make	guess	rocket

Be careful! The joins in sloped writing are exactly the same as the upright joins you have learned.

EXTENSION

Choose the correct word from the **Extra** above to finish these sentences. Copy the sentences into your book.
Remember to slope your writing slightly to the right.

1 Dad wanted to ____ a birthday cake.

2 Annie's ____ was in a mess.

3 The magician took a ____ from his pocket.

24 25

Developing Skills

Focus

- Explain that the main task in this lesson is to practise sloping letters slightly to the right. Sloping writing helps you to write with more speed. Ask children why and when this might be useful.
- Add that sloped writing makes handwriting look more 'grown up'.
- Demonstrate slanted letters, e.g. **it**, on the board. Point out that the join is the same, but the letters slope slightly to the right. Stress that all letters must have the same slope.
- Show children that their paper will need to be angled slightly to the left if they are right-handed, and slightly to the right if they are left-handed. Remind them to sit and hold their pens correctly.
- Ask children to finger trace over the large sloped **it** join.
- Demonstrate the patterns. Suggest children practise on their whiteboards before copying them.
- Encourage the class to slope their patterns evenly, quickly and smoothly and to the right.

Extra

- Discuss plurals. Most words add **s**.
- Extend the activity to talk about words ending with **ss**. Explain that these add **es** when plural, e.g. **dress** – **dresses**.
- Model writing the first column of words on the board. Write each word in upright writing and then sloped. Use a ruler to draw lines to demonstrate the slope.

cake bake make

- Ask the children to copy the words into their books.

Extension

- Read the sentences.
- The children should choose the correct words from the Extra section to make sense of the sentence in the context.
- Model writing the first sentence on the board.
- Ask the children to copy the completed sentences into their books, remembering to slope their writing.

Resources and Assessment

Focus

More practice in sloping writing to the right. Words adding **s**, **es** and **ies**. Tracing and copying patterns and words.

10 Focus Resource Book 1

Name Date

A Trace and write the pattern and letters.

B Trace and write the words.

Practising writing with a slope.

Extension

Poem provides practice sloping writing to the right. Copying poem; checking angle of sloped writing.

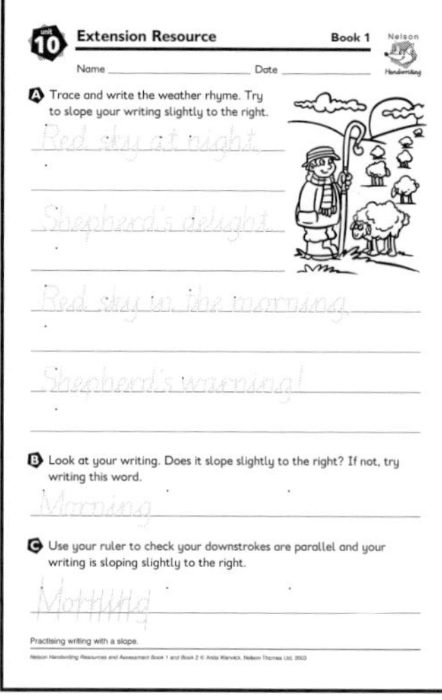

10 Extension Resource Book 1

Name Date

A Trace and write the weather rhyme. Try to slope your writing slightly to the right.

Red sky at night,
Shepherd's delight.
Red sky in the morning,
Shepherd's warning!

B Look at your writing. Does it slope slightly to the right? If not, try writing this word.

Morning

C Use your ruler to check your downstrokes are parallel and your writing is sloping slightly to the right.

Practising writing with a slope.

Assessment

- The pattern slopes evenly to the right.
- The letters slope forward slightly.
- All letters have the same slope.

UNIT 11

Objectives

- To practise the first and third joins to the letter **e**.
- To practise sloping letters forward slightly.

Spelling links

- apostrophe of contraction

Nelson theme – mazes

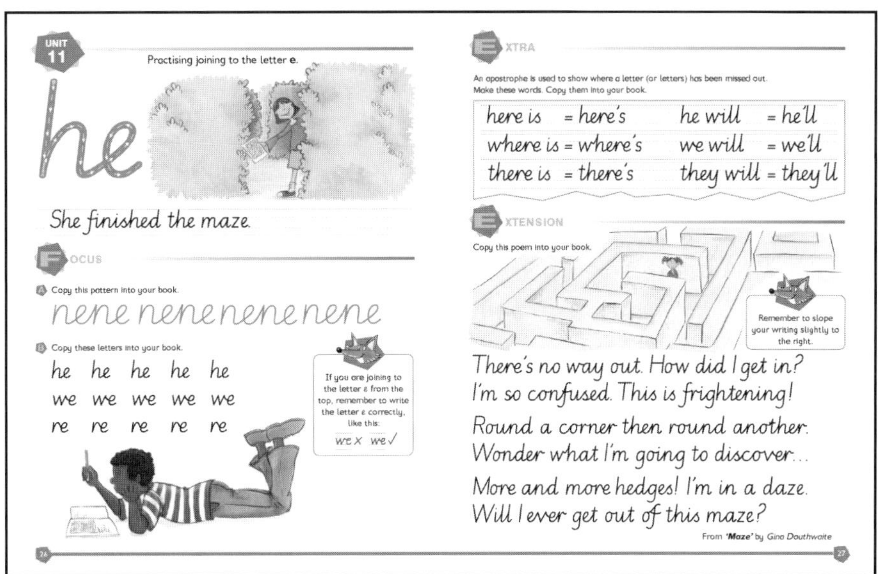

UNIT 11 Practising joining to the letter **e**.

he

She finished the maze.

FOCUS

A Copy this pattern into your book.

nene nenenenenene

B Copy these letters into your book.

he he he he he
we we we we we
re re re re re

If you are joining to the letter e from the top, remember to write the letter e correctly, like this: we✗ we✓

EXTRA

An apostrophe is used to show where a letter (or letters) has been missed out. Make these words. Copy them into your book.

here is = here's	he will = he'll
where is = where's	we will = we'll
there is = there's	they will = they'll

EXTENSION

Copy this poem into your book.

Remember to slope your writing slightly to the right.

There's no way out. How did I get in?
I'm so confused. This is frightening!
Round a corner then round another.
Wonder what I'm going to discover...
More and more hedges! I'm in a daze.
Will I ever get out of this maze?

From '**Maze**' by Gina Douthwaite

26 27

Developing Skills

Focus

- Before the lesson, draw four lines and write the whole class sentence on the board.
- Explain that one objective of this lesson is to practise sloping letters slightly to the right.
- Demonstrate the sloped letters **he** on the board.
- Point out that the join is the same as in upright writing, but the letters slope slightly to the right.
- Ask the class to point out, then underline, the **he** joins in the whole class sentence: **She**, **finished**, **the**.
- Model the joins **he**, **we** and **re**.
- The joins from the letters **w** and **r** are tricky joins. Remind the children that the joining line must go down when you have finished forming the first letter, ready to join to the letter **e**. Refer to the fox box.
- Tell the children to finger trace over the large **he** join.
- Demonstrate the pattern. Suggest children practise on their whiteboards before copying the pattern.
- Encourage the class to slope their pattern and joins evenly, quickly and smoothly and to the right.

Extra

- Discuss the use of apostrophes when we join two or more words. Some letters are missed out when a con-traction is formed, e.g. **here is** = **here's**. Explain that the apostrophe is shaped like a comma and it is written just below the top line.
- Model writing the first column of words on the board, using sloped writing.
- Also demonstrate the **ll**, e.g. **we will** = **we'll**.
- Ask the children to copy the contractions.

Extension

- Read the poem.
- Model writing the first line on the board. Remind children to slope their writing when they copy the poem.

Resources and Assessment

Focus

More practice sloping writing to the right and joining **he**, **we** and **re**. Copying patterns, joins and words.

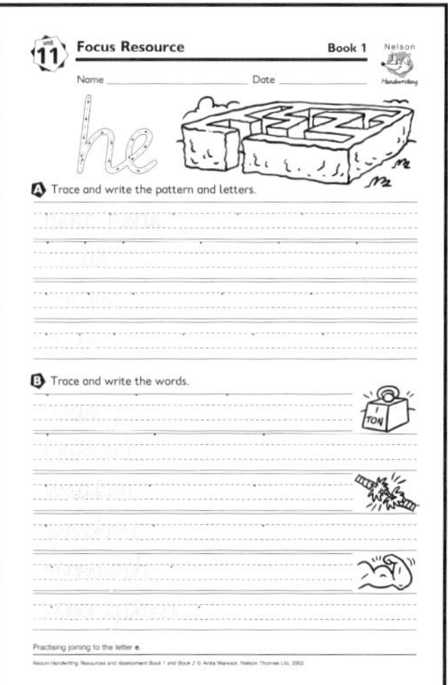

11 Focus Resource Book 1

Name Date

he

A Trace and write the pattern and letters.

B Trace and write the words.

Extension

More practice using apostrophes and contractions. Sloping writing to the right.

11 Extension Resource Book 1

Name Date

These words are contractions.

she's	you've	I've	we'll
they've	we're	you're	he'll

Trace and write the words. Write in the correct contraction from above.

Contraction

Assessment

- The letters slope forward slightly and have the same slope.
- The correct use of the first join to the letter **e**.
- The correct use of the third join to the letter **e**.

UNIT 12

Objectives

- To practise the fourth and third joins from the letter **f**.
- To write capital letters correctly.

UNIT 12

Practising joining from the letter f.

ft

People fled swiftly from the maze.

FOCUS

A Copy this pattern into your book.

B Copy these letters into your book.

fte fte fte fte fte
fir fir fir fir fir
fin fin fin fin fin

EXTRA

Certain words and phrases can be used in sentences to give a 'time' meaning. Copy these words into your book.

Remember to slope your writing slightly to the right.

after first then
after a while firstly suddenly
afterwards finally once

EXTENSION

Choose a word from the Extra above to finish these sentences.
Copy the sentences into your book.
Remember to start each sentence with a capital letter.

1 ____ there was a frightening beast called the Minotaur. He was half bull and half human.

2 Theseus went into the labyrinth to find the Minotaur and ____ he killed him.

3 ____ Theseus followed the string Ariadne had given him and escaped.

Spelling links

- time words and phrases
- common suffixes

Nelson theme – mazes

Developing Skills

Focus

- Before the lesson, draw four lines and write the whole class sentence on the board.
- Tell the class that this lesson practises joining from the letter **f**.
- You will need to use four lines to demonstrate the correct formation of the letter **f**.
- Point out that the join from the letter **f** can be diagonal or horizontal.
- Model the joins **fte**, **fir**, **fin**.
- Remind children that the letter **t** is not as tall as the letter **f**.
- Mention that the horizontal join from the letter **f** helps leave a consistent space between the letters.
- Ask the class to finger trace over the large **ft** join.
- Demonstrate the pattern and ask the children to practise on their whiteboards before copying it into their books.
- Encourage them to slope the pattern evenly, quickly and smoothly and to the right.

Extra

- Model writing the time words. Point out that the **wh** join is similar to the **ft** join.
- Ask the children to copy the words into their books, bearing in mind the two ways to join from the letter **f**.
- *Extension activity*: talk about the consonant suffix **ly** on the end of **first**, **final** and **sudden**. Point out that the suffix is added without changing the root word. Ask pairs of children to make a list of words to which the suffix **ly** can be added (*e.g.* ***like, real, week, kind, friend, actual, proper***). What happens if a word ends in **y**? (*the* **y** *changes to* *i, e.g.* ***day*** – ***daily***)

Extension

- Read the sentences.
- Model writing the first sentence on the board. Remind children to slope their writing when they copy the sentences.
- Choose a word from the Extra section to complete the sentence.
- Ask the children to complete and copy all the sentences into their books, making sure the capital letters are properly formed and the correct height.

Resources and Assessment

Focus

Practice joining **aft** and **fin** in words. Tracing and copying pattern, joins and words.

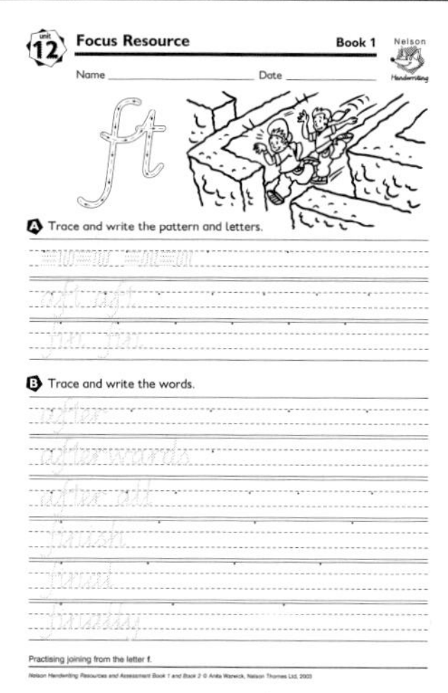

12 Focus Resource Book 1 Nelson Handwriting

Name ____ Date ____

ft

A Trace and write the pattern and letters.

B Trace and write the words.

Practising joining from the letter f.

Extension

Practice of horizontal joins from **f**. Practice of diagonal join **fl**. Copying poem.

12 Extension Resource Book 1 Nelson Handwriting

Name ____ Date ____

Trace and write the sentence.

Friendly Frederick
Fuddlestone
could fiddle on
his funny bone

From 'Friendly Frederick Fuddlestone' by Arnold Lobel

Practising joining from the letter f.

Assessment

- The correct use of the fourth join for **ft**.
- The correct use of the third join for **fi**.
- Capital letters are the correct height.

NIT 13

Objectives

- To form and join the silent letters **w** and **k** correctly.
- To join **w** and **r** using the third join.

Spelling links

- silent letters **w** and **k**

Nelson theme – hands

UNIT 13 Practising writing silent letters.

wr

The knight wrote letters every night.

FOCUS

A Copy this pattern into your book.

wrwr wrwr wrwr wrwr

B Copy these letters into your book.

wra wra wra wra wra
wri wri wri wri wri
kni kni kni kni kni

EXTRA

Copy these words into your book.

wrap	write	knit
wrapping	writing	knitting
wrapper	writer	knitter

Remember, the join helps you leave the correct space between the letter w and the letter r, like this: wrap

EXTENSION

Copy this tongue-twister into your book.

A right-handed fellow named Wright,
In writing 'write' always wrote 'rite'
Where he meant to write right.
If he'd written 'write' right,
Wright would not have
wrought rot writing 'rite.

'Mr Wright' by Joseph Rosenbloom

Remember to slope your writing slightly to the right.

30 31

Developing Skills

Focus

- Before the lesson, draw four lines and write the whole class sentence on the board.
- Tell the class that this lesson will focus on silent letters in words.
- Make clear that we do not pronounce every letter in each word. The letters we do not pronounce are known as silent letters.
- Ask the class if they can identify the silent letters in the words in the whole class sentence (***k** and **w***).
- Model the joins **wr** and **kn**.
- Point out that the join from **w** to **r** is the third join. It is a horizontal join and it dips down then goes back up, just like **r** to **a** and **r** to **i**, which are the same join.
- Also remind children about the height and formation of the letter **k**. Point out that the join is the diagonal join, from **k** to **n** and **n** to **i**.
- Point out that a join helps leave a consistent space between letters.
- Ask the children to finger trace over the large **wr** join.
- Demonstrate the pattern. Children can practise on their whiteboards before copying the pattern into their books.
- Encourage the children to slope the pattern evenly, quickly and smoothly to the right.

Extra

- Model writing the first column of words on the board.
- Remind the children about the silent letters being practised in this lesson.
- Ask the children to copy the words into their books.
- *Extension activity:* using a dictionary ask the group to make a list of words beginning with a silent **g**, e.g. **gnat**, **gnaw**, **gnome**.

Extension

- Read the tongue twister and talk about the spellings.
- Model writing the first line on the board. Remind children to slope their writing.
- Ask the children to copy the rhyme into their books.

Resources and Assessment

Focus

More practice with silent letters through a picture/word matching activity.

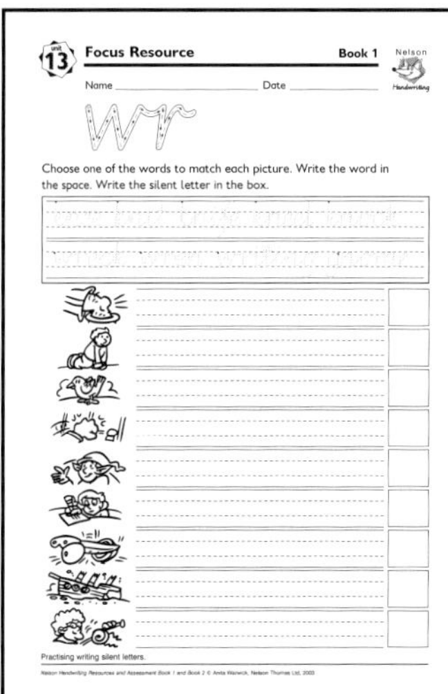

13 Focus Resource Book 1 Nelson Handwriting

Name ______ Date ______

wr

Choose one of the words to match each picture. Write the word in the space. Write the silent letter in the box.

Practising writing silent letters.

Extension

Further work on silent letters. Ask the children to notice and comment on the silent letters. Can they see patterns? Do they know of other examples? Tracing and/or copying words and joins, sloping writing to the right.

13 Extension Resource Book 1 Nelson Handwriting

Name ______ Date ______

A Trace and write the words.

B Write each word from above in the correct column.

wre	kne	wro

Practising writing silent letters.

Assessment

- The correct use of the third join from **w** to **r** and from **r** to **a**.
- All letters are joined, except the break letters.
- The letter **k** is formed and joined correctly.

UNIT 14

Objectives

- To practise joining double letters.
- To use the four handwriting joins correctly.

UNIT 14

Practising forming double letters correctly.

ff

The fluffy bunny was very small.

FOCUS

Copy this pattern into your book.

uuu ssss uuu ssss

Copy each of these sets of letters into your book three times.

ii ll tt
rr nn mm
cc oo dd
ss ff ee

EXTRA

Copy these words into your book.

ball	guess	off
call	dress	offer
fall	press	cliff

EXTENSION

Copy this poem into your book.

I like my fingers.
They grip a ball,
Turn a page,
Break a fall,
Help whistle
A call.

From *'Mark's Fingers'* by Mary O'Neill

Remember to slope your writing slightly to the right.

Spelling links

- double letters
- spelling pattern **le**

Nelson theme– hands

Developing Skills

Focus

- Before the lesson, draw four lines and write the whole class sentence on the board.
- Explain that in this lesson the children are going to practise forming and joining double letters.
- Demonstrate the letters **ff** on the board.
- Point out that the join is made from the crossbar on the **f** to the top of the next **f**.
- Ask the children to underline the double letters in the whole class sentence, i.e. **ff** in **fluffy**, **nn** in **bunny** and **ll** in **small**.
- Model the pattern and the joins.
- Point out that these letters are all joined using either a diagonal or horizontal joining line. The joining line helps you to leave a space between letters.
- Ask the class to finger trace over the large **ff** join.
- Children should practise the pattern and the joins on their whiteboards before copying them into their books.

Extra

- Model writing the first row of words on the board.
- Point out where the letter **f** begins and finishes.
- Remind the class to be careful with the **re** join: it's tricky!
- The words to be copied contain all four handwriting joins. Tell the children to bear this in mind as they copy the words into their books.
- *Extension activities:* encourage the children to add words of their own to the list. They could make a list of words containing other double letters, e.g. **tt**, **mm**, **oo**. Can they turn any of the words into plurals? (*Add* **s** *or* **es** *– but no plural for* ***off***.)

Extension

- Read the poem and model writing it on the board.
- Remind children to slope their writing when they copy the poem.
- Extension activity: children could draw round their hands and write their own poem about what their hands can do.

Resources and Assessment

Focus

Practice with double letters **dd**, **oo**, **rr**, **tt**. Comment that the **le** ending produces an extra syllable. Tracing and copying joins and words, sloping writing slightly to the right.

14 Focus Resource Book 1

Name Date

ff

A Trace and write the pattern and letters.

B Trace and write the words.

Practising forming double letters correctly.

Extension

More practice joining double consonants within words. Writing a list poem.

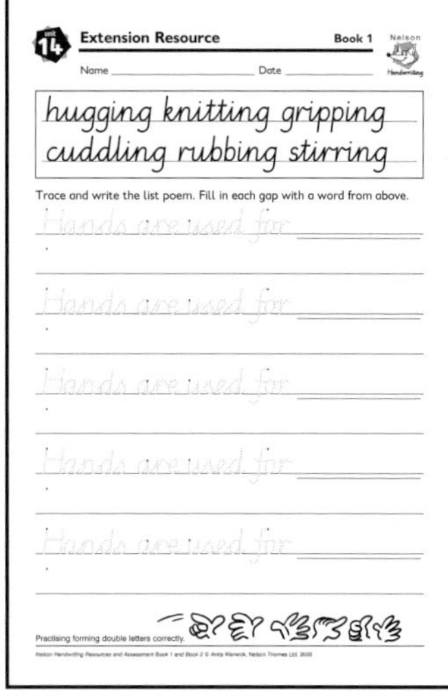

14 Extension Resource Book 1

Name Date

hugging knitting gripping
cuddling rubbing stirring

Trace and write the list poem. Fill in each gap with a word from above.

Hands are used for
Hands are used for
Hands are used for
Hands are used for
Hands are used for

Practising forming double letters correctly.

Assessment

- The letter **f** is formed and joined correctly.
- The correct use of the first join to the letters **i**, **n**, **m**, **c**, **d**, **s** and **e** and the second join to **l** and **t**.
- The correct use of the third join to the letters **r** and **o**.

NIT 15

Objectives

- To leave a consistent space between letters.
- To leave a consistent space between words.

Spelling links

- **ew**, **ev** and **ex**

Nelson theme – storms

UNIT 15 Practising spacing letters consistently.

ew

"Phew, the storm is over," said Matthew.

FOCUS

A Copy this pattern into your book.

ewew ewew ewew ewew

B Copy these letters into your book.

ew ew ew ew ew
ev ev ev ev ev
ex ex ex ex ex

Remember, the join helps you leave the correct space between your letters.

XTRA

Copy these words into your book.

new	even	flex
blew	ever	next
flew	every	text

XTENSION

Copy this poem into your book.

Through every nook and every cranny
The wind blew in on poor old Granny;
Around her knees, into each ear
(And up her nose as well, I fear).

From 'Granny' by Spike Milligan

Check you have joined your letters carefully and sloped your writing slightly to the right.

Developing Skills

Focus

- Before the lesson, draw four lines and write the whole class sentence on the board.
- Talk about space between letters and words and remind the class that the joining line helps leave a consistent space between letters.
- Underline the **ew** joins in the whole class sentence. Point out that the joins from **s** to **t** in the word **storm** and **a** to **t** in **Matthew** are the second join and **o** to **r** in **storm** and **v** to **e** in **over** are the third join. All these joins help you leave a consistent space between letters.
- Model the pattern. Point out that **ew** is an easier join than **we**: the pen must come down after the letter **e** to join the **w** to the **e**. To make this join correctly the letter **e** begins about halfway up its own letter height.
- Remind the class that the letter **x** does not join to the next letter.
- Ask the children to finger trace over the large **ew** join.
- Children can practise the pattern and the joins on their whiteboards before copying them into their books. Remind them to slope their writing slightly to the right.

Extra

- Model writing the words on the board. Point out that **v** to **e** and **w** to **e** are tricky joins.
- Tell the children to copy the words into their books.
- *Extension activity:* in pairs, see if the children can add words of their own to the list.

Extension

- Read the poem.
- Model writing the first two lines of the poem on the board.
- Emphasise that the space between each word must be consistent. As a rough guide, leave a space the size of the letter **o** between words. To illustrate this point write the letter **o** between each word, using a different coloured pen. Is there a consistent space between the words?
- Ask the children to copy the poem into their books, sloping their writing slightly to the right.

Resources and Assessment

Focus

More practice joining letters **ew**, **ev** and **ex**. Tracing and copying joins and words.

15 Focus Resource Book 1

Name Date

A Trace and write the pattern and letters.

B Trace and write the words.

Practising spacing letters consistently.

Extension

Copying poem – check for consistent space between letters.

15 Extension Resource Book 1

Name Date

Trace and write the poem.

By Andrea Shavick

Practising spacing letters consistently.

Assessment

- The correct use of the first join to the letters **w**, **v** and **x**.
- Consistent space between letters, with all except break letters joined.
- Consistent space between words.

UNIT 16

Objectives

- To ensure letters are consistent in size and proportion.
- To ensure letters with ascenders are the correct height and size.

Spelling links

- common suffixes

Nelson theme – storms

UNIT 16

Practising writing letters with ascenders in proportion.

th

Lightning flickers and thunder crashes.

FOCUS

A Copy this pattern into your book.

ul ul ul ul

B Copy these letters into your book.

th th th th th
ht ht ht ht ht
fl fl fl fl fl

The letters b, d, h, f, k and l all have ascenders. The letter t also has an ascender but it is not as tall.

EXTRA

Make these words. Copy them into your book.
Remember to slope your writing slightly to the right.

light+ly = lightly	light+er = lighter
tight+ly = tightly	tight+er = tighter
bright+ly = brightly	bright+er = brighter

EXTENSION

Copy this poem into your book. Remember to leave the correct space between your letters and between your words.

See lightning is flashing,
The forest is crashing,
The rain will come dashing,
A flood will be rising anon;
The heavens are scowling,
The thunder is growling,
The loud winds are howling,
The storm has come suddenly on!

From 'The Storm' by Sara Coleridge

36 37

Developing Skills

Focus

- Before the lesson, draw four lines and write the whole class sentence on the board.
- Tell the class that the lesson will focus on making sure ascenders are written in proportion.
- Write the letters with ascenders on the board. Remind the children that **b**, **d**, **h**, **f**, **k** and **l** all have ascenders and start at the top line. The letter **t** also has an ascender, but it is not as tall as the rest.
- Point out the letter **f** has an ascender and a descender.
- Model the pattern and the joins on the board.
- Ask the class to finger trace over the large **th** join.
- Suggest they practise the pattern and joins on their whiteboards before copying them into their books.
- Encourage the children to slope their pattern and letters evenly and smoothly and to the right.

Extra

- Model writing the words on the board. Talk about the height and size of letters with ascenders.
- Point out that the letters **g** and **y** are actually the same size as the letters with ascenders – but their tails go below the line.
- Ask the children to copy the words carefully into their books, focusing on keeping the letters in proportion.
- *Extension activity:* talk about how adding a suffix to a word affects its meaning, e.g. **ly** means 'in this way'. Look at the words **light** and **tight**. Make a list of words ending with the suffixes **ful** and/or **less**. Again comment on the effect on meaning.

Extension

- Read the poem.
- Model writing the first verse on the board. Point out the size and height of the ascenders compared to the small letters.
- Remind the group of the lesson objectives and of the need to slope their writing when they copy the poem.
- Tell the children to copy the poem on to plain paper with guidelines underneath, to practise and assess whether the ascenders are written in proportion to the other letters.

Resources and Assessment

Focus

More practice writing letters with ascenders in proportion. Tracing and copying words.

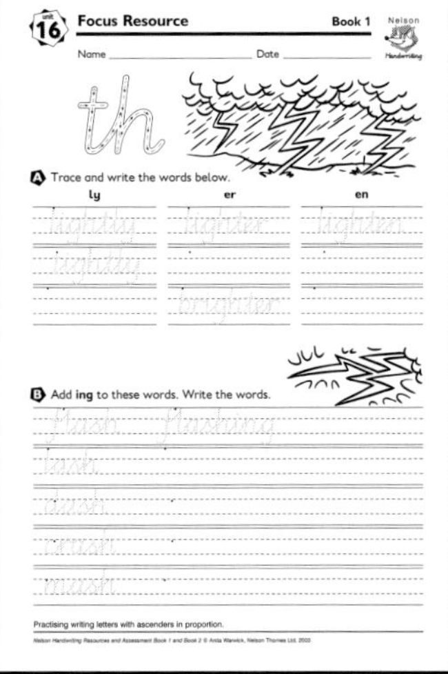

16 Focus Resource Book 1

Name Date

th

A Trace and write the words below.

ly er en

B Add ing to these words. Write the words.

Practising writing letters with ascenders in proportion.

Extension

Further practice of words with suffix **ly**. Completing and copying sentences.

16 Extension Resource Book 1

Name Date

A Add ly to each adjective to make the adverb. Write the words.

Adjective	Adverb
loud	loudly
neat	
slow	
quiet	
quick	

B Trace and write the sentences. Fill in each gap with an adverb from above.

1 The pop group played the drums

2 Sacha writes very

Practising writing letters with ascenders in proportion.

Assessment

- The letter **t** is the correct height and size.
- The other letters with ascenders are almost twice the height of small letters.
- All the letters slope slightly to the right.

NIT 17

Objectives

- To ensure letters are consistent in size and proportion.
- To use the diagonal joining line from the letter **a**.

Spelling links

- compound words

Nelson theme – tea

UNIT 17 Practising joining from the letter **a**.

ac

Hot tea in a teacup.

FOCUS

A Copy this pattern into your book.

acac acac acac acac

B Copy these letters into your book.

ac ac ac ac ac
ag ag ag ag ag
af af af af af

EXTRA

Use the words in the box to make compound words starting with tea.
Copy the compound words into your book.
The first one is done to help you.

pot spoon cup time

Remember, t is not as tall as other letters with ascenders.

1 teapot

EXTENSION

Put these instructions for making tea into the correct order.
Copy them into your book.

- Put two teabags into the teapot.
- Stir the tea.
- Pour the tea into some cups.
- Add milk, sugar or lemon.
- Fill the kettle with water. Switch it on.
- Pour the boiling water into the teapot.

Remember to slope your writing slightly to the right.

Developing Skills

Focus

- Before the lesson, draw four lines and write the whole class sentence on the board.
- Explain that the focus of the lesson will be joining from the letter **a**.
- Ask the class to tell you the small letters of the alphabet.
- Demonstrate the size of these letters by writing them between the middle lines on the board.
- Model the pattern and the joins on the board. Point out that the joining line meets the letters **c** and **g** about halfway up the letter, whereas it meets the **f** at x-height.
- Mention that the letter **g** has a descender. Its body is the same height as the small letters, but its descender goes below the line.
- Ask the class to finger trace over the large **ac** join. Suggest they practise the pattern and joins on their whiteboards before copying them into their books.

Extra

- Model writing the words on the board.
- Explain that a compound word is a word made up of two separate words.
- Ask the children if they can join any two words you have written to make a compound word.
- Model writing the compound word.
- Ask the children to copy the compound words into their books, making sure that their letters are in proportion and that they are joining from the letter **a** correctly.
- *Extension activity:* ask pairs of children to make a list of compound words.

Extension

- Ask the group how they would make a cup of tea.
- Read the instructions for making tea.
- Which instruction comes first? Model writing the first sentence on the board. Comment on the size and height of the letters.
- Tell the children to copy the instructions into their books in the correct order, remembering to slope their writing.

Resources and Assessment

Focus

Tracing and/or copying words containing **ac**, **ag** and **af**.

17 Focus Resource Book 1

Name Date

ac

A Trace and write the pattern and letters.

B Trace and write the words.

Practising joining from the letter **a**.

Extension

Sequence instructions for making a jam sandwich.

17 Extension Resource Book 1

Name Date

These instructions for making a jam sandwich have got mixed up.
Write the sentences in the correct order.
Remember to leave a consistent space between your letters and words.

Then put jam on one slice.
First get two slices of bread.
Put the slices together.
Cut it into sandwiches.
Next put butter on each slice.

Practising joining from the letter **a**.

Assessment

- The letter **t** is the correct height and size.
- The small letters are all the same height.
- The diagonal join from **a** meets the joining letter halfway up a small letter or at the x-height of the letters **f** and **t**.

NIT 18

Objectives

- To ensure capital letters are formed correctly and do not join.
- To ensure capital letters are consistent in size and proportion.

UNIT 18

Practising forming capital letters.

W

We have Earl Grey tea or Oolong tea.

FOCUS

A Copy this pattern into your book.

≡OIIIIO ≡OIIIIO ≡OIIIIO ≡OIIIIO

B Copy these sets of capital letters into your book.

OOO CCC GGG QQQ SSS

EEE FFF HHH III LLL TTT

AAA KKK MMM NNN

BBB DDD PPP RRR

JJJ UUU VVV WWW

XXX YYY ZZZ

Remember, capital letters are the same height as ascenders and do not join.

EXTRA

Names of countries begin with a capital letter.
Copy these names into your book.

Indonesia	China
Georgia	Sri Lanka
India	Japan

Remember to slope your writing slightly to the right.

EXTENSION

A comma is used to separate each word in a list, like this:

Tea is grown in India, Indonesia, Japan, Sri Lanka, China and Georgia.

Copy these sentences into your book. Add in the missing commas.

1 Tea is grown in India Indonesia Japan Sri Lanka China and Georgia.
2 Tea leaves are grown picked dried and then packed.
3 There are many flavours of tea including Oolong Assam Darjeeling and Earl Grey.

Spelling links

- short words within longer words

Nelson theme – tea

Developing Skills

Focus

- Before the lesson, draw four lines and write the whole class sentence on the board.
- Tell the class that the focus of the lesson will be capital letters.
- Begin by writing capital letters on the lines on the board to demonstrate their height and size. Ask the children when we use capital letters.
- Model the pattern on the board.
- Explain that the capital letters in the Focus section are grouped in a way that makes them easier to write.
- Suggest the children practise the pattern and the capital letters on their whiteboards before copying them into their books.
- Encourage the children to slope their pattern and letters evenly, smoothly and to the right.

Extra

- Model writing the words on the board. Explain that these are the names of places where tea is grown.
- Ask the children to copy the names into their books, paying special attention to the formation of the capital letters.
- *Extension activity:* can the group find any small words within these words? Ask them to underline any they find, e.g. **on** in **Indonesia**. Explain that finding short words in longer words can help with spelling.

Extension

- Model writing the first sentence on the board.
- Point out that a comma is used to separate words in a list.
- Demonstrate writing a comma. Show how it sits on the baseline.
- Point out the size and height of the capital letters.
- Tell the group to copy the sentences, adding in the missing commas and remembering to slope their writing.

Resources and Assessment

Focus

More practice forming capital letters. Tracing and copying alphabet. Writing own name and address.

18 Focus Resource Book 1

Name Date

A Trace and write the pattern and letters.

B Write your name and address. Put capital letters in the correct places.

Practising forming capital letters.

Extension

Shape poem to copy.

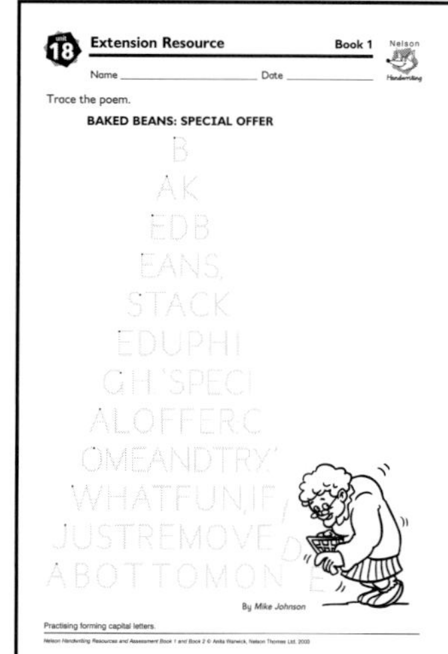

18 Extension Resource Book 1

Name Date

Trace the poem.

BAKED BEANS: SPECIAL OFFER

B
AK
EDB
EANS
STACK
EDUPHI
GH 'SPECI
ALOFFERC
OMEANDTRY'
WHATFUN,IF,
JUSTREMOVE
ABOTTOMON

By Mike Johnson

Practising forming capital letters.

Assessment

- The capital letters start at the top line.
- The capital letters are consistent in size and proportion.
- The capital letters do not join.

NIT 19

Objectives

- To practise writing decorated capital letters.
- To use decorated capital letters in presentation.

Spelling links

- short words within longer words

Nelson theme – books

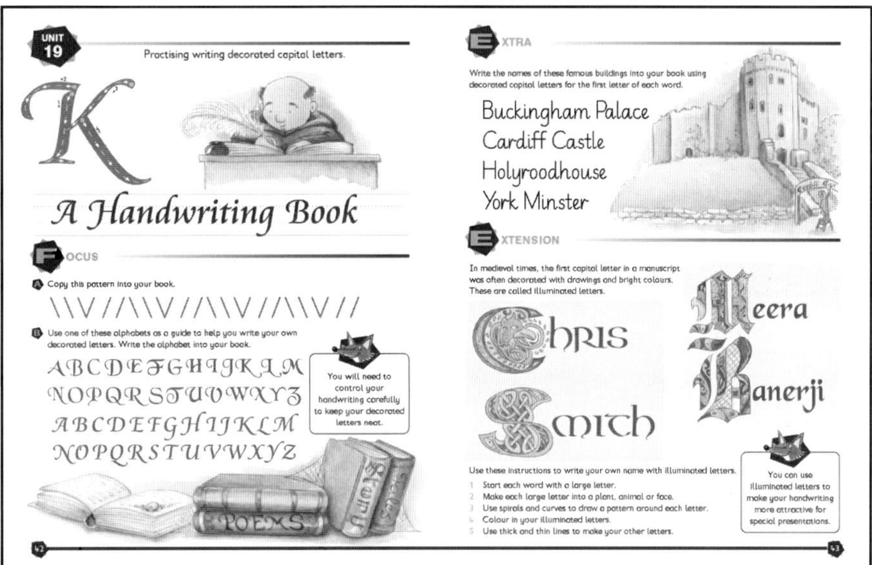

UNIT 19

Practising writing decorated capital letters.

A Handwriting Book

FOCUS

A Copy this pattern into your book.

\\V//\\V//\\V//\\V//

B Use one of these alphabets as a guide to help you write your own decorated letters. Write the alphabet into your book.

ABCDEFGHIJKLM
NOPQRSTUVWXYZ
ABCDEFGHIJKLM
NOPQRSTUVWXYZ

You will need to control your handwriting carefully to keep your decorated letters neat.

42

EXTRA

Write the names of these famous buildings into your book using decorated capital letters for the first letter of each word.

Buckingham Palace
Cardiff Castle
Holyroodhouse
York Minster

EXTENSION

In medieval times, the first capital letter in a manuscript was often decorated with drawings and bright colours. These are called illuminated letters.

Chris Smith

Meera Banerji

Use these instructions to write your own name with illuminated letters.

1 Start each word with a large letter.
2 Make each large letter into a plant, animal or face.
3 Use spirals and curves to draw a pattern around each letter.
4 Colour in your illuminated letters.
5 Use thick and thin lines to make your other letters.

You can use illuminated letters to make your handwriting more attractive for special presentations.

43

Developing Skills

Focus

- Before the lesson, draw four lines and write the whole class sentence on the board.
- Demonstrate a few of the decorated capital letters. Point out that these letters are the same height and size as the alphabet capitals in Unit 18, although they can be written above and below the line, e.g. the letter **H**.
- Explain that it is usually the first capital letter, and sometimes the last one in a word, that is a decorated capital.
- Ask children when they think we might use a decorated capital letter.
- Model the pattern on the board. Suggest the children practise the pattern and the capital letters on their whiteboards before copying them into their books.

Extra

- Model writing one of the words on the board, using a decorated capital at the beginning of each word.
- The children could write each letter of the words as a decorated capital.
- *Extension activity:* can the children identify any small words within these words? Tell them to underline any they find, e.g. **Car** in **Cardiff**. Explain that finding short words in longer words can help with spelling.

Extension

- Illuminated letters were used in medieval times. Show children pictures of some examples or create your own.
- Read the instructions at the bottom of the page.
- Tell the children to practise writing these letters on plain paper, using felt-tip pens or paints.
- *Extension activity:* have fun with different computer fonts. Many of them are very attractive.

Resources and Assessment

Focus

Practise decorated capitals.

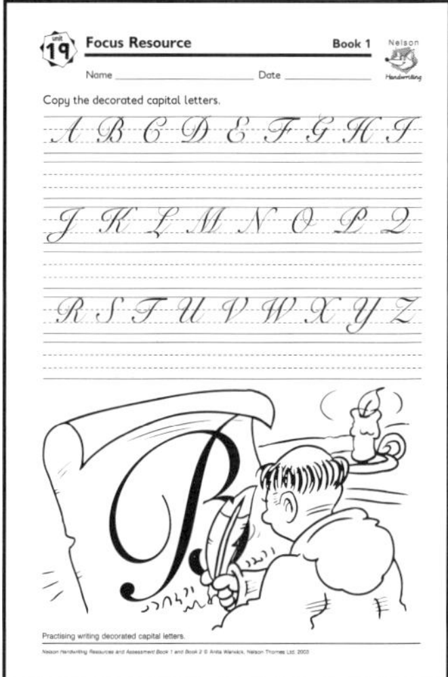

19 Focus Resource Book 1

Name Date

Copy the decorated capital letters.

A B C D E F G H I
J K L M N O P Q
R S T U V W X Y Z

Practising writing decorated capital letters.

Extension

Using decorated capitals to help make a piece of writing look attractive. Copying poem on to plain paper with guidelines underneath.

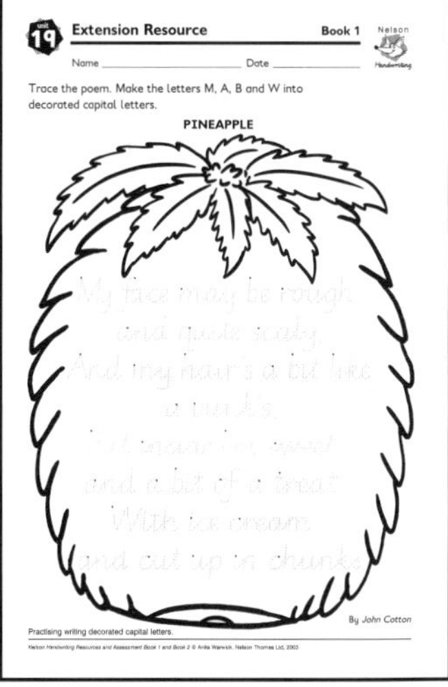

19 Extension Resource Book 1

Name Date

Trace the poem. Make the letters M, A, B and W into decorated capital letters.

PINEAPPLE

By John Cotton

Practising writing decorated capital letters.

Assessment

- The capital letters are consistent in size and proportion.
- The capital letters do not join.

NIT 20

Objectives

- To practise writing punctuation marks.
- To write exclamation marks.

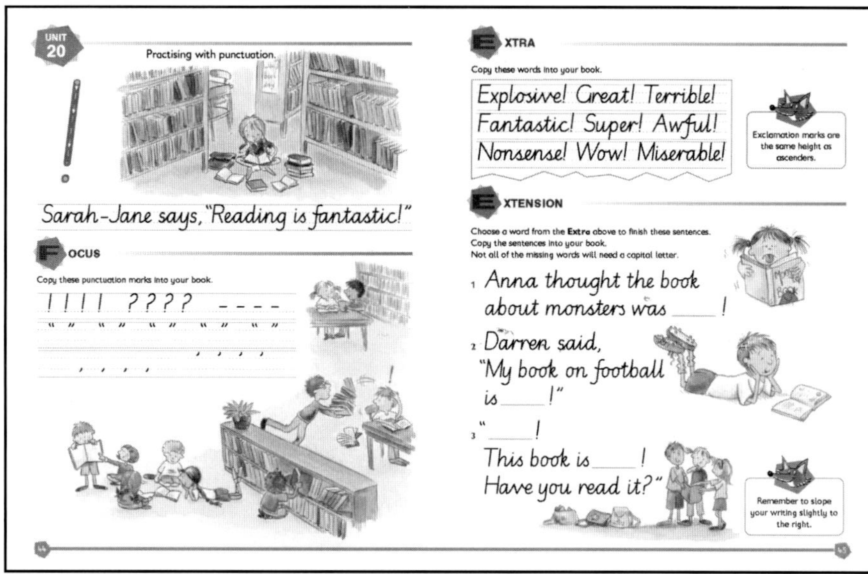

UNIT 20

Practising with punctuation.

Sarah-Jane says, "Reading is fantastic!"

FOCUS

Copy these punctuation marks into your book.

! ! ! ! ? ? ? ? - - - -

XTRA

Copy these words into your book.

Explosive! Great! Terrible!
Fantastic! Super! Awful!
Nonsense! Wow! Miserable!

Exclamation marks are the same height as ascenders.

XTENSION

Choose a word from the Extra above to finish these sentences. Copy the sentences into your book. Not all of the missing words will need a capital letter.

1 Anna thought the book about monsters was ____!

2 Darren said, "My book on football is ____!"

3 "____! This book is ____! Have you read it?"

Remember to slope your writing slightly to the right.

Spelling links

- prefixes **non** and **ex**

Nelson theme – books

Developing Skills

Focus

- Before the lesson, draw four lines and write the whole class sentence on the board.
- Tell the class that they will be focusing on making punctuation marks in this lesson.
- Discuss the exclamation mark. When is it used? Explain that it is as tall as an ascender and finishes above the full stop. Point out how similar it is, in size, to the question mark.
- Ask children to name the other punctuation marks in the whole class sentence.
- Explain the role of each punctuation mark in the sentence.
- Note that the exclamation mark is written inside the speech marks. Emphasise that all punctuation of spoken text is written inside the speech marks, e.g. question mark, comma and full stop.
- Demonstrate the formation of these marks on the lines.
- Ask the children if they can change the whole class sentence into a question. Invite one child to come and write the question on the board.
- Talk about when the apostrophe might be used. Model some examples.
- Tell the children to copy the punctuation marks into their books.

Extra

- Model writing some of the words with the exclamation marks on the board.
- Tell the children to copy the words into their books.
- *Extension activity:* point out that the word **nonsense** has the prefix **non**, which means 'not' or 'the opposite of'. Can pairs of children make a list of words with the prefix **non**? Ask them to repeat the exercise for the prefix **ex** (as in **explosive**), meaning 'out' or 'outside of'.

Extension

- Read the sentences.
- Ask the children to choose a word from the Extra section to complete the sentences.
- Model writing the first sentence on the board.
- Remind the group to slope their writing slightly to the right as they copy the sentences into their books.

Resources and Assessment

Focus

Copying question marks and questions. Writing answers between the lines.

20 Focus Resource — Book 1

Name ____ Date ____

Trace and write the questions. Write your own answer underneath.

Practising with punctuation.

Extension

Copying sentences, inserting missing speech marks.

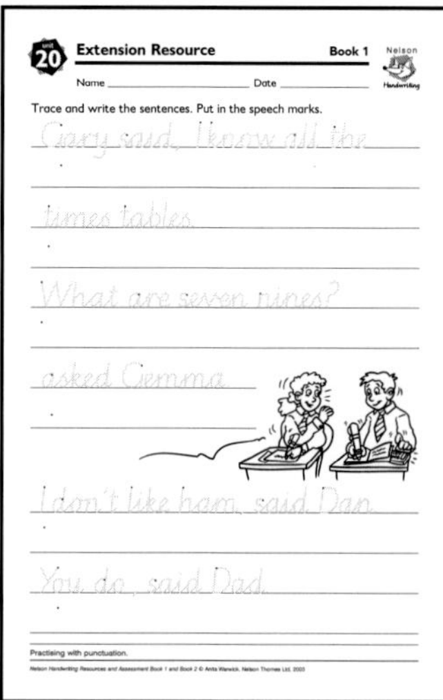

20 Extension Resource — Book 1

Name ____ Date ____

Trace and write the sentences. Put in the speech marks.

Gary said, I know all the times tables

What are seven nines? asked Gemma

I don't like ham, said Dan

You do, said Dad

Practising with punctuation.

Assessment

- The punctuation marks are the correct height and size.
- The punctuation marks are positioned correctly.

HECK-UP

Objectives

Explain to the pupils that this exercise is an assessment activity. The objective is to assess what the pupils can do and where they need extra practice. This exercise will help assess each pupil's ability to form and use the four handwriting joins. Ask pupils to look at the checklist on the back of the flap to remind themselves of the important points.

CHECK-UP

FOCUS

Copy these patterns into your book.

nnnn nnnn nnnn nnnn
ffff ffff ffff ffff
lele lele lele lele
wrwr wrwr wrwr wrwr
ulul ulul ulul ulul
acac acac acac acac

EXTRA

Copy these words into your book.

January February March
April May June
July August September
October November December

Copy these words into your book.

Monday Tuesday
Wednesday Thursday
Friday Saturday
Sunday

EXTENSION

Copy this poem into your book.

Thirty days hath September,
April, June and November.
All the rest have thirty-one
Except February alone,
Which has twenty-eight days clear,
And twenty-nine in each leap year.
(Anonymous)

Focus

Ask the pupils to copy the patterns into their books. The patterns are an important part of helping pupils to learn to join letters. The patterns need to be made smoothly, with the letter shapes the correct height and spaces between the letters and between pattern blocks.

Extra

Ask the pupils to copy the months of the year and days of the week into their books. The words in this section contain all four handwriting joins.

Extension

Ask the pupils to copy the poem into their books.

Assessment

- is the writing easy to read?
- Are the letters well shaped and clear?
- Are the letters consistent in size and proportion?
- Are any letters too tall or too short?
- Are the capital letters formed correctly?
- Are the four handwriting joins made correctly?

- For more Assessment see *Resources and Assessment Book 1 and Book 2*

SCOPE AND SEQUENCE
DEVELOPING SKILLS BOOK TWO

Page	Focus	Extra	Extension	Focus resource	Extension resource
4-5 Flashback	*Flashback*	*Flashback*	*Flashback*	*Flashback*	*Flashback*
6-7 Unit 1 Vikings	practising consistency in size and proportion of letters: rr ll tt dd	copy words ending in ing	copy passage	trace and copy pattern, double consonants and words	copy passage
8-9 Unit 2 Vikings	practising using a diagonal joining line: ship, ment, ness, less	add suffix and copy words	choose words and copy sentences	trace and copy pattern, suffixes and words	choose correct words, complete and copy sentences
10-11 Unit 3 China and India	practising leaving an equal space between letters: ary, ery, cry, dry	copy words ending in ary	copy postcard and fill in missing letters	trace and copy pattern and words ending with ary, ery, cry, dry	choose correct words, complete and copy sentences
12-13 Unit 4 China and India	practising joining to the letter y: ly, ily, ity, ify	add suffix to words, remove e in words ending in e before adding suffix, copy words	choose words and copy sentences	trace and copy pattern and words ending with ily, ity, ify	choose correct words, complete and copy sentences
14-15 Unit 5 Flood	practising using a horizontal joining line: row, now, how, bow	change one letter to show a change of tense and copy words	choose words and copy sentences	trace and copy pattern and words featuring row, now, how and bow	match and copy words in past and present tense
16-17 Unit 6 Flood	practising the size and height of letters: ried, ries, rief	change y to i before adding es or ed, leave y when adding ing, copy words	copy poem	trace and copy pattern and words ending with ried and ries	complete tables adding s, ed and ing to words
18-19 Unit 7 Fireworks	practising joining from the letter i: lig, rig, nig, mig	copy words ending in ight and ite	copy poem	trace and copy pattern, make and copy words ending with ight, write own sentence	complete and copy sentences choosing missing ight or ite word
20-21 Unit 8 Fireworks	practising joining to and from the letter v: live, tive, sive, five	copy words made from explode and act	choose words and copy sentences	trace and copy pattern and words ending with ive and tive, write own sentence	complete and copy sentences choosing a word ending with sive or tive
22-23 Unit 9 Castles	practising consistency in forming and joining letters: ear, are, rew, new	copy homophones	choose words and copy sentences	trace and copy pattern, make and copy words ending with ear and are	practise writing homophones using ee and ea words, write own sentence
24-25 Unit 10 Castles	practising speedwriting: speedily, quickly, swiftly, briskly	use speedwriting to copy 'directional' words	put instructions in correct order and copy in speedwriting	copy sentences to practise speedwriting	copy passage and work out writing speed

Page	Focus	Extra	Extension	Focus resource	Extension resource
26-27 Unit 11 Rubbish and Pollution	practising crossing double tt on completing the word: itt, utt, att, ott	copy two-syllable words containing double consonants	copy poem	trace and copy pattern, copy words containing att and ott	copy poem
28-29 Unit 12 Rubbish and Pollution	practising joining to and from the letter e: rec, red, ved, ves	add s and d to words ending in e, drop e and add ing, copy words	copy poem	trace and copy pattern, copy words ending with f, fe that change to ves in the plural	copy poem
30-31 Unit 13 Snow	practising joining to and from the letter w: owf, owb, owm, owd	copy compound words including the word snow	copy haiku poem	trace and copy pattern and compound words using base words ward and work	copy haiku and cinquain poems
32-33 Unit 14 Snow	practising joining to the letter a from the letter w: wan, was, wav, wax	copy words beginning with wa	copy poem	trace and copy pattern and words containing wa, write own sentence	complete and copy sentences choosing a word containing wa
34-35 Unit 15 Bridges and Fire	practising speedwriting	copy shortened words	copy message using speedwriting and shortened words	write the meaning of a detective's notes	practise speedwriting to write a pizza order
36-37 Unit 16 Bridges	practising printing	copy printed 'rhyming' words	put captions in correct order and copy them	use print to write labels on a street plan	use print to write the names of cities on a map
38-39 Unit 17 Famous Author	practising drafting and editing	write new draft about Roald Dahl	copy corrected draft about Roald Dahl	write a neat copy, with corrected spellings, of the first draft of a story	write a neat copy of the first draft of a story choosing words to replace ones crossed out
40-41 Unit 18 Famous Author	practising speedwriting	copy words and their abbreviations	use shortened words in a list of ingredients for a hot chocolate drink and copy list	writing numerals and number words 11-20	write notes from a newspaper article
42-43 Unit 19 Country Pursuits	practising joining to the letter t: its, lts, tts, uts	choose the correct word its or it's and copy sentences	copy poem	choose words and complete sentences	copy poem
44-45 Unit 20 Country Pursuits	practising printing	draw and print rosettes	design a poster	copy the print alphabet and numerals	copy poster
46-48 Check-up	*Check-up*	*Check-up*	*Check-up*	*Check-up*	*Check-up*

FLASHBACK

Objectives

Explain to pupils that this exercise is an assessment activity. The lesson objective is to assess what the pupils can do from Book 1 and where they need the extra practice. This exercise will help assess each pupil's ability to form and use the four handwriting joins. Ask pupils to look at the checklist on the back of the flap to remind themselves of the important points.

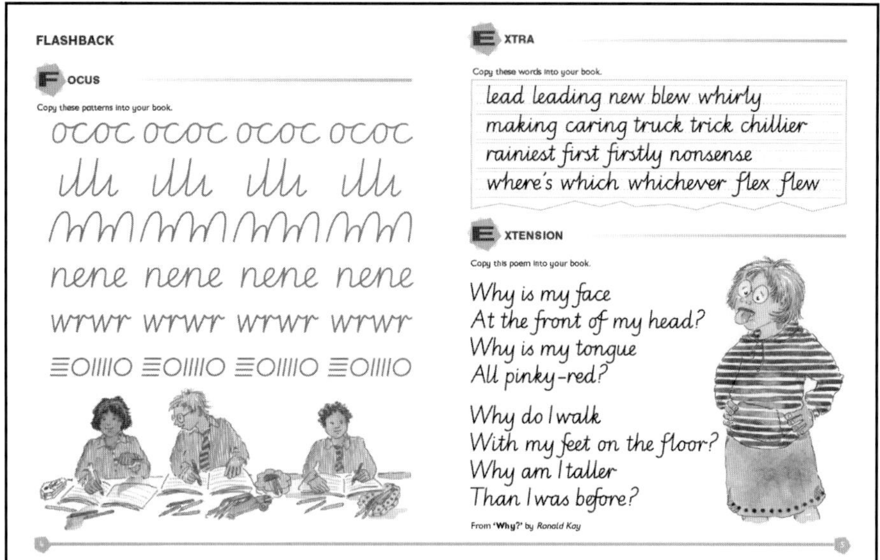

FLASHBACK

FOCUS

Copy these patterns into your book.

ocoo ocoo ocoo ocoo

ulu ulu ulu ulu

nene nene nene nene

wrwr wrwr wrwr wrwr

≡OIIIIO ≡OIIIIO ≡OIIIIO ≡OIIIIO

XTRA

Copy these words into your book.

lead leading new blew whirly
making caring truck trick chillier
rainiest first firstly nonsense
where's which whichever flex flew

XTENSION

Copy this poem into your book.

Why is my face
At the front of my head?
Why is my tongue
All pinky-red?

Why do I walk
With my feet on the floor?
Why am I taller
Than I was before?

From 'Why?' by Ronald Kay

Focus

Ask the pupils to copy the patterns into their book. The patterns are an important part of helping pupils to learn to join letters. The patterns need to be made smoothly, with the letter shapes the correct height and spaces between the letters and between pattern blocks. These patterns are sloped and will help pupils to write with an even slope. The last pattern will give children suitable practice for printing letters.

Extra

Ask the pupils to copy these words into their books. The words in this section contain all four handwriting joins and include double letters, some punctuation and difficult joins.

Extension

Ask the pupils to copy the poem into their books. This poem incorporates punctuation marks introduced in Book 1.

Assessment

- Are the letters formed correctly?
- Are any letters too tall or too short?
- Do the descenders fall below the line?
- Is there a consistent space between letters and words?
- Does the handwriting have an even slope?
- Are the four handwriting joins made correctly?

UNIT 1

Objectives

- To form and write letters to the correct height.
- To form and write letters to the correct size.

Spelling links

- two-syllable words containing double consonants

Nelson theme – Vikings

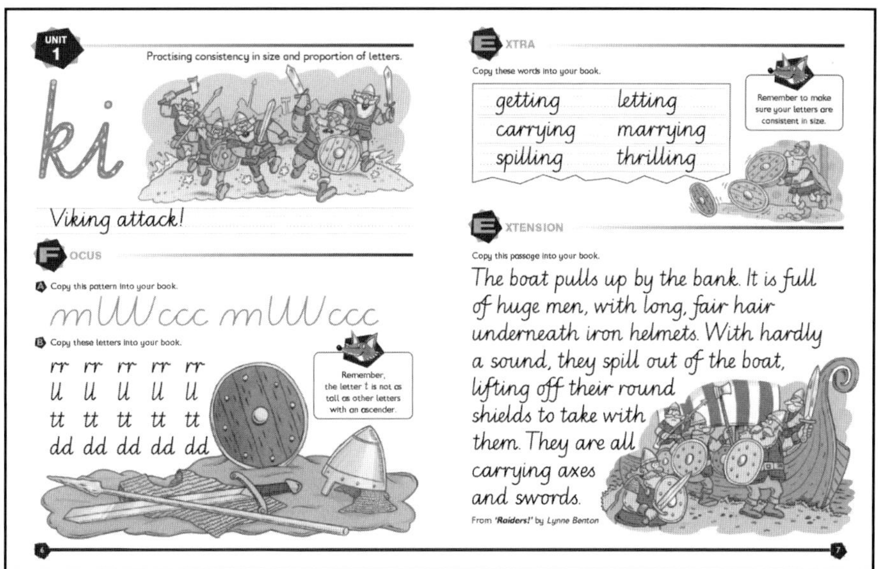

UNIT 1

Practising consistency in size and proportion of letters.

ki

Viking attack!

FOCUS

A Copy this pattern into your book.

mllllccc mllllccc

B Copy these letters into your book.

rr rr rr rr rr
ll ll ll ll ll
tt tt tt tt tt
dd dd dd dd dd

Remember, the letter t is not as tall as other letters with an ascender.

EXTRA

Copy these words into your book.

getting letting
carrying marrying
spilling thrilling

Remember to make sure your letters are consistent in size.

EXTENSION

Copy this passage into your book.

The boat pulls up by the bank. It is full of huge men, with long, fair hair underneath iron helmets. With hardly a sound, they spill out of the boat, lifting off their round shields to take with them. They are all carrying axes and swords.

From *'Raiders!'* by *Lynne Benton*

4 7

Developing Skills

Focus

- Before the lesson, draw four lines and write the whole class sentence on the board.
- Start by discussing the letters **ki**. Point out that the letter **k** is a tall letter, but the body of the letter **k** is the same height as the letter **i**. Remind them that the size and proportion of letters is important.
- Explain that the join is a diagonal join made from the bottom of the letter **k** to the top of the letter **i**. Both letters sit on the baseline.
- Look at the words in the whole class sentence. What can the children tell you about the size and proportion of these letters?
- Model the pattern and the letters on the board.
- Ask the children to practise the pattern and joining **rr**, **ll**, **tt** and **dd** on their individual whiteboards before copying them into their books.

Extra

- Model writing the words on the board.
- Distinguish between long and short vowels. Discuss how short vowels in the middle of words are followed by two consonants, e.g. **marrying**.
- Point out that letters need to be consistent in size and height. This is much easier when writing between lines, but remind the children that handwriting practice needs to be transferred to writing on plain paper, writing in other subjects, etc.
- Ask the group to copy the words into their books.

Extension

- Read the passage.
- Model the first sentence on the board, commenting on the type of joining lines you are using.
- Point out the fox box and remind the class to keep letters a consistent size.
- Suggest that the group copy this passage on to plain paper with guidelines, to ensure letters are consistent in size and proportion even when there are no lines.
- *Extension activity:* brainstorm double-consonant words, e.g. **happy**, **funny**. Use a dictionary to help find the words.

Resources and Assessment

Focus

More practice ensuring letters are consistent in size and proportion. Tracing and/or copying pattern, letters, and words containing double consonants.

1 Focus Resource Book 2

Name Date

ki

A Trace and write the pattern and letters.

B Trace and write the words.

Practising consistency in size and proportion of letters.

Extension

Further practice ensuring letters are consistent in size and proportion. Copying a passage of text.

1 Extension Resource Book 2

Name Date

Copy the passage.

Erik was a Viking warrior. His ship was called the Golden Dragon. The ship's figurehead was a fierce monster carved out of wood and covered with gold leaf.

Practising consistency in size and proportion of letters.

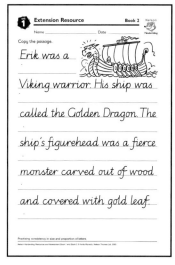

Assessment

- The double consonants are consistent in shape and size.
- All small letters are the same height.
- The letter **t** is not as tall as the other letters with ascenders.

NIT 2

Objectives

- To practise the first join.
- To practise the second join.

Spelling links

- suffixes: **ship**, **hood**, **ness**, **less**, **ment**

Nelson theme – Vikings

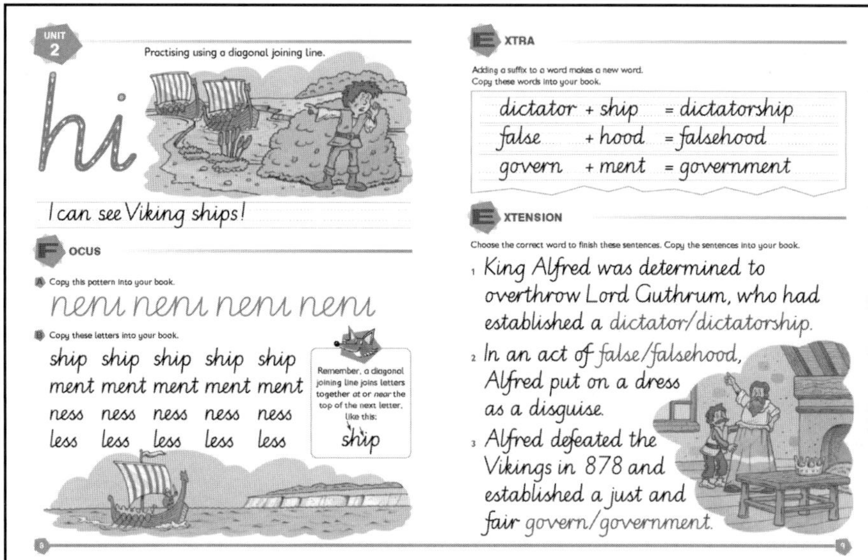

UNIT 2

Practising using a diagonal joining line.

hi

I can see Viking ships!

FOCUS

A Copy this pattern into your book.

neni neni neni neni

B Copy these letters into your book.

ship ship ship ship ship
ment ment ment ment ment
ness ness ness ness ness
less less less less less

Remember, a diagonal joining line joins letters together at or near the top of the next letter, like this: ship

EXTRA

Adding a suffix to a word makes a new word.
Copy these words into your book.

dictator + ship = dictatorship
false + hood = falsehood
govern + ment = government

EXTENSION

Choose the correct word to finish these sentences. Copy the sentences into your book.

1 King Alfred was determined to overthrow Lord Guthrum, who had established a dictator/dictatorship.
2 In an act of false/falsehood, Alfred put on a dress as a disguise.
3 Alfred defeated the Vikings in 878 and established a just and fair govern/government.

8 9

Developing Skills

Focus

- Before the lesson, draw four lines and write the whole class sentence on the board.
- Begin by referring to the **hi** join at the top of page 8. Point out that the letter **h** is a tall letter. The join is made from the bottom of the letter **h** to the top of the letter **i**, using the first join. Both letters sit on the baseline.
- Look at the words in the whole class sentence. Ask the children to tell you which letters have been joined using the diagonal join, e.g. **ca**, **an**, **se**.
- Model the pattern and the suffixes. Discuss the fox box.
- Ask children to practise the pattern and the suffixes on their individual whiteboards before copying them into their books.

Extra

- Model writing the words on the board.
- Brainstorm words with the suffix **ship**, e.g. **membership**, **ownership**, **partnership**.
- Ask the children to copy the words into their books.
- *Extension activity:* make a list of words with the suffix **ment**. Repeat for the suffix **hood**.

Extension

- Read the sentences. The children should choose the correct word to finish each sentence.
- Model writing the first sentence on the board, commenting on the use of the diagonal joins whenever they occur.
- Ask the children to copy the sentences into their books.

Resources and Assessment

Focus

More practice using a diagonal joining line. Copying pattern, suffixes, and words with the suffixes **ship**, **ment**, **ness** and **less**.

2 Focus Resource Book 2

Name Date

hi

A Trace and write the pattern and letters.

B Trace and write the words.

Practising using a diagonal joining line.

Extension

Further practice writing suffixes and using the diagonal joining line. Identifying the missing word and copying completed sentence.

2 Extension Resource Book 2

Name Date

A suffix such as **ship**, **hood** or **ness** appears at the end of a word. Copy this sentence. Choose the correct word.

Legend has it that King Alfred was so busy thinking about fighting that he burned some cakes in a fit of (absent minded/ absent mindedness).

Practising using a diagonal joining line.

Assessment

- The first and second diagonal joining lines are used correctly.
- Suffixes are formed and joined correctly.

UNIT 3

Objectives

- To practise the third join.
- To ensure equal space is left between letters.

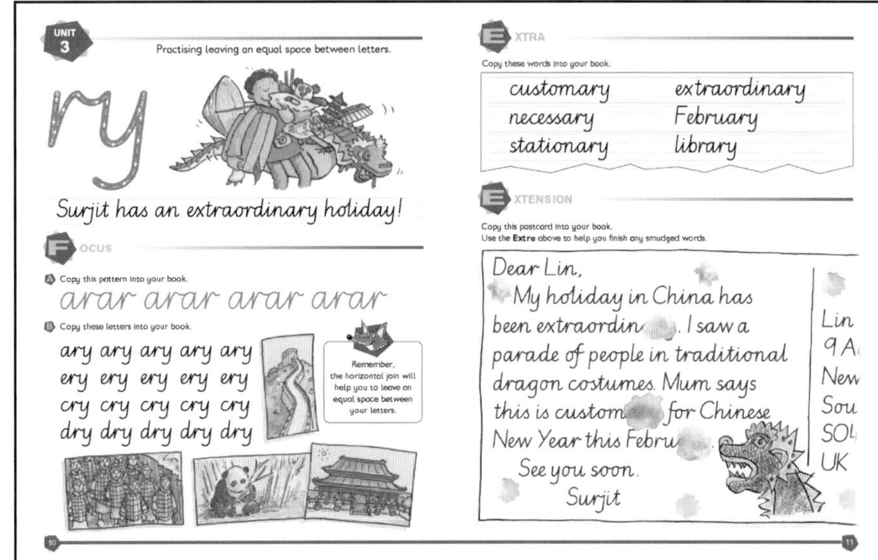

UNIT 3 Practising leaving an equal space between letters.

ry

Surjit has an extraordinary holiday!

FOCUS

A Copy this pattern into your book.

arar arar arar arar

B Copy these letters into your book.

ary ary ary ary ary
ery ery ery ery ery
cry cry cry cry cry
dry dry dry dry dry

Remember, the horizontal join will help you to leave an equal space between your letters.

EXTRA

Copy these words into your book.

customary extraordinary
necessary February
stationary library

EXTENSION

Copy this postcard into your book.
Use the Extra above to help you finish any smudged words.

Dear Lin,
My holiday in China has been extraordin . I saw a parade of people in traditional dragon costumes. Mum says this is custom for Chinese New Year this Febru .
See you soon.
Surjit

Spelling links

- suffixes **al**, **ary**, **ic**

Nelson theme – China and India

Developing Skills

Focus

- Discuss the **ry** join at the top of page 10. Point out that the two letters are the same height, but the letter **y** has a descender, which falls below the baseline. The letter **r** and the body of the letter **y** both sit on the baseline. The join is made from the exit stroke of the letter **r** to the start of the letter **y**. It is a horizontal joining line, which also helps to leave a space between the letters.
- Point out the space between **j** and **i** and between **x** and **t** in the whole class sentence. There is no joining line from the **j** or the **x**. Discuss how it helps you to leave a space between letters when there is a joining line.
- Look at the words in the whole class sentence. Ask the children to tell you which letters have been joined using the horizontal join, (*e.g.* ***rj*** *,* ***ra****,* ***or****,* ***rd****,* ***ry***).
- Model the pattern and the groups of letters and discuss the fox box.
- Ask the class to practise the pattern and joins on their individual whiteboards before copying them into their books.

Extra

- Model writing the words on the board. Can the group think of any more words ending in **ary**? (*e.g.* ***dictionary***)
- Repeat for the suffix **ery**.
- Ask the children to copy the words into their books, taking care to leave equal space between letters.
- *Extension activity:* make a list of words with the suffix **ic**.

Extension

- Read Surjit's postcard and write it on the board. Underline words with the suffix **ary**.
- Remind the children to leave an equal space between letters as they copy the text of the postcard into their books.

Resources and Assessment

Focus

More practice leaving an equal space between letters. Tracing and/or copying pattern and words with suffixes **ary**, **ery**, **cry** and **dry**.

3 Focus Resource Book 2

Name Date

ry

A Trace and write the pattern and letters.

B Trace and write the words.

Practising leaving an equal space between letters

Extension

Choosing the correct **ary** word to complete sentence. Copying words and sentence into books.

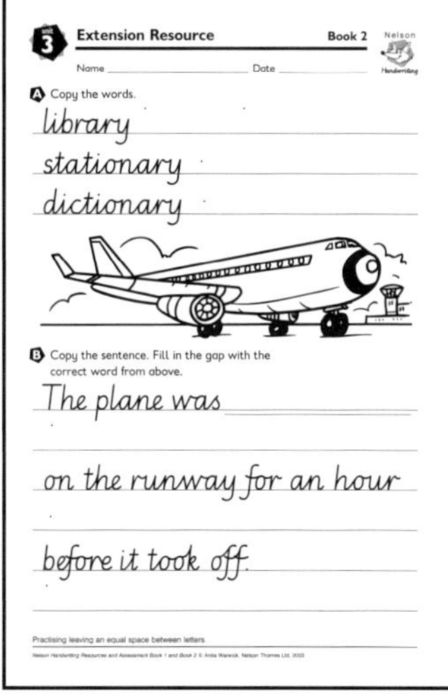

3 Extension Resource Book 2

Name Date

A Copy the words.

library
stationary
dictionary

B Copy the sentence. Fill in the gap with the correct word from above.

The plane was
on the runway for an hour
before it took off.

Practising leaving an equal space between letters

Assessment

- The horizontal and diagonal joins are used correctly.
- Suffixes are formed and joined correctly.
- Equal space is allowed between letters.

UNIT 4

Objectives

- To join to the letter **y** using the first join.
- To join to the letter **y** using the third join.
- To ensure adequate space is left between letters and between words.

Spelling links

- suffixes: **ify**, **ity**

Nelson theme – China and India

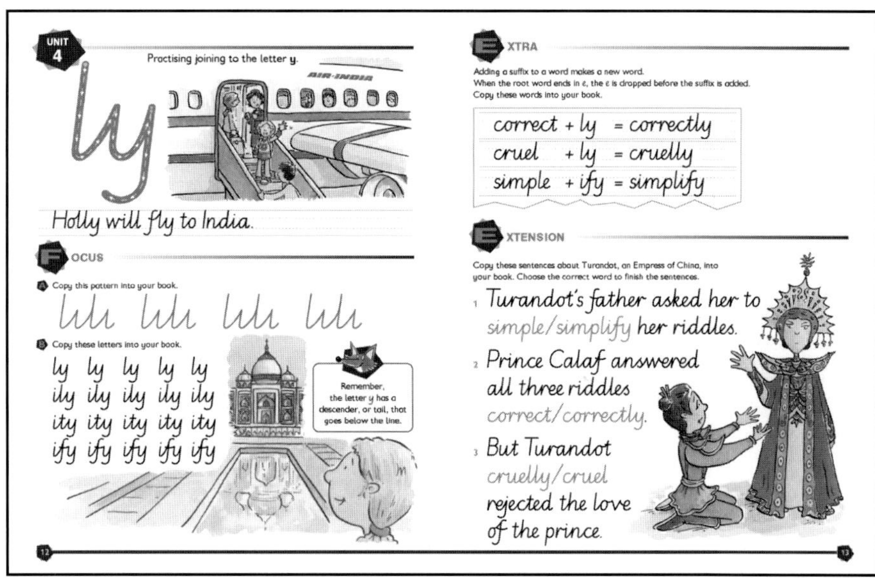

UNIT 4

Practising joining to the letter y.

ly

Holly will fly to India.

FOCUS

A Copy this pattern into your book.

lılı lılı lılı lılı

B Copy these letters into your book.

ly ly ly ly ly
ily ily ily ily ily
ity ity ity ity ity
ify ify ify ify ify

Remember, the letter y has a descender, or tail, that goes below the line.

EXTRA

Adding a suffix to a word makes a new word.
When the root word ends in e, the e is dropped before the suffix is added.
Copy these words into your book.

correct + ly = correctly
cruel + ly = cruelly
simple + ify = simplify

EXTENSION

Copy these sentences about Turandot, an Empress of China, into your book. Choose the correct word to finish the sentences.

1 Turandot's father asked her to simple/simplify her riddles.
2 Prince Calaf answered all three riddles correct/correctly.
3 But Turandot cruelly/cruel rejected the love of the prince.

12 13

Developing Skills

Focus

- Before the lesson, draw four lines and write the whole class sentence on the board.
- Start by discussing the **ly** join. Point out that the letter **l** is a tall letter that starts at the top line. The letter **l** and the body of the letter **y** sit on the baseline. The descender of the letter **y** falls below the baseline. The join is made from the bottom of the letter **l** to the top of the letter **y** –the first join.
- Look at the words in the whole class sentence. Underline the **ly** joins.
- Model the pattern and the letters on the board. Refer the class to the fox box as you write the joins to **y**.
- Ask the children to practise the pattern and joins on their individual whiteboards before copying them into their books.

Extra

- Model writing the words with suffixes on the board.
- Point out that the words **correct**, **cruel** and **simple** are adjectives. By adding the suffix **ly**, the first two become adverbs (**correctly** and **cruelly**). Removing the **e** in **simple** and adding **ify** gives us the verb **simplify**.
- Ask the group to copy the new words into their books, paying particular attention to the **ly** and **fy** joins.
- Extension activity: make a list of nouns with the suffix **ity**, e.g. **purity**, **sanity**. Comment on how the **e** has been removed from the adjectives **pure** and **sane** to form these nouns.

Extension

- Read the sentences and choose the verb to complete them.
- Remind children to leave enough space between their letters and their words as they copy the sentences into their books.

Resources and Assessment

Focus

Further practice joining to the letter **y**. Tracing and/or copying pattern, suffixes, and words with suffixes **ily**, **ity** and **ify**.

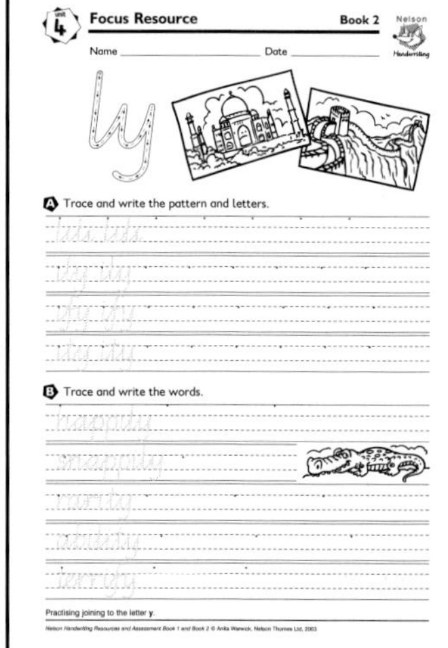

4 Focus Resource Book 2

Name Date

ly

A Trace and write the pattern and letters.

B Trace and write the words.

Practising joining to the letter y.

Extension

More practice joining to the letter **y**. Choosing the correct word; copying completed sentences.

4 Extension Resource Book 2

Name Date

A Copy the words.

pure purify
speed speedily
terror terrify

B Copy the sentences. Fill in each gap with the correct word from above.

1 People can ride bicycles to move around ____.

2 The water in many rivers is not ____.

Practising joining to the letter y.

Assessment

- The first and third joins are used correctly to join to the letter **y**.
- Suffixes are formed and joined correctly.
- Equal space is allowed between letters.

UNIT 5

Objectives

- To use the third join.
- To ensure adequate space is left between letters and words.

Spelling links

- irregular tense changes, e.g. go/went, can/could

Nelson theme – flood

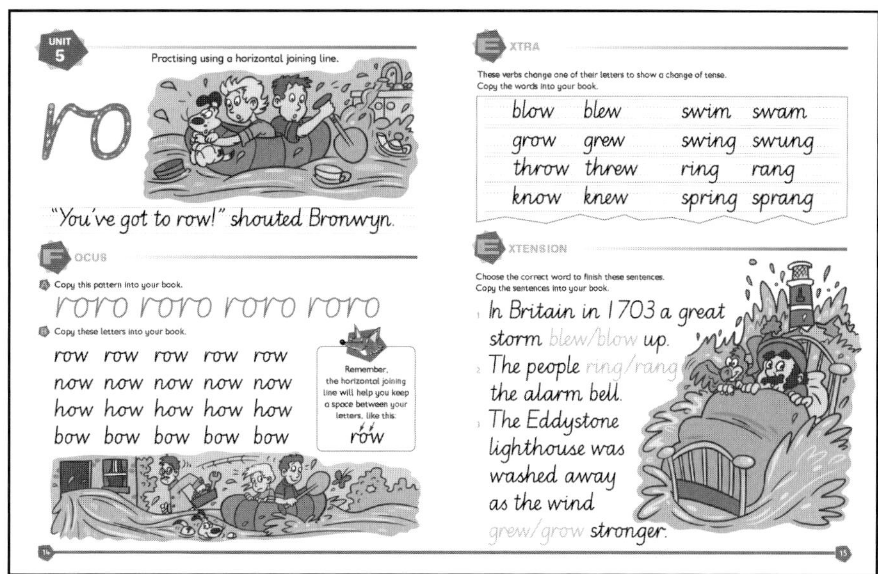

UNIT 5

Practising using a horizontal joining line.

ro

"You've got to row!" shouted Bronwyn.

FOCUS

A Copy this pattern into your book.

roro roro roro roro

B Copy these letters into your book.

row row row row row
now now now now now
how how how how how
bow bow bow bow bow

Remember, the horizontal joining line will help you keep a space between your letters, like this: row

EXTRA

These verbs change one of their letters to show a change of tense. Copy the words into your book.

blow	blew	swim	swam
grow	grew	swing	swung
throw	threw	ring	rang
know	knew	spring	sprang

EXTENSION

Choose the correct word to finish these sentences. Copy the sentences into your book.

1. In Britain in 1703 a great storm blew/blow up.
2. The people ring/rang the alarm bell.
3. The Eddystone lighthouse was washed away as the wind grew/grow stronger.

Developing Skills

Focus

- Before the lesson, draw four lines and write the whole class sentence on the board.
- Discuss the **ro** join. Point out that the letters are both small letters. Demonstrate how they sit on the baseline. The join is made from the top of the letter **r** to the top of the letter **o**. Notice how the join from the **r** dips down then goes back up, ready to meet the **o** in a horizontal join.
- Look at the words in the whole class sentence. Ask a few children to come to the board and underline the eight horizontal joins *(**ou**, **ve**, **ot**, **ro**, **ow**, **ou**, **ro**, **wy**)*.
- Model the pattern and the letters and discuss the fox box.
- Ask the children to practise the pattern and joins on their whiteboards before copying them into their books.

Extra

- Discuss the regular past tense ending **ed**.
- Brainstorm verbs with irregular tense endings, e.g **grow**, **grew**.
- Model writing the words on the board.
- Point out the horizontal joins **ro** and **ow**.
- Mention also the tricky **we** and **re** joins. Remind the children that the pen goes down ready to join to the **e** about halfway down.
- Ask the children to copy the words into their books.

Extension

- Read the sentences and choose the correct tense for the verb.
- Remind children to make sure they leave equal space between their letters as they copy the sentences into their books.

Resources and Assessment

Focus

More practice using a horizontal joining line. Copying pattern and words featuring **row**, **now**, **how** and **bow**.

5 Focus Resource — Book 2 — Nelson Handwriting

Name ________ Date ________

ro

A Trace and write the pattern and letters.

B Trace and write the words.

Practising using a horizontal joining line.

Extension

Matching present tense words to past tense words. Writing the pairs of words, ensuring letters are the correct height.

5 Extension Resource — Book 2 — Nelson Handwriting

Name ________ Date ________

These are present-tense words.

ring blow sing take fight
sell tell have shake buy

These are past-tense words.

blew rang sang sold told had
took shook fought bought

Match each past-tense word to its present-tense word. Write the pairs of words.

Present	Past	Present	Past
blow	blew		took

Practising using a horizontal joining line.

Assessment

- The correct use of the third join.
- The letter **e** is formed correctly following the third join.
- Equal space is allowed between letters.

NIT 6

Objectives

- To form letters to the correct height and size.

Spelling links

- regular verb endings: **s**, **ed**, **ing**

Nelson theme – flood

UNIT 6 Practising the size and height of letters.

ri

She cried floods of tears.

FOCUS

A Copy this pattern into your book.

riri riri riri riri

B Copy these letters into your book.

ried ried ried ried ried
ries ries ries ries ries
rief rief rief rief rief

EXTRA

Copy these words into your book.

cry cries cried crying
dry dries dried drying
try tries tried trying
fry fries fried frying

Remember, the descender, or tail, on a letter goes below the line.

EXTENSION

Copy this poem into your book.
Write the title in capital letters.

BOO HOO

Mabel cried as she stood
by the window,
Mabel cried as she stood
by the door.
Mabel cried and her tears
filled three buckets;
Mabel cried as she sat on the floor.

By Arnold Spilka

Developing Skills

Focus

- Before the lesson, draw four lines and write the whole class sentence on the board.
- Begin by commenting on the letters **ri**. Both are small letters, the same height as the other small letters in the alphabet, i.e. **a**, **c**, **e**, **m**, **n**, **o**, **s**, **u**, **v**, **w**, **x**, **z**.
- Model writing all the small letters on the board, between the lines.
- Point out that the **r** to **i** join is the third join made from the top of the letter **r** to the top of the letter **i**. Note how the join from the **r** dips down then goes back up, ready to meet the letter **i** (just like **r** to **o** in Unit 5).
- Look at the words in the whole class sentence. Discuss the size and height of the letters: capital letters are as tall as ascenders; the letter **f** has both an ascender and a descender; ascenders are almost twice the height of small letters.
- Model the pattern on the board. Draw attention to the fact that the **i** to **r** join is the first join while **r** to **i** is the third join.
- Write the groups of letters on the board, commenting on their size and height.
- Ask the children to practise the pattern and joins on their whiteboards before copying them into their books.

Extra

- Model writing the words on the board. Comment on the endings in each case. Emphasise that, in words ending with **y**, the **y** changes to **i** before adding **es** or **ed**.
- Talk about the height of the letters, particularly of the letter **t** and the other ascenders.
- Notice how letters are similar in size, e.g. **g** and **y**, **c** and **e**.

Extension

- Read the poem.
- Model the first three lines, commenting on the height and size of the letters as you write.
- Ask the children to copy the poem into their books or on to plain paper with guidelines.

Resources and Assessment

Focus

More practice of **ri** join. Copying pattern, letters, and words ending **ried** and **ries**.

6 Focus Resource Book 2

Name ______ Date ______

A Trace and write the pattern and letters.

B Trace and write the words.

Practising the size and height of letters.

Extension

Completing table of verb families adding **s**, **ed** and **ing** to words.

6 Extension Resource Book 2

Name ______ Date ______

Most words add **s**, **ed** or **ing** to show tenses. Fill in the correct words.

	s	ed	ing
cook	cooks	cooked	cooking
book			
stay			
play			

With short vowels, double the final consonant before adding **ed** or **ing**.

	ed	ing
hop	hopped	hopping
stop		
drop		

If a word ends in **e**, avoid **ee** by dropping one **e**.

	s	ed
save	saves	saved
pave		
wave		

Practising the size and height of letters.

Assessment

- All the small letters are the same height and size.
- The ascenders (except **t**) are almost twice the height of small letters.
- The letters with descenders are the same size as those with ascenders, but the descender goes below the line.

UNIT 7

Objectives

- To join from the letter **i** using the diagonal joining line.
- To join to the letter **g** from the letter **i**.

Spelling links

- common letter strings, e.g. **ight**

Nelson theme – fireworks

UNIT 7 Practising joining from the letter i.

ig

Sparklers are little bright lights.

FOCUS

A Copy this pattern into your book.

ıtıg ıtıg ıtıg ıtıg

B Copy these letters into your book.

lig lig lig lig lig
rig rig rig rig rig
nig nig nig nig nig
mig mig mig mig mig

Remember, when you join from the letter i to the letter g, go to the top and then back round, like this: ig

EXTRA

Make these words. Copy them into your book.

Remember, the letter g has a descender, or tail, that goes below the line.

l + ight = light   wh + ite = white
n + ight = night   k + ite = kite
fr + ight = fright   b + ite = bite

EXTENSION

Copy this poem into your book. Write the title in capital letters.

FIREWORKS

Use your best handwriting when you want to present neat, careful work.

They rise like sudden fiery flowers
That burst upon the night,
Then fall to earth in burning showers
Of crimson, blue, and white.

from 'Fireworks' by James Reeves

18 19

Developing Skills

Focus

- Before the lesson, draw four lines and write the whole class sentence on the board.
- Start by talking about the letters **i** and **g**. Point out that both letters are the same height, but the **g** has a descender, which goes below the baseline.
- Demonstrate this join on the board. Comment that it is the same join as **io**, **ia**, **id** or **ic**. This diagonal joining line joins these letters together; it also helps leave a space between the letters.
- Ask the class to look at the whole class sentence and find words containing a join from the letter **i**. Discuss the fact that since the letter **i** finishes at the bottom, the join is always upwards and diagonal to the next letter. If the next letter is a tall letter, e.g. **t**, the joining line meets the ascender at approximately x-height.
- Model the pattern and the groups of letters on the board.
- Point out that all the joins are diagonal except the **ri** join in **rig**, which is the horizontal join.
- Ask the children to practise the pattern and letters on their whiteboards before copying them into their books.

Extra

- Make a class list of words ending in **ight**.
- Make connections to words that follow the same pattern but are spelled differently, e.g. **white**, **kite**, **bite**. Point out that **ight** and **ite** sound the same.
- Model writing the six words on the board.
- Ask the children to copy the words into their books.

Extension

- Read the poem.
- Model writing the first two lines.
- Identify all the words in the poem that contain a join from the letter **i**, e.g. **rise**, **like**, **fiery**, **night**. Remind the group that all these joins are diagonal joins.
- Ask the children to copy the poem into their books or on to plain paper with guidelines.

Resources and Assessment

Focus

More practice of the letter string **ight**. Tracing and copying pattern, letters and words. Creating a sentence using a word ending in **ight**.

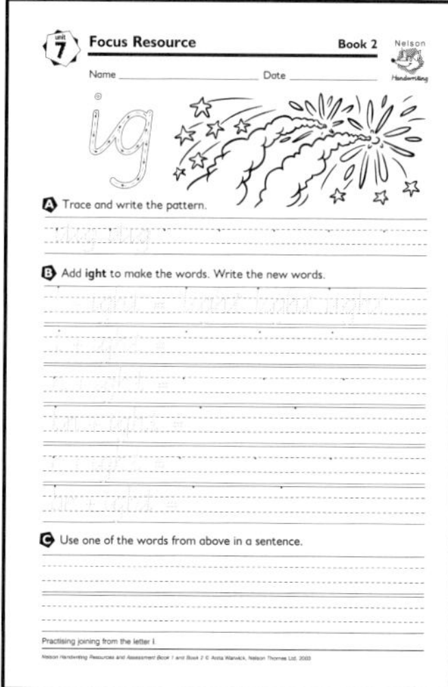

7 Focus Resource Book 2 Nelson Handwriting

Name Date

ig

A Trace and write the pattern.

B Add **ight** to make the words. Write the new words.

C Use one of the words from above in a sentence.

Practising joining from the letter i

Extension

Choosing between **ight** and **ite** words to complete sentences. Writing completed sentences.

7 Extension Resource Book 2 Nelson Handwriting

Name Date

A Most words ending in the 'ight' sound use **ight**. A handful of words use **ite**. Copy the words.

night   white
knight   bite
fight   rite
slight   mite

B Copy the sentences. Fill in each gap with the correct word from above.

1 Snow is ______.

2 The ______ grasped his sword and began to ______.

Practising joining from the letter i

Assessment

- The descender of the letter **g** falls below the baseline.
- The correct formation of the **it** join. It does not join to the bottom of the **t**.
- The join to the letter **t** is made at x-height.

UNIT 8

Objectives

- To join to the letter **v** using the first join.
- To join from the letter **v** to the letter **e** using the third join.

Spelling links

- suffixes: **ing**, **ive**, **tion**, **sion**

Nelson theme – fireworks

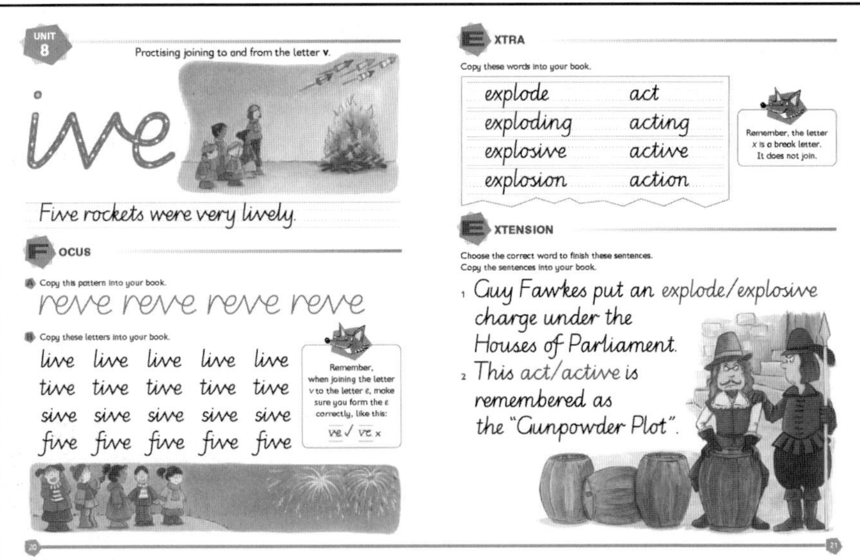

UNIT 8 Practising joining to and from the letter **v**.

ive

Five rockets were very lively.

FOCUS

A Copy this pattern into your book.

reve reve reve reve

B Copy these letters into your book.

live live live live live
tive tive tive tive tive
sive sive sive sive sive
five five five five five

Remember, when joining the letter v to the letter e, make sure you form the e correctly, like this: ve ✓ ve ✗

EXTRA

Copy these words into your book.

explode	act
exploding	acting
explosive	active
explosion	action

Remember, the letter x is a break letter. It does not join.

EXTENSION

Choose the correct word to finish these sentences. Copy the sentences into your book.

1 Guy Fawkes put an explode/explosive charge under the Houses of Parliament.
2 This act/active is remembered as the "Gunpowder Plot".

20 21

Developing Skills

Focus

- Write the whole class sentence on the board as the class watch. Explain that the pen dips down after writing the letters **v** and **r** to enable the letter **e** to be formed correctly.
- Talk about the joins at the top of page 20.
- Use a coloured pen to illustrate that the **iv** join is made from the bottom of the letter **i** to the top of the letter **v** using a diagonal joining line.
- Use a different coloured pen to demonstrate the horizontal **ve** join. This is a tricky join as the pen must dip down to enable the letter **e** to be formed correctly.
- Look at the whole class sentence together. Underline the letters **ve** in **five**, **very** and **lively**. Also underline the **re** in **were**.
- Model the pattern on the board. Note that **re** and **ve** are horizontal joins, while **ev** is a diagonal join.
- Ask the children to practise the pattern and joins on their whiteboards before copying them into their books.
- Tell the class to copy the whole class sentence into their books as well.

Extra

- Model writing the words **explode**, **exploding**, **explosive** and **explosion** on the board.
- Explain that deleting the final **e** is common in root words, e.g. **explode**/**exploding**.
- Point out that words ending with **sion** are often formed from verbs ending in **d** or **de**, e.g. **extend** – **extension**, explode – **explosion**.
- Remind the group how to join to and how to form the letter **x**. Look at the fox box and talk about break letters.

Extension

- Read the sentences.
- Model writing the first sentence, commenting on the **ive** letter pattern, the height and size of the letters and the two types of join involved.
- Ask the children to copy both sentences into their books, choosing the correct word to complete the sentence in each case.

Resources and Assessment

Focus

More practice joining to and from the letter **v** in words ending in **ive** and **tive**. Writing a sentence using one of the words ending in **ive**.

8 Focus Resource Book 2 Nelson Handwriting

Name ________ Date ________

ive

A Trace and write the pattern.

B Add **ive** or **tive** to make the words. Write the new words.

C Use one of the words from above in a sentence.

Practising joining to and from the letter v.

Extension

Further practice using words ending in **sive** and **tive**. Copying sentences, adding missing word.

8 Extension Resource Book 2 Nelson Handwriting

Name ________ Date ________

A Copy the words.

massive
relative
competitive
expensive

B Copy the sentences. Fill in each gap with the correct word from above.

1 I built a ________ tower with all the bricks in the box.
2 The magician made the ________ watch disappear.

Practising joining to and from the letter v.

Assessment

- The letter **e** is formed correctly following the letters **v** and **r**.
- The letters **i**, **v** and **e** are the same height and size.
- The first join is used to join **i** to **v**.

NIT 9

Objectives

- To make all small letters the same height and size.
- To use the horizontal and diagonal joining lines to join small letters.

Spelling links

- common homophones, e.g. **knew/new**

Nelson theme – castles

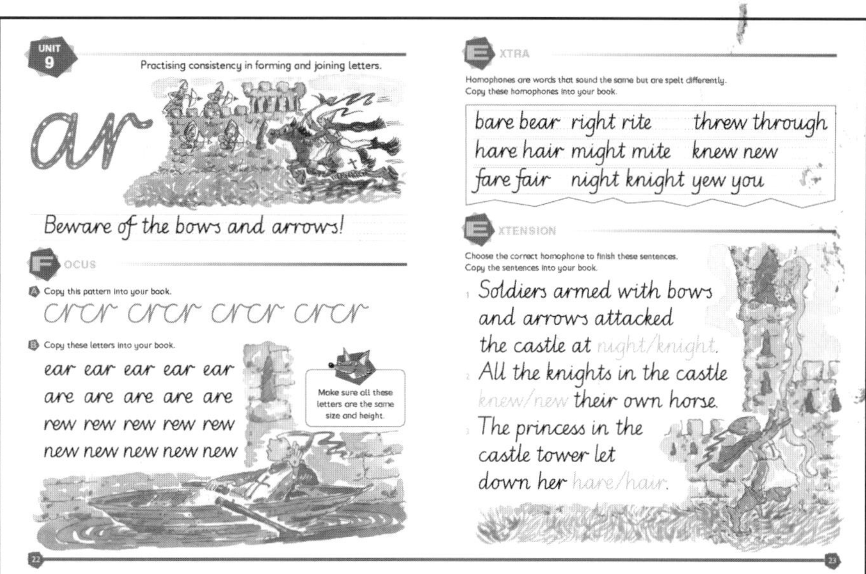

UNIT 9

Practising consistency in forming and joining letters.

ar

Beware of the bows and arrows!

FOCUS

A Copy this pattern into your book.

crcr crcr crcr crcr

B Copy these letters into your book.

ear ear ear ear ear
are are are are are
rew rew rew rew rew
new new new new new

Make sure all these letters are the same size and height.

XTRA

Homophones are words that sound the same but are spelt differently.
Copy these homophones into your book.

bare bear right rite threw through
hare hair might mite knew new
fare fair night knight yew you

XTENSION

Choose the correct homophone to finish these sentences.
Copy the sentences into your book.

Soldiers armed with bows and arrows attacked the castle at night/knight.
All the knights in the castle knew/new their own horse.
The princess in the castle tower let down her hare/hair.

22 23

Developing Skills

Focus

- Write the whole class sentence between four lines on the board as the children watch. Explain that the small letters are the same height and size. Point out the horizontal and diagonal joining lines. Ask the class to point out which letters are not small *(**B**, **f**, **t**, **h**, **b** and **d**)*.
- Discuss the size of the letters **ar** and the diagonal join. Remind the children that **a** and **r** are small letters and are the same height as the other small letters in the alphabet.
- Model writing all the small letters on the board, between the lines.
- Note that the join is made from the bottom of the letter **a** to the top of the letter **r**, using the first join.
- Model the pattern on the board. Underline the diagonal joins in one colour and the horizontal joins in a different colour.
- Write up each group of letters, commenting on the size and height of the letters and the joins used.
- Ask the children to practise the pattern and joins on their individual whiteboards.
- The children should then copy them into their books.

Extra

- Discuss the meaning of the word homophone.
- Model writing the first set of words in a column on the board (**bare**/**bear**, **hare**/**hair** and **fare**/**fair**).
- Ask the children to think of sentences using the words in the correct context.
- Tell them to write the words into their books, remembering that small letters are the same height and size.

Extension

- Read the three sentences connected with castles.
- Ask the children to copy the sentences into their books, choosing the correct word to complete the sentence in each case.
- Remind the children to pay particular attention to how they join small letters.

Resources and Assessment

Focus

More practice forming and joining small letters using words ending with **ear** (diagonal joins) and words ending with **are** (diagonal and horizontal joins).

9 Focus Resource Book 2

Name Date

ar

A Trace and write the pattern and letters.

B Trace and write the words.

Practising consistency in forming and joining letters.

Extension

Further practice forming and joining small letters. Writing homophones. Writing sentences using homophones.

9 Extension Resource Book 2

Name Date

A Copy the words.

see	meet
week	feet
tee	leek
seem	flee
reed	been
peel	reel

B Change the **ee** in each word to **ea**. Write the new words.

sea

C Write a sentence containing 'sea' and 'see'.

Practising consistency in forming and joining letters.

Assessment

- All small letters are the same height and size.
- The horizontal joining line is used correctly.
- The diagonal joining line is used correctly.

NIT 10

Objectives

- To write at different speeds for different purposes.
- To write quickly and legibly.

Spelling links

- suffixes, e.g. **ly**

Nelson theme – castles

UNIT 10 Practising speedwriting.

Turn right to get to the castle.

FOCUS

A Copy this pattern into your book.

uuu uuu uuu uuu

B Copy these words in speedwriting into your book.

speedily speedily speedily
quickly quickly quickly
swiftly swiftly swiftly
briskly briskly briskly

You use speedwriting when you need to write something quickly, such as directions. Your handwriting doesn't have to be neat but it must be readable.

EXTRA

A Copy these words in speedwriting into your book.

through beneath
behind across
left right up down

B See how many times you can write the words in one minute.

EXTENSION

Put these instructions in the correct order.
Use speedwriting to copy the instructions into your book.

1 Follow the stairs up to the top of the tower to find two doors.
2 Go through the green door on the right.
3 Bring the drawbridge down to cross the moat.
4 The treasure is behind the throne on the left.

24 25

Developing Skills

Focus

- Explain the concept of writing at different speeds for different purposes, e.g. writing notes and messages quickly.
- Write the whole class sentence on the board – quickly. Point out that we don't need to use our best writing at all times.
- Think about occasions when we need to write quickly.
- Stress that even quick writing must be legible.
- Model the pattern on the board. Point out that joining your writing helps you to write more quickly.
- Talk about the consonant suffix **ly** as you write the four adverbs on the board. Explain that **ly** can usually be added without changing the base word, unless the adjective ends in **y**. In this case the y changes to an **i**, e.g. **speedily**.
- Ask the children to practise the pattern and words on their whiteboards before copying them into their books.

Extra

- Explain that the aim of this exercise is to write the words quickly while making sure that they are easy to read.
- Point out that it helps to slant writing slightly to the right (about 8 degrees when speedwriting).
- Demonstrate the first three words on the board.
- Ask the children to use speedwriting to copy the words into their books.

Extension

- Explain to the group that we might use speedwriting to write instructions – especially if someone is giving us instructions over the telephone.
- The instructions in this exercise need to be written in the correct order.
- Ask the children to use speedwriting to copy the sentences, in the correct order, into their books.

Resources and Assessment

Focus

Several opportunities to copy a sentence quickly but legibly.

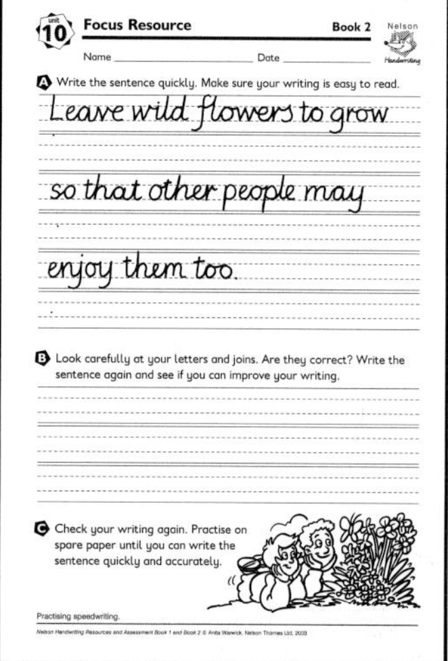

10 Focus Resource Book 2

Name Date

A Write the sentence quickly. Make sure your writing is easy to read.

Leave wild flowers to grow so that other people may enjoy them too.

B Look carefully at your letters and joins. Are they correct? Write the sentence again and see if you can improve your writing.

C Check your writing again. Practise on spare paper until you can write the sentence quickly and accurately.

Practising speedwriting.

Extension

Copying a passage quickly but legibly. Formula for finding writing speed.

10 Extension Resource Book 2

Name Date

A Copy this passage quickly but neatly.

The tallest living animal in the world is the giraffe. The longest animal ever recorded is the bootlace worm. One of these worms was washed ashore in Scotland. People could not believe its length.

B Now time yourself. To find out your writing speed, count the letters and divide them by the number of minutes.

My writing speed is letters per minute.

Practising speedwriting.

Assessment

- Writing slants slightly to the right.
- The child is writing quickly and well.
- Writing is legible, the correct joins are used and letters are formed correctly.

NIT 11

Objectives

- To join the letter **t** to another **t** using the second join.
- To cross the letter **t** on completing the word.

Spelling links

- two-syllable words containing double consonants, e.g. **litter**

Nelson theme – rubbish and pollution

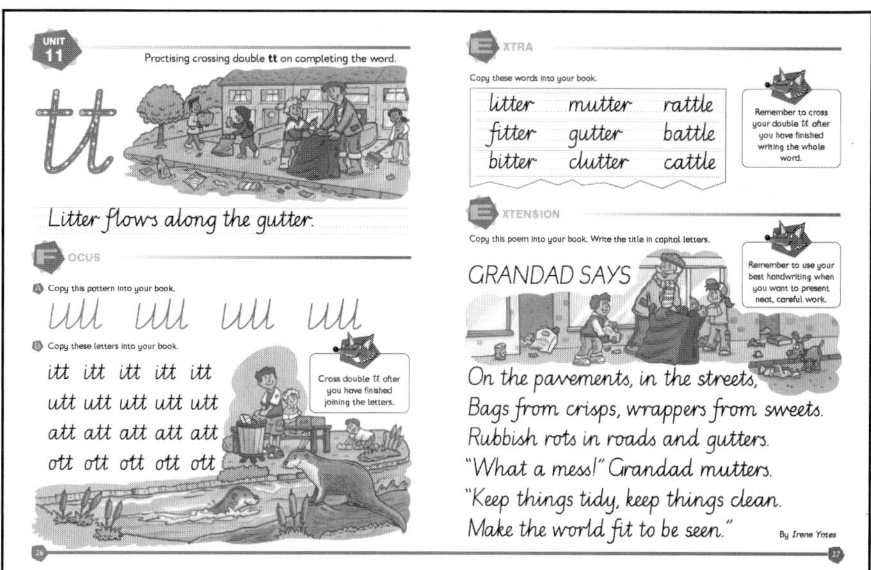

UNIT 11 Practising crossing double **tt** on completing the word.

tt

Litter flows along the gutter.

FOCUS

A Copy this pattern into your book.

ul ul ul ul

B Copy these letters into your book.

itt itt itt itt itt
utt utt utt utt utt
att att att att att
ott ott ott ott ott

Cross double tt after you have finished joining the letters.

EXTRA

Copy these words into your book.

litter	mutter	rattle
fitter	gutter	battle
bitter	clutter	cattle

Remember to cross your double tt after you have finished writing the whole word.

EXTENSION

Copy this poem into your book. Write the title in capital letters.

Remember to use your best handwriting when you want to present neat, careful work.

GRANDAD SAYS

On the pavements, in the streets,
Bags from crisps, wrappers from sweets.
Rubbish rots in roads and gutters.
"What a mess!" Grandad mutters.
"Keep things tidy, keep things clean.
Make the world fit to be seen."

By Irene Yates

26 27

Developing Skills

Focus

- Before the lesson, draw four lines and write the whole class sentence on the board. Point out that the letter **t** is crossed on completing the word.
- Explain to the class that if you stop in the middle of a word to cross the letter **t**, you interrupt the flow and speed of the sentence and the joining of the letters.
- Point out that the two **t**s at the top of the page are joined using a diagonal joining line, which meets the second **t** at approximately x-height.
- The letter **t** is crossed just above the x-height guideline.
- Model the pattern and each set of letters on the board.
- Ask the children to practise the pattern and joins on their individual whiteboards before copying them into their books.

Extra

- Point out that all these words contain short vowels and that short vowels in the middle of words are followed by two consonants, e.g. **dinner**, **bitter**, **written**; long vowels are followed by one, e.g. **diner**, **biter**, **writing**.
- Model writing the first column of words on the board. Point out that the **t**s are crossed after the word has been written.
- Also point out that the letter **t** is not quite as tall as the letter **l**.
- Ask the group to copy the words into their books.

Extension

- Read the poem.
- Ask the children to copy the poem into their writing books or on to a piece of plain paper with guidelines underneath.
- Remind them to cross the letter **t** when they have finished the word and not before.

Resources and Assessment

Focus

Further practice joining to the letter **t** and crossing the **t** on completing the word. Copying words containing the letters **att** and **ott**.

11 Focus Resource Book 2 Nelson Handwriting

Name Date

A Trace and write the pattern and letters.

B Trace and write the words.

Practising crossing double tt on completing the word

Extension

Reading and copying poem containing words with **t** and **tt**. Further practice crossing the letter **t** on completing the word.

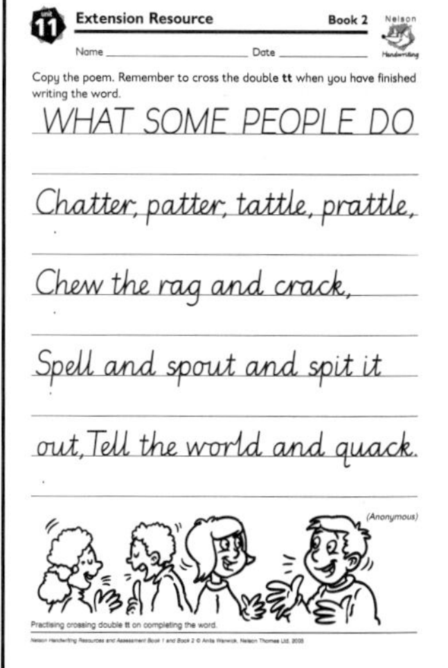

11 Extension Resource Book 2 Nelson Handwriting

Name Date

Copy the poem. Remember to cross the double **tt** when you have finished writing the word.

WHAT SOME PEOPLE DO

Chatter, patter, tattle, prattle,
Chew the rag and crack,
Spell and spout and spit it
out, Tell the world and quack.

(Anonymous)

Practising crossing double tt on completing the word

Assessment

- All the letters are joined, except break letters and capitals.
- The letter **t** is joined to the letter **t** at approximately x-height and is not as tall as the other letters with ascenders.
- The letter **t** is crossed on completing the word.

UNIT 12

Objectives

- To join to the letter **e** using the third join.
- To join from the letter **e** using a diagonal join.

Spelling links

- regular verb endings **s**, **ed**, **ing**

Nelson theme – rubbish and pollution

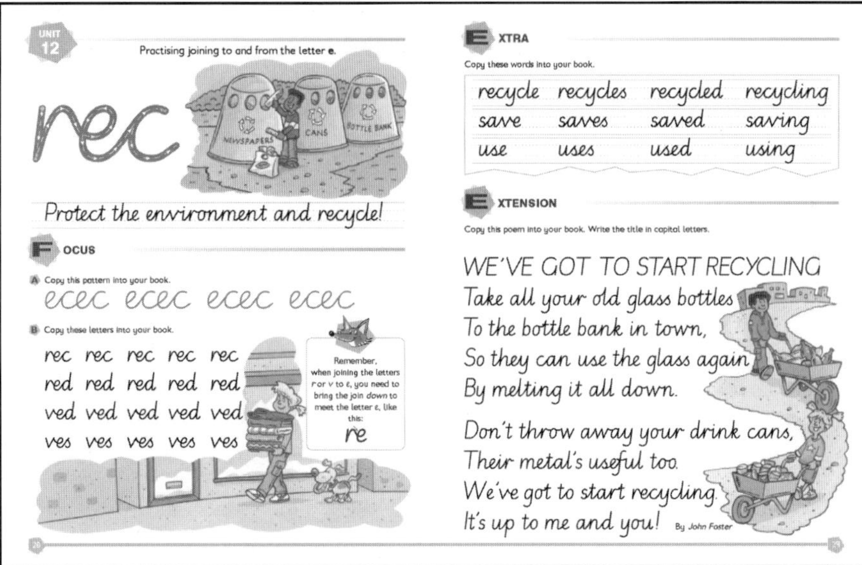

Developing Skills

Focus

- Write the whole class sentence on the board. Ask the children to look at each word and identify which join has been used to join to and from the letter **e**.
- Look at the **re** join. Remind the children that this is a tricky join – you need to bring the joining line down to meet the start of the letter **e**. If you don't bring the joining line down, the letter **e** will not be formed correctly.
- Joining from the letter **e** is easier. It is the first join. Look at the letters **rec**. Point out that the join from **e** to **c** is made halfway up the letter **c**.
- After the join from **e** to **c** and from **e** to **d**, the pen comes back round to complete the letter.
- Model the pattern on the board.
- Now model each set of letters, commenting that since the letters **v** and **r** finish at the top – and the letter **e** starts near the bottom line – the pen must come down to enable the letter **e** to be formed correctly.
- Ask the children to practise the pattern and letters on their whiteboards before copying them into their books.

Extra

- Look at the three rows of words and talk about how the endings are added in each of the four cases. Point out that most verbs simply add **s** and **ed**. But if a word ends in **e**, the double **e** is avoided by dropping one as necessary *(e.g.* ***recycled/saved/used****)*. If a word ends in **e**, the **e** is dropped when **ing** is added.
- Model writing the first row of words on the board. Point out the **re** and **ec** joins.
- Ask the children to copy the words into their books, taking care with the joins to and from **e**.

Extension

- Read the poem.
- Ask the group to copy the poem into their ordinary writing books or on to a piece of plain paper with guidelines.
- Remind them to make sure they join to and from the letter **e** correctly.

Resources and Assessment

Focus

Further practice of the **ves** ending using words changing from **f** to **v** in the plural. Copying pattern and words.

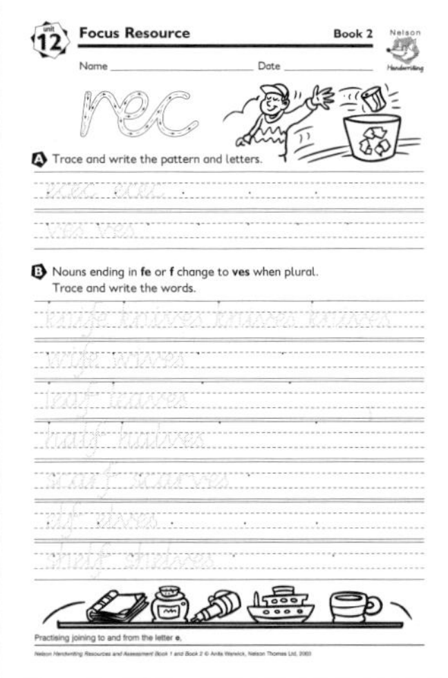

Extension

More practice joining to and from the letter **e**. Copying poem.

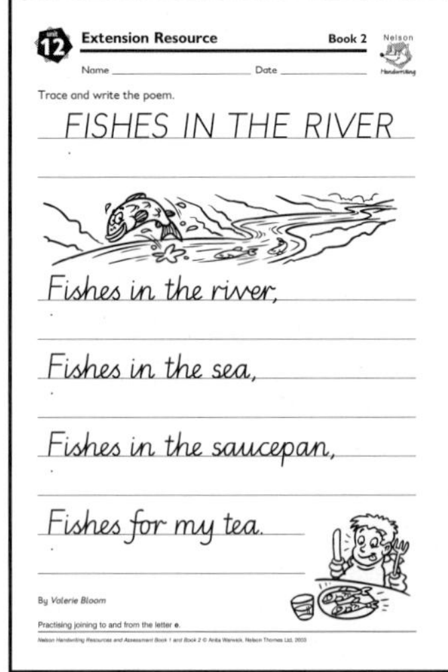

Assessment

- The correct **re** and **ve** joins – with the letter **e** correctly formed.
- The correct join from the letter **e** and correct formation of letter **d** in all **ed** joins.

UNIT 13

Objectives

- To join to and from the letter **w** using the third join.
- To join from the letter **w** using the fourth join (diagonal join).
- To leave a space between letters.

Spelling links

- compound words

Nelson theme – snow

UNIT 13

Practising joining to and from the letter **w**.

owf

A snowfall can be fun!

FOCUS

A Copy this pattern into your book.

owow owow owow owow

B Copy these letters into your book.

owf owf owf owf owf
owb owb owb owb owb
owm owm owm owm owm
owd owd owd owd owd

Remember, the horizontal join will help you to keep the correct space between your letters.

EXTRA

Copy these compound words into your book.

snowfall snowman snowflake
snowball snowdrift snowdrop

EXTENSION

A haiku is a single-verse poem with three lines. Lines one and three each contain five syllables and line two contains seven syllables. Copy this haiku into your book. Write the title in capital letters.

Remember to use your best handwriting when you want to present neat, careful work.

HAIKU
Snowman in a field
listening to the raindrops
wishing him farewell

By Roger McGough

30 31

Developing Skills

Focus

- Write the whole class sentence on the board. Point out that the **ow** join (in the word **snowfall**) is the third join, which helps leave a space between letters. Explain that in the **wf** join the pen dips down before joining to the letter **f** near the top.
- Discuss the **owf** group of letters. Point out that the joins help to create a space between the letters, ensuring that the letters do not touch.
- Point out the horizontal join from **o** to **w** does not go straight across, but dips down slightly.
- Mention that the **wf** join is also tricky. It does not go straight from the end of the letter **w** to the top of the letter **f**, but the exit stroke from the **w** dips down slightly before the diagonal join is made to near the top of the letter **f**.
- Model the pattern on the board. Comment on the horizontal joins between the letters and the equal spaces between the letters.
- Demonstrate each set of letters and ask the children to practise them on their whiteboards.
- Tell them to copy the pattern and the letters into their books.

Extra

- Model writing some of the words on the board.
- Identify the different elements of the compound words.
- Explain that most compound words simply add two base words together without modification.
- Discuss the height and size of the letter **f**.
- Point out that the letter **b** is a break letter and does not join to the next letter.

Extension

- Read the haiku.
- Ask the class to copy the poem into their ordinary writing books or on to a piece of plain paper with guidelines.
- Remind them to take care with joining to and from the letter **w**.

Resources and Assessment

Focus

More practice joining to and from the letter **w**. Copying compound words.

13 Focus Resource Book 2

Name Date

owf

A Trace and write the pattern.

B Trace and write the words.

Extension

Further practice joining to and from the letter **w**. Copying a haiku; completing pattern. Copying a cinquain; completing pattern. Making up own cinquain.

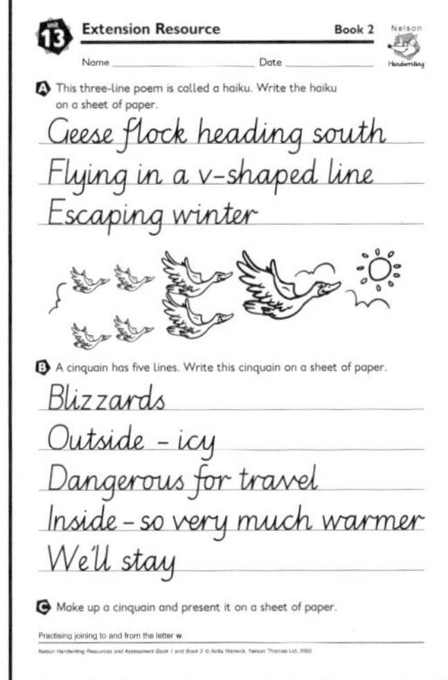

13 Extension Resource Book 2

Name Date

A This three-line poem is called a haiku. Write the haiku on a sheet of paper.

Geese flock heading south
Flying in a v-shaped line
Escaping winter

B A cinquain has five lines. Write this cinquain on a sheet of paper.

Blizzards
Outside – icy
Dangerous for travel
Inside – so very much warmer
We'll stay

C Make up a cinquain and present it on a sheet of paper.

Assessment

- The correct **ow** join using the third join.
- Consistently equal space between the letters **o** and **w**.
- The correct **wf** join, using the fourth join.

UNIT 14

Objectives

- To join to the letter **a** using the third join.
- To leave a space between the letters **w** and **a**.

Spelling links

- letter strings within words, e.g. **wa**

Nelson theme – snow

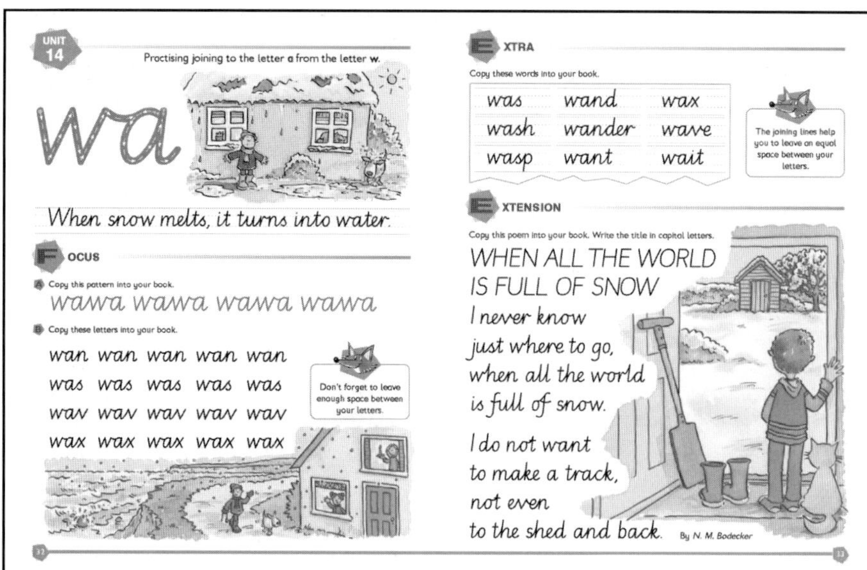

UNIT 14

Practising joining to the letter a from the letter w.

wa

When snow melts, it turns into water.

FOCUS

A Copy this pattern into your book.

wawa wawa wawa wawa

B Copy these letters into your book.

wan wan wan wan wan

was was was was was

wav wav wav wav wav

wax wax wax wax wax

Don't forget to leave enough space between your letters.

EXTRA

Copy these words into your book.

was	wand	wax
wash	wander	wave
wasp	want	wait

The joining lines help you to leave an equal space between your letters.

EXTENSION

Copy this poem into your book. Write the title in capital letters.

WHEN ALL THE WORLD
IS FULL OF SNOW
I never know
just where to go,
when all the world
is full of snow.
I do not want
to make a track,
not even
to the shed and back.

By N. M. Bodecker

Developing Skills

Focus

- Write the whole class sentence on the board. Point out that the **w** is joined to the letter **a** (in **water**) using a horizontal joining line.
- Discuss the **wa** join. Point out that the letters are joined using a horizontal join. The join dips down, then goes back up and over to the start of the letter **a**.
- The join ensures the letters do not touch each other. Mention that many people do not make this join correctly and the letters touch each other.
- Model the pattern and each set of letters on the board.
- Ask the children to practise the pattern and joins on their individual whiteboards.
- Tell them to copy the pattern and letters into their books.

Extra

- Discuss the fact that the **a** in **wa** often make a long flat **a** sound.
- Model writing the words **was**, **wash** and **wasp** in a column on the board. Remind the children that the joining line helps them to leave an equal space between letters.
- Ask the children to copy the words into their books.

Extension

- Read the poem.
- Ask the group to copy the poem into their ordinary writing books or on to a piece of plain paper with guidelines underneath.
- Tell them you will be checking to see if the **wa** join in **want** and the **ra** join in **track** have been made correctly.

Resources and Assessment

Focus

More practice joining to the letter **a** from the letter **w**. Copying words. Creating a sentence using one of the words.

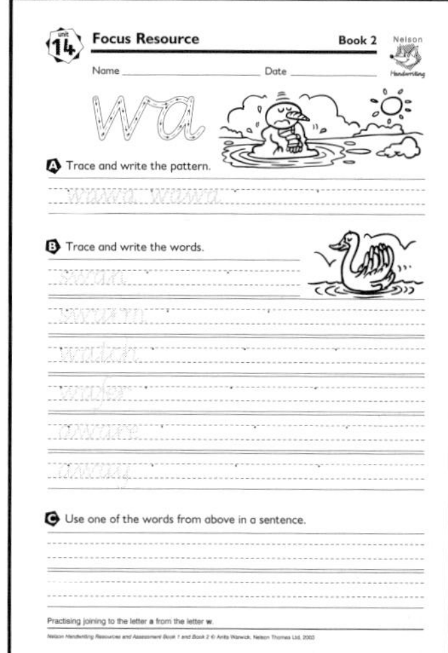

14 Focus Resource Book 2

Name Date

wa

A Trace and write the pattern.

B Trace and write the words.

C Use one of the words from above in a sentence.

Practising joining to the letter a from the letter w.

Extension

More practice writing **wa** at the beginning or middle of a word. Copying the words into the correct column to complete the table.

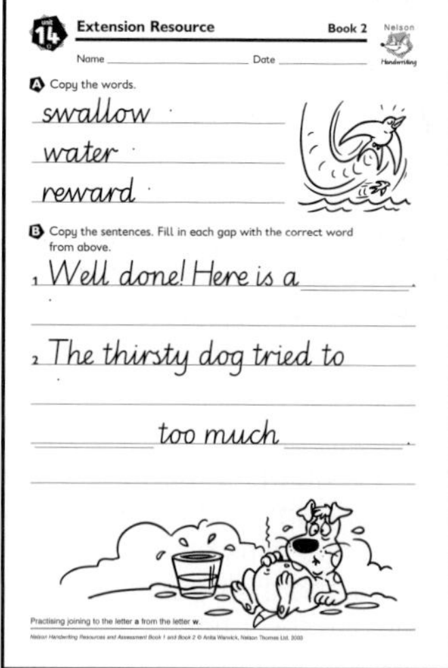

14 Extension Resource Book 2

Name Date

A Copy the words.

swallow

water

reward

B Copy the sentences. Fill in each gap with the correct word from above.

1 Well done! Here is a ______.

2 The thirsty dog tried to ______ too much.

Practising joining to the letter a from the letter w.

Assessment

- The letters **w** and **a** are joined using the third join.
- There is space between the letters **w** and **a** (i.e. the letters do not touch).
- The letters **w** and **a** are the same height.

UNIT 15

Objectives

- To write quickly and legibly.

Spelling links

- apostrophe of contraction

Nelson theme – bridges and fire

UNIT 15

Practising speedwriting.

Urgent message!

FOCUS

A Copy this pattern into your book.

dd dd dd dd

B Copy these words in speedwriting into your book.

department
ten o'clock
accident and emergency
as soon as possible

Remember, you use speedwriting when you need to write something quickly, such as a note. Your handwriting doesn't have to be neat but it must be readable.

EXTRA

The words below have a shortened form, which is useful in speedwriting. Copy the words into your book.

Road = Rd
number = no.
we will = we'll
there is = there's
as soon as possible = a.s.a.p.
ten o'clock tonight = 10.00p.m.
accident and emergency = A and E

EXTENSION

Copy this message into your book in speedwriting. Use the shortened forms from the Extra above.

Urgent message
Ten o'clock tonight
There is a fire at the old bridge on London Road. Send out fire engine number three as soon as possible.
We will contact the accident and emergency department to let them know.

Developing Skills

Focus

- Write the whole class phrase on the board quickly in front of the class.
- Compile a list of situations demanding speedwriting, e.g. making lists, making notes, taking telephone messages, drafting stories.
- Model the pattern on the board.
- Model writing each word. Ask the children if they can think of a quicker way of writing these words that might help them if they were making notes or taking a message.
- Write the abbreviated forms on the board.
- Ask children to practise the pattern on their individual whiteboards.
- Tell them to copy the pattern and words into their books.

Extra

- Point out that these words all have a shortened form, which is useful in speedwriting.
- Model writing the words and their shortened forms.
- Ask the children to copy the word abbreviations into their books.

Extension

- Read the message.
- Discuss which words could be shortened.
- Ask the children to copy the message into their books using the shortened forms from the Extra section.
- Tell the children to use speedwriting for this exercise.

Resources and Assessment

Focus

Writing out detective's quick notes in full.

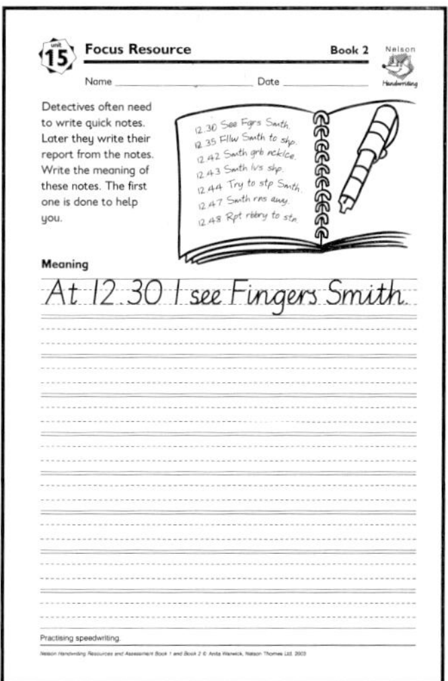

15 Focus Resource Book 2 Nelson Handwriting

Name ______ Date ______

Detectives often need to write quick notes. Later they write their report from the notes. Write the meaning of these notes. The first one is done to help you.

12.30 See Fgrs Smth.
12.35 Fllw Smth to shp.
12.42 Smth grb ncklce.
12.43 Smth lvs shp.
12.44 Try to stp Smth.
12.47 Smth rns awy.
12.48 Rpt rbbry to stn.

Meaning

At 12.30 I see Fingers Smith.

Practising speedwriting.

Nelson Handwriting Resources and Assessment Book 1 and Book 2 © Anita Warwick, Nelson Thornes Ltd, 2003

Extension

Making quick notes for two pizza orders taken over the telephone.

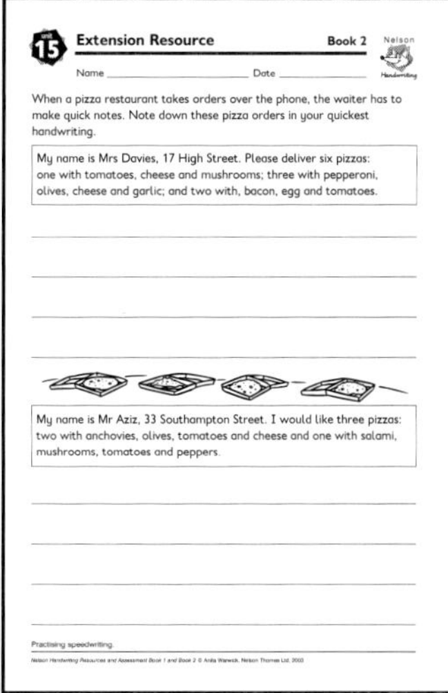

15 Extension Resource Book 2 Nelson Handwriting

Name ______ Date ______

When a pizza restaurant takes orders over the phone, the waiter has to make quick notes. Note down these pizza orders in your quickest handwriting.

My name is Mrs Davies, 17 High Street. Please deliver six pizzas: one with tomatoes, cheese and mushrooms; three with pepperoni, olives, cheese and garlic; and two with, bacon, egg and tomatoes.

My name is Mr Aziz, 33 Southampton Street. I would like three pizzas: two with anchovies, olives, tomatoes and cheese and one with salami, mushrooms, tomatoes and peppers.

Practising speedwriting.

Nelson Handwriting Resources and Assessment Book 1 and Book 2 © Anita Warwick, Nelson Thornes Ltd, 2003

Assessment

- The writing slants slightly to the right.
- The letters are joined correctly.
- The writing is quick but legible.

UNIT 16

Objectives

- To write the print alphabet.
- To use print letters to write a caption.

Spelling links

- occurrence of certain letters within words, e.g. **k**; deduce some of the conventions for using them at the beginning, middle and end of words.

Nelson theme – bridges

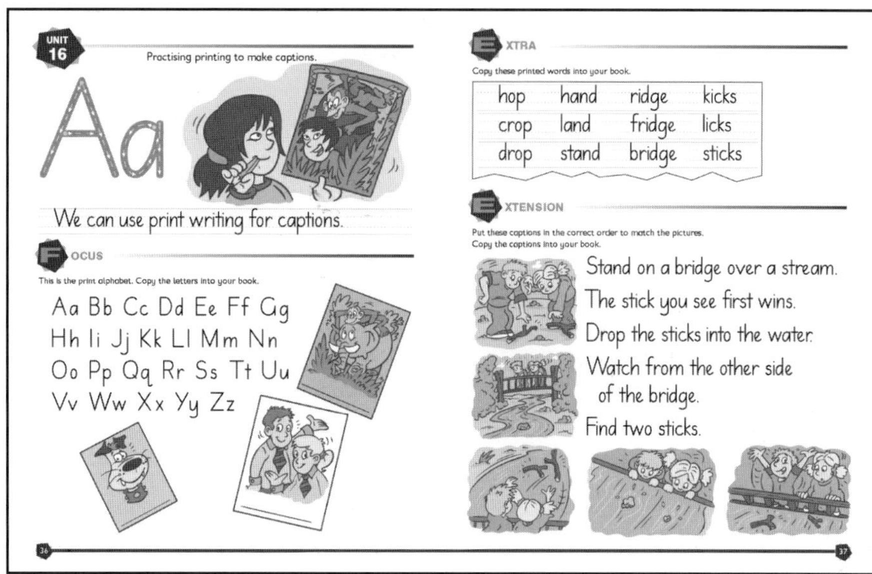

Developing Skills

Focus

- Write the printed whole class sentence on the board.
- Discuss the difference between lower case print letters and lower case letters for handwriting *(i.e. there are no exit flicks and the letters* ***f*** *and* ***k*** *are shaped differently)*.
- Ask when we might want to use print script *(e.g. for filling in forms, writing labels, labelling a parcel, labelling a diagram or illustration, writing captions)*.
- Look at the print alphabet.
- Model writing some of the print alphabet, both capital and lower case letters, on the board.
- Point out that the capital letters are the same as for joined writing.
- Ask the class to practise writing the print alphabet on their whiteboards before copying it into their books.

Extra

- Model writing the first column (**hop**, **crop**, **drop**). Point out that the letter **p** has a descender – its tail goes below the line.
- Next write the last column of words on the board (**kicks**, **licks**, **sticks**).
- *Extension activity:* either brainstorm a list of words containing the letter **k** or ask the class to write a list on their whiteboards using print letters.
- Discuss where **k** most frequently appears within words and what letters most frequently precede or follow it. Point out that **k** is often preceded by **l**, **r**, **n** and **c** at the end of words, and that it is rarely preceded by a vowel (**wok** and **yak** are exceptions).
- Ask the children to use print letters to copy the words in columns into their books.

Extension

- Read the instructions.
- Look at the pictures and discuss the correct order.
- Ask the children to copy the captions into their books, making sure the order matches the pictures.

Resources and Assessment

Focus

Using print to write the labels in the correct places on a street plan.

Extension

Using print to write the names of cities in the correct places on a map of Europe.

Assessment

- The letters are the correct height and size.
- Print letters do not have an exit flick.
- The letters **f** and **k** are printed correctly.

NIT 17

Objectives

- To write in different ways for different audiences and purposes.
- To practise drafting and editing.

Spelling links

- regular spelling rules, e.g. add **es** in plural of most words ending in **ch**

Nelson theme – Roald Dahl

UNIT 17

Practising drafting and editing.

Roald Dahl wrote famously funny books.

FOCUS

These words have been edited.
Write the corrected words into your book.

toock b/st funy
b/ok gest bunney
loook quyst runey

Correcting your writing in the first draft will help you produce a neat and tidy final draft.

EXTRA

This draft has been edited.
Write the new draft into your book.

Roald
R. Dahl was born in 1817 and died
the
in 1990. He wrote funniast
children's books in the world!
In 1964 he wrote his bst-selling book
'Charlie and the Chocolate Factry'.

EXTENSION

Use your best handwriting to copy this final draft into your book.

My favourite Roald Dahl book is 'The Twits'. It is about Mr and Mrs Twit and the tricks they play on each other. The worm spaghetti was the best trick and made me laugh!

Developing Skills

Focus

- Before the lesson, draw four lines and write the whole class sentence on the board.
- Talk about writing in different ways for different audiences and purposes. Explain that the way we write depends on what we are writing and who is going to read it
- Use the edited words to introduce the idea of drafting. Think about an author writing the first draft of a story. Discuss other occasions when drafting might be useful, e.g. when planning stories, writing down a recipe, making quick notes or doing other written work.

Extra

- Further practice is given with edited words. These words enable children to practise editing a first draft.
- Model writing the first sentence asking the children to suggest the corrections.
- Tell the children to write the draft into their book, remembering to make the corrections and not copy out the errors

Extension

- This is an example of the final stage of drafting and editing: making the final neat copy.
- Read the three sentences about Roald Dahl.
- Ask the children to copy the draft neatly into their books.

Resources and Assessment

Focus

Writing a neat copy from a corrected first draft.

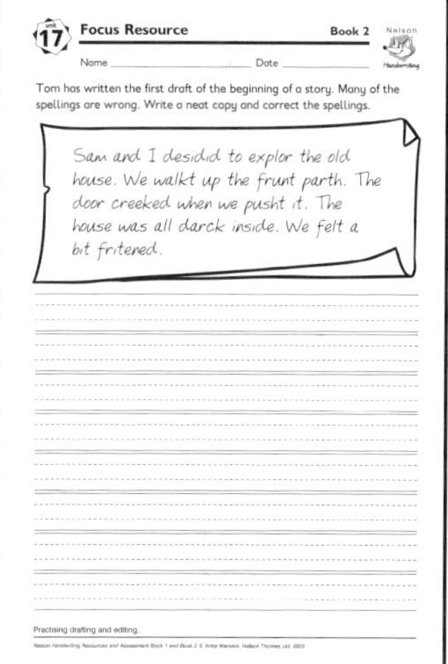

17 Focus Resource Book 2

Name ______ Date ______

Tom has written the first draft of the beginning of a story. Many of the spellings are wrong. Write a neat copy and correct the spellings.

Sam and I desidid to explor the old house. We walkt up the frunt parth. The door creeked when we pusht it. The house was all darck inside. We felt a bit fritened.

Practising drafting and editing.

Extension

Writing a neat copy from a partially corrected first draft.

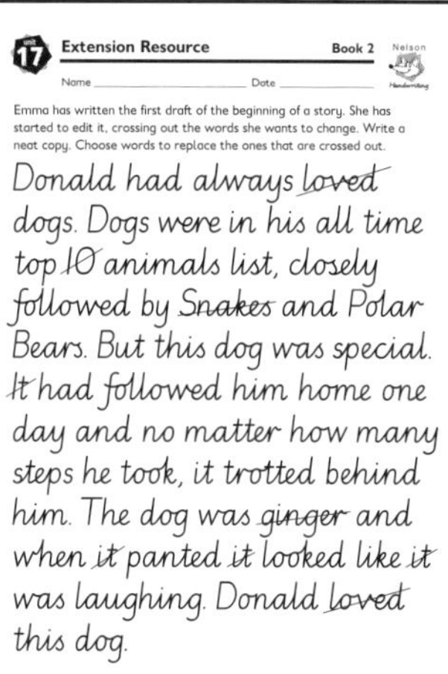

17 Extension Resource Book 2

Name ______ Date ______

Emma has written the first draft of the beginning of a story. She has started to edit it, crossing out the words she wants to change. Write a neat copy. Choose words to replace the ones that are crossed out.

Donald had always ~~loved~~ dogs. Dogs were in his all time top ~~10~~ animals list, closely followed by ~~Snakes~~ and Polar Bears. But this dog was special. ~~It~~ had followed him home one day and no matter how many steps he took, it trotted behind him. The dog was ~~ginger~~ and when ~~it~~ panted ~~it~~ looked ~~like it~~ was laughing. Donald ~~loved~~ this dog.

Practising drafting and editing.

Assessment

- Corrections are made accurately.
- The corrected words are written neatly and with the same style as the rest of the handwriting.

UNIT 18

Objectives

- To practise speedwriting.
- To use shortened forms of words.

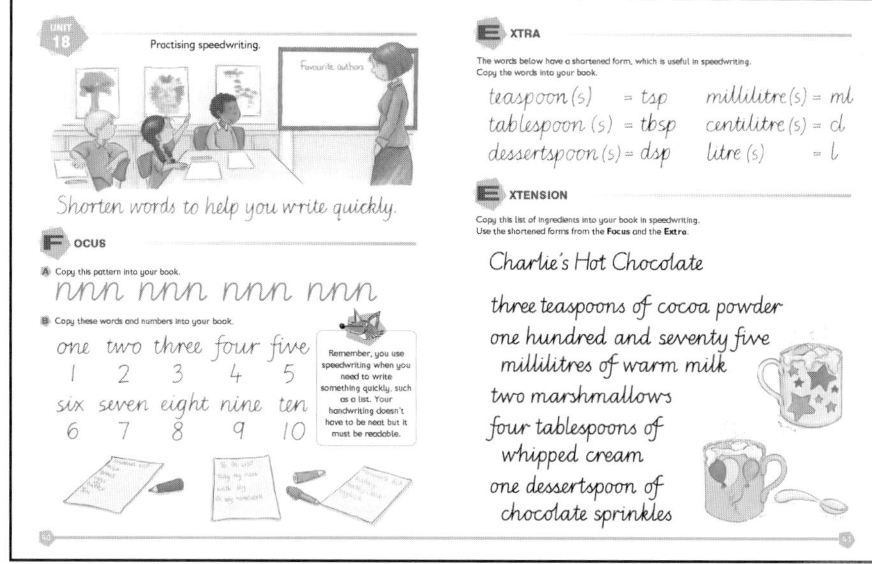

UNIT 18

Practising speedwriting.

Shorten words to help you write quickly.

FOCUS

A Copy this pattern into your book.

nnn nnn nnn nnn

B Copy these words and numbers into your book.

one two three four five
1 2 3 4 5
six seven eight nine ten
6 7 8 9 10

Remember, you use speedwriting when you need to write something quickly, such as a list. Your handwriting doesn't have to be neat but it must be readable.

EXTRA

The words below have a shortened form, which is useful in speedwriting. Copy the words into your book.

teaspoon(s) = tsp
tablespoon(s) = tbsp
dessertspoon(s) = dsp
millilitre(s) = ml
centilitre(s) = cl
litre(s) = l

EXTENSION

Copy this list of ingredients into your book in speedwriting. Use the shortened forms from the Focus and the Extra.

Charlie's Hot Chocolate

three teaspoons of cocoa powder
one hundred and seventy five millilitres of warm milk
two marshmallows
four tablespoons of whipped cream
one dessertspoon of chocolate sprinkles

Spelling links

- Compound words

Nelson theme – Roald Dahl

Developing Skills

Focus

- Before the lesson, draw four lines and write the whole class sentence on the board.
- Remind the class that joining letters and slanting writing slightly to the right will help them write quickly.
- Writing a numeral, instead of the word, also helps when you need to write quickly.
- Model writing the words **one** to **ten**. Point out that all the letters join, except for **g** in **eight**.
- Write the numerals. Point out that numerals are as tall as ascenders.
- Demonstrate the pattern on the board. Note that the diagonal joining line joins to the top of the letter **n**, not to the bottom. Write the pattern quickly to encourage writing at speed yet maintaining legibility.
- Ask the children to copy the pattern on to their whiteboards or into their books quickly and legibly.
- Tell them to copy the words and numerals into their books.

Extra

- Discuss how abbreviations, e.g. **tsp** for **teaspoon** are useful when you want to write something quickly.
- Ask the class for a list of words and how they could be shortened, e.g. when writing out a recipe. They could work in pairs, using their whiteboards.
- Model writing the words and their shortened forms.
- Point out that the words **teaspoon**, **tablespoon** and **dessertspoon** are all compound words. Discuss whether **millilitre** and **centilitre** are compound words.
- Point out that the letters in the shortened form of the word still join.
- Ask the children to copy the words into their books.

Extension

- Discuss the ingredients for 'Charlie's Hot Chocolate'.
- Ask the group which words could be shortened.
- Tell them to copy the list of ingredients using the shortened forms for words, as appropriate.

Resources and Assessment

Focus

Writing the number words **eleven** to **twenty** and the shortened forms, i.e. numerals **11**–**20**.

18 Focus Resource — Book 2

Name ____ Date ____

When you need to write quickly, use numerals instead of number words.

A Write the numerals as fast as you can.

B Write the number words as fast as you can.

Practising speedwriting

Extension

Reading newspaper article about a fire. Writing quick notes the reporter might have made at the scene.

18 Extension Resource — Book 2

Name ____ Date ____

Reporters have to write quickly. They often use notes. This is a reporter's finished article.

A Underline the main points in the article.

I ARRIVED AT THE SCENE of the fire at 10 o'clock at 15 Brookside. The fire brigade arrived at 10.05. At 10.06 I saw flames coming through the roof. A woman appeared at an upstairs window and screamed. By 10.08 the firefighters were using water hoses on the fire. A crowd had gathered. At 10.10 a ladder went up and a firefighter climbed it. At 10.12 he reached the upstairs window. Flames appeared behind the woman. At 10.13 the firefighter carried the woman down. She was put in an ambulance and taken to the QE II hospital.

B Now finish the notes from which the article was written.

10.00 Arr. at fr. 15 Brksd.
10.05 Fr. bdgd. arr.

Practising speedwriting

Assessment

- The letters are joined and slanting slightly to the right.
- The children are writing quickly and legibly.
- Shortened forms have been used correctly.

NIT 19

Objectives

- To write the letter **t** correctly.
- To join and cross the letter **t** correctly.

Spelling links

- possessive **its** and contraction **it's**.

Nelson theme – country pursuits

UNIT 19 Practising joining to the letter **t**.

it

It's up to us to protect the countryside.

FOCUS

A Copy this pattern into your book.

B Copy these letters into your book.

its its its its its
lts lts lts lts lts
tts tts tts tts tts
uts uts uts uts uts

Remember, the letter t is not as tall as other letters with an ascender.

EXTRA

its and it's are often confused but
it's = it is and its = belonging to it
Choose the correct word to finish each sentence. Copy the sentences into your book.

1 We saw a bird make its/it's nest in the tree.
2 Its/It's important to take your litter home with you.

Remember to use your best handwriting when you want to present neat, careful work.

EXTENSION

Copy this poem into your book. Write the title in capital letters.

WE MUST PROTECT THE COUNTRYSIDE
We must protect the countryside –
The flowers and the trees.
We must protect the animals.
It's up to you and me.
Don't throw litter on the ground.
Please put it in a bin,
And close the gate behind you
To keep the cattle in. By John Foster

Developing Skills

Focus

- Write the whole class sentence on the board. Point out that the letter **t** is crossed after you have finished writing the word.
- Discuss the use of the apostrophe when writing **it's**. Explain that **it's** is the contracted form of **it is**.
- Discuss the height and size of the letter **t**. It is not as tall as the ascenders of other letters.
- Demonstrate the pattern. Note the different height of the lines and the diagonal joining lines.
- Suggest the children practise the pattern on their whiteboards.
- Model writing each set of letters.
- Ask the class to copy the pattern and letters into their books.

Extra

- Discuss the difference between **it's** and **its**. Point out that these two words are often confused but **it's** is the contracted form of **it is** while **its** means 'belonging to it'.
- Read the sentences – discuss which word is correct.
- If time, model writing the sentences on the board.
- Ask the children to choose the correct word and copy the sentences into their books.

Extension

- Read the poem.
- Tell the children to copy the poem into their books.

Resources and Assessment

Focus

More practice forming and joining the letter **t** using the words **its** and **it's**. Copying sentences and inserting correct word.

19 Focus Resource Book 2

Name Date

it

A Trace and write the words.

B Trace and write the sentences. Fill in each gap with the correct word from above.

1

2

Practising joining to the letter t

Extension

More practice joining to the letter **t**. Copying poem, crossing the letter **t** after writing the word.

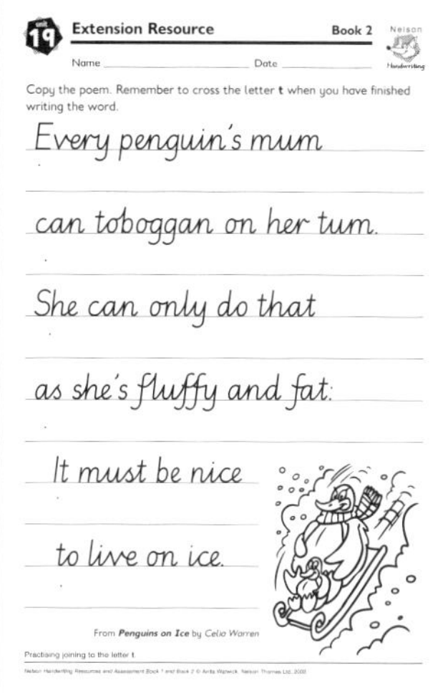

19 Extension Resource Book 2

Name Date

Copy the poem. Remember to cross the letter t when you have finished writing the word.

Every penguin's mum
can toboggan on her tum.
She can only do that
as she's fluffy and fat.
It must be nice
to live on ice.

From *Penguins on Ice* by Celia Warren

Practising joining to the letter t

Assessment

- The join to the letter **t** is made at x-height.
- The letter **t** is the correct height and size.
- The letter **t** is crossed after the word has been written and the cross is just above the x-height.

SCOPE AND SEQUENCE
DEVELOPING SKILLS BOOK THREE

Page	Focus	Extra	Extension	Focus resource	Extension resource
4-5 Flashback	*Flashback*	*Flashback*	*Flashback*	*Flashback*	*Flashback*
6-7 Unit 1 Disasters	ensuring letters are consistent in height and size	add suffixes ing and ed to words	copy poem	copy words ending with single consonant preceded by short vowel, double the final consonant to add ing and ed	copy passage and ensure letters are consistent in height and size
8-9 Unit 2 Disasters	practising with punctuation	use an apostrophe to show where letters have been missed out	copy sentences	copy sentences and put in exclamation mark	copy sentences and add an apostrophe in the correct place
10-11 Unit 3 Journeys	practising break letters	copy alliterative sentences	copy extract	copy break letters, form plural of words ending in o	practise break letters, copy words and write dictionary definition
12-13 Unit 4 Journeys	practising joining from the letter m; writing definitions of four words	choose words and copy sentences	copy extract	use the diagonal line to join from the letter m (to make sure there is a space between letters)	practise using diagonal joining lines and copy poem
14-15 Unit 5 Space and planets	ensuring the ascender on the letter t is the correct height	choose words and copy sentences	copy extract	add the prefix inter to words	practise ensuring letter t is not as tall as other letters with an ascender and copy extract
16-17 Unit 6 Space and planets	practising spacing within words	copy words using diagonal and horizontal joining lines	choose correct words to finish sentences, copy sentences	practise spacing within words, use suffixes tion and sion	practise leaving spaces within words, write definitions for words beginning with prefix tele
18-19 Unit 7 London	developing fluency	choose words and copy sentences	copy poem	develop fluency, add s to make plurals	practise writing fluently and legibly and copy poem
20-21 Unit 8 London	practising writing a playscript; writing definitions of five words	copy a playscript	copy play extract	practise writing a playscript	finish writing a playscript
22-23 Unit 9 Flight	practising printing	make a timeline with labels in print handwriting	copy newspaper report	use print to write the names of countries in the correct place on a map	print instructions for making a compass
24-25 Unit 10 Flight	practising forming and joining the letter f	copy homophones, choose correct homophone and copy sentences	copy tongue-twister	practise forming and joining the letter f, drop f and add ves to make plurals	practise forming and joining the letter f and copy poem

Page	Focus	Extra	Extension	Focus resource	Extension resource
26-27 Unit 11 Night	practising presentation	copy words, choose word from Focus section with similar meaning and copy	copy poem on to plain paper and decorate with border	read and copy two poems and add decoration	copy a poem, paying particular attention to presentation
28-29 Unit 12 Night	practising writing shape poems; copying antonyms in a style of writing suited to each word	copy shape poem	copy shape poem	copy shape poem	copy shape poem
30-31 Unit 13 Australia	practising printing; copying address label in print handwriting	draw picture and print labels	match labels to pictures and print labels	practise printing, copy print letters and print names and addresses	use the print alphabet to copy signs seen in the environment
32-33 Unit 14 Australia	practising speedwriting; copying patterns	copy list of words, dotting i and crossing t on completing the word to increase speed	copy extract from a holiday notebook in speedwriting	practise patterns to help speedwriting, double the final consonant to add ing, ed or er to words	copy patterns and sentences to practise smoothness and steadiness, calculate and record writing speed
34-35 Unit 15 Caribbean	practising writing decorated capital letters	copy words from poem and decorate the first letter of each word	copy poem and use decorated capital letters to start each line	practise writing capital letters with flourishes, copy an acrostic poem and use decorated capitals	use another style of decorated capital letters to practise writing the names of famous buildings
36-37 Unit 16 Caribbean	practising writing letters; practising writing addresses correctly	copy letter endings such as yours faithfully and kind regards	copy letter on to blank paper and set out correctly	practise copying a letter in best handwriting	finish writing a letter and fill in the missing details
38-39 Unit 17 Strange stories and mythical creatures	practising paragraphs	copy a list of features, use it to write a paragraph describing a Martian	copy sentences and divide them into two paragraphs	copy a paragraph and remember to indent the first word	rewrite the information as two paragraphs
40-41 Unit 18 Strange stories and mythical creatures	practising presentation; copying border patterns	copy first verse of poem on to plain paper and try to get the spacing even	copy second verse of poem and add decorative border	copy a poem and a limerick, finish decorating their borders	copy shape poem
42-43 Unit 19 Religion	revising difficult joins ve, we, oe, fe, re; copying words that drop e when ing is added	choose words and copy passage	copy poem	practise forming difficult joins, add vowel and consonant suffixes to words ending with e	copy poem
44-45 Unit 20 Religion	looking at different handwriting styles; joining from break letters	add suffixes ful and less to words and copy in a different handwriting style	copy sentences about three religions in different writing styles	copy rhyme in usual handwriting style, then practise adding loops from g and y	copy poem in usual handwriting style, then join from b and p and add loops from f and g
46-48 Check-up	*Check-up*	*Check-up*	*Check-up*	*Check-up*	*Check-up*

FLASHBACK

Objectives

Explain to the pupils that this exercise is an assessment activity. The objective is to assess what the pupils can do from Book 2 and where they need the extra practice. This exercise will help assess each pupil's ability to form and use the four handwriting joins. Ask pupils to look at the checklist on the back of the flap to remind them of the important points.

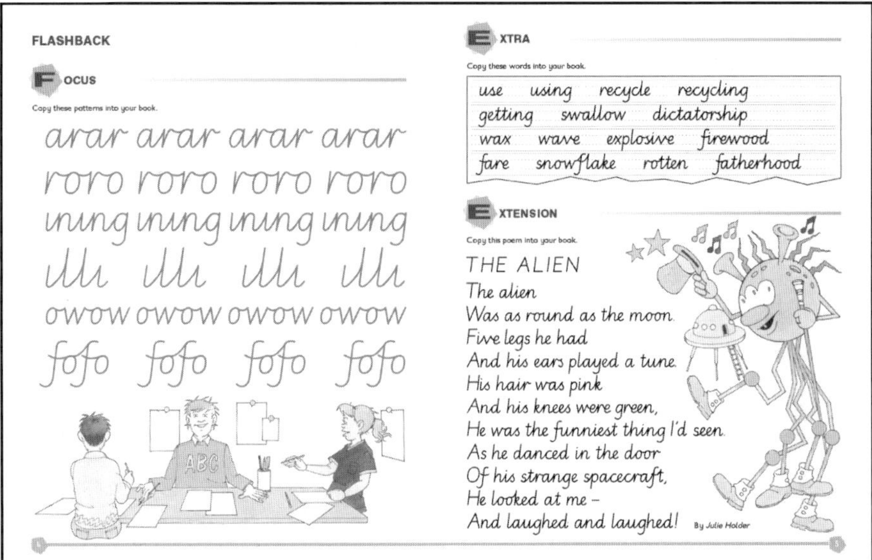

FLASHBACK

FOCUS

Copy these patterns into your book.

arar arar arar arar
roro roro roro roro
ining ining ining ining
lli lli lli lli
owow owow owow owow
fofo fofo fofo fofo

EXTRA

Copy these words into your book.

use using recycle recycling
getting swallow dictatorship
wax wave explosive firewood
fare snowflake rotten fatherhood

EXTENSION

Copy this poem into your book.

THE ALIEN
The alien
Was as round as the moon
Five legs he had
And his ears played a tune.
His hair was pink
And his knees were green,
He was the funniest thing I'd seen.
As he danced in the door
Of his strange spacecraft,
He looked at me –
And laughed and laughed!

By Julie Holder

Focus

Ask the pupils to copy the patterns into their book. The patterns are an important part of helping pupils to learn to join letters. The patterns need to be made smoothly, with the letter shapes the correct height, and spaces between the letters and between pattern blocks. These patterns are sloped and will help pupils write with an even slope.

Extra

Ask the pupils to copy these words into their books. The words in this section contain all four handwriting joins as well as some double letters, break letters and difficult joins.

Extension

Ask the pupils to copy the poem and its heading into their books. This poem incorporates a variety of punctuation marks.

Assessment

- Are the correct joins used?
- Are the letters formed correctly?
- Are any letters too tall or too short?
- Do the descenders fall below the line?
- Is there a consistent space between letters and words?
- Does the handwriting have an even slope?

- For more Assessment see *Resources and Assessment Book 3 and Book 4*

UNIT 1

Objectives

- To ensure all small letters are consistent in height and size.
- To ensure letters with descenders and ascenders are consistent in height and size.

Spelling links

- short vowel words doubling the final consonant before adding **ing** or **ed**

Nelson theme – disasters

UNIT 1 Ensuring letters are consistent in height and size.

A big wind is blowing.

FOCUS

Copy these words into your book.

mop mopping mopped
hop hopping hopped
shop shopping shopped
stop stopping stopped

Remember, the letter *p* has a descender, or tail, that goes below the line.

EXTRA

Add the suffix *ing* and then the suffix *ed* to these words. Write the words into your book. The first one is done to help you.

flow row crow tow
flowing
flowed

EXTENSION

Copy this poem into your book.

HURRICANE!
Shut the windows
Bolt the doors
Big rain coming
Climbing up the mountain.
Branches falling
Raindrops flying
Tree tops swaying
People running
Big wind blowing
Hurricane! On the mountain. By Dionne Brand

Remember to use your best handwriting when you want to present neat, careful work.

Developing Skills

Focus

- Write the lesson objectives on the board.
- Point out that the small letters are the same height and size, i.e. **i**, **w**, **n**, **s**, **o**. Emphasise that the **i** is the same height as, for example, the **n**.
- Discuss the height of letters with descenders, e.g. **g**. The body of these letters is the same height as the x-height, but they also have a descender which falls below the baseline.
- Comment on the fact that if you measured a letter with a descender and a letter with an ascender they would be the same height.
- Point out that a letter with an ascender is nearly twice the height of a small letter.
- Point out that the word **mop** contains a short vowel (if necessary, discuss the difference between long and short vowel sounds). All the Focus words end in a single consonant preceded by a short vowel. These words double the consonant before adding **ing** or **ed**.
- Tell the children to practise the words on their whiteboards before copying them into their books.

Extra

- Explain that these words all contain long vowel sounds. Point out that words ending in a consonant and preceded by a long vowel sound simply add **ing** or **ed**. Sound out the short and long vowel words in the Focus and Extra sections to help children understand the difference.
- Demonstrate writing the word **flow** – compare the height and size of the letter **f** with the letter **l**.
- Ask the children to add the missing suffixes and copy the words into their books.

Extension

- Read the poem and talk about the words that obey the spelling rules discussed above.
- Model the title and the first two lines on the board.
- Remind children to make sure their letters are consistent in height and size as they copy the poem into their books or on to plain paper with guidelines underneath.

Resources and Assessment

Focus

Further practice ensuring letters are consistent in height and size. Copying words ending in a single consonant preceded by a short vowel – the consonant is doubled before adding **ing** or **ed**.

1 Focus Resource Book 3 Nelson Handwriting

Name ______ Date ______

Words that have a short vowel before ending in a single consonant double the consonant before adding **ing** or **ed**.

Copy these words.

hum	humming	hummed
hug	hugging	hugged
beg	begging	begged
pot	potting	potted
wrap	wrapping	wrapped
trap	trapping	trapped

Ensuring letters are consistent in height and size.

Nelson Handwriting Resources and Assessment Book 3 and Book 4 © Anita Warwick, Nelson Thomes Ltd. 2003

Extension

Further practice in consistent letter formation. Copying passage.

1 Extension Resource Book 3 Nelson Handwriting

Name ______ Date ______

A Read this passage.

Gale Warning!

When the air moves about we say that the wind is blowing. Sometimes the air moves slowly and we get a gentle breeze. Sometimes it moves very quickly and storms and hurricanes occur.

In 1805, a British admiral called Sir Francis Beaufort worked out what happened at sea when the air moved at different speeds. The Beaufort Scale was adapted for the effects of wind on land and is still in use today.

B Copy the passage. Make sure your letters are consistent in height and size.

Ensuring letters are consistent in height and size.

Assessment

- All the small letters are the same height and size.
- All ascenders except that of **t** are almost twice the height of small letters.
- All letters with descenders are the same height as letters with ascenders.

UNIT 2

Objectives

- To form speech marks and apostrophes correctly.
- To ensure exclamation marks are the correct height and size.

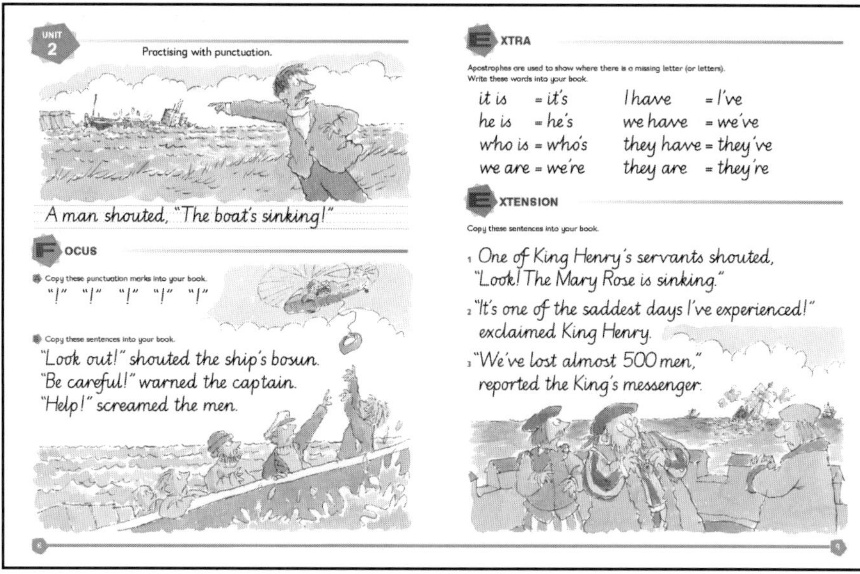

UNIT 2

Practising with punctuation.

A man shouted, "The boat's sinking!"

FOCUS

A Copy these punctuation marks into your book.

"!" "!" "!" "!" "!"

B Copy these sentences into your book.

"Look out!" shouted the ship's bosun.
"Be careful!" warned the captain.
"Help!" screamed the men.

EXTRA

Apostrophes are used to show where there is a missing letter (or letters).
Write these words into your book.

it is	= it's	I have	= I've
he is	= he's	we have	= we've
who is	= who's	they have	= they've
we are	= we're	they are	= they're

EXTENSION

Copy these sentences into your book.

1 One of King Henry's servants shouted, "Look! The Mary Rose is sinking."
2 "It's one of the saddest days I've experienced!" exclaimed King Henry.
3 "We've lost almost 500 men," reported the King's messenger.

Spelling links

- apostrophe of contraction

Nelson theme – disasters

Developing Skills

Focus

- Write the lesson objectives on the board.
- Write the whole class sentence on the board.
- Explain how and where speech marks are written, i.e. just below the top line (it may be useful to write 66 and 99 to help the children form the marks correctly).
- Explain the use of the exclamation mark. It is used here because the man is shouting that the boat is sinking.
- Point out that the exclamation mark is written before the final speech mark. It is the same height as an ascender, and the dot is made on the line in the same place as the full stop.
- Model writing the first sentence on the board.
- Suggest the children practise on their white-boards before copying the punctuation marks and sentences into their books.

Extra

- Discuss when apostrophes are used.
- Demonstrate writing an apostrophe just below the top line.
- Write the words and contractions on the board.
- Ask the children to copy the words with apostrophes into their books.

Extension

- Read the sentences.
- Discuss the use of commas, speech marks and exclamation marks.
- Tell the children to copy the sentences into their books.

Resources and Assessment

Focus

More practice writing speech marks and exclamation marks. Copying sentences and inserting exclamation marks.

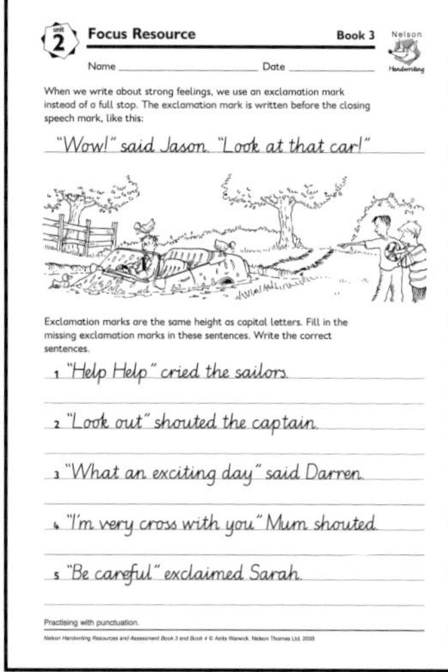

2 Focus Resource Book 3 Nelson Handwriting

Name ______ Date ______

When we write about strong feelings, we use an exclamation mark instead of a full stop. The exclamation mark is written before the closing speech mark, like this:

"Wow!" said Jason. "Look at that car!"

Exclamation marks are the same height as capital letters. Fill in the missing exclamation marks in these sentences. Write the correct sentences.

1 "Help Help" cried the sailors.
2 "Look out" shouted the captain.
3 "What an exciting day" said Darren.
4 "I'm very cross with you" Mum shouted.
5 "Be careful" exclaimed Sarah.

Practising with punctuation.

Nelson Handwriting Resources and Assessment Book 3 and Book 4 © Anita Warwick, Nelson Thomas Ltd, 2003

Extension

Practice in the two uses of the apostrophe. Copying sentences, adding missing apostrophes.

2 Extension Resource Book 3 Nelson Handwriting

Name ______ Date ______

An apostrophe looks like a comma, but it is the same height as an ascender. It shows that a letter or letters have been left out of a word or that someone owns something, like this:

I didn't want it. (The letter o has been left out.)
That is John's dinner. (The dinner belongs to John.)

A Copy these sentences. Add an apostrophe where a letter or letters have been left out.

1 Now were getting somewhere
2 That wasnt a very good idea.
3 Hes running very fast.
4 I think well still be late

B Copy these sentences. Add an apostrophe to show that someone owns something.

1 The cat is Dans pet.
2 Emilys perfect pet is a guinea pig
3 We thought the guinea pigs name was Lucy
4 But Lucy is the cats name!

Practising with punctuation.

Nelson Handwriting Resources and Assessment Book 3 and Book 4 © Anita Warwick, Nelson Thomas Ltd, 2003

Assessment

- The correct formation of speech marks.
- Speech marks and apostrophes are written just below the top line.
- Exclamation marks are the same height as ascenders, with the dot on the line.

NIT 3

Objectives

- To practise break letters.
- To ensure only a small space is left after each break letter.

Spelling links

- words ending in vowels other than **e**

Nelson theme – journeys

UNIT 3

Practising break letters.

Billy bounced his ball on Brighton beach.

FOCUS

A Copy these words into your book.

bhaji *pizza*
ciabatta *pasta*
chapatti *poppadom*

Remember, the break letters are *b, g, j, p, q, x, y* and *z*. No joins are made from these letters.

B Use a dictionary to sort the words in **A** into two groups – foods from Italy and foods from India. Write the two lists into your book and remember to give each list a heading.

10

EXTRA

A series of words beginning with the same initial sound is called alliteration. Copy these alliterative sentences into your book.

1 *Sombreros, sofas and sunbeds are ideal for siestas.*
2 *Kevin and Kim saw kangaroos, kiwis and koalas.*
3 *Pizza is perfect for peckish people.*

EXTENSION

This extract about a circus in Japan is from Jules Verne's famous book ***'Around the World in Eighty Days'***. Copy the extract into your book.

Remember, no join is made after a break letter.

The musicians, he said, took up their places and the full orchestra, with bongos, banjos, pianos, piccolos, tambourines and cellos began to play furiously.

We saw men and women with long noses. The noses were really pieces of bamboo five, six, or even ten feet long, some of them straight, others bent, some smooth, others covered with tattoos.

11

Developing Skills

Focus

- Write the lesson objectives on the board.
- Remind the children about break letters. Ask the children to tell you the names of these letters (***b**, **g**, **j**, **y**, **b**, **p**, **q**, **z***).
- Explain that the letters **g**, **j**, **q** and **y** are not joined to the letter that follows because they finish with a descender. Joining from the base of the descender to the correct point on the next letter would either double the gap between the letters or halve the angle of the join.
- The letters **b** and **p** are not joined to the following letter because their final curve goes against the flow of writing. (This is also true of the letter **s**, but because it is used so frequently, it is treated as an exception.)
- The letter **z** is not joined to the next letter because it is made up of straight lines and adding an exit flick would alter its shape.
- The **x** is not joined because the second stroke finishes on the left, making it impossible to join.
- Model writing the food words on the board.
- Suggest the children practise the words on their whiteboards before copying them into their books.

Extra

- Read and discuss the alliterative sentences.
- Point out that most nouns ending in **a**, **i** or **o** form their plural by adding **s**. There are some exceptions: some words ending in **o** take **es** in the plural, e.g. **tomatoes**.
- Model the first sentence on the board. Point out that the letter **b** is a break letter. Stress that not too large a space should be left after a break letter because the whole word must read as a single unit.
- Ask the children to copy the sentences into their books.

Extension

- This is an extract from *Around the World in 80 Days*.
- Read the extract. Discuss plurals that obey the spelling rules discussed in the Extra section.
- Remind the children to take care with break letters as they copy the extract into their books.

Resources and Assessment

Focus

Further practice writing break letters, ensuring letters are consistent in height and size. Copying plurals of words ending in the letter **o**.

unit 3 **Focus Resource** **Book 3** Nelson Handwriting

Name ____________ Date ____________

A Break letters do not join. Copy the break letters.

b p g q j x y z

B Most nouns ending in **o** form their plural by adding **s**. Copy these singular and plural words.

yoyo	*yoyos*	
banjo	*banjos*	
bongo	*bongos*	
zero	*zeros*	
zoo	*zoos*	
igloo	*igloos*	
patio	*patios*	
piano	*pianos*	
gecko	*geckos*	

Practising break letters.

Nelson Handwriting Resources and Assessment Book 3 and Book 4 © Anita Warwick, Nelson Thornes Ltd, 2003

Extension

Further practice writing words containing break letters. Writing definitions of imported words.

unit 3 **Extension Resource** **Book 3** Nelson Handwriting

Name ____________ Date ____________

A Write each word on the line below it.

	Definition
banjo	
bongo	
gecko	
matzo	
yoyo	
piazza	
pizza	
samba	
puma	
pagoda	

B Look up each word in a dictionary and write the definition beside it.

Practising break letters.

Nelson Handwriting Resources and Assessment Book 3 and Book 4 © Anita Warwick, Nelson Thornes Ltd, 2003

Assessment

- The break letters are not joined.
- Only a small space is left after each break letter and the word reads as a unit.
- The break letters are the correct height and size.

UNIT 4

Objectives

- To use the diagonal joining line to join from the letter **m**.

Spelling links

- 'soft' **c** before **i**, e.g. **circumference**

Nelson theme – journeys

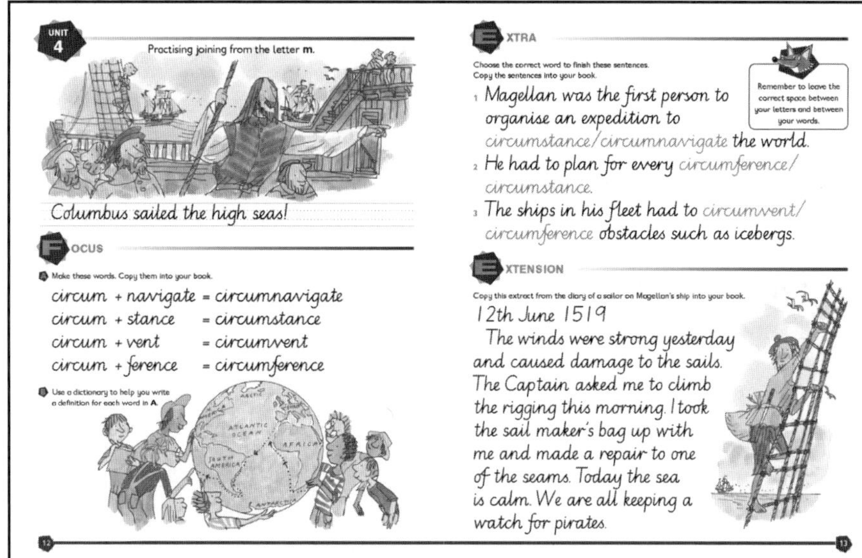

UNIT 4

Practising joining from the letter **m**.

Columbus sailed the high seas!

FOCUS

A Make these words. Copy them into your book.

circum + navigate = circumnavigate
circum + stance = circumstance
circum + vent = circumvent
circum + ference = circumference

B Use a dictionary to help you write a definition for each word in **A**.

EXTRA

Choose the correct word to finish these sentences.
Copy the sentences into your book.

Remember to leave the correct space between your letters and between your words.

1 Magellan was the first person to organise an expedition to circumstance/circumnavigate the world.
2 He had to plan for every circumference/circumstance.
3 The ships in his fleet had to circumvent/circumference obstacles such as icebergs.

EXTENSION

Copy this extract from the diary of a sailor on Magellan's ship into your book.

12th June 1519
The winds were strong yesterday and caused damage to the sails. The Captain asked me to climb the rigging this morning. I took the sail maker's bag up with me and made a repair to one of the seams. Today the sea is calm. We are all keeping a watch for pirates.

12 13

Developing Skills

Focus

- Write the lesson objectives on the board.
- Write the whole class sentence on the board between four lines.
- Point out that the join from the letter **m** is the second join from the exit stroke to near the x-height of the letter **b**.
- Look at the words in part A. Explain that **circum** is a prefix meaning *round*.
- Model writing the words on the board.
- Point out that the join from the bottom of the letter **m** must go up to the top of the x-height of the next letter and not join to the bottom.
- Remind the children that the join helps to leave the correct space between letters.
- Tell the children to practise the words on their whiteboards before copying them into their books.
- Tell the children to use a dictionary to find a definition for each word.
- Ask the children which pronunciation rule they think applies to words with the **ci** pattern. Can they think of other **c** words that belong to the **ci** group? E.g. **ce** words ***(celery, centre, cereal)***, **cy** words ***(cyclist, cyclone)***. Compare these groups with words beginning with **ca**, **co**, **cu**.

Extra

- Read the sentences.
- The children should choose the correct word to finish each sentence.
- Ask the children to copy the sentences into their books, remembering to pay attention to the joins from the letter **m**.

Extension

- Read the extract from the diary of one of the sailors who travelled with Magellan.
- Point out the words that contain the letter **m**.
- Model writing the first sentence on the board.
- Remind children that they need to slope their writing slightly to the right and join all letters, except break letters and capitals.
- Ask the class to copy the extract into their books.

Resources and Assessment

Focus

More practice joining from the letter **m**, using the prefix **auto** meaning *self*. Copying words.

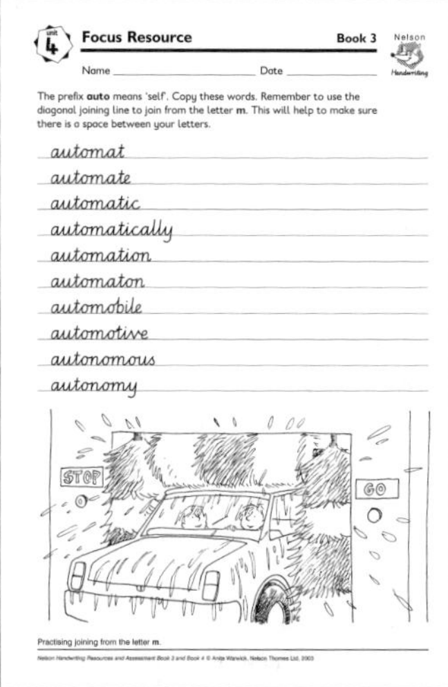

unit 4 **Focus Resource** Book 3 Nelson Handwriting

Name ______ Date ______

The prefix **auto** means 'self'. Copy these words. Remember to use the diagonal joining line to join from the letter **m**. This will help to make sure there is a space between your letters.

automat
automate
automatic
automatically
automation
automaton
automobile
automotive
autonomous
autonomy

Practising joining from the letter **m**.

Nelson Handwriting Resources and Assessment Book 3 and Book 4 © Anita Warwick, Nelson Thornes Ltd, 2003

Extension

Further practice writing words containing the letter **m** and other diagonal joins. Copying verses, using best handwriting.

unit 4 **Extension Resource** Book 3 Nelson Handwriting

Name ______ Date ______

Copy these verses on to a sheet of paper in your best handwriting.
Arrange your page attractively with good margins and some decoration.

The Owl and the Pussy-cat went to sea
In a beautiful pea-green boat,
They took some honey and plenty of money,
Wrapped up in a five-pound note.

The Owl looked up to the stars above,
And sang to a small guitar,
"O lovely Pussy! O Pussy, my love,
What a beautiful Pussy you are,
You are,
You are!
What a beautiful Pussy you are!"

From **'The Owl and the Pussy-cat'** by *Edward Lear*

Practising joining from the letter **m**.

Nelson Handwriting Resources and Assessment Book 3 and Book 4 © Anita Warwick, Nelson Thornes Ltd, 2003

Assessment

- The letter **m** is the correct height and size.
- The letter **m** is joined to the next letter using the correct diagonal joining line.
- The correct space is left between letter **m** and the next letter.

UNIT 5

Objectives

- To form and write the letter **t** correctly.
- To ensure all ascenders, except **t**, are same height and size.

Spelling links

- prefix **inter**

Nelson theme – space and planets

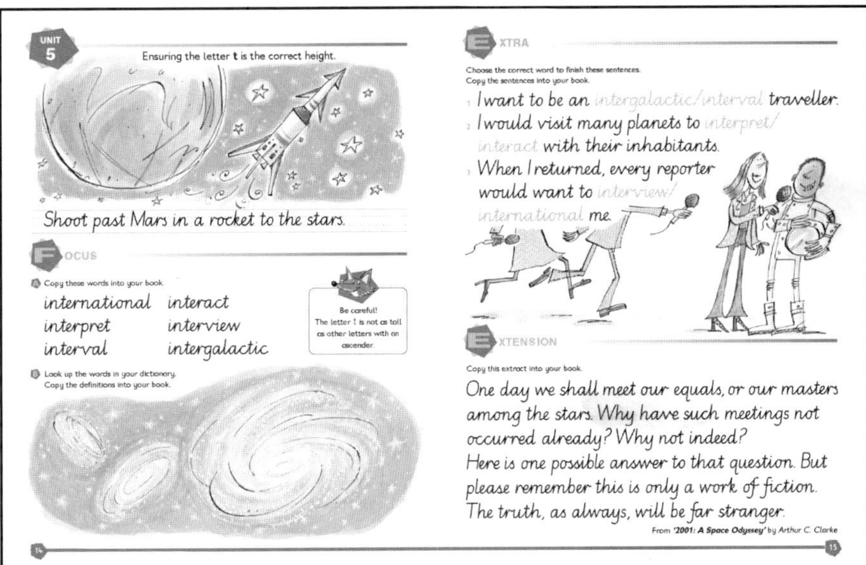

UNIT 5 Ensuring the letter **t** is the correct height.

Shoot past Mars in a rocket to the stars.

FOCUS

A Copy these words into your book.

international interact
interpret interview
interval intergalactic

Be careful! The letter t is not as tall as other letters with an ascender.

B Look up the words in your dictionary. Copy the definitions into your book.

EXTRA

Choose the correct word to finish these sentences. Copy the sentences into your book.

1 I want to be an intergalactic/interval traveller.
2 I would visit many planets to interpret/interact with their inhabitants.
3 When I returned, every reporter would want to interview/international me.

EXTENSION

Copy this extract into your book.

One day we shall meet our equals, or our masters among the stars. Why have such meetings not occurred already? Why not indeed?
Here is one possible answer to that question. But please remember this is only a work of fiction.
The truth, as always, will be far stranger.

From '2001: A Space Odyssey' by Arthur C. Clarke

14 15

Developing Skills

Focus

- Write the lesson objectives on the board.
- Write the whole class sentence on the board between four lines. Point out that the letter **t** is not as tall as the other letters with ascenders, e.g. **h** in **Shoot** and **k** in **rocket**.
- Remind the children that the letter **t** is not crossed until the word has been completed.
- Look at the words to copy. Explain that **inter** is a prefix meaning *between*.
- Model writing the words on the board, commenting as you do so that the cross on the letter **t** is made just above the x-height line.
- Suggest the children practise the words on their whiteboards before copying them into their books.
- Tell them to use a dictionary to find definitions for the words.

Extra

- Read the sentences, choosing the correct word to complete each sentence.
- Point out the height of the letter **t** compared with the ascenders of other letters.
- Ask the children to copy the sentences into their books.

Extension

- Read the extract from *2001: A Space Odyssey*.
- Point out instances of the letter **t**.
- Model writing the first sentence on the board.
- Remind children the letter **t** is crossed only when the word has been completed.
- Ask them to remember to slope their writing slightly to the right and to join all letters, except break letters and capitals.
- Tell the children to copy the extract into their books.

Resources and Assessment

Focus

More practice forming and crossing the letter **t** correctly. Adding the prefix **inter** and copying words.

5 Focus Resource Book 3

Name ______ Date ______

The prefix **inter** means 'between'. Add **inter** to each word and write the new word two or three times. The first one is done to help you.

act interact interact interact
active
change
connect
face
lock
mission
mix
national
relate
view
weave

Ensuring the letter t is not as tall as other letters with an ascender

Extension

Further practice ensuring the letter **t** is not as tall as ascenders. Copying the account of the first moon landing as neatly as possible.

5 Extension Resource Book 3

Name ______ Date ______

Copy this passage. Remember to make sure the letter **t** is not as tall as other letters with an ascender.

The First Steps on the Moon
The door of the Apollo 11 lunar module opened and Neil Armstrong emerged. He carried a backpack containing enough oxygen for four hours. Armstrong unveiled a television camera so the world could witness his first step. "That's one small step for a man, and one giant leap for mankind," he said. It was 21 July 1969. All around the world people marvelled at this great achievement and wondered what the next step would be.

Ensuring the letter t is not as tall as other letters with an ascender

Assessment

- The letter **t** is the correct height and size.
- The letter **t** is crossed when children have finished writing the word.
- The ascenders are the correct height and size, i.e. nearly twice the height of small letters (except for **t**).

NIT 6

Objectives

- To ensure letters do not touch each other.
- To leave a correct space between letters within words.

Spelling links

- suffix **ation**
- prefix **tele**

Nelson theme – space and planets

UNIT 6

Practising spacing within words.

Twinkle, twinkle, little star.

FOCUS

A Copy these letters into your book.

ation ation ation ation ation

Look at how the joining line goes up to the top of the next letter. This helps to make sure the spacing within a word is consistent.

B Copy these words into your book.

constellation station
relaxation education
habitation nation

EXTRA

A Copy these words into your book.

telephone
television
telepathic
telescope
telephoto

Remember to join your letters using the diagonal and horizontal joining lines.

B Use a dictionary to help you make a list of other words that use the prefix tele.

EXTENSION

Choose the correct word to finish these sentences.
Copy the sentences into your book.

1 A telegraph/telescope can help you see constellations.
2 A telephoto/television lens enables you to photograph distant objects.
3 Many people watched the first man walking on the moon on their television/telephone.

Remember to leave a consistent space between letters within words.

Developing Skills

Focus

- Write the lesson objectives on the board.
- Write the whole class sentence on the board between four lines. Recap the point of the last lesson, i.e. the ascender of the letter **t** is not as tall as the other ascenders.
- Point out that joining lines help to leave the correct space between letters. If we join correctly, letters will not touch each other.
- Look at the letter pattern. Explain that **ation** is a suffix.
- Read the words. Point out that a long **a** sound is often followed by **tion**.
- Model writing the words on the board, reiterating that the diagonal joins go to the top or near the top of the x-height of the next letter and not to the bottom.
- The other join is the horizontal join – this join is tricky but it helps create a space between letters and ensures letters do not touch, e.g. **on** in **ation**.
- Ask the children to practise writing and joining the letters and the words on their whiteboards before copying the words into books.

Extra

- Read the words containing the prefix **tele**.
- Ask the children if they can work out its meaning *(distant)*.
- Model writing the words. Point out the horizontal and diagonal joins.
- Talk about the break letters. Mention how care must be taken to leave the correct amount of space after a break letter.
- Ask the children to copy the words into their books.

Extension

- Read the sentences.
- The children should choose the correct word to finish each sentence.
- Remind children they need to slope their writing slightly to the right and join all letters, except break letters and capitals.
- Tell the children to copy the completed sentences into their books, remembering that letters must not touch.

Resources and Assessment

Focus

More practice leaving the correct space between letters, using suffixes **tion** and **sion**. Copying words, and underlining suffixes.

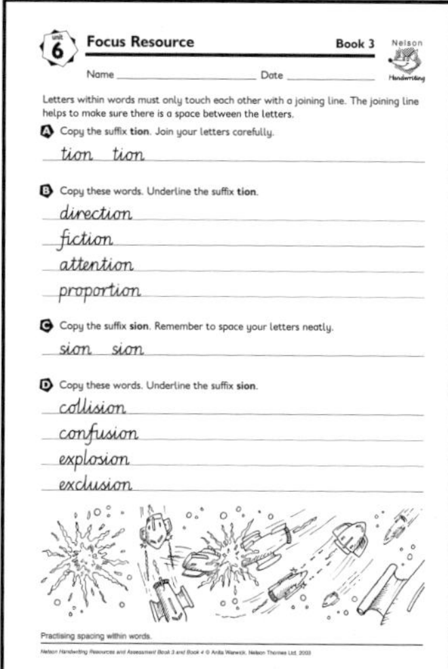

6 Focus Resource Book 3

Name ______ Date ______

Letters within words must only touch each other with a joining line. The joining line helps to make sure there is a space between the letters.

A Copy the suffix **tion**. Join your letters carefully.

tion tion

B Copy these words. Underline the suffix **tion**.

direction
fiction
attention
proportion

C Copy the suffix **sion**. Remember to space your letters neatly.

sion sion

D Copy these words. Underline the suffix **sion**.

collision
confusion
explosion
exclusion

Practising spacing within words.

Extension

Further practice leaving a correct space between letters. Matching words and dictionary definitions using best handwriting.

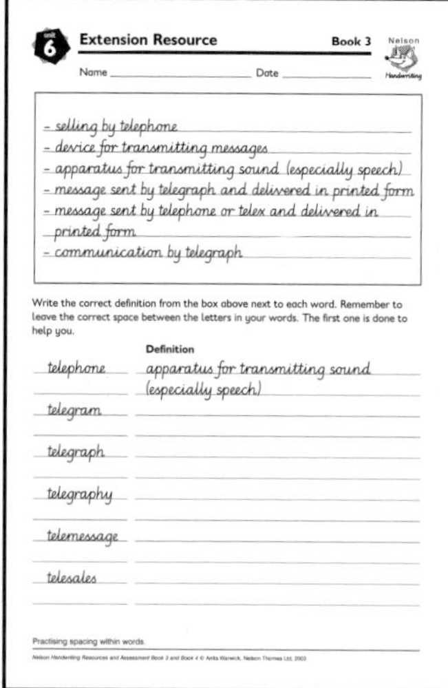

6 Extension Resource Book 3

Name ______ Date ______

- selling by telephone
- device for transmitting messages
- apparatus for transmitting sound (especially speech)
- message sent by telegraph and delivered in printed form
- message sent by telephone or telex and delivered in printed form
- communication by telegraph

Write the correct definition from the box above next to each word. Remember to leave the correct space between the letters in your words. The first one is done to help you.

	Definition
telephone	apparatus for transmitting sound (especially speech)
telegram	
telegraph	
telegraphy	
telemessage	
telesales	

Practising spacing within words.

Assessment

- The letters do not touch.
- The correct formation of horizontal joins.
- The letters using the diagonal join are joined at or near the top of the x-height of the next letter, *not* at the bottom.

UNIT 7

Objectives

- To build up handwriting speed, fluency and legibility.

Spelling links

- Regular plurals ending in **s**

Nelson theme – London

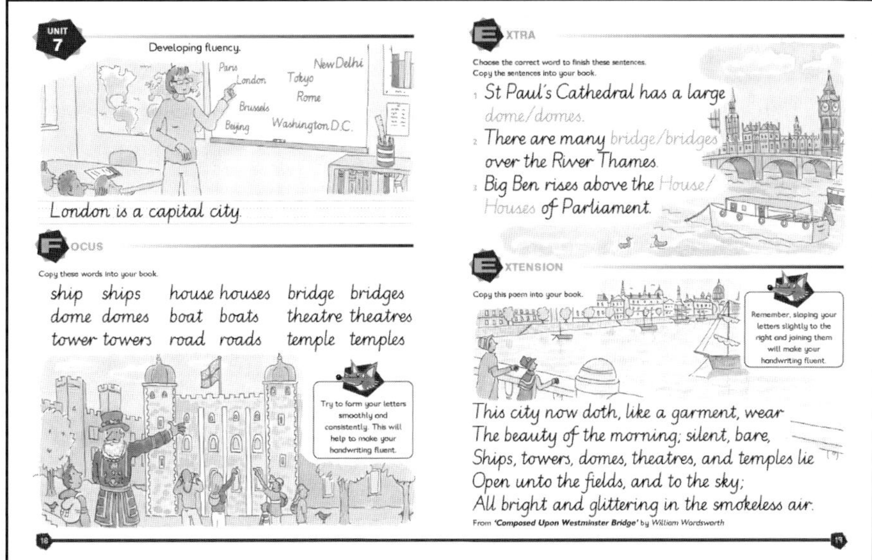

UNIT 7

Developing fluency.

London is a capital city.

FOCUS

Copy these words into your book.

ship ships house houses bridge bridges
dome domes boat boats theatre theatres
tower towers road roads temple temples

Try to form your letters smoothly and consistently. This will help to make your handwriting fluent.

EXTRA

Choose the correct word to finish these sentences. Copy the sentences into your book.

1 St Paul's Cathedral has a large dome/domes.
2 There are many bridge/bridges over the River Thames.
3 Big Ben rises above the House/Houses of Parliament.

EXTENSION

Copy this poem into your book.

Remember, sloping your letters slightly to the right and joining them will make your handwriting fluent.

This city now doth, like a garment, wear
The beauty of the morning; silent, bare,
Ships, towers, domes, theatres, and temples lie
Open unto the fields, and to the sky;
All bright and glittering in the smokeless air.

From 'Composed Upon Westminster Bridge' by William Wordsworth

18 19

Developing Skills

Focus

- Write the lesson objectives on the board.
- Write the whole class sentence on the board between four lines. Point out that the writing is slanting (about 8 degrees to the right from the vertical). Remind the class that slanting helps build up speed.
- Point out that joining letters also helps you to write more quickly– every time you finish writing a letter you take your pen back up to the top to write the next (unless it is the letter **d** or **e**).
- Remind children not to lift their pen off the paper as this hampers joining letters and prevents build-up of speed and fluency.
- Remind the children that sitting properly is important, as well as holding the pen correctly and having the paper at the correct angle.
- Model writing the plural words on the board.
- Suggest the children practise the words on their whiteboards – writing with speed, fluency and legibility. Remind them to form their letters smoothly and consistently
- Tell the children to copy the plurals into their books.

Extra

- Read the sentences.
- The children should choose the correct word to finish each sentence.
- Model writing the first sentence. Reiterate that writing smoothly and ensuring letters are consistent in height and size helps fluency and speed.
- Ask the children to copy the sentences into their books, bearing in mind all the pointers for writing fluently and quickly.

Extension

- Read the poem.
- Remind children that they need to slope their writing slightly to the right and join all letters, except break letters and capitals.
- Encourage the children to try to build up their handwriting speed whilst ensuring their writing is fluent, consistent and legible.
- Tell the children to copy the poem into their books.

Resources and Assessment

Focus

More practice developing fluency. Adding **s** to make plurals of words, using slanted writing to achieve speed whilst ensuring legibility.

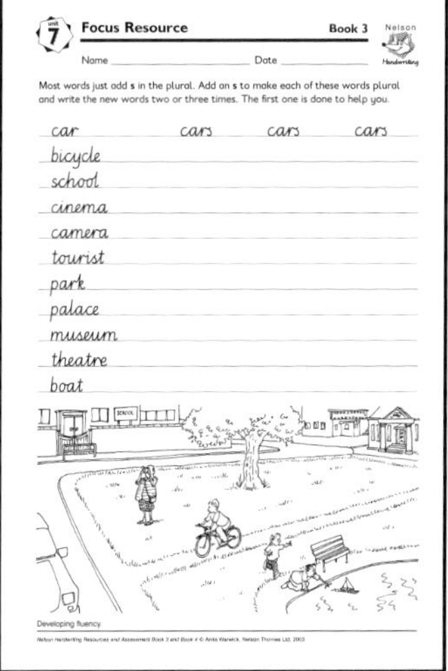

7 Focus Resource Book 3 Nelson Handwriting

Name Date

Most words just add s in the plural. Add on s to make each of these words plural and write the new words two or three times. The first one is done to help you.

car cars cars cars
bicycle
school
cinema
camera
tourist
park
palace
museum
theatre
boat

Developing fluency

Extension

Further practice writing with speed, fluency and legibility. Copying poem, taking care to join letters correctly, slanting writing slightly.

7 Extension Resource Book 3 Nelson Handwriting

Name Date

Copy this poem on to a sheet of plain paper.

BALLOONING OVER LONDON

The mist has cleared and far below
We see the snake-like river flow.

And though it's huge, the London Eye
Looks like a toy from way up high.

There's Nelson's Column – and dare we scare
The hordes of pigeons in Trafalgar Square?

We hover an hour (the air's not chilly)
Then pick up speed over Piccadilly.

Now hold on tight – we're drifting down
Above the Thames that runs through town.

Back where we started – who would have thought?
We land with a bump at Hampton Court!

By Ronald Kay

Developing fluency

Assessment

- The letters slant slightly to the right.
- All letters are joined correctly.
- Writing is legible and the height and size of letters is consistent.

UNIT 8

Objectives

- To use a range of presentational skills when writing.
- To use capital letters for headings and sub-headings.

Nelson theme – London

UNIT 8

Practising writing a playscript.

HAMLET: To be, or not to be, that is the question.

FOCUS

A Copy these words into your book.

ACT ACT ACT
SCENE SCENE SCENE
ENTER ENTER ENTER
EXIT EXIT EXIT
SOLUS SOLUS SOLUS

B Use a dictionary to help you write a definition for each of the words in A.

EXTRA

The story in a play is told through the words the characters say. Their words are set out in a special way. Copy this playscript into your book.

SHAKESPEARE: We are building our new theatre by the Thames in Southwark.
JOHN: What will you call the theatre?
SHAKESPEARE: The Globe.

EXTENSION

Copy this play extract into your book. Remember to use capital letters for the scene and the character's name.

Capital letters are as tall as ascenders.

SCENE I London. A street.

GLOUCESTER:
Now is the winter of our discontent
Made glorious summer by this sun of York;
And all the clouds that lour'd over our house
In the deep bosom of the ocean buried.

From '*Richard III*' (Act 1, scene 1) by *William Shakespeare*

Developing Skills

Focus

- Write the lesson objectives on the board.
- Write the whole class sentence on the board between four lines. Point out that this is a line from a play and that the story in a play is told through the speeches of the characters.
- List the conventions used when writing a play script, e.g. character names are sometimes written in capitals like sub-headings.
- Write the play script words on the board, reminding the class that capital letters are the same height as ascenders.
- Suggest the children practise the words on individual whiteboards before copying them into their books.
- Tell them to look up the meaning of the words in a dictionary.

Extra

- Discuss the section of play script, reinforcing the conventions of presentation and layout of dialogue.
- Ask the children to copy the speeches into their books, paying careful attention to the capital letters for the characters' names.

Extension

- Read the play extract.
- Ask the children to copy the extract into their books, using capital letters for the scene and character name.

Resources and Assessment

Focus

More practice writing a play script. Reading and copying play script, as well as observing conventions of presentation and layout.

Unit 8 Focus Resource Book 3 Nelson Handwriting

Name ______ Date ______

The story in a play is told through the speeches of the characters. The speeches are set out like this:

ROBIN: Stand back and let the better man cross!
STRANGER: I AM the better man, so get out of my way!

Copy the next part of the play.

ROBIN: You talk like a coward.
STRANGER: I am no coward.

Practising writing a playscript.

Nelson Handwriting Resources and Assessment Book 3 and Book 4 © Anita Warwick, Nelson Thomes Ltd. 2003

Extension

Further practice in presenting a play script, continuing dialogue in own words.

Unit 8 Extension Resource Book 3 Nelson Handwriting

Name ______ Date ______

Three members of a football team wanted to buy a new strip for the team. They discussed how to raise the money and decided on a garage sale. They asked their teammates to collect second-hand toys and sports equipment. James' parents agreed to let them have the sale in their garage. The three team members raised enough money to buy a new strip for everyone in the team.

Make up a playscript for this story to show how the children organised the garage sale and what happened. The script has been started for you.

The Garage Sale
JAMES: I think our team needs a new strip.
SAM: Bright green with a black collar and black sleeves would look good.
SEAN: We'll need a lot of money. How can we get it?

Continue on a sheet of paper if necessary.

Practising writing a playscript.

Nelson Handwriting Resources and Assessment Book 3 and Book 4 © Anita Warwick, Nelson Thomes Ltd. 2003

Assessment

- All capital letters are the same height and size.
- The capital letters are as tall as ascenders.
- The writing is set out correctly as a play script.

UNIT 9

Objectives

- To revise the print letters.
- To use print letters when writing labels and headings.

Nelson theme – flight

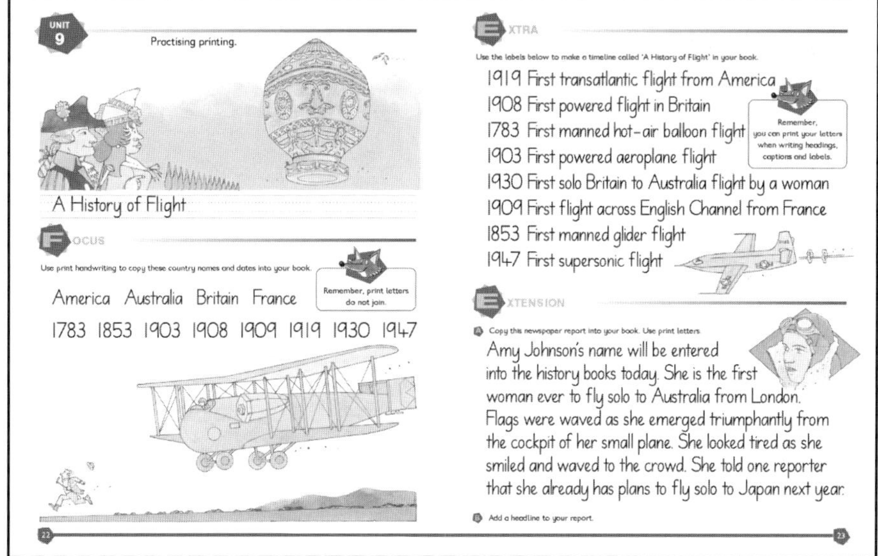

UNIT 9 Practising printing.

A History of Flight

FOCUS

Use print handwriting to copy these country names and dates into your book.

America Australia Britain France

Remember, print letters do not join.

1783 1853 1903 1908 1909 1919 1930 1947

22

EXTRA

Use the labels below to make a timeline called 'A History of Flight' in your book.

1919 First transatlantic flight from America
1908 First powered flight in Britain
1783 First manned hot-air balloon flight
1903 First powered aeroplane flight
1930 First solo Britain to Australia flight by a woman
1909 First flight across English Channel from France
1853 First manned glider flight
1947 First supersonic flight

Remember, you can print your letters when writing headings, captions and labels.

EXTENSION

A Copy this newspaper report into your book. Use print letters.

Amy Johnson's name will be entered into the history books today. She is the first woman ever to fly solo to Australia from London. Flags were waved as she emerged triumphantly from the cockpit of her small plane. She looked tired as she smiled and waved to the crowd. She told one reporter that she already has plans to fly solo to Japan next year.

B Add a headline to your report.

23

Developing Skills

Focus

- Write the lesson objectives on the board.
- Write the whole class heading on the board between four lines and ask the children when they might use print script (*writing instructions, labels, captions, headings*).
- Remind the children that print letters are very plain, making them easy to read quickly.
- Write the country names and dates on the board, using print script.
- Point out that the numerals are the same height and size as capital letters.
- Encourage the children to practise writing the words on their whiteboards before copying them into their books.

Extra

- Read the labels and talk about timelines.
- Ask the children to copy the labels, putting them in the correct order to make a timeline called, 'The History of Flight'.

Extension

- Read the newspaper report about Amy Johnson's solo flight to Australia.
- Ask the children to suggest a headline for the report.
- Tell the class to copy the report using print letters, adding their own headline.
- Remind them that reports in newspapers are written using a printed font.

Resources and Assessment

Focus

More practice printing. Using small print to write city names in the correct places on a map.

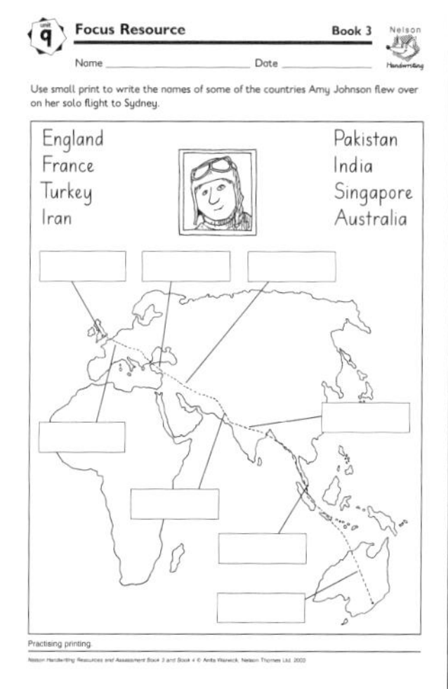

Unit 9 Focus Resource Book 3 Nelson Handwriting

Name ______ Date ______

Use small print to write the names of some of the countries Amy Johnson flew over on her solo flight to Sydney.

England
France
Turkey
Iran

Pakistan
India
Singapore
Australia

Practising printing.

Extension

Copying in print script instructions for making a simple compass.

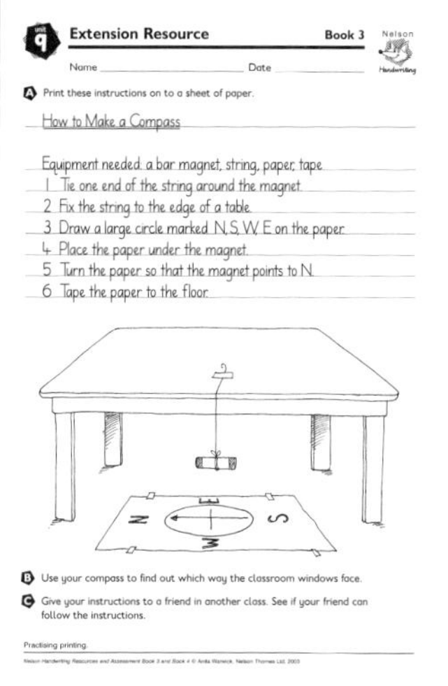

Unit 9 Extension Resource Book 3 Nelson Handwriting

Name ______ Date ______

A Print these instructions on to a sheet of paper.

How to Make a Compass

Equipment needed: a bar magnet, string, paper, tape
1 Tie one end of the string around the magnet.
2 Fix the string to the edge of a table.
3 Draw a large circle marked N, S, W, E on the paper.
4 Place the paper under the magnet.
5 Turn the paper so that the magnet points to N.
6 Tape the paper to the floor.

B Use your compass to find out which way the classroom windows face.

C Give your instructions to a friend in another class. See if your friend can follow the instructions.

Practising printing.

Assessment

- The print letters are clear and formed correctly.
- All capital letters are as tall as ascenders.
- All numerals are same height as capital letters.

NIT 10

Objectives

- To form the letter **f** correctly.
- To join to and from the letter **f** correctly.

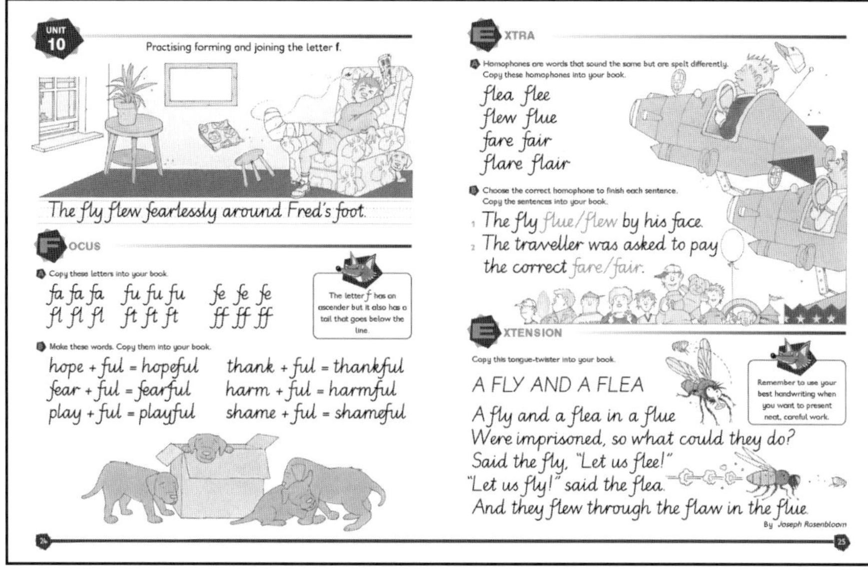

UNIT 10 Practising forming and joining the letter f.

The fly flew fearlessly around Fred's foot.

FOCUS

Copy these letters into your book.

fa fa fa fu fu fu fe fe fe
fl fl fl ft ft ft ff ff ff

The letter f has an ascender but it also has a tail that goes below the line.

Make these words. Copy them into your book.

hope + ful = hopeful thank + ful = thankful
fear + ful = fearful harm + ful = harmful
play + ful = playful shame + ful = shameful

EXTRA

Homophones are words that sound the same but are spelt differently. Copy these homophones into your book.

flea flee
flew flue
fare fair
flare flair

Choose the correct homophone to finish each sentence. Copy the sentences into your book.

1 The fly flue/flew by his face.
2 The traveller was asked to pay the correct fare/fair.

EXTENSION

Copy this tongue-twister into your book.

Remember to use your best handwriting when you want to present neat, careful work.

A FLY AND A FLEA

A fly and a flea in a flue
Were imprisoned, so what could they do?
Said the fly, "Let us flee!"
"Let us fly!" said the flea.
And they flew through the flaw in the flue.

By Joseph Rosenbloom

24 25

Spelling links

- homophones

Nelson theme – flight

Developing Skills

Focus

- Write the lesson objectives on the board.
- Write the whole class sentence on the board between four lines, pointing out the height and size of the letter **f**. It has an ascender and a descender, which goes below the baseline, as well as a straight back.
- Comment on the join. Unlike the letter **t**, the letter **f** is crossed and joined from the cross, straight after the letter itself has been formed.
- Demonstrate the series of joins: some are horizontal (**fa**, **fi**, **fe**, **fr**); some are from the cross of the **f** to the top of the next letter (**fl**, **ff**).
- Remind the children that although **fe** is a horizontal join, the pen must be brought down to enable the letter **e** to be formed correctly.
- Suggest the children practise forming and joining the letter **f** on their whiteboards.
- Discuss the **ful** words. Point out that the double **l** in **full** becomes a single **l** when used as a suffix.
- Ask the children to copy the six adjectives into their books.

Extra

- Talk about homophones. Ask the children if they can remember what they are. *(Words that sound the same but are spelt differently.)*
- Read the words and ask the children if they can think of more homophones.
- Model writing the words on the board. Point out that the letters **f** and **l** should reach the same height and the small letters (**a**, **e**, **i**, **r**) are the same height and size as each other.
- Ask the children to copy the homophones into their books.
- Then tell the children to copy the sentences into their books, choosing the correct homophone in each case.

Extension

- Read the tongue twister.
- Model writing the first two lines.
- Ask the children to copy the tongue twister into their books, bearing in mind the correct formation of the letter **f**.

Resources and Assessment

Focus

More practice forming and joining the letter **f**. Copying singular nouns ending in **f** that change to **ves** in the plural.

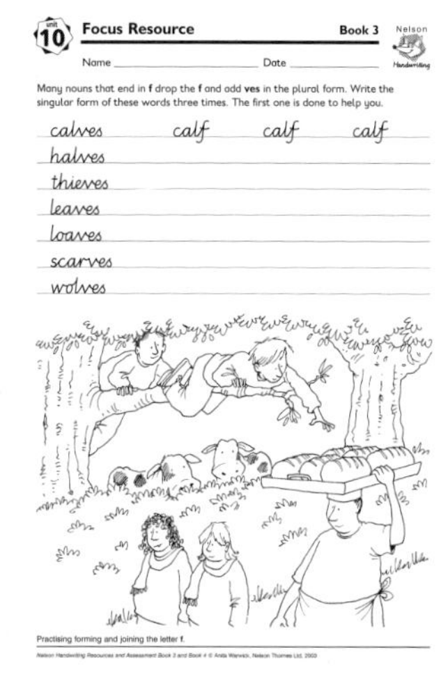

10 Focus Resource Book 3 Nelson Handwriting

Name Date

Many nouns that end in f drop the f and add ves in the plural form. Write the singular form of these words three times. The first one is done to help you.

calves calf calf calf
halves
thieves
leaves
loaves
scarves
wolves

Practising forming and joining the letter f.

Extension

Further practice joining from the letter **f**. Copying poem.

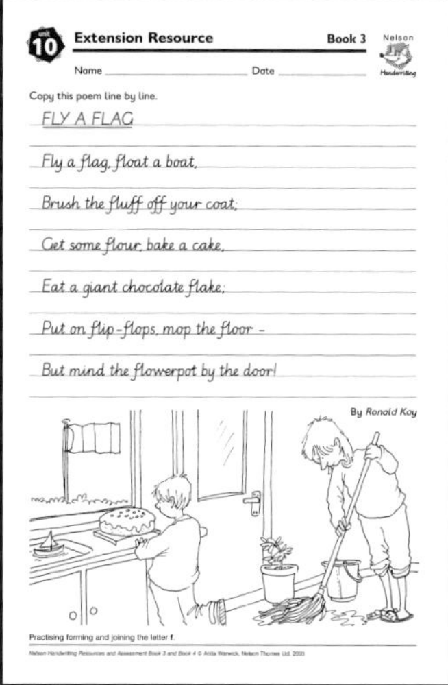

10 Extension Resource Book 3 Nelson Handwriting

Name Date

Copy this poem line by line.

FLY A FLAG

Fly a flag, float a boat,
Brush the fluff off your coat,
Get some flour, bake a cake,
Eat a giant chocolate flake,
Put on flip-flops, mop the floor –
But mind the flowerpot by the door!

By Ronald Kay

Practising forming and joining the letter f.

Assessment

- The letter **f** is as tall as the letter **l**.
- The letter **f** has a straight back and its descender goes below the baseline.
- Correct joins to and from the letter **f**.

NIT 11

Objectives

- To think carefully about how to present a poem.
- To think about spacing and margins.

Practising presentation.

That night the moonlight was very bright.

FOCUS

Copy these letters into your book.

ight ight ight ight ight

Copy these words into your book.

light sight might
plight slight flight
right bright fright

Remember, the letter g has a descender, or tail, that goes below the line.

XTRA

Copy these words into your book. Beside each word, write the word from the Focus on page 26 that has the same meaning. The first one is done to help you.

shiny bright	fear
small	flying
illumination	correct

XTENSION

Copy this poem on to plain paper. Draw a border around the edge to decorate your poem.

NIGHT COMES...

Night comes
leaking
out of the sky.

Stars come
peeking.

Moon comes
sneaking,
silvery-sly.

Who is
shaking,
shivery-
quaking?

Who is afraid
of the night?

Not I.

By Beatrice Schenk de Regniers

When using plain paper, place guidelines underneath to help keep your handwriting neat.

26 27

Spelling links

- common letter strings with different pronunciations

Nelson theme – night

Developing Skills

Focus

- Write the lesson objectives on the board.
- Write the whole class sentence on the board between four lines, underlining the words that end in **ight**.
- Model writing the letter strings and words on the board. Discuss the meaning of each word.
- Point out the size and height of the letters. Remind children the ascender of the letter **t** is not as tall as the ascenders of other letters.
- Ask the children if they can think of any more words ending in **ight**.
- Point out that an **e** before **igh** usually gives a long **a** sound, e.g. **weight**, **freight**, **neighbour**.
- Ask the class to copy the nine Focus words into their books.
- Use the poem in the Extension section to talk about generous margins and spacing.
- Read the poem and think about how you would present it.

Extra

- Read the words and discuss which words in the Focus section have a similar meaning.
- Ask the children to find a match in each case and to write both sets of words into their books.

Extension

- Ask the children to read and copy the poem, thinking carefully about presentation and use of capital letters.
- Encourage the children to think about the margins on each side of the poem, the spacing and the decoration.
- Tell the children to use plain paper, with guidelines underneath.

Resources and Assessment

Focus

Practice with writing and presentation. Copying two poems, thinking about spacing and adding decoration.

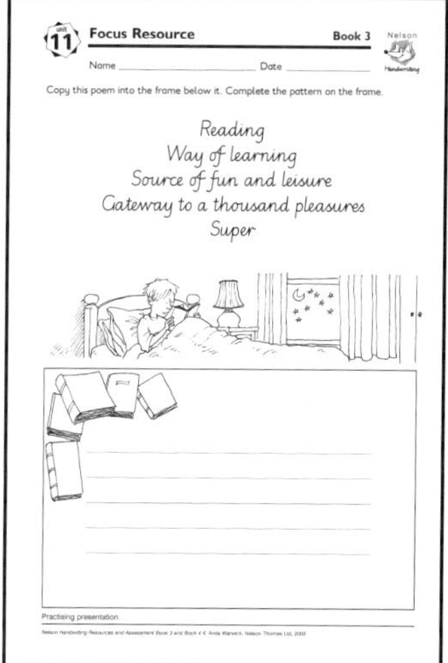

11 Focus Resource Book 3

Name Date

Copy this poem into the frame below it. Complete the pattern on the frame.

Reading
Way of learning
Source of fun and leisure
Gateway to a thousand pleasures
Super

Practising presentation

Extension

More practice with presentation. Copying poem, thinking carefully first about how to present it.

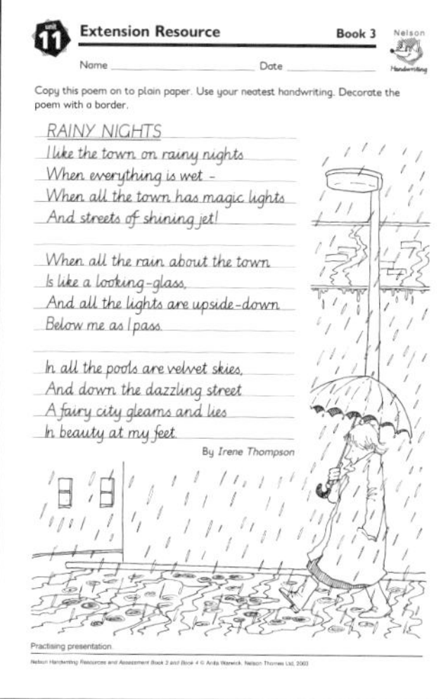

11 Extension Resource Book 3

Name Date

Copy this poem on to plain paper. Use your neatest handwriting. Decorate the poem with a border.

RAINY NIGHTS

I like the town on rainy nights
When everything is wet –
When all the town has magic lights
And streets of shining jet!

When all the rain about the town
Is like a looking-glass,
And all the lights are upside-down
Below me as I pass.

In all the pools are velvet skies,
And down the dazzling street
A fairy city gleams and lies
In beauty at my feet.

By Irene Thompson

Practising presentation

Assessment

- The correct space between letters (letters within words should not touch), words and verses.
- The correct use of the margin.
- Capital letters are used correctly.

NIT 12

Objectives

- To think carefully about how to present words.
- To use capital letters to make a poem more powerful.

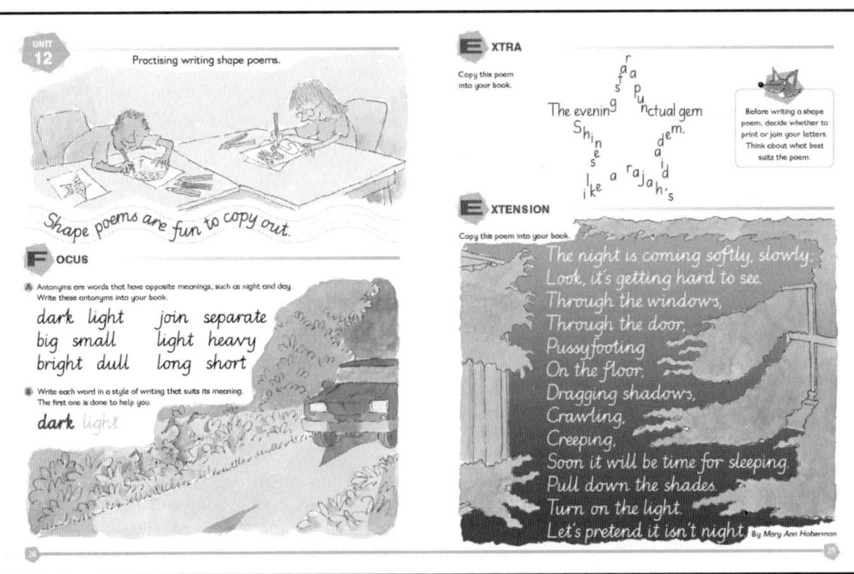

UNIT 12

Practising writing shape poems.

Shape poems are fun to copy out.

FOCUS

A Antonyms are words that have opposite meanings, such as night and day. Write these antonyms into your book.

dark light join separate
big small light heavy
bright dull long short

B Write each word in a style of writing that suits its meaning. The first one is done to help you.

dark light

EXTRA

Copy this poem into your book.

The evening star's a punctual gem.
Shines like a rajah's diadem.

Before writing a shape poem, decide whether to print or join your letters. Think about what best suits the poem.

EXTENSION

Copy this poem into your book.

The night is coming softly, slowly;
Look, it's getting hard to see.
Through the windows,
Through the door,
Pussyfooting
On the floor,
Dragging shadows,
Crawling,
Creeping,
Soon it will be time for sleeping.
Pull down the shades,
Turn on the light.
Let's pretend it isn't night.
By Mary Ann Hoberman

Spelling links

- antonyms

Nelson theme – night

Developing Skills

Focus

- Write the lesson objectives on the board.
- Write the whole class sentence on the board between four lines.
- Brainstorm a list of subjects suitable for shape poems, e.g. snakes, clouds, fireworks.
- If time permits, create a class shape poem.
- Look at the set of antonyms: words with opposite meanings, e.g. **night** and **day**.
- Discuss writing each word in a style that suits its meaning. Look at the words **dark** and **light**.
- Ask the children to practise on their own whiteboards and then to share their ideas.
- Tell the children to copy the antonyms on to paper or into their books.

Extra

- Read the poem and discuss its shape.
- Notice how the words on the theme of a star are shaped to reinforce and illustrate the theme.
- Point out the use of unjoined letters.
- Discuss the need to plan carefully how to present the words before writing. It might be useful to pencil an outline first and to work out spacing. Point out that spacing the letters is important, especially when writing a shape poem with letters that do not join.
- Ask the children to copy the poem.

Extension

- Tell the children to read and copy the poem, thinking carefully about presentation and use of capital letters.
- Encourage the children to think about the margins either side of the poem, as well as its spacing and decoration. Use plain paper, with guidelines underneath.

Resources and Assessment

Focus

Copying shape poem about fruit salad.

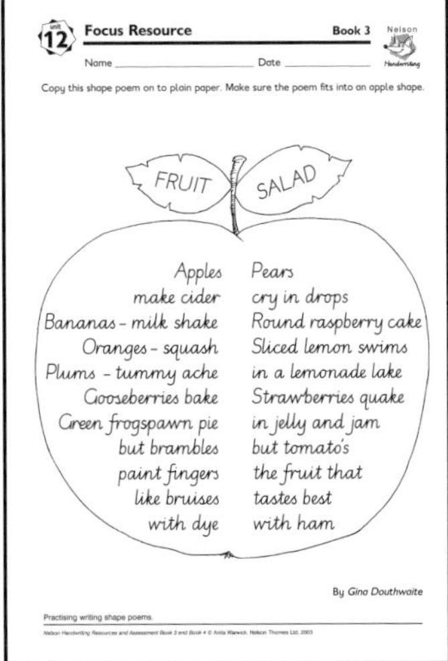

12 Focus Resource Book 3 Nelson Handwriting

Name Date

Copy this shape poem on to plain paper. Make sure the poem fits into an apple shape.

FRUIT SALAD

Apples
make cider
Bananas - milk shake
Oranges - squash
Plums - tummy ache
Gooseberries bake
Green frogspawn pie
but brambles
paint fingers
like bruises
with dye

Pears
cry in drops
Round raspberry cake
Sliced lemon swims
in a lemonade lake
Strawberries quake
in jelly and jam
but tomato's
the fruit that
tastes best
with ham

By Gina Douthwaite

Practising writing shape poems.

Extension

Copying shape poem about pollution. Writing own shape poem.

12 Extension Resource Book 3 Nelson Handwriting

Name Date

Copy this shape poem on to plain paper.

POLLUTION

SMOKE SMOKE SMOKE SMOOO
SMOKE SMOKE SMOKE SMOOO
DUST
GRIT
ACID
RAIN
BLOW
WIND
KILL
MAIM
DRIP
LEAK
FALL
RAIN
ATOM
BOMB
BURN
FLAME
CREEPING CRAWLING
OOZING SEEPING
SMELLING SWELLING
WAILING WEEPING
TECHNOLOGICALLY SPEAKING
PROGRESS IS ITS NAME

Practising writing shape poems.

Assessment

- The correct space between letters (letters within words should not touch), words and verses.
- The correct use of the margin.
- Capital letters used correctly.

UNIT 13

Objectives

- To revise print letters.
- To use print script to write labels.

Nelson theme – Australia

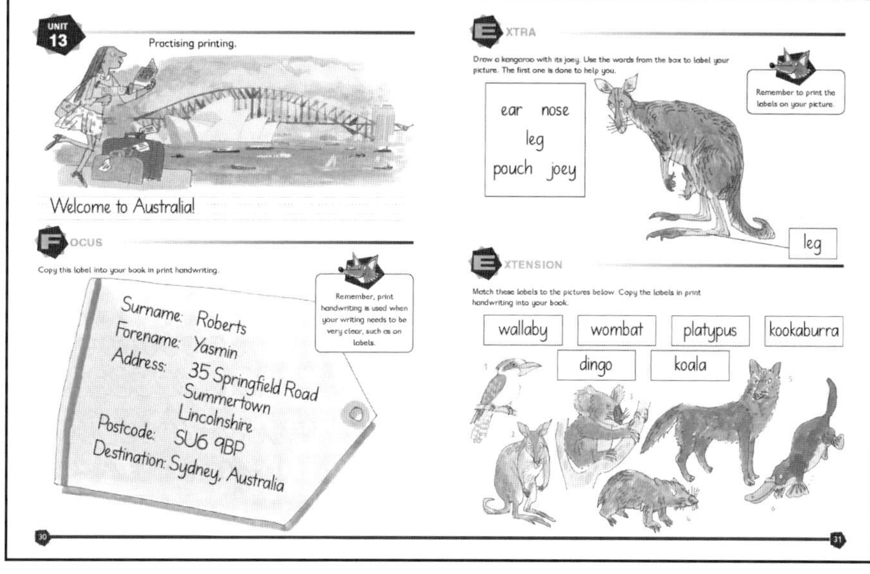

UNIT 13 Practising printing.

Welcome to Australia!

FOCUS

Copy this label into your book in print handwriting.

Surname: Roberts
Forename: Yasmin
Address: 35 Springfield Road
Summertown
Lincolnshire
Postcode: SU6 9BP
Destination: Sydney, Australia

Remember, print handwriting is used when your writing needs to be very clear, such as on labels.

EXTRA

Draw a kangaroo with its joey. Use the words from the box to label your picture. The first one is done to help you.

ear nose
leg
pouch joey

Remember to print the labels on your picture.

leg

EXTENSION

Match these labels to the pictures below. Copy the labels in print handwriting into your book.

wallaby wombat platypus kookaburra dingo koala

30 31

Developing Skills

Focus

- Write the lesson objectives on the board.
- Write the whole class sentence on the board between four lines, making clear that it is written in print script. Discuss the fact that most environmental signs are written in print. Why might this be? (*Because print is easy to read.*)
- Read the name and address on the label, which provides practice in writing most of the print letters.
- Model writing your school address on the board.
- Ask the children to practise on their whiteboards before copying the label into their books.

Extra

- Read the words in the box.
- Point out that labels need to be printed clearly.
- Tell the children to draw a kangaroo and label their picture using the words from the box.

Extension

- Tell the children to match the labels to the pictures.
- Model writing the picture number and matching the correct label.
- Ask the children to copy the labels in print writing into their books.

Resources and Assessment

Focus

Extra practice in writing all the print letters and in printing addresses.

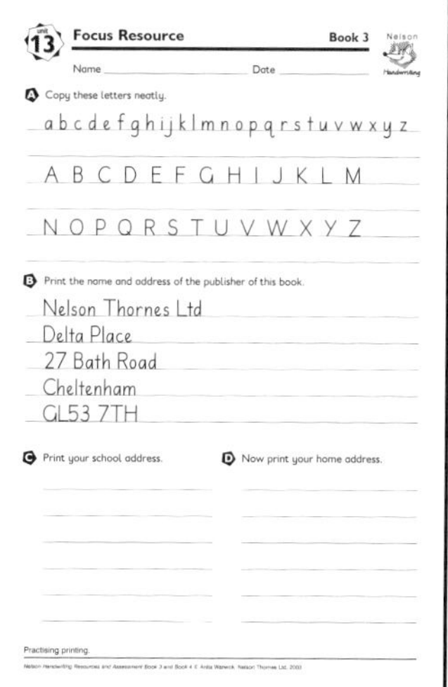

13 Focus Resource Book 3

Name Date

A Copy these letters neatly.

a b c d e f g h i j k l m n o p q r s t u v w x y z

A B C D E F G H I J K L M

N O P Q R S T U V W X Y Z

B Print the name and address of the publisher of this book.

Nelson Thornes Ltd
Delta Place
27 Bath Road
Cheltenham
GL53 7TH

C Print your school address. D Now print your home address.

Practising printing

Extension

Remind children that the print alphabet is often used for signs and notices in the environment. Brainstorm signs they might have seen. Copying signs neatly, using the print alphabet.

Printing eight more notices that they might see in the local environment.

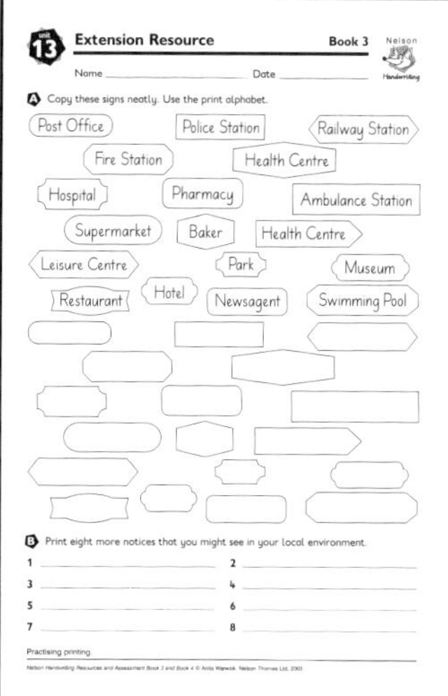

13 Extension Resource Book 3

Name Date

A Copy these signs neatly. Use the print alphabet.

Post Office, Police Station, Railway Station, Fire Station, Health Centre, Hospital, Pharmacy, Ambulance Station, Supermarket, Baker, Health Centre, Leisure Centre, Park, Museum, Restaurant, Hotel, Newsagent, Swimming Pool

B Print eight more notices that you might see in your local environment.

1 2
3 4
5 6
7 8

Practising printing

Assessment

- Print letters are written clearly.
- The capital letters are almost twice the size of small letters.

UNIT 16

Objectives

- To explore the conventions of letter writing.
- To set out a letter clearly and neatly.

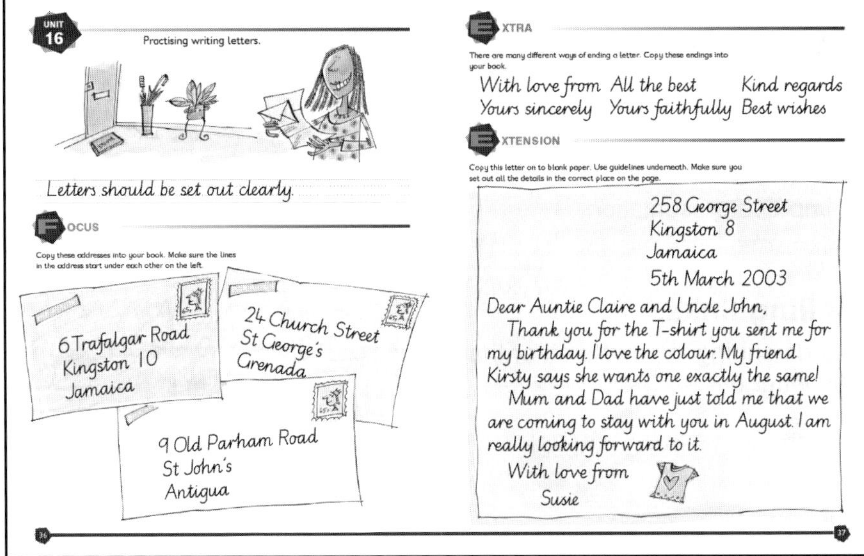

UNIT 16

Practising writing letters.

Letters should be set out clearly.

FOCUS

Copy these addresses into your book. Make sure the lines in the address start under each other on the left.

6 Trafalgar Road
Kingston 10
Jamaica

24 Church Street
St George's
Grenada

9 Old Parham Road
St John's
Antigua

EXTRA

There are many different ways of ending a letter. Copy these endings into your book.

With love from All the best Kind regards
Yours sincerely Yours faithfully Best wishes

EXTENSION

Copy this letter on to blank paper. Use guidelines underneath. Make sure you set out all the details in the correct place on the page.

258 George Street
Kingston 8
Jamaica
5th March 2003

Dear Auntie Claire and Uncle John,
Thank you for the T-shirt you sent me for my birthday. I love the colour. My friend Kirsty says she wants one exactly the same!
Mum and Dad have just told me that we are coming to stay with you in August. I am really looking forward to it.
With love from
Susie

36 37

Spelling links

- unstressed vowels in polysyllabic words, e.g. **faithfully**, **sincerely**

Nelson theme – the Caribbean

Developing Skills

Focus

- Write the lesson objectives on the board.
- Study and discuss the layout of the letter in the Extension section.
- Point out the conventions of writing a letter, such as where to write the address, date, etc.
- Note how friendly and chatty the letter is. Why is this?
- Discuss the addresses in the Focus section.
- Point out that the address is neatly aligned to the left and that the names of houses, cottages, streets and towns begin with a capital letter.
- Point out that postcodes in Great Britain always use capital letters.
- Ask the children to copy the addresses into their books.

Extra

- Discuss the different ways of ending a letter. Ask the children for ideas.
- Explain that formal letters, when we do not know the person we are writing to, usually end with **Yours faithfully** (**f** for **formal** and **f** for **faithfully** is a good way to remember).
- If we know the person we are writing to, but not very well, we usually end the letter **Yours sincerely**.
- Discuss the spellings of the words **faithfully** and **sincerely** – they are both polysyllabic words and they contain unstressed vowels (i.e. **i** in **faithfully**, **e** in **sincerely**).
- Ask the children to suggest how the spellings of these words might be memorised, e.g. exaggerated pronunciation, breaking them down into syllables – **faith** - **full** - **y** or **faith** - **fully**. A helpful tactic is to say the word as it sounds and refer to the root word.
- Ask the children to copy the different ways of ending a letter into their books, remembering that they begin with a capital letter.

Extension

- Tell the children to copy the letter on to plain paper, using guidelines underneath.
- Remind them to set the letter out neatly and to use their best handwriting.

Resources and Assessment

Focus

More practice writing a letter. Copying an invitation.

16 Focus Resource Book 3 Nelson Handwriting

Name ______ Date ______

Copy this letter on to a sheet of paper in your best handwriting. Put guidelines underneath. Notice how the letter is set out.

17 Wheatsheaf Lane,
Southdell AL4 7BC
15th August 2003

Dear Alex,
One of my friends owns a hot-air balloon. He has invited me to go with him on a flight over the countryside. He plans to go on Saturday, and says that you are invited too. Would you like to come? Ask your parents if you can come and let me know by Friday evening.
Love to everyone,
Uncle John

Practising writing letters.

Nelson Handwriting Resources and Assessment Book 3 and Book 4 © Anita Warwick, Nelson Thornes Ltd. 2003

Extension

Copying the beginning of a letter. Completing the letter in best handwriting.

16 Extension Resource Book 3 Nelson Handwriting

Name ______ Date ______

A newspaper has invited children to write a letter about their favourite television programme. The writer of the best letter will win tickets to see the programme being recorded. Write a letter about your favourite programme. Use the letter below as a starting point. Remember to put in your address and the date.

Dear Sir,
My name is ______ and I am ___ years old. I will try my hardest to write a good letter as I would really love to win this competition and go to see my favourite programme being recorded.

Practising writing letters.

Nelson Handwriting Resources and Assessment Book 3 and Book 4 © Anita Warwick, Nelson Thornes Ltd. 2003

Assessment

- The letter is set out clearly and neatly.
- The address and date are written correctly.
- Capital letters and numerals are the correct height and size.

UNIT 17

Objectives

- To understand what a paragraph is and to write one.
- To indent the first line of a paragraph.

Spelling links

Nelson theme – strange stories and mythical creatures

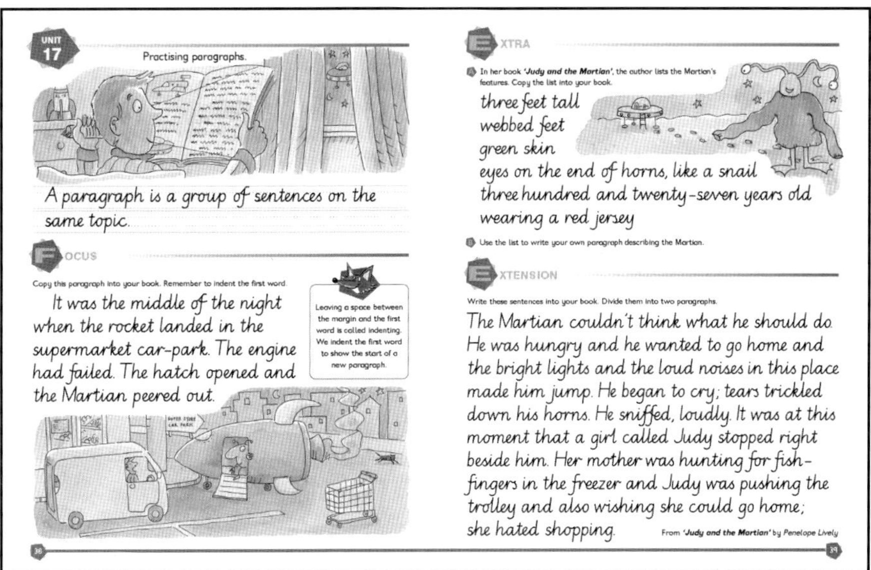

UNIT 17

Practising paragraphs.

A paragraph is a group of sentences on the same topic.

FOCUS

Copy this paragraph into your book. Remember to indent the first word.

It was the middle of the night when the rocket landed in the supermarket car-park. The engine had failed. The hatch opened and the Martian peered out.

Leaving a space between the margin and the first word is called indenting. We indent the first word to show the start of a new paragraph.

EXTRA

In her book 'Judy and the Martian', the author lists the Martian's features. Copy the list into your book.

three feet tall
webbed feet
green skin
eyes on the end of horns, like a snail
three hundred and twenty-seven years old
wearing a red jersey

Use the list to write your own paragraph describing the Martian.

EXTENSION

Write these sentences into your book. Divide them into two paragraphs.

The Martian couldn't think what he should do. He was hungry and he wanted to go home and the bright lights and the loud noises in this place made him jump. He began to cry; tears trickled down his horns. He sniffed, loudly. It was at this moment that a girl called Judy stopped right beside him. Her mother was hunting for fish-fingers in the freezer and Judy was pushing the trolley and also wishing she could go home; she hated shopping.

From 'Judy and the Martian' by Penelope Lively

Developing Skills

Focus

- Write the lesson objectives on the board.
- Encourage children to volunteer suggestions for what a paragraph is.
- Read the paragraph provided. Ask the children what the main idea in this paragraph is.
- Point out that when we write a paragraph it starts on a new line and it is indented. Draw attention to the fox box definition of indenting.
- Model indenting this paragraph on the board.
- Ask the children to copy the paragraph into their books.

Extra

- Read the list of features that the author uses to describe the Martian.
- Ask the children to copy the list and then write one paragraph to describe the Martian using some of the features listed.
- Remind the children to indent the paragraph.

Extension

- Read the sentences.
- Ask the children if they can identify two main ideas – one for each paragraph.
- Tell them to copy the passage, dividing it into two paragraphs.
- Remind the children to start each paragraph on a new line and to indent it.

Resources and Assessment

Focus

More practice writing a paragraph. Copying a paragraph about the care of dogs. Writing a second paragraph about the care of cats or another pet.

17 Focus Resource — Book 3

Name ____ Date ____

A Copy this paragraph neatly. Remember to indent the first word.

Looking After a Dog

A pet dog needs regular meals and clean water to drink. Its diet should include meat, biscuits and vegetables. Tinned and dried dog food provide all these. A dog also needs plenty of exercise and regular grooming and it must, of course, be house-trained.

B Now write a paragraph about looking after a cat or another pet. Use a separate sheet of paper. Remember to indent the first word.

Practising paragraphs.

Extension

Further practice writing paragraphs – an opportunity for a sustained piece of handwriting. Rewriting information about science fiction writers as two paragraphs.

17 Extension Resource — Book 3

Name ____ Date ____

Rewrite this information as two paragraphs.

Nicholas Fisk has written around 40 books, including many science-fiction titles for older children. He completed his first book when he was only nine years old! He has tried many different jobs including acting and playing jazz, but he likes writing best. However, Nicholas Fisk doesn't like his books to be labelled as sci-fi. He says his books are written from the point of view of 'If...' because then anything can happen in them. He enjoys writing for young people because they find it easier than adults to accept the unconventional.

Practising paragraphs with indentation.

Assessment

- Each new paragraph starts on a new line.
- The first line of each new paragraph is indented.
- Writing is neat, joined and legible.

UNIT 18

Objectives

- To explore aspects of presentation.
- To present writing attractively.

Nelson theme – strange stories and mythical creatures

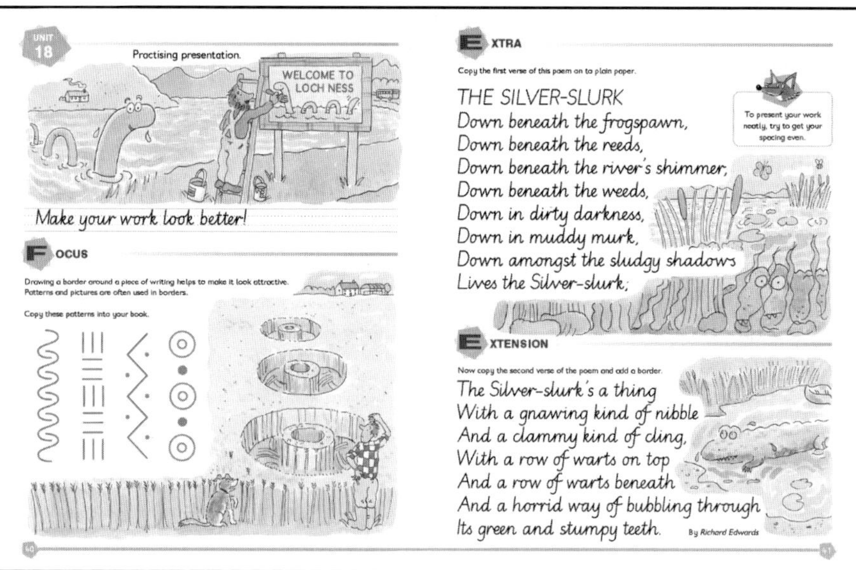

UNIT 18 Practising presentation.

Make your work look better!

FOCUS

Drawing a border around a piece of writing helps to make it look attractive. Patterns and pictures are often used in borders.

Copy these patterns into your book.

EXTRA

Copy the first verse of this poem on to plain paper.

To present your work neatly, try to get your spacing even.

THE SILVER-SLURK
Down beneath the frogspawn,
Down beneath the reeds,
Down beneath the river's shimmer,
Down beneath the weeds,
Down in dirty darkness,
Down in muddy murk,
Down amongst the sludgy shadows
Lives the Silver-slurk.

EXTENSION

Now copy the second verse of the poem and add a border.

The Silver-slurk's a thing
With a gnawing kind of nibble
And a clammy kind of cling,
With a row of warts on top
And a row of warts beneath
And a horrid way of bubbling through
Its green and stumpy teeth.
By Richard Edwards

40 41

Developing Skills

Focus

- Write the lesson objectives on the board.
- Ask children for suggestions of how to present writing attractively.
- Suggest they could try:
  - writing on plain paper, with guidelines
  - leaving wide margins
  - adding flourishes
  - decorating the capitals
  - adding patterned borders
  - writing inside a shape
  - curving the lines of writing (shape poems)
- Discuss drawing borders around a piece of writing to help it took more attractive.
- Look at the patterns provided.
- Tell the children to practise these patterns on their whiteboards and experiment with other ideas of their own.
- Ask the class to copy the patterns carefully into their books.

Extra

- Read and discuss the poem. Are shape poems an effective way of enhancing meaning?
- Curving the lines of writing can make writing look attractive. Discuss how tricky this can be.
- Ask the class to suggest what they would need to do to ensure writing looks neat and well presented, i.e. need to pencil feint lines on page in shape and to plan the spacing of letters and words before beginning to write.
- Tell the children to copy the poem on to plain paper.

Extension

- Read and discuss the rest of the poem.
- Look at the letter shapes. Encourage the children to practise these either on their whiteboards or on plain scrap paper.
- Ask them to copy the rest of the poem on to plain paper.

Resources and Assessment

Focus

More practice making a border to help present writing attractively. Copying a limerick inside a frame.

18 Focus Resource Book 3 Nelson Handwriting

Name ____ Date ____

Copy this limerick into the frame below it. Complete the pattern on the frame.

THERE WAS A YOUNG LADY OF RIGA

There was a young lady of Riga
Who rode with a smile on a tiger;
They returned from the ride,
With the lady inside,
And the smile on the face of the tiger.
(Anonymous)

Practising presentation.

Extension

Further practice presenting writing attractively. Copying shape poem carefully, adhering to the shape.

18 Extension Resource Book 3 Nelson Handwriting

Name ____ Date ____

Copy this poem carefully on to plain paper. Notice the shape of the poem. Does it remind you of the way seals move?

SEAL
See how he dives
From the rocks with a zoom!
See how he darts
Through his watery room,
Past crabs and eels
And green seaweed,
Past fluffs of sandy
Minnow feed!
See how he swims
With a swerve and a twist,
A flip of the flipper,
A flick of the wrist!
Quicksilver-quick,
Softer than spray,
Down he plunges
And sweeps away.
By William Jay Smith

Practising presentation.

Assessment

- The writing is carefully planned.
- The writing is neat and tidy.
- The letters are consistent in size and height.

UNIT 19

Objectives

- To revise the third join.
- To practise joining to the letter **e**.

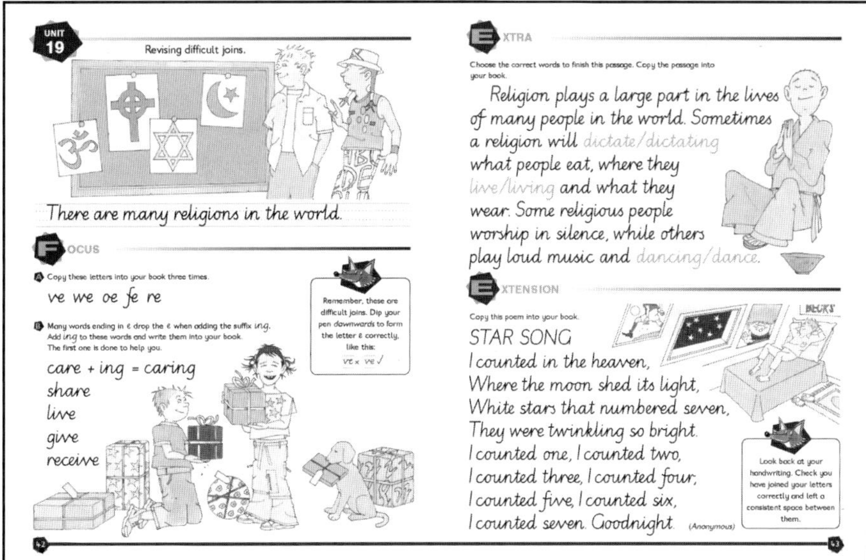

UNIT 19

Revising difficult joins.

There are many religions in the world.

FOCUS

A Copy these letters into your book three times.

ve we oe fe re

B Many words ending in e drop the e when adding the suffix ing.
Add ing to these words and write them into your book.
The first one is done to help you.

care + ing = caring
share
live
give
receive

Remember, these are difficult joins. Dip your pen *downwards* to form the letter e correctly, like this:
ve × ve ✓

EXTRA

Choose the correct words to finish this passage. Copy the passage into your book.

Religion plays a large part in the lives of many people in the world. Sometimes a religion will dictate/dictating what people eat, where they live/living and what they wear. Some religious people worship in silence, while others play loud music and dancing/dance.

EXTENSION

Copy this poem into your book.

STAR SONG
I counted in the heaven,
Where the moon shed its light,
White stars that numbered seven,
They were twinkling so bright.
I counted one, I counted two,
I counted three, I counted four,
I counted five, I counted six,
I counted seven. Goodnight. (Anonymous)

Look back at your handwriting. Check you have joined your letters correctly and left a consistent space between them.

42 43

Spelling links

- spelling patterns of consonants

Nelson theme – religion

Developing Skills

Focus

- Write the whole class sentence on the board, underlining the tricky horizontal joins.
- Look at the joins to the letter **e**. Remind the class that this is a tricky join: the pen must be brought down to enable the letter **e** to be formed correctly.
- Demonstrate the joins **ve**, **we**, **oe**, **fe**, **re**.
- Ask some children to demonstrate the correct joining of these letters on the board.
- Point out that many words ending in **e** drop the **e** when adding **ing**.
- Model writing the **ing** words on the board.
- Ask the children to copy the letters and words into their books.

Extra

- Read and discuss the passage.
- Ask the children to copy the passage, choosing the correct word to complete the sentences and remembering to take extra care when joining to the letter **e**.
- Remind the children to slope their writing slightly to the right and to leave a consistent space between letters and between words.

Extension

- Read the poem together.
- Ask the children to copy the poem into their books, watching out for any tricky horizontal joins to the letter **e**.

Resources and Assessment

Focus

More practice revising difficult joins. Copying words and adding suffixes **ed** and **ing** to other words, dropping **e** as appropriate.

19 Focus Resource Book 3 Nelson Handwriting

Name ____________ Date ____________

A Copy these words.

live	lived	lively
love	loved	lovely
brave	braved	bravely

B Drop the final **e** and then add the suffix **ed** to these words.
Write each new word three times.

care
stare
share

C Drop the final **e** and then add the suffix **ing** to these words.
Write each new word three times.

weave
welcome
wedge

Revising difficult joins.

Nelson Handwriting Resources and Assessment Book 3 and Book 4 © Anita Warwick, Nelson Thornes Ltd, 2003

Extension

Further practice joining to the letter **e**. Copying poem.

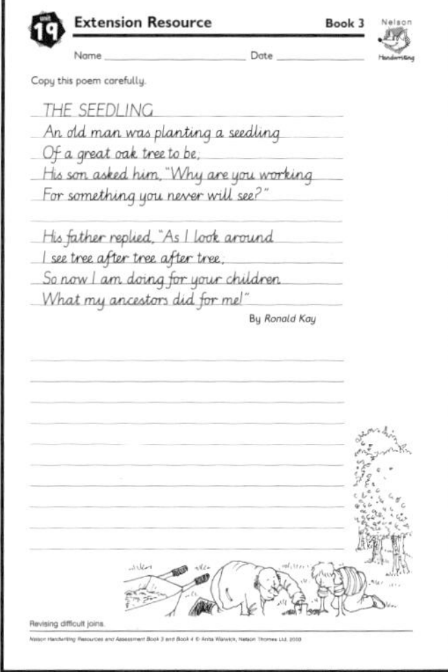

19 Extension Resource Book 3 Nelson Handwriting

Name ____________ Date ____________

Copy this poem carefully.

THE SEEDLING
An old man was planting a seedling
Of a great oak tree to be;
His son asked him, "Why are you working
For something you never will see?"

His father replied, "As I look around
I see tree after tree after tree,
So now I am doing for your children
What my ancestors did for me!"

By *Ronald Kay*

Revising difficult joins.

Nelson Handwriting Resources and Assessment Book 3 and Book 4 © Anita Warwick, Nelson Thornes Ltd, 2003

Assessment

- The correct horizontal join to the letter **e**.
- The letter **e** is the correct shape and size.
- Writing is joined and there is a consistent space between letters and between words.

UNIT 20

Objectives

- To develop a personal writing style.

Nelson theme – Religion

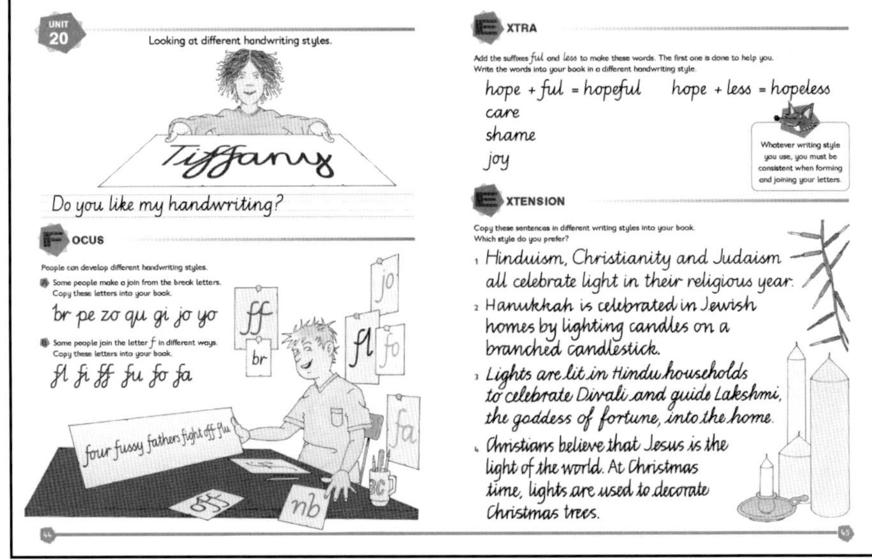

UNIT 20

Looking at different handwriting styles.

Tiffany

Do you like my handwriting?

FOCUS

People can develop different handwriting styles.

A Some people make a join from the break letters. Copy these letters into your book.

br pe zo qu gi jo yo

B Some people join the letter f in different ways. Copy these letters into your book.

fl fi ff fu fo fa

XTRA

Add the suffixes ful and less to make these words. The first one is done to help you. Write the words into your book in a different handwriting style.

hope + ful = hopeful hope + less = hopeless

care

shame

joy

Whatever writing style you use, you must be consistent when forming and joining your letters.

XTENSION

Copy these sentences in different writing styles into your book. Which style do you prefer?

1 Hinduism, Christianity and Judaism all celebrate light in their religious year.

2 Hanukkah is celebrated in Jewish homes by lighting candles on a branched candlestick.

3 Lights are lit in Hindu households to celebrate Divali and guide Lakshmi, the goddess of fortune, into the home.

4 Christians believe that Jesus is the light of the world. At Christmas time, lights are used to decorate Christmas trees.

Developing Skills

Focus

- Explain to the children that the objective of this lesson is to build on all that has been learned using *Nelson Handwriting* and explore different styles of writing.
- Point out that legibility and fluency are very important when writing in a personal style.
- Model joining the break letters **b**, **p**, **z**, **q**, **g**, **j** and **y**.
- Point out that joining from break letters can help you write more quickly as you do not have to lift your pen off the page.
- Demonstrate by writing some words containing the break letters on the board.
- There is more than one way of adding a loop to the letter **f**. Demonstrate the examples to the children.
- Tell the children to copy the joins into their books

Extra

- Ask the class to make the words and copy them into their books while experimenting with different handwriting styles.
- In one example they may just want to join the letters **j**, **p** or **y** and write the remaining letters in Nelson Script. In another, they may want to loop the letter **f**.
- Point out that to develop an individual style takes practice regardless of the style chosen. This is because it is very important that letters are formed and joined using a consistent approach, i.e. letters are consistent in height, shape, size and the way they are joined.

Extension

- Tell the children to copy the sentences into their book in the four different styles. This will give them the chance to explore different joins and loops.
- Talk to the children about the style they preferred and how they could incorporate any of these handwriting features into their personal handwriting style.

Resources and Assessment

Focus

More practice developing an individual style with examples of looped joins.

20 Focus Resource Book 3 Nelson Handwriting

Name ______ Date ______

A Copy this rhyme in your usual handwriting style.

A blink, I think, is the same as a wink,
A blink is a wink that grew,
For a wink you blink with only one eye,
For a blink you wink with two.

By *Jacqueline Segal*

Some people develop their writing by adding loops to **f**, **g**, **j** and **y**.

A blink, I think, is the same as a wink,
A blink is a wink that grew,
For a wink you blink with only one eye,
For a blink you wink with two.

B Now try writing the rhyme with loops.

Looking at different handwriting styles.

Nelson Handwriting Resources and Assessment Book 3 and Book 4 © Anita Warwick, Nelson Thomes Ltd, 2003

Extension

Further practice with joins after **p** and **b**, as well as words with looped joins. Practising writing poem in an individual style on plain paper to develop a personal writing style.

20 Extension Resource Book 3 Nelson Handwriting

Name ______ Date ______

A Copy this poem on to a sheet of paper in your usual handwriting style.

HUMPTY DUMPTY WENT TO THE MOON
Humpty Dumpty went to the moon
On a supersonic spoon.
He took some porridge and a tent
But when he landed
The spoon got bent.
Humpty said he didn't care
And for all I know
He's still up there.

By *Michael Rosen*

Some people develop their handwriting by adding loops to **f**, **g**, **j** and **y** and joining from **b** and **p**, like this:

HUMPTY DUMPTY WENT TO THE MOON
Humpty Dumpty went to the moon
On a supersonic spoon.
He took some porridge and a tent
But when he landed
The spoon got bent.
Humpty said he didn't care
And for all I know
He's still up there.

B Copy this version of the poem on to another sheet of paper. Make sure you add the loops and the joins from **b** and **p**.

Looking at different handwriting styles.

Nelson Handwriting Resources and Assessment Book 3 and Book 4 © Anita Warwick, Nelson Thomes Ltd, 2003

Assessment

- Loops are formed correctly.
- The letters are a consistent height and size.
- Joins are consistently formed.

HECK-UP

Objectives

Explain to the pupils that this exercise is an assessment activity. The objective is to assess what the pupils can do and where they need extra practice. This exercise will help assess each pupil's ability to form and use the four handwriting joins. Ask pupils to look at the checklist on the back of the flap to remind them of the important points.

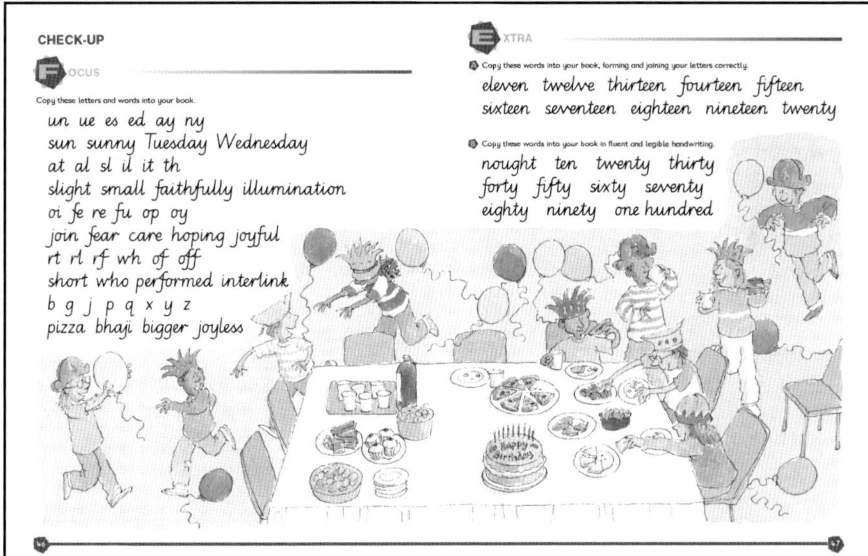

CHECK-UP

FOCUS

Copy these letters and words into your book.

un ue es ed ay ny
sun sunny Tuesday Wednesday
at al sl il it th
slight small faithfully illumination
oi fe re fu op oy
join fear care hoping joyful
rt rl rf wh of off
short who performed interlink
b g j p q x y z
pizza bhaji bigger joyless

EXTRA

A Copy these words into your book, forming and joining your letters correctly.

eleven twelve thirteen fourteen fifteen
sixteen seventeen eighteen nineteen twenty

B Copy these words into your book in fluent and legible handwriting.

nought ten twenty thirty
forty fifty sixty seventy
eighty ninety one hundred

46 47

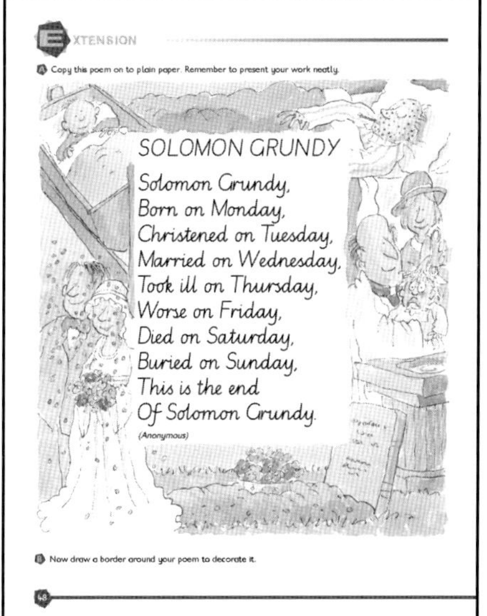

EXTENSION

A Copy this poem on to plain paper. Remember to present your work neatly.

SOLOMON GRUNDY

Solomon Grundy,
Born on Monday,
Christened on Tuesday,
Married on Wednesday,
Took ill on Thursday,
Worse on Friday,
Died on Saturday,
Buried on Sunday,
This is the end
Of Solomon Grundy.
(Anonymous)

B Now draw a border around your poem to decorate it.

48

Focus

Ask the pupils to copy the letters and words into their books. The letter shapes should be the correct height with correct spaces between the letters and between letter blocks and words. The handwriting should also have a consistent slope. The last two rows contain break letters which should not join.

Extra

Ask the pupils to copy the words into their books. The words in this section contain all four handwriting joins, and also include double letters, difficult joins and break letters.

Extension

Ask the pupils to copy the poem into their book. The poem contains a mixture of capital and lowercase letters and should also be presented neatly. The pupils are also asked to give the poem a border to add to the presentation.

Assessment

- Do all letters joins apart from break and capital letters?
- Are the correct joins used?
- Are the letters well shaped and clear?
- Are letters consistent in size and proportion?
- Are any letters too tall or too short?
- Does the handwriting have a consistent slope?
- Are the capital letters the correct height and size?

- For more Assessment see *Resources and Assessment Book 3 and Book 4*

SCOPE AND SEQUENCE
DEVELOPING SKILLS BOOK FOUR

Page	Focus	Extra	Extension	Focus resource	Extension resource
4-5 Flashback	*Flashback*	*Flashback*	*Flashback*	*Flashback*	*Flashback*
6-7 Unit 1 Wartime	revising sloped writing	choose words using the prefixes aero, trans and micro and copy sentences	copy passage about codes, using fluent and legible handwriting	practise making patterns and letters with a slope, copy words with a prefix	revise sloped letters
8-9 Unit 2 Wartime	ensuring letters are the correct height and size	choose words using the prefix counter and copy sentences	copy passage, ensuring letters are the correct height and size	practise making patterns and letters the correct height and size	copy poem, ensuring letters are correct height and size
10-11 Unit 3 Shipwrecks	practising spacing	practise writing speech marks	use notes to write a short biography, remembering to leave a space between letters	copy words containing unstressed vowels, join letters correctly to ensure correct spacing	write out sentences, adding speech marks and leaving a correct space between letters and words
12-13 Unit 4 Shipwrecks	practising speedwriting	finish writing notes	copy reporter's finished article	underline main points in article and write the notes from which it was written	copy passage quickly but neatly
14-15 Unit 5 Victorians	practising drafting and editing	copy and edit the first draft of newspaper article	write final draft of newspaper article	correct the spelling mistakes and write a paragraph about Brunel in best handwriting	edit first draft of a short biography about Darwin, copy corrected final draft in best handwriting
16-17 Unit 6 Victorians	practising writing capital letters	copy sentences and insert the missing capital letters	copy passage from Mary Seacole's autobiography	copy poem	copy extract and insert the missing capital letters
18-19 Unit 7 Mysteries and the unexplained	practising fluency	copy sentences and insert a descriptive word from Focus section	copy passage, using quick, fluent and legible handwriting	choose a verb to complete each sentence, change the ending to ed or ing, copy sentences	practise writing fluently and legibly, copy poem
20-21 Unit 8 Mysteries and the unexplained	practising paragraphs	write information as two paragraphs	write an account of a Yeti hunt as three paragraphs	copy paragraph about the Sphinx in best handwriting	divide passage about standing stones into two paragraphs, copy them in best handwriting
22-23 Unit 9 Aliens	practising keeping letters in the correct proportion	choose the correct word, either with prefix un or not, and copy passage	copy poem	copy sentences, inserting correct word containing prefix dis	copy poem
24-25 Unit 10 Aliens	practising presentation	copy text for birthday party invitation	design and make an invitation to an Aliens Fancy Dress Party	copy/design a certificate for winning fancy dress competition	Write and present a thank-you letter, write a reply to letter

Page	Focus	Extra	Extension	Focus resource	Extension resource
26-27 Unit 11 Safety first	practising writing instructions	copy sentences and insert the correct connective word	put instructions from The Green Cross Code in correct order and copy them	use connectives to join sentences about firework safety	follow instructions for designing a poster about a fireworks display
28-29 Unit 12 Safety first	practising writing instructions	copy instructions for cyclists turning right at a road junction	design and make a leaflet about buying and maintaining a bicycle	put instructions for making a pizza in the correct order and copy	design a poster about wearing seat belts
30-31 Unit 13 Ancient Greece	practising presenting a project (handwriting for different purposes)	read and make notes on passage about the origin of the Olympic Games	use best handwriting to write a passage about the Olympic Games then and now from notes	put the rocket launches that led up to the first moon landing in the correct order on a chart	copy poem about how it might feel to land on the moon in best handwriting
32-33 Unit 14 Ancient Greece	practising fluency	copy passage, inserting the pronouns he or him to make it easier to read	copy extract about Narcissus in fluent, joined and legible writing	use fluent handwriting to copy passage about the Ancient Greeks	use fluent handwriting to copy passage about Medusa, underline pronouns
34-35 Unit 15 Cliffs and treasure	practising writing double letters	choose correct word and copy sentences	copy passage containing words with double letters	choose synonyms, copying double letters within words carefully	copy poem, underline words with double letters
36-37 Unit 16 Cliffs and treasure	practising speedwriting	write out notes in full, using neat handwriting	copy sentences quickly, using abbreviations as necessary	copy two sentences quickly but legibly to find writing speed	copy quickly a list of 20 words to do with treasure
38-39 Unit 17 Cats	ensuring letters are in the correct proportion	choose the correct word to complete each simile	think of a simile to finish sentences, copy sentences with letters the correct shape, size and height	choose a word to complete each simile	copy similes, ensuring letters are in correct proportion, and match sentences with similes
40-41 Unit 18 Cats	practising presentation	copy list of kennings about a cat, thinking carefully about presentation	write own kennings poem and illustrate it	put acrostic poem about cats in correct order, copy it and make it attractive	copy poem and illustrate it
42-43 Unit 19 Travellers' tales	practising printing	copy advert, using the print alphabet	copy poster, using the print alphabet	use print letters to copy fact sheet about a theme park	copy chart showing prices of two-day breaks at different hotels
44-45 Unit 20 Travellers' tales	developing an individual handwriting style	copy sentences in different styles of writing	copy extract, using own preferred style of writing	copy poem, making joins after the letters b and p and loops from f, g and j	copy lines, making joins after b and p and loops from f, g and y
46-48 Check-up	*Check-up*	*Check-up*	*Check-up*	*Check-up*	*Check-up*

FLASHBACK

Objectives

Explain to pupils that this exercise is an assessment activity. The objective is to assess what the pupils can do from Book 3 and where they need the extra practice. This exercise will help assess each pupil's ability to form and use the four handwriting joins. Ask pupils to look at the checklist on the back of the flap to remind them of the important points.

FLASHBACK

FOCUS

A Copy these patterns into your book.

amamam wewewewe

B Copy these words into your book. Make sure all your letters are the correct height and size.

twenty forty Monday Wednesday
family familiar heavy heavily

C Copy these words into your book. Make sure your writing is sloped slightly to the right.

faithfully sincerely fitter fittest
light heavy join constellation

EXTRA

Copy these words into your book using fluent and legible handwriting. Check you are making the joins correctly.

mine my yes no his new
near he her plane plain
dull night theatre boats
shop shopping nation
bright far long knives
hopeful share sharing
dark old short fearful
flew flue who's whose
telephone relaxed lizard
joyful bright flying queen

EXTENSION

Copy this poem into your book.

The city mouse eats bread and cheese;
The garden mouse eats what he can;
We will not grudge him seeds and stocks,
Poor little timid furry man.

From *'The City Mouse and the Garden Mouse'* by Christina Rossetti

Focus

Ask the pupils to copy the patterns and words into their books. The patterns need to be made smoothly and will consolidate the handwriting skills required for fluent writing. Some of the patterns are also useful practice for creating borders to help with the presentation of work.

Extra

Ask the pupils to copy these words into their books. The words in this section contain all four handwriting joins as well as double letters, difficult joins and break letters.

Extension

Ask the pupils to copy the poem into their book. This poem incorporates a variety of punctuation marks.

Assessment

- Are the correct joins used?
- Are the letters formed correctly?
- Are any letters too tall or too short?
- Do the descenders fall below the line?
- Is there a consistent space between letters and words?
- Does the handwriting have an even slope?

- For more Assessment see *Resources and Assessment Book 3 and Book 4*

UNIT 1

Objectives

- To slope joined writing slightly to the right.
- To sit correctly.
- To position the paper correctly.

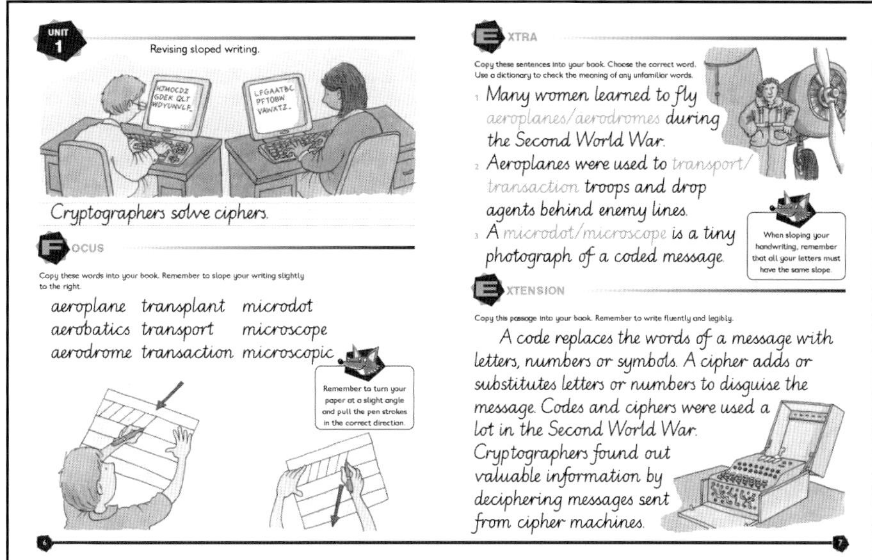

Spelling links

- prefixes

Nelson theme – wartime

Developing Skills

Focus

- Write the whole class sentence on the board and share the lesson objectives with the children; explain that this is a revision lesson.
- Ask the class if they can list the benefits of sloped writing *(it is an aid to quicker writing and makes handwriting look more grown up)*.
- Emphasise the need to sit correctly and position the paper properly.
- Explain that the joins and the spacing of words and letters should not change.
- Model some of the words with the same prefix, e.g. **aeroplane**, **aerodrome**.
- Point out that the correct angle of the slope should not be more than 8 degrees from the vertical.
- Discuss words with the same prefix and invite the children to identify the meaning in each case, e.g. **micro** *(small)*, **aero** *(air)*, **trans** *(across)*.
- Ask the children to practise the words on their whiteboards before copying them neatly into their books. Remind the children that their writing should slope forwards not backwards.
- *Extension activity:* ask the children to generate more words containing the prefixes. Encourage them to use dictionaries to research clusters of words.

Extra

- Read the sentences.
- Ask the children to choose the correct word to complete each sentence, using a dictionary to help them.
- Tell the children to copy the sentences into their books. Remind them to sit properly, angle their paper correctly and give all their letters the same slope.

Extension

- Read the passage about codes.
- Demonstrate the first sentence on the board.
- Ask the children to copy the passage, sloping their writing, and writing fluently and legibly.

Resources and Assessment

Focus

More practice writing letters and words in sloped writing. Copying sloping patterns and words with different prefixes.

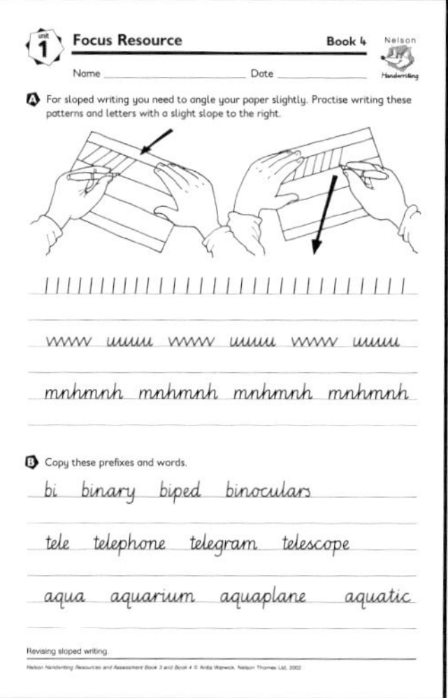

Extension

Further practice writing with a slope.

Assessment

- The child is sitting properly with their paper angled correctly.
- The writing is joined and spaced correctly.
- The writing slopes slightly to the right (no more than 8 degrees from the vertical).

NIT 2

Objectives

- To ensure small letters are consistent in height and size.
- To ensure letters with descenders and ascenders are consistent in height and size.

UNIT 2 Ensuring letters are the correct height and size.

The defence was too strong for the attacking force.

FOCUS

Copy these words into your book. Make sure all your letters are the correct height and size.

counteract counterbalance counterfeit
countermove counterweight counterfoil
counterpoise countermeasure countermand

Be careful, these letters should all be the same height: acemnorsuvwxz

EXTRA

Copy these sentences into your book. Use a dictionary to help you choose the correct word.

1 The captain was cross because he had been paid in counterbalance/counterfeit money.
2 The village planned to counteract/counterfoil the invasion of the army.
3 The fort was filled with soldiers as a countermeasure/counterpoise.

EXTENSION

Copy this passage into your book. Remember to make your letters the correct height and size.

Instead of hillforts, the Iron Age people in Scotland and Wales built small circular stone forts for defence. In the north of Scotland and the islands, chiefs defended their homes with tall circular towers. These are called brochs and many can still be seen. The best example is on Mousa Island in the Shetland Isles.

From 'Places of Defence' by Gillian Clegg

Remember, the descender, or tail, on these letters falls below the line: fgjpqy

Spelling links

- prefixes

Nelson theme – wartime

Developing Skills

Focus

- Share the lesson objectives with the children.
- Discuss the height of the letters with descenders, e.g. **p** and **g**. The body of these letters is the same height as the small letters, but they also have a descender, which falls below the baseline.
- Mention that if a letter with a descender were placed beside a letter with an ascender they would be the same size.
- Point out that a letter with an ascender, e.g. **k**, is nearly twice the height of a small letter, but its body is the same height as a small letter.
- Remind the children that ensuring letters are consistent in height and size is important.
- Model writing the first line of words on the board.
- Talk about the letter **f**, which is a letter with both an ascender and a descender.
- Point out that the words all begin with the same prefix, counter, which means opposite, against. What do these words mean? Can you think of any more words starting with **counter**? Encourage the children to use a dictionary to check definitions.
- Suggest the class practise the words on their whiteboards before copying them into their books.

Extra

- Read the sentences.
- Ask the children to choose the correct word to complete each sentence, using a dictionary to help them.
- Tell the children to copy the sentences into their books, making sure their letters are consistently sized and spaced.
- Remind them to slope their writing slightly to the right.

Extension

- Read the passage. Ask the children to point out the words with descenders.
- Model writing the first two sentences on the board. Mention that the ellipsis means that part of the original text has been left out.
- Ask the children to copy the passage into their book, or on to plain paper with guidelines.

Resources and Assessment

Focus

More practice ensuring letters are consistent in height and size. Copying patterns and letters.

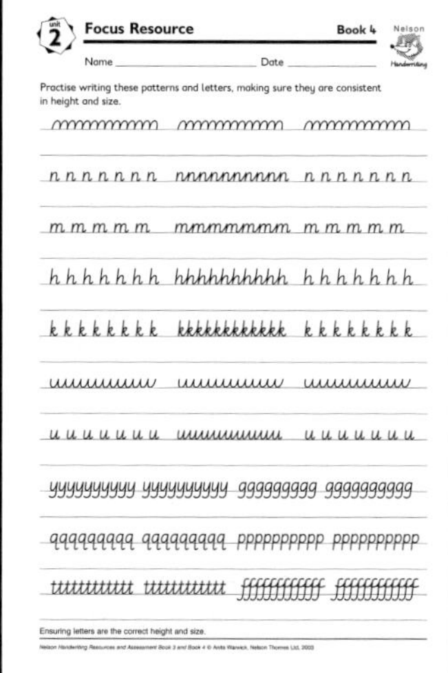

2 Focus Resource Book 4 Nelson Handwriting

Name ______ Date ______

Practise writing these patterns and letters, making sure they are consistent in height and size.

nnnnnnn nnnnnnnnnn nnnnnnn
mmmmm mmmmmmmm mmmmm
hhhhhhh hhhhhhhhhh hhhhhhh
kkkkkkk kkkkkkkkkkk kkkkkkk
uuuuuuu uuuuuuuuuu uuuuuuu
yyyyyyyyy yyyyyyyyy ggggggggg ggggggggg
qqqqqqqqq qqqqqqqqq ppppppppp ppppppppp
tttttttttt tttttttttt fffffffff fffffffff

Ensuring letters are the correct height and size.

Extension

Further practice of the lesson objectives. Copying poem containing word **counteract**.

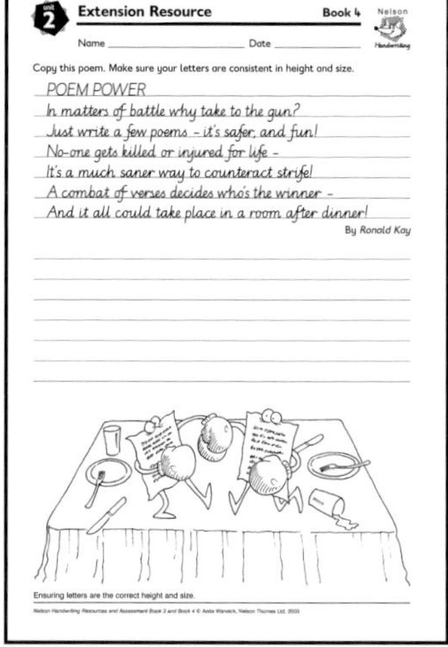

2 Extension Resource Book 4 Nelson Handwriting

Name ______ Date ______

Copy this poem. Make sure your letters are consistent in height and size.

POEM POWER
In matters of battle why take to the gun?
Just write a few poems – it's safer, and fun!
No-one gets killed or injured for life –
It's a much saner way to counteract strife!
A combat of verses decides who's the winner –
And it all could take place in a room after dinner!

By Ronald Kay

Ensuring letters are the correct height and size.

Assessment

- All small letters are the same height and size.
- The letters with ascenders (except for **t**) are almost twice the height of small letters.
- The letters with descenders are the same size as those with ascenders.

UNIT 3

Objectives

- To ensure a correct space is left between letters.
- To ensure a correct space is left between words.

Spelling links

- unstressed vowels

Nelson theme – shipwrecks

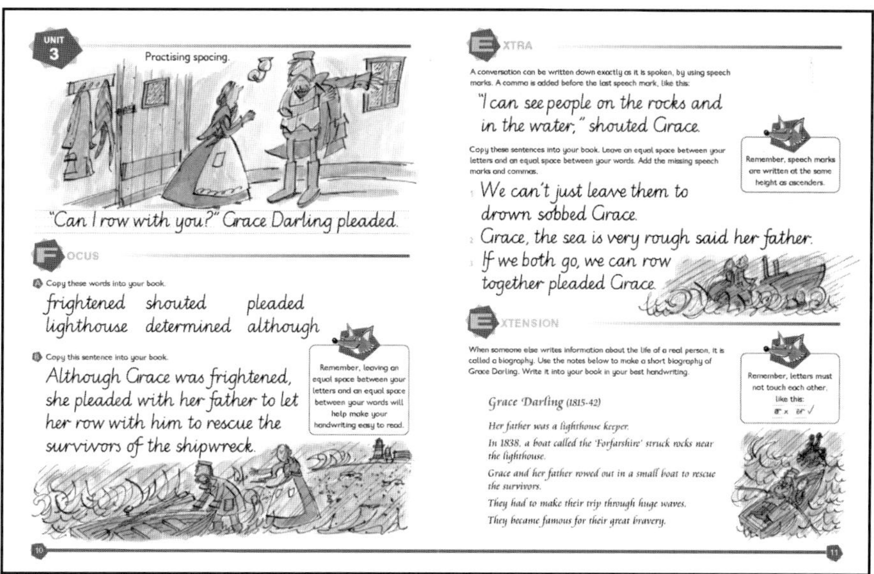

UNIT 3

Practising spacing.

"Can I row with you?" Grace Darling pleaded.

FOCUS

A Copy these words into your book.

frightened shouted pleaded
lighthouse determined although

B Copy this sentence into your book.

Although Grace was frightened, she pleaded with her father to let her row with him to rescue the survivors of the shipwreck.

Remember, leaving an equal space between your letters and an equal space between your words will help make your handwriting easy to read.

10

EXTRA

A conversation can be written down exactly as it is spoken, by using speech marks. A comma is added before the last speech mark, like this:

"I can see people on the rocks and in the water," shouted Grace.

Copy these sentences into your book. Leave an equal space between your letters and an equal space between your words. Add the missing speech marks and commas.

1 We can't just leave them to drown sobbed Grace.
2 Grace, the sea is very rough said her father.
3 If we both go, we can row together pleaded Grace.

Remember, speech marks are written at the same height as ascenders.

EXTENSION

When someone else writes information about the life of a real person, it is called a biography. Use the notes below to make a short biography of Grace Darling. Write it into your book in your best handwriting.

Grace Darling (1815-42)

Her father was a lighthouse keeper.

In 1838, a boat called the 'Forfarshire' struck rocks near the lighthouse.

Grace and her father rowed out in a small boat to rescue the survivors.

They had to make their trip through huge waves.

They became famous for their great bravery.

Remember, letters must not touch each other, like this:

11

Developing Skills

Focus

- Write the objectives for the lesson on the board.
- Write up the whole class sentence, explaining how words that are spoken are enclosed in speech marks.
- Point out that speech marks do not touch letters, just as letters do not touch each other.
- Talk about leaving the correct space between letters; using the joining line helps to ensure the correct amount of space is left and letters do not touch each other.
- Write an example of letters touching, e.g. **a** and **n**, and then write the same two letters with a diagonal join.
- Discuss spacing between words.
- Demonstrate writing the Focus words on the board. Suggest to the class that they practise on their whiteboards before copying the words and the sentence into their books.
- *Extension activity:* point out that these words contain unstressed vowels, e.g. **fright<u>e</u>n<u>e</u>d**. Ask the children to underline the unstressed vowel in each word.

Extra

- Explain that speech marks are written at the same height as the top of ascenders.
- Remind the children to space their letters and words carefully as they copy the sentences.
- Tell them to position the missing speech marks and commas correctly.

Extension

- Discuss what a biography is.
- Read the information about Grace Darling.
- Tell the children that you want them to write a short biography of Grace Darling using the information given.
- Model writing the title and the first two lines of her biography on the board.
- Point out that the diagonal joins help ensure letters are correctly spaced within the word.
- Ask the children to write the biography into their books, or on to plain paper with guidelines.

Resources and Assessment

Focus

More practice leaving space between letters. Writing words containing unstressed vowels, joining letters correctly to ensure they do not touch. Underlining unstressed vowels.

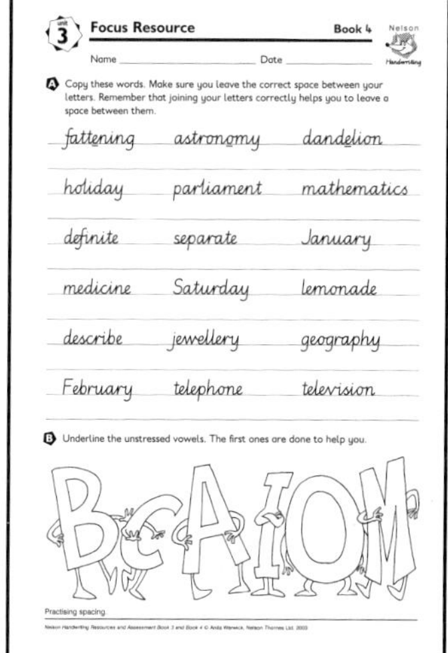

3 Focus Resource Book 4 Nelson Handwriting

Name ______ Date ______

A Copy these words. Make sure you leave the correct space between your letters. Remember that joining your letters correctly helps you to leave a space between them.

fattening astronomy dandelion
holiday parliament mathematics
definite separate January
medicine Saturday lemonade
describe jewellery geography
February telephone television

B Underline the unstressed vowels. The first ones are done to help you.

Practising spacing.

Extension

Further practice leaving correct space between letters and words and writing speech marks. Adding speech marks to show the beginning and end of direct speech.

3 Extension Resource Book 4 Nelson Handwriting

Name ______ Date ______

When writing down exactly what is spoken, we use speech marks to show the beginning and end of the direct speech.

Copy these sentences. Leave the correct space between letters and the correct space between words. Add the commas, full stops and speech marks, like this:

Grace yelled, "I can see some survivors."

1 Dad, keep rowing shouted Grace
2 How much further is it? asked her father
3 We're nearly there exclaimed Grace
4 Thank you for saving us sobbed the survivors
5 Three of you sit at the front said Grace and the rest sit behind me
6 Dad, I know it's hard said Grace but we're nearly home

Practising spacing.

Assessment

- The letters are joined correctly using horizontal and diagonal joining lines.
- The letters do not touch each other.
- The correct space is left between words.

UNIT 4

Objectives

- To write quickly but legibly.
- To use speedwriting to make notes.

Spelling links

- unstressed vowels

Nelson theme – shipwrecks

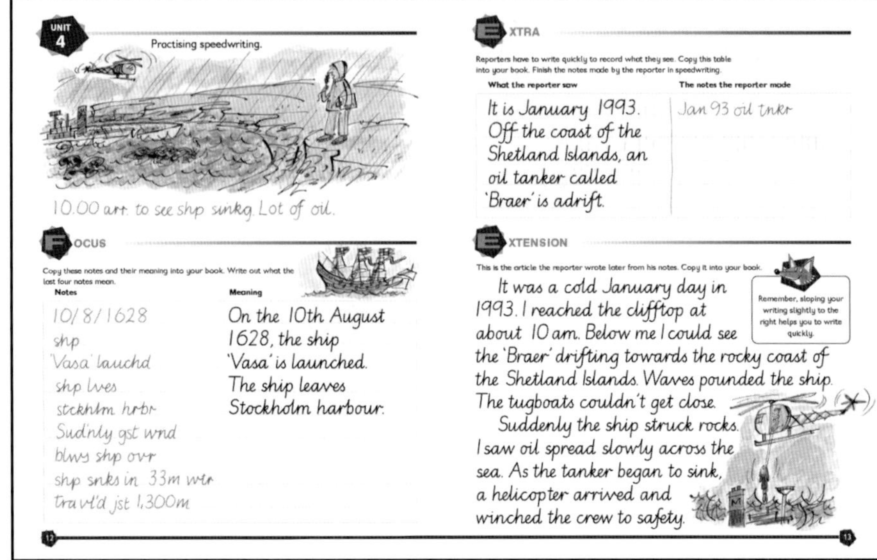

UNIT 4 Practising speedwriting.

10.00 arr to see ship sinkg Lot of oil.

FOCUS

Copy these notes and their meaning into your book. Write out what the last four notes mean.

Notes	Meaning
10/8/1628	On the 10th August
ship	1628, the ship
'Vasa' lauchd	'Vasa' is launched.
shp lves	The ship leaves
stckhlm hrbr	Stockholm harbour.
Sudnly gst wnd	
blws shp ovr	
shp snks in 33m wtr	
travl'd jst 1,300m	

EXTRA

Reporters have to write quickly to record what they see. Copy this table into your book. Finish the notes made by the reporter in speedwriting.

What the reporter saw	The notes the reporter made
It is January 1993. Off the coast of the Shetland Islands, an oil tanker called 'Braer' is adrift.	Jan 93 oil tnkr

EXTENSION

This is the article the reporter wrote later from his notes. Copy it into your book.

It was a cold January day in 1993. I reached the clifftop at about 10 am. Below me I could see the 'Braer' drifting towards the rocky coast of the Shetland Islands. Waves pounded the ship. The tugboats couldn't get close.

Suddenly the ship struck rocks. I saw oil spread slowly across the sea. As the tanker began to sink, a helicopter arrived and winched the crew to safety.

Remember, sloping your writing slightly to the right helps you to write quickly.

12 13

Developing Skills

Focus

- Share the lesson objectives with the children.
- Write the whole class sentence on the board, explaining the abbreviations as you write.
- Talk about when we might need to write quickly, e.g. when making lists, notes, or taking telephone messages. Ask for other suggestions.
- Emphasise that even when we write quickly, our writing still needs to be legible.
- Study and discuss the sample notes and their meaning.
- Discuss which words might contain unstressed vowels and comment that these words might be tricky to spell; suggest a dictionary might be needed to check, e.g. **travelled**.
- Ask the children to write out in full what the last three notes might mean.
- Remind the children to slope their writing slightly to the right. This will also help them write more quickly.

Extra

- Study and discuss the Focus section example.
- Ask the children to model this exercise on that example.
- Tell them to draw two columns in their books. In one column they should copy what the reporter saw and in the other they need to finish making the reporter's notes, using speedwriting.

Extension

- Read the reporter's finished article.
- Model writing the first sentence on the board.
- Remind the children to slope their writing slightly to the right and use their best handwriting as they copy the finished article into their books.

Resources and Assessment

Focus

Underlining the main points in a newspaper article about the *Titanic*. Writing the notes from which the article might have been written.

Focus Resource Book 4 Nelson Handwriting

Name ________ Date ________

A Reporters have to write quickly. They often use notes. This is a reporter's finished article about the sinking of the *Titanic* in 1912. Underline the main points in the article.

Mr C.H. Stengal, a first-class passenger who was on board the *Titanic* the night it sank, said that when the *Titanic* struck the iceberg the impact was terrific, and great blocks of ice were thrown on the deck, killing a number of people. The stern of the vessel rose in the air, and people ran shrieking from their berths below. Women and children were quickly placed in boats by the sailors, who like their officers, it was stated, were heard to threaten that they would shoot male passengers if they attempted to get in the boats ahead of the women. Indeed, it was said that shots were actually heard.

B Write the notes from which the article was written. The first ones are done to help you.

Mr C H Stengal 1st cls pass

Titanic struck iceberg impact terrific

blocks ice thrown on dck

Practising speedwriting.

Extension

Copying a passage quickly but legibly.

Extension Resource Book 4 Nelson Handwriting

Name ________ Date ________

Copy this passage quickly but neatly.

At 12.30 a.m. on 4 April 2001 the ship lost power in both her engines and began to float helplessly towards the rocks. The wind was blowing at gale force. Waves over 25 metres high were crashing over the ship. At 12.40 a.m. a terrific bang was heard. The ship had hit a rock and there was a large hole in her side. Water began to pour into the hull as the passengers and crew ran towards the lifeboats. At 1.00 a.m. a helicopter arrived at the scene and began to winch the passengers and crew to safety. Miraculously, everyone survived.

Practising speedwriting.

Assessment

- The writing is done quickly, but is legible.
- Notes are used to help write quickly.
- Best handwriting is used to write the finished article.

UNIT 5

Objectives

- To understand that the way we write depends on what we are writing and who is going to read it.
- To understand that drafting and editing are part of the handwriting process.

Nelson theme – Victorians

UNIT 5

Practising drafting and editing.

Drafting your writing helps you get it right.

FOCUS

The three stages of drafting, editing and final copy are below. Look at them and write the final copy into your book.

Isimbard Kingdom Brunell was 1 of Britains gretest engineaRs.

a
Isimbard Kingdom Brunell
one a
was 1 of Britain's gretest
e
engineaRs.

Isambard Kingdom Brunel was one of Britain's greatest engineers.

When writing a first draft, you do not need to use your best handwriting as no one else is going to read it.

EXTRA

Read this draft. Some of the draft has been edited. Copy the draft into your book and correct the rest of the mistakes.

a
Isimbard Kingdom Brunell was 1 of Britains gretest enginears. 1826 he began working on the thames tunnel. It took allmost 18 years to finish bcause walls kept collapsing. It is still used today as part off London's underground railway.

EXTENSION

This tribute to Isambard Kingdom Brunel has been drafted and edited. Write the final copy into your book.

a e
By his defth the greatist off
i s
Britain's engeneers had been
Brunel
lost. He was a man with striking originality of
g is
thoutht, bold in her plans but right.

14 15

Developing Skills

Focus

- Share the lesson objectives with the children as you write the whole class sentence on the board.
- Explain what drafting and editing are.
- Talk about writing in different ways for different audiences and purposes.
- Use the activity to discuss drafting.
- Ask the children to think of other occasions when drafting might be useful, e.g when planning stories or other written work.
- Tell the children to copy the corrected draft into their books, using their best handwriting.

Extra

- Tell the children to copy out this extract of a first draft of a newspaper report.
- Point out that first draft would not need to be done in best handwriting.
- Explain that there are mistakes in this piece of writing and they will have to edit it, checking and correcting spellings and punctuation.

Extension

- Ask the children to read the edited extract about Brunel.
- Point out that as it is a first draft they will need to read it carefully and look at the corrections which have to be made.
- Ask them to write out the final copy using their best handwriting.

Resources and Assessment

Focus

Correcting spelling mistakes in first draft of a paragraph about Brunel. Writing corrected draft in best handwriting.

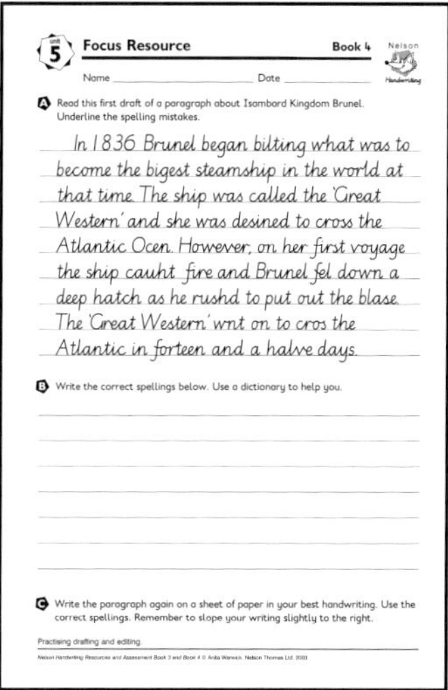
Unit 5 **Focus Resource** Book 4 Nelson Handwriting

Name ______ Date ______

A Read this first draft of a paragraph about Isambard Kingdom Brunel. Underline the spelling mistakes.

In 1836 Brunel began bilting what was to become the bigest steamship in the world at that time. The ship was called the 'Great Western' and she was desined to cross the Atlantic Ocen. However, on her first voyage the ship cauht fire and Brunel fel down a deep hatch as he rushd to put out the blase. The 'Great Western' wnt on to cros the Atlantic in forteen and a halve days.

B Write the correct spellings below. Use a dictionary to help you.

C Write the paragraph again on a sheet of paper in your best handwriting. Use the correct spellings. Remember to slope your writing slightly to the right.

Practising drafting and editing

Nelson Handwriting Resources and Assessment Book 3 and Book 4 © Anita Warwick, Nelson Thomas Ltd. 2003

Extension

Further practice correcting a first draft – about another Victorian, Charles Darwin. Identifying and correcting spelling errors. Copying corrected draft in best handwriting.

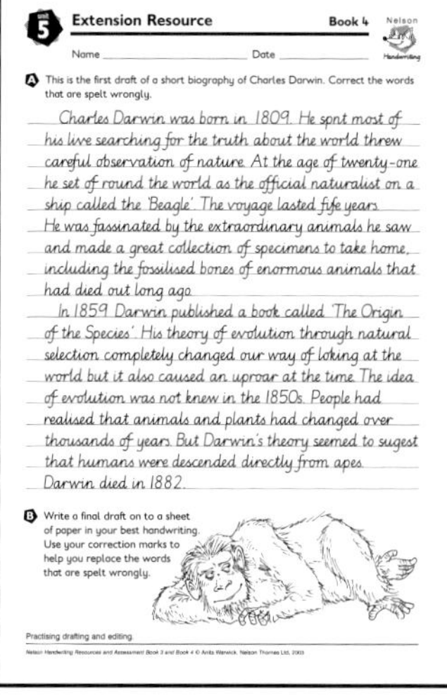
Unit 5 **Extension Resource** Book 4 Nelson Handwriting

Name ______ Date ______

A This is the first draft of a short biography of Charles Darwin. Correct the words that are spelt wrongly.

Charles Darwin was born in 1809. He spnt most of his live searching for the truth about the world threw careful observation of nature. At the age of twenty-one he set of round the world as the official naturalist on a ship called the 'Beagle'. The voyage lasted fife years. He was fassinated by the extraordinary animals he saw and made a great collection of specimens to take home, including the fossilised bones of enormous animals that had died out long ago.

In 1859 Darwin published a book called 'The Origin of the Species'. His theory of evolution through natural selection completely changed our way of loking at the world but it also caused an uproar at the time. The idea of evolution was not knew in the 1850s. People had realised that animals and plants had changed over thousands of years. But Darwin's theory seemed to sugest that humans were descended directly from apes. Darwin died in 1882.

B Write a final draft on to a sheet of paper in your best handwriting. Use your correction marks to help you replace the words that are spelt wrongly.

Practising drafting and editing

Nelson Handwriting Resources and Assessment Book 3 and Book 4 © Anita Warwick, Nelson Thomas Ltd. 2003

Assessment

- Best handwriting used for final draft.
- Children have edited their work, using a dictionary to check and correct spellings.
- The writing slopes slightly to the right in the notes.

UNIT 6

Objectives

- To form capital letters correctly.
- To ensure capital letters are the same height as ascenders.

Nelson theme – Victorians

UNIT 6

Practising writing capital letters.

Mary Seacole was a famous Victorian.

FOCUS

Here is each capital letter with its lower-case version. Copy the letters three times into your book.

Aa Bb Cc Dd Ee Ff Gg Hh Ii Jj
Kk Ll Mm Nn Oo Pp Qq Rr Ss
Tt Uu Vv Ww Xx Yy Zz

EXTRA

These sentences show what Mary Seacole did. Copy them into your book. Add the missing capital letters. The first one is done to help you.

I knew the hospitals in the Crimea were filthy and rat-infested.

1 i volunteered my services to the army, but i was rejected.

2 so i travelled to the crimea and opened the british hotel.

3 wherever i went i took medicines and food for the soldiers.

Remember, capital letters are the same height as ascenders.

EXTENSION

This is an extract from Mary Seacole's account of her own life, her autobiography. Copy the extract into your book. Make sure your capital letters are as tall as ascenders.

The first day that I approached the wharf (at Balaclava) a party of sick and wounded had just arrived. Seeing a poor artilleryman. I ran up to him at once, and eased the stiff dressing. and well was I rewarded when the poor fellow's groans subsided into a restless easy mutter.

From *'Wonderful Adventures of Mrs Seacole in Many Lands'*

Remember, capital letters are break letters.

Developing Skills

Focus

- List the objectives for the lesson on the board.
- Write the whole class sentence on the board, explaining that capital letters are the same height as ascenders.
- Remind the class when capital letters are used.
- Model writing some capital letters and their lower-case versions. Pick out the letters that are trickier to form, e.g. **G**, **K**, **P**, **R**, **Y**.
- Suggest the children practise writing these letters on their whiteboards.
- Tell the children to copy all the capital letters, and their lower-case versions, into their books.

Extra

- Read the sentences.
- Discuss the missing capital letters.
- Model writing the first sentence on the board, inserting capital letters in the correct place.
- Ask the children to copy the sentences into their books, inserting the missing capital letters.

Extension

- Read the extract from Mary Seacole's autobiography.
- Model writing the first sentence on the board.
- Ask the children to copy the extract into their books, or on to plain paper with guidelines underneath, using their best handwriting.

Resources and Assessment

Focus

Copying alphabet acrostic poem using all 26 capital letters.

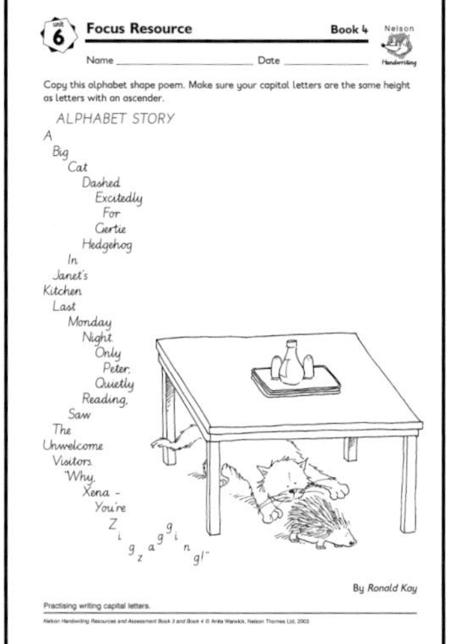

unit 6 **Focus Resource** Book 4 Nelson Handwriting

Name ______ Date ______

Copy this alphabet shape poem. Make sure your capital letters are the same height as letters with an ascender.

ALPHABET STORY

A
Big
Cat
Dashed
Excitedly
For
Gertie
Hedgehog
In
Janet's
Kitchen
Last
Monday
Night.
Only
Peter,
Quietly
Reading,
Saw
The
Unwelcome
Visitors.
"Why,
Xena -
You're
Zigzagging!"

By *Ronald Kay*

Practising writing capital letters.

Nelson Handwriting Resources and Assessment Book 3 and Book 4 © Anita Warwick, Nelson Thornes Ltd, 2003

Extension

Further practice with capital letters. Copying a newspaper extract, inserting capital letters.

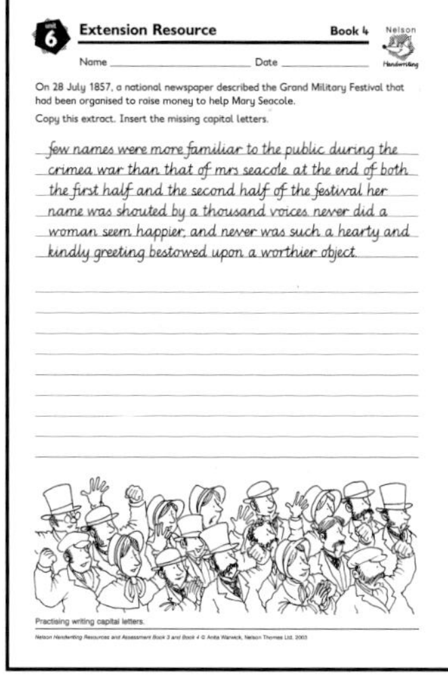

unit 6 **Extension Resource** Book 4 Nelson Handwriting

Name ______ Date ______

On 28 July 1857, a national newspaper described the Grand Military Festival that had been organised to raise money to help Mary Seacole.

Copy this extract. Insert the missing capital letters.

few names were more familiar to the public during the crimea war than that of mrs seacole at the end of both the first half and the second half of the festival her name was shouted by a thousand voices never did a woman seem happier, and never was such a hearty and kindly greeting bestowed upon a worthier object.

Practising writing capital letters.

Assessment

- The capital letters are formed correctly.
- The capital letters almost twice the height of the x-height.
- The capital letters are used correctly.

UNIT 7

Objectives

- To write fluently and legibly.
- To slope writing slightly to the right.

UNIT 7 Practising fluency.

Fluent writing flows quickly!

FOCUS

Copy these words into your book. Remember to join your letters.

stare whine crackle whistle
stared whined crackled whistled
staring whining crackling whistling

Sloping your writing and forming your joins correctly will help make your handwriting fluent.

XTRA

Use a word from the Focus on page 18 to finish these sentences. Copy the sentences into your book. Remember to write fluently and legibly.

1 The wind ______ through the trees.
2 I could hear a dog ______ in the distance.
3 Suddenly I heard the log fire ______.
4 Then I saw two eyes ______ at me.

XTENSION

Copy this passage into your book using fluent handwriting.

There were strange whining noises and odd whistling sounds that Imran couldn't identify. He felt a shiver run down his spine. What could the noises be? He crept forward. Suddenly he heard a loud moan from somewhere beneath his feet. Could there be dungeons under the castle floor? If so, who or what was down there?

Remember to use your best handwriting when you want to present neat, careful work.

18 19

Spelling links

- verbs which drop final **e** when adding **ed**, and **ing**

Nelson theme – mysteries and the unexplained

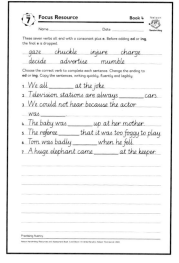

Developing Skills

Focus

- Share the lesson objectives with the class.
- Write the whole class sentence on the board, pointing out that sloping writing slightly to the right is an aid to quicker, more fluent writing.
- Emphasise the need to sit correctly and position the paper correctly.
- Stress that the joins should not change as you increase your writing speed. Nor should the spacing of words and letters be affected by writing faster.
- Model writing some of the verbs on the board.
- Point out that verbs ending in **e** drop the **e** when adding the suffix **ed**, e.g. **stare/stared**, **crackle/crackled**.
- Remind the children that verbs ending in **e** also drop the **e** when adding **ing**, e.g. **stare/staring**.
- Suggest the children practise these words on their whiteboards.
- Ask them to copy the words neatly into their books.

Extra

- Read the sentences.
- Ask the children to suggest words from the Focus section to complete the sentences.
- Model writing the first sentence on the board, pointing out that fluent writing is still neat and legible.
- Ask the children to copy the sentences into their books.

Extension

- Read the passage, which is a descriptive extract from a story.
- Remind the children of the objectives of the lesson.
- Ask them to copy the passage in a fluent, neat and legible handwriting style.
- Writing should slope slightly to the right, and be joined, neat and legible.

Resources and Assessment

Focus

Completing sentences by choosing verbs from a list, changing the ending to **ed** or **ing**. Copying sentences quickly and fluently.

7 Focus Resource — Book 4 — Nelson Handwriting

Name ______ Date ______

These seven verbs all end with a consonant plus **e**. Before adding **ed** or **ing**, the final **e** is dropped.

gaze chuckle injure charge decide advertise mumble

Choose the correct verb to complete each sentence. Change the ending to **ed** or **ing**. Copy the sentences, writing quickly, fluently and legibly.

1 We all ______ at the joke.
2 Television stations are always ______ cars.
3 We could not hear because the actor was ______.
4 The baby was ______ up at her mother.
5 The referee ______ that it was too foggy to play.
6 Tom was badly ______ when he fell.
7 A huge elephant came ______ at the keeper.

Practising fluency

Extension

Copying a poem, practising sloping writing, joining letters, writing quickly and fluently.

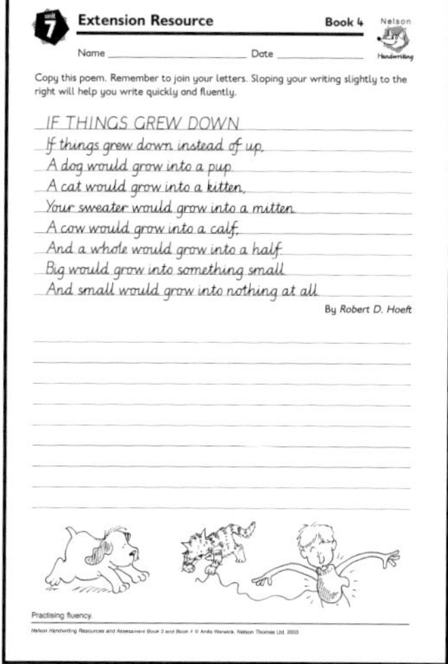

7 Extension Resource — Book 4 — Nelson Handwriting

Name ______ Date ______

Copy this poem. Remember to join your letters. Sloping your writing slightly to the right will help you write quickly and fluently.

IF THINGS GREW DOWN
If things grew down instead of up
A dog would grow into a pup
A cat would grow into a kitten
Your sweater would grow into a mitten
A cow would grow into a calf
And a whole would grow into a half
Big would grow into something small
And small would grow into nothing at all

By Robert D. Hoeft

Practising fluency

Assessment

- Use a ruler to check that the letters are sloping to the right (no more than 8 degrees from the vertical) and that the slope is even.
- Children write quickly and join their letters.

NIT 8

Objectives

- To write in indented paragraphs.
- To identify key ideas in a text and use paragraphing.

Nelson theme – mysteries and the unexplained

UNIT 8

Practising paragraphs.

Paragraphs help you to organise your writing.

FOCUS

Copy this paragraph into your book in your best handwriting.

The Loch Ness Monster is believed to live in a loch, or lake, in Scotland. Some people claim they have seen it. Some have even taken photographs of a strange dark shape.

Remember to indent the first word of each paragraph.

EXTRA

Write the sentences below into your book. Divide the sentences into two paragraphs. Remember to start each new paragraph on a new line and indent the first word.

The Abominable Snowman, or the Yeti, is said to be a huge, hairy, human-like creature living in the Himalayas. In 1957, an explorer set out on a Yeti hunt after five local people had been killed. But he didn't find the Yeti.

EXTENSION

Write the sentences below into your book. Divide the sentences into three paragraphs.

In 1951, a climber took photographs of huge footprints in the snow. Could these have been made by the Yeti? An expert on snow explained that footprints made by a smaller animal could have started to melt in the midday sun and frozen again at night. Each time this happened, the footprints would have got bigger until they looked enormous. High in the mountains, the air is very thin. The lack of oxygen can make people imagine strange things.

20 21

Developing Skills

Focus

- List the lesson objectives on the board.
- Write up the whole class sentence, explaining how a paragraph is a group of sentences about the same idea.
- Point out that each new paragraph starts on a new line and is indented (this term will need explaining).
- Study and discuss the passage. Encourage the children to volunteer suggestions as to what the main idea of each paragraph is.
- Ask the children to copy the paragraphs in their best handwriting.

Extra

- Read the information about the Abominable Snowman.
- Point out that the information can be written as two paragraphs.
- Ask the children to identify the two key ideas, and then divide the passage into two paragraphs.
- Tell them to copy the information as two paragraphs, using their best handwriting and remembering to indent each paragraph.

Extension

- Read the rest of the account.
- Ask the children to identify three paragraphs.
- Tell them to copy the three paragraphs into their books.

Resources and Assessment

Focus

Copying a passage about the Sphinx, using best handwriting and remembering to indent first line.

unit 8 **Focus Resource** Book 4 Nelson Handwriting

Name ______________ Date ______________

Copy this paragraph neatly. Remember to indent the first word.

The pyramids of Giza are guarded by a huge sphinx. This massive stone statue of a lion has the head of a man, who may be the pharaoh Khafra. The Great Sphinx was probably built on Khafra's orders. It looks east, towards the rising sun. For most of the last 4,500 years it has been covered in sand.

Practising paragraphs.

Nelson Handwriting Resources and Assessment Book 3 and Book 4 © Anita Warwick, Nelson Thomes Ltd, 2003

Extension

Dividing passage about standing stones into two paragraphs. Copying paragraphs in best handwriting.

unit 8 **Extension Resource** Book 4 Nelson Handwriting

Name ______________ Date ______________

Read this passage. Divide the passage into two paragraphs, each about a different main idea. Write the two paragraphs. Remember to indent the first word of each paragraph.

Many stone temples were built on Malta between 3600 BC and 2500 BC. The oldest have walls at least 6m long and 3.5m tall. The most impressive temple is the Hypogeum, carved on three levels deep underground. Later, wood or stone circles called henges, such as Stonehenge in England, were built. Stonehenge was built over many centuries from about 2800 BC to 1400 BC. The first Stonehenge was a circular earthwork made up of a bank and ditch. Later, large blocks of shaped stones were put up.

Practising paragraphs.

Nelson Handwriting Resources and Assessment Book 3 and Book 4 © Anita Warwick, Nelson Thomes Ltd, 2003

Assessment

- Each new paragraph begins on a new line.
- Each paragraph is indented.
- Children understand the key idea in each paragraph.

UNIT 9

Objectives

- To ensure all small letters are the same height and size.
- To form ascenders and descenders in correct proportion.

Spelling links

- prefixes

Nelson theme – aliens

UNIT 9

Practising keeping letters in the correct proportion.

ufologist

Form your letters neatly and consistently.

FOCUS

A These prefixes make a word have the opposite meaning. Copy them into your book.

un de dis anti il

B Add the prefix *un* to the words below. Write the words into your book. The first one is done to help you.

un + happy = unhappy

kind
educated
helpful
identified
familiar

When you join the letter *f* to *a*, *u*, or *i*, the horizontal joining line helps you form the next letter in the correct proportion, like this: *fa fu fi*

22

EXTRA

Copy this passage into your book. Choose the correct word.

A big mystery that has so far remained solved/unsolved is this: what are the identified/unidentified flying objects that have been seen in the sky? Some people have said that they are usual/unusual cloud formations. Ufologists usually/unusually claim that the Earth is being watched by alien intelligences. If so, what do these aliens want? Will we ever discover the truth?

EXTENSION

Copy this poem on to plain paper. Keep your letters in the correct proportion.

UNIDENTIFIED FLYING OBJECT

There
in the night sky
with lights flashing
it swoops from high to low –
and straight away it's identified
as an unfamiliar
UFO!

By Ronold Kay

Remember, capital letters are as tall as ascenders.

23

Developing Skills

Focus

- Share the lesson objectives with the class and write the whole class sentence on the board.
- Make sure the children understand that capital letters and letters with ascenders (except **t**) are almost twice the x-height, and that letters with descenders are almost the same size as letters with ascenders, but their descenders go below the baseline.
- Study and discuss the five prefixes listed.
- Model writing the prefixes on the board. Talk about the relative height of the letters, e.g. the letter **d** is almost twice the height of the letter **e**, and small letters are all the same height.
- Encourage the children to volunteer suggestions for words that could have the prefixes **un**, **de**, **dis**, **anti** or **il** added. The children could work in pairs, or use a dictionary, or write words on their whiteboards.
- Ask the children to copy the prefixes and words into their books.

Extra

- Read the passage.
- Discuss the words with the prefix **un**.
- Model writing the first sentence on the board, emphasising the relative heights of the letters.
- Ask the children to copy the passage into their books, remembering to keep their letters in proportion.

Extension

- Read the poem.
- Tell the group to copy the poem on to plain paper, with guidelines underneath.
- Remind them to form and join their letters carefully.

Resources and Assessment

Focus

Practice of the prefix **dis**. Inserting correct words into sentences. Copying sentences, ensuring the letters are in correct proportion.

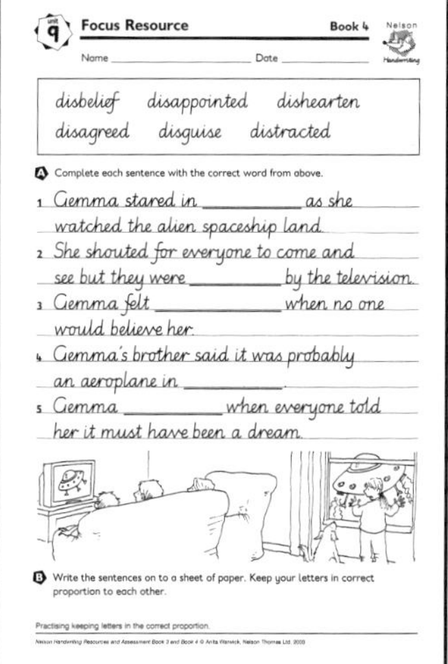

Unit 9 Focus Resource Book 4 Nelson Handwriting

Name ______ Date ______

disbelief disappointed dishearten
disagreed disguise distracted

A Complete each sentence with the correct word from above.

1 Gemma stared in ______ as she watched the alien spaceship land.
2 She shouted for everyone to come and see but they were ______ by the television.
3 Gemma felt ______ when no one would believe her.
4 Gemma's brother said it was probably an aeroplane in ______.
5 Gemma ______ when everyone told her it must have been a dream.

B Write the sentences on to a sheet of paper. Keep your letters in correct proportion to each other.

Practising keeping letters in the correct proportion.

Nelson Handwriting Resources and Assessment Book 3 and Book 4 © Anita Warwick, Nelson Thomas Ltd. 2003

Extension

More practice writing letters in correct proportion by copying poem.

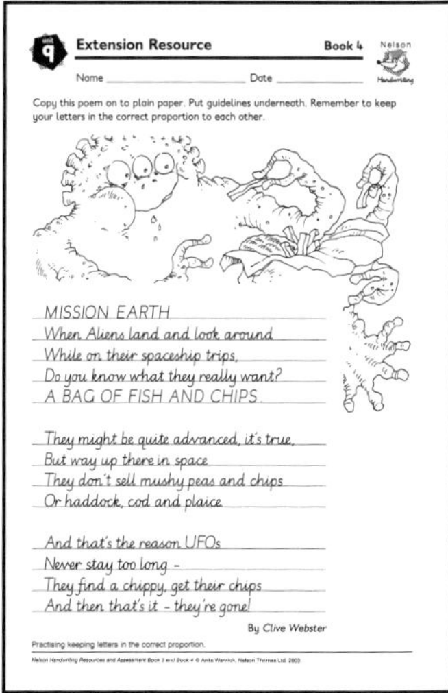

Unit 9 Extension Resource Book 4 Nelson Handwriting

Name ______ Date ______

Copy this poem on to plain paper. Put guidelines underneath. Remember to keep your letters in the correct proportion to each other.

MISSION EARTH
When Aliens land and look around
While on their spaceship trips,
Do you know what they really want?
A BAG OF FISH AND CHIPS.

They might be quite advanced, it's true,
But way up there in space
They don't sell mushy peas and chips
Or haddock, cod and plaice.

And that's the reason UFOs
Never stay too long –
They find a chippy, get their chips
And then that's it – they're gone!

By Clive Webster

Practising keeping letters in the correct proportion.

Nelson Handwriting Resources and Assessment Book 3 and Book 4 © Anita Warwick, Nelson Thomas Ltd. 2003

Assessment

- The capital letters are the same height as letters with ascenders.
- The ascenders are almost twice the x-height.
- Letters with descenders are the same size as those with ascenders, but the descenders go below the baseline.

UNIT 10

Objectives

- To present a piece of writing attractively.
- To design a party invitation.

Spelling links

- party invitation words

Nelson theme – aliens

UNIT 10

Practising presentation.

FOCUS

Practise drawing different borders on a piece of paper. You can use borders when you want to present a piece of writing attractively.

EXTRA

Practise writing this text on to plain paper.

You are invited to my
ALIENS
fancy dress birthday party
on Saturday June 15th at 4 pm
at 29 The Spinneys, Chipping Aston.
From Stuart Stevens

R.S.V.P.

Draw some guidelines in pencil on your paper. This will help you keep your letters the correct height and size and your writing straight across the paper.

EXTENSION

Use these instructions to design and make an invitation to 'An aliens fancy dress party' on a piece of plain paper. Don't forget to say who the invitation is for, what it is to, the day, the time, where it will take place, and who it is from.

1 Plan where your writing will go.
2 Pencil in the borders and colour them.
3 Lightly pencil in some guidelines. Use a ruler to make sure the lines are the same width apart.
4 Write in your text.
5 Rub out the pencil lines.

You are less likely to smudge your work if you start at the top left-hand corner.

This was written with a fine pen nib.
This was written with a medium pen nib.
This was written with a broad pen nib.

24 25

Developing Skills

Focus

- Talk about the lesson objectives, suggesting that borders can be used around a piece of writing to help make it look attractive.
- Model drawing some different border designs on the board.
- Discuss a border design for a party invitation.
- Ask the children to practise drawing different types of borders on their whiteboards and show them to the rest of the class.
- Tell them to draw a border design for a party invitation on a piece of paper.

Extra

- Draw three pencil lines on the board to show how to help make letters the correct height and size. Point out that, as a rough guide, tall letters are almost twice the height of small letters.
- Model writing some of the party invitation text.

Extension

- Explain that when designing a party invitation you need to plan the layout of the writing.
- First you need to make a rough draft of what you want to write.
- Next you need to use a ruler and draw some lines on the paper. It is useful to draw three feint lines with a pencil, for each line of writing. These lines will help make the small letters and the tall letters the correct, uniform height.
- Model drawing three lines on the board, measuring the height of the lines.
- Point out that spacing between lines is also important; to get this right you need to decide how many lines you want to fit on the page.
- You can begin writing at the side of the paper or, if you want to centre the text, you can calculate using 4mm per letter. Count the letters and spaces in the line of text and multiply by 4. Measure the width of the page and subtract the space needed for the writing. Then divide by 2; this tells you where to begin to write. It is only a rough guide, but it will centre the writing and help make it look attractive.
- Model writing the first line of text.

Resources and Assessment

Focus

Copying a certificate for winning a fancy dress competition.

unit 10 **Focus Resource** Book 4 Nelson Handwriting

Name ______________ Date ______________

Copy this certificate into the space below and decorate it with your own border.

CERTIFICATE
Winner of the Aliens Fancy Dress Competition
Name ______________
Congratulations!
You have won first prize in the
Aliens Fancy Dress Competition.

Practising presentation.

Nelson Handwriting Resources and Assessment Book 3 and Book 4 © Anita Warwick, Nelson Thornes Ltd, 2003

Extension

Writing and presenting a thank you letter.

unit 10 **Extension Resource** Book 4 Nelson Handwriting

Name ______________ Date ______________

A Copy this letter on to the notepaper below.

28 Ashley Croft
Oxford OX2 HRD
16th October 2003

Dear Stuart,
Thank you for inviting me to your birthday party.
I had a great time. The Aliens Fancy Dress Competition was fun, even though my hair is still purple!
Dad says you can stay next weekend. Can you come?
Best wishes from
Andrew

B Now write a reply on a sheet of paper. Remember the address and the date.

Practising presentation.

Nelson Handwriting Resources and Assessment Book 3 and Book 4 © Anita Warwick, Nelson Thornes Ltd, 2003

Assessment

- Feint pencil lines drawn to help make letters correct height and size.
- The writing is well spaced out on page.
- A border is used to help make the invitation look attractive.

UNIT 11

Objectives

- To use bullet points to separate sentences in instructional text.
- To write instructions using best handwriting.

Spelling links

- connectives

Nelson theme – safety first

UNIT 11 Practising writing instructions

Cross the road safely!

FOCUS

Copy these connective words into your book.

so but however
also because furthermore
or before otherwise
and therefore as well as

Remember, the letter f is a tall letter and its tail falls below the line.

EXTRA

Bullet points are often used to separate instructions. Copy these sentences into your book. Choose the correct connective word.

- Use a pedestrian crossing, otherwise/because choose a place where you can see in all directions.
- Always listen, otherwise/because sometimes you can hear traffic before you see it.

Take care! You must leave the same space between the bullet point and the first letter in each sentence.

EXTENSION

Put these instructions from The Green Cross Code into the correct order and number them. Copy the instructions into your book in your best handwriting.

Stop just before you get to the kerb.
First find a safe place to cross.
If traffic is coming, let it pass.
Look all around for traffic and listen.
When it is safe, go straight across the road – do not run.

26 27

Developing Skills

Focus

- List the lesson objectives on the board.
- Remind, or explain to, the children about connectives.
- Brainstorm a list of connectives and write them on the board.
- Consider the features of connectives: some are simple words, e.g. **and**, **so**; some are connective phrases, e.g. **as well as**; some are compound words, e.g. **furthermore**
- Ask the children to copy the list of connectives carefully into their books, using their best handwriting.

Extra

- Discuss the use of bullet points.
- Point out that bullet points are often used in instructional text to separate sentences.
- Tell the class to ensure that a consistent space is left between the bullet point and the first letter of each sentence.
- Read the sentences and ask the children to suggest which connective completes each sentence.
- Tell the children to copy the sentences, remembering to join their letters, slope their writing slightly to the right and leave a consistent space between words.

Extension

- Read the Green Cross Code rules.
- Remind the children that these are the rules we should all follow when we cross a road.
- The rules have been muddled. Ask the children to suggest the correct order.
- Tell them to write the rules in the correct order, numbering them and using their best handwriting.

Resources and Assessment

Focus

Practice with connectives. Using a connective to join two sentences about firework safety precautions.

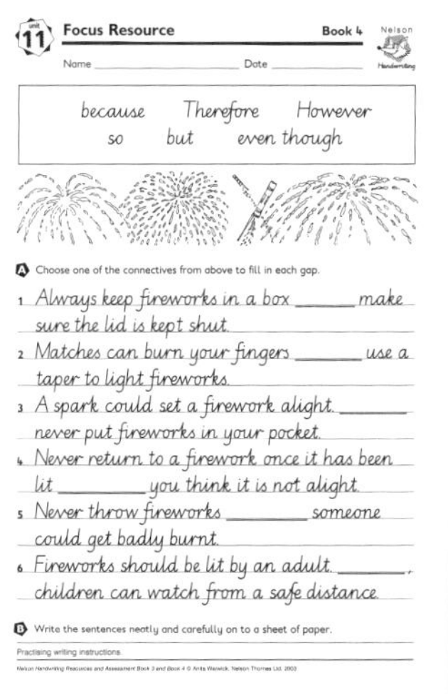

11 Focus Resource Book 4 Nelson Handwriting

Name ______ Date ______

because Therefore However
so but even though

A Choose one of the connectives from above to fill in each gap.

1 Always keep fireworks in a box ______ make sure the lid is kept shut
2 Matches can burn your fingers ______ use a taper to light fireworks
3 A spark could set a firework alight ______ never put fireworks in your pocket
4 Never return to a firework once it has been lit ______ you think it is not alight
5 Never throw fireworks ______ someone could get badly burnt
6 Fireworks should be lit by an adult ______, children can watch from a safe distance

B Write the sentences neatly and carefully on to a sheet of paper.

Practising writing instructions

Nelson Handwriting Resources and Assessment Book 3 and Book 4 © Anita Warwick, Nelson Thornes Ltd. 2003

Extension

Following instructions for designing and making a poster about a firework display.

11 Extension Resource Book 4 Nelson Handwriting

Name ______ Date ______

A Follow these instructions to help you design and make your own poster.

1 Make a rough draft of what you want to write and draw on your poster.
2 If you want a border, draw a margin in faint pencil all the way round your paper.
3 Decide how many lines of writing you want to fit on the page.
4 Using a ruler and pencil, draw three faint lines for each line of writing. These lines will help to make all your letters the correct height and size.
5 You need to centre each line of your text. Allow 4mm for each letter and 4mm for each space between the letters. For each line, count the letters in your text and add the number of spaces. Then multiply by 4.
6 Measure the width of the page in mm. Take away the space needed for the text (in 5 above) and then divide by 2. This is the distance from the left of the page, where you start to write. This is only a rough guide but it will help you centre your writing and make it look attractive.
7 Have a go! You may need several attempts to get the design the way you want it to look.
8 When you have finished, rub out all the pencil lines.

Firework Display
Roundwood Park
Sunday 3rd November 2002
7.30 pm
Admission £3.00

B Now write some instructions on how to design and make a birthday card. Remember to number them.

Practising writing instructions

Assessment

- The letters in the connectives are joined correctly.
- A consistent space is left between the bullet point and first letter of each sentence.
- The instructions are in the correct order and have been written in best handwriting.

UNIT 12

Objectives

- To use bullet points, or numbers, to separate sentences.
- To design and make an instructional leaflet, using best handwriting.

UNIT 12 Practising writing instructions.

Cyclists should always wear a helmet.

FOCUS

A Copy these instructions into your book.

Check! Wait! Stop! Dismount! Choose! Watch! Steer! Disappear!

B Think of four more instruction words. Write them into your book.

EXTRA

These instructions are for cyclists wanting to turn right. Copy them into your book. Add bullet points.

Check the traffic, signal, and move to the centre of the road.
Wait until there is a safe gap in the traffic before turning.
Stop and wait on the left until there is a safe gap in the traffic.
Dismount and push your bicycle across the road.

Remember to space out your instructions to make them clear.

EXTENSION

Design and make a leaflet called 'Buying a bicycle'. Plan your page. Decide where your writing will go. Will you use print writing or sloped and joined writing?

Write down the title of the leaflet. You need to include this advice for buyers:

- Check the cycle is the right size for you.
- Check the saddle and handlebars are the right height.
- Check the lights and reflectors are working properly.
- Check the brakes and gears are working efficiently.
- Check the tyres are inflated to the right pressure.

Remember to add bullet points or numbers if you want information to stand out.

Spelling links

- instructional words

Nelson theme – safety first

Developing Skills

Focus

- Write the objectives and the whole class sentence for the lesson on the board.
- Model writing the one-word instructions on the board.
- Suggest that the children practise writing these words, with the letters to the correct height and size, on their whiteboards.
- Remind the children that capital letters should be around twice the height of small letters.
- Tell the children to write the words carefully into their books, using their best handwriting.

Extra

- Discuss the use of bullet points.
- Point out that bullet points are often used in instructional text to separate sentences. A consistent space is left between the bullet point and the first letter of each sentence.
- Read the sentences and ask the children to copy them into their books adding either bullet points or numbers.
- Remind the children to join their letters, slope writing slightly to the right and leave a consistent space between words.

Extension

- The task is to design and make a leaflet about buying and maintaining a bicycle.
- Read the information provided.
- Ask the children for ideas regarding the design of the leaflet.
- Suggest they make a rough draft.
- Once they have finalised their design, they should copy it out in their best handwriting.
- Remind the children they may use either joined or printed handwriting, or a mixture of both. However, the handwriting must be neat and legible with consistent spacing between letters and words.

Resources and Assessment

Focus

Putting instructions for making a pizza in correct order. Copying instructions.

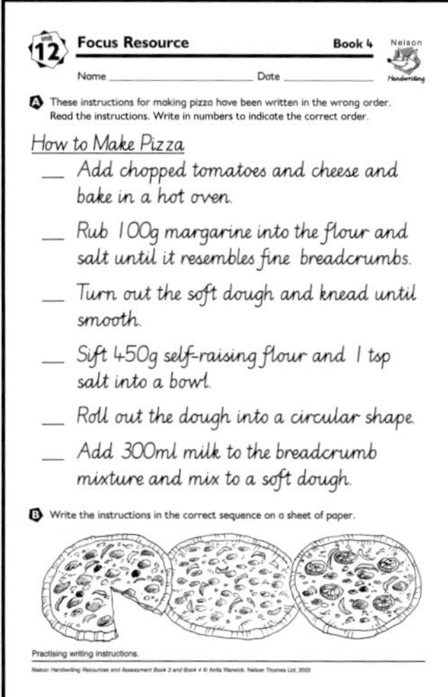

Unit 12 Focus Resource Book 4 Nelson Handwriting

Name ______________ Date ______________

A These instructions for making pizza have been written in the wrong order. Read the instructions. Write in numbers to indicate the correct order.

How to Make Pizza

__ Add chopped tomatoes and cheese and bake in a hot oven.

__ Rub 100g margarine into the flour and salt until it resembles fine breadcrumbs.

__ Turn out the soft dough and knead until smooth.

__ Sift 450g self-raising flour and 1 tsp salt into a bowl.

__ Roll out the dough into a circular shape.

__ Add 300ml milk to the breadcrumb mixture and mix to a soft dough.

B Write the instructions in the correct sequence on a sheet of paper.

Practising writing instructions.

Nelson Handwriting Resources and Assessment Book 3 and Book 4 © Anita Warwick, Nelson Thomas Ltd, 2003

Extension

Designing and making a poster about use of seat belts. Practice with bullet points and neat, careful handwriting.

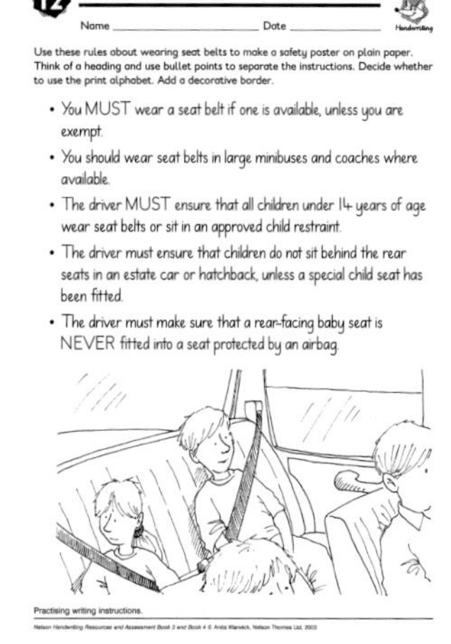

Unit 12 Extension Resource Book 4 Nelson Handwriting

Name ______________ Date ______________

Use these rules about wearing seat belts to make a safety poster on plain paper. Think of a heading and use bullet points to separate the instructions. Decide whether to use the print alphabet. Add a decorative border.

- You MUST wear a seat belt if one is available, unless you are exempt.
- You should wear seat belts in large minibuses and coaches where available.
- The driver MUST ensure that all children under 14 years of age wear seat belts or sit in an approved child restraint.
- The driver must ensure that children do not sit behind the rear seats in an estate car or hatchback, unless a special child seat has been fitted.
- The driver must make sure that a rear-facing baby seat is NEVER fitted into a seat protected by an airbag.

Practising writing instructions.

Assessment

- All letters are the correct height and size.
- Consistent space is left between bullet point/number and the first letter of sentence.
- Pencil lines drawn on the leaflet plan to help with design and layout.

NIT 13

Objectives

- To use different handwriting for different purposes.
- To make notes about what you have read.

Nelson theme – Ancient Greece

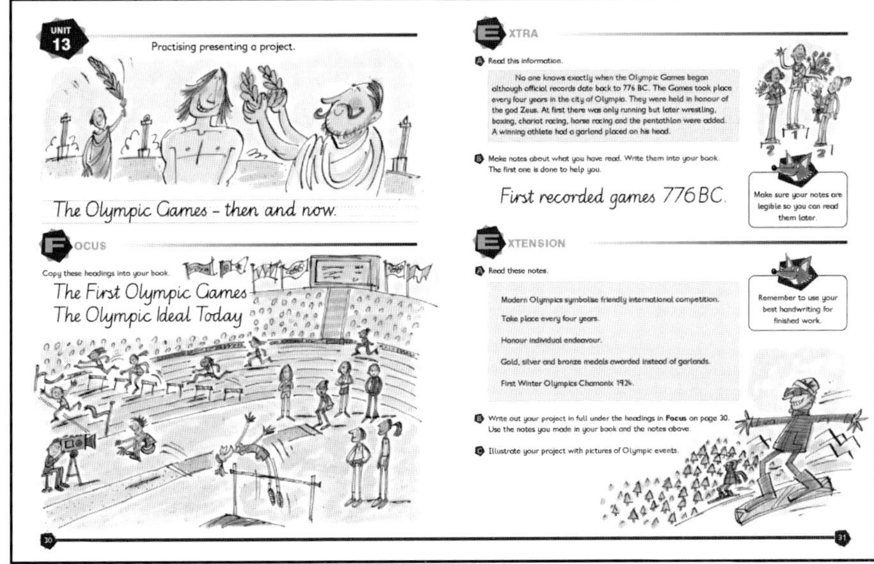

Practising presenting a project.

The Olympic Games – then and now.

FOCUS

Copy these headings into your book.

The First Olympic Games

The Olympic Ideal Today

EXTRA

A Read this information.

No one knows exactly when the Olympic Games began although official records date back to 776 BC. The Games took place every four years in the city of Olympia. They were held in honour of the god Zeus. At first there was only running but later wrestling, boxing, chariot racing, horse racing and the pentathlon were added. A winning athlete had a garland placed on his head.

B Make notes about what you have read. Write them into your book. The first one is done to help you.

First recorded games 776 BC.

Make sure your notes are legible so you can read them later.

EXTENSION

A Read these notes.

Modern Olympics symbolise friendly international competition.

Take place every four years.

Honour individual endeavour.

Gold, silver and bronze medals awarded instead of garlands.

First Winter Olympics Chamonix 1924.

Remember to use your best handwriting for finished work.

B Write out your project in full under the headings in **Focus** on page 30. Use the notes you made in your book and the notes above.

C Illustrate your project with pictures of Olympic events.

30 31

Developing Skills

Focus

- Share the lesson objectives with the children.
- Write the whole class sentence on the board.
- Explain that we use different handwriting for different purposes. Ask for volunteers to suggest when we use best handwriting, speedwriting, notes, etc.
- Read the chapter headings about the Olympic Games.
- Tell the children to copy the headings into their books, using best handwriting.
- Remind the children that best handwriting should slant slightly to the right, and be joined, fluent and legible, with letters the correct shape, height and size.

Extra

- Discuss making notes.
- Point out that when we write notes we do not need to use our best handwriting as no one else is going to read it. However, the writing should be legible as we have to be able to read it.
- When we write notes, we usually have to write quickly. Remind the children to continue to join their letters, as joined writing helps you to write quickly and fluently.
- Read the passage.
- Point out that when we write notes we pick out the main points.
- Ask the children to make notes about what they have read. It may help to model some notes on the board.
- Remind the children that handwriting, although not their best when making notes, must still be precise and legible.

Extension

- Read the notes about the Olympic Ideal Today. Ask the children to write a passage in full, using the notes.
- Remind the children that when writing a passage in full to insert into a project, they should use their best handwriting.
- The first draft, which will need editing and correcting, can be in rough, but the children must use their best handwriting for the final draft.

Resources and Assessment

Focus

More practice presenting a project. Sequencing events leading to the 1969 moon landing.

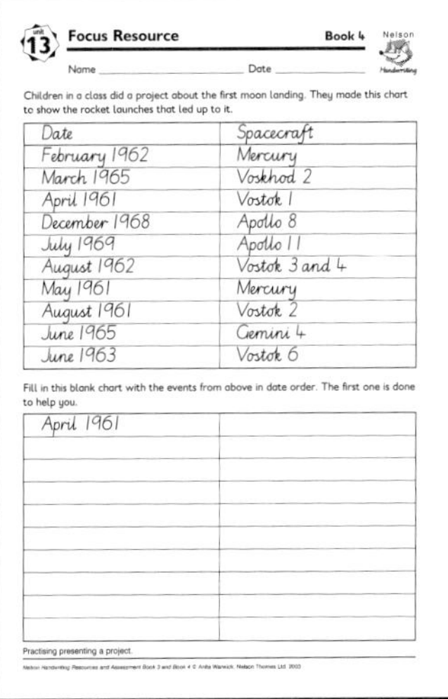

13 **Focus Resource** **Book 4** Nelson Handwriting

Name ______________ Date ______________

Children in a class did a project about the first moon landing. They made this chart to show the rocket launches that led up to it.

Date	Spacecraft
February 1962	Mercury
March 1965	Voskhod 2
April 1961	Vostok 1
December 1968	Apollo 8
July 1969	Apollo 11
August 1962	Vostok 3 and 4
May 1961	Mercury
August 1961	Vostok 2
June 1965	Gemini 4
June 1963	Vostok 6

Fill in this blank chart with the events from above in date order. The first one is done to help you.

April 1961	

Practising presenting a project.

Nelson Handwriting Resources and Assessment Book 3 and Book 4 © Anita Warwick, Nelson Thornes Ltd 2003

Extension

Sustained writing practice copying a poem about how it might feel to land on the moon.

13 **Extension Resource** **Book 4** Nelson Handwriting

Name ______________ Date ______________

These verses are about how it might feel to land on the moon. Copy them neatly on to a sheet of paper. Draw a border to suit the verses.

ASTRONAUTS AND CROSSES

I lay down by the Sea of Tranquillity
And drew pictures in the dust –
A house with a chimney, two windows, a door,
A path, some flowers, a tree
I have had some time now to adjust
I won't see my world any more,
Except from a distance, like a misty beacon.

I imagined a game of lunar football
A visored striker ghosting through
Defenders, in slow motion, to shoot
The golden goal to beat them all,
Like a fiery comet swerving through the blue
Spectators in their spacesuits might be mute,
But the scorer would be over the moon.

By Paul Sidley

Practising presenting a project.

Nelson Handwriting Resources and Assessment Book 3 and Book 4 © Anita Warwick, Nelson Thornes Ltd 2003

Assessment

- Notes are made using quick but legible handwriting.
- The first draft is edited and corrected.
- Best handwriting is used to write the final copy.

UNIT 14

Objectives

- To write quickly, fluently and legibly.

Nelson theme – Ancient Greece

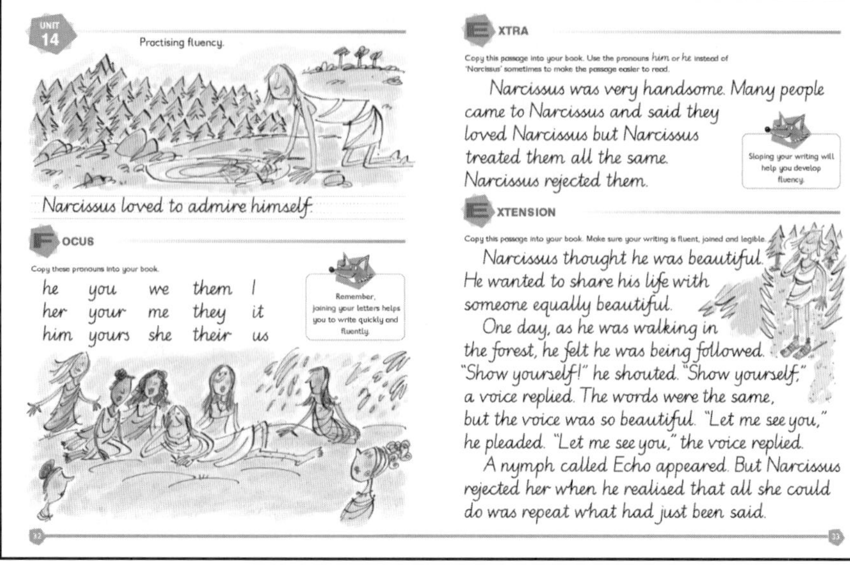

Unit 14 Practising fluency.

Narcissus loved to admire himself.

FOCUS

Copy these pronouns into your book.

he you we them I
her your me they it
him yours she their us

Remember, joining your letters helps you to write quickly and fluently.

EXTRA

Copy this passage into your book. Use the pronouns *him* or *he* instead of 'Narcissus' sometimes to make the passage easier to read.

Narcissus was very handsome. Many people came to Narcissus and said they loved Narcissus but Narcissus treated them all the same. Narcissus rejected them.

Sloping your writing will help you develop fluency.

EXTENSION

Copy this passage into your book. Make sure your writing is fluent, joined and legible.

Narcissus thought he was beautiful. He wanted to share his life with someone equally beautiful.

One day, as he was walking in the forest, he felt he was being followed. "Show yourself!" he shouted. "Show yourself," a voice replied. The words were the same, but the voice was so beautiful. "Let me see you," he pleaded. "Let me see you," the voice replied.

A nymph called Echo appeared. But Narcissus rejected her when he realised that all she could do was repeat what had just been said.

32 33

Developing Skills

Focus

- Explain that the lesson will focus on writing quickly, fluently and legibly.
- Model writing the whole class sentence in this way.
- Point out that to write fluently you need to keep your pen on the paper and join letters correctly.
- Remind the class to go back and cross the **t**'s and dot the **i**'s at the end of the sentence to increase fluency.
- Ask the children to write the heading as quickly as they can, making sure it is still neat and legible.
- Remind the children when pronouns are used and model some of these on the board.
- Suggest the children practise writing these words on their whiteboards.
- Ask them to copy the words neatly into their books, ensuring a consistency in size, spacing and speed.

Extra

- Read the passage about Narcissus.
- Ask the children which words we could use to replace Narcissus. How does this make it easier to read?
- Remind the children to position the paper correctly to aid fluency.
- Ask the children to copy the sentences into their books replacing Narcissus with an appropriate pronoun.

Extension

- Read the passage from the Greek myth about Narcissus.
- Remind the children of the objectives of the lesson.
- Model the first sentence to show fluency, returning at the end of a sentence to cross **t**'s and dot **i**'s.
- Ask them to copy the passage in a fluent, neat and legible handwiting style.

Resources and Assessment

Focus

More practice writing fluently. Copying passage about Ancient Greece, remembering to join letters correctly, slope writing slightly to the right and ensure letters are consistent in height and size.

Unit 14 Focus Resource Book 4 Nelson Handwriting

Name ______ Date ______

Copy this passage. Remember to join your letters at or near the top, to slope your writing slightly to the right and to write fluently and legibly.

Over a period of 2,000 years, the Ancient Greeks laid many of the foundations of the modern world. Some of their ideas about medicine, mathematics, and government are still in use today. They also introduced theatre, new ways in art, and building styles that can still be seen around us. Theirs was a civilisation of spectacular achievements as they travelled, traded and fought their way through the known world.

Practising fluency

Nelson Handwriting Resources and Assessment Book 3 and Book 4 © Anita Warwick, Nelson Thornes Ltd. 2003

Extension

Further practice writing fluently. Copying passage about the Ancient Greek legend of Medusa. Underlining pronouns.

Unit 14 Extension Resource Book 4 Nelson Handwriting

Name ______ Date ______

A Copy this Ancient Greek legend about Medusa on to a sheet of paper. Use neat, fluent handwriting. Remember to slope your writing slightly to the right and to join your letters correctly.

Medusa was one of three monsters called the Gorgons. They had the bodies of women, snakes for hair, teeth like the tusks of wild boars, sharp claws and wings of gold. Anyone who dared to look at the face of a Gorgon was turned to stone in horror.

The young hero Perseus was on a quest to kill Medusa. Fortunately, he had the help of the gods. Athena, the goddess of war, went with him on his journey. Hermes, messenger of the gods, gave him a sharp knife to cut off her head. Some nymphs gave him a pair of winged sandals so that he could fly, a magic helmet to make him invisible, and a special pouch to keep Medusa's head in if he was successful.

One final gift was from Athena herself. She handed Perseus a shield. "It contains no magic, but it is vital to your task," she explained.

"It's beautiful," said Perseus, admiring the gleaming shield. The bronze was so highly polished that he could see his face in it.

"Use it as a mirror," said the goddess, and the young hero understood.

From **'Ancient Greek Myths and Legends'** by *Philip Ardagh*

B Underline the pronouns. The first few are done to help you.

Practising fluency

Nelson Handwriting Resources and Assessment Book 3 and Book 4 © Anita Warwick, Nelson Thornes Ltd. 2003

Assessment

- The writing slopes slightly to the right.
- The letters are joined in a uniform style with all small letters being the same height and size.
- There is evidence of speed and fluency to the writing.

UNIT 15

Objectives

- To write and join double letters correctly.
- To ensure double letters are correct size and height.

Spelling links

Nelson theme – cliffs and treasure

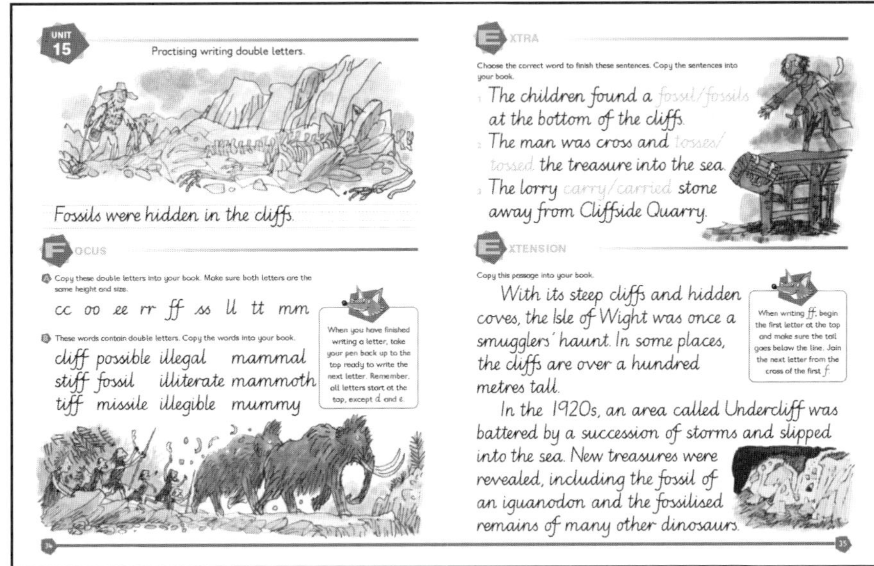

UNIT 15

Practising writing double letters.

Fossils were hidden in the cliffs.

FOCUS

A Copy these double letters into your book. Make sure both letters are the same height and size.

cc oo ee rr ff ss ll tt mm

B These words contain double letters. Copy the words into your book.

cliff possible illegal mammal
stiff fossil illiterate mammoth
tiff missile illegible mummy

When you have finished writing a letter, take your pen back up to the top ready to write the next letter. Remember, all letters start at the top, except d and e.

EXTRA

Choose the correct word to finish these sentences. Copy the sentences into your book.

1 The children found a fossil/fossils at the bottom of the cliffs.
2 The man was cross and tosses/tossed the treasure into the sea.
3 The lorry carry/carried stone away from Cliffside Quarry.

EXTENSION

Copy this passage into your book.

With its steep cliffs and hidden coves, the Isle of Wight was once a smugglers' haunt. In some places, the cliffs are over a hundred metres tall.

In the 1920s, an area called Undercliff was battered by a succession of storms and slipped into the sea. New treasures were revealed, including the fossil of an iguanodon and the fossilised remains of many other dinosaurs.

When writing ff, begin the first letter at the top and make sure the tail goes below the line. Join the next letter from the cross of the first f.

Developing Skills

Focus

- Write the whole class sentence on the board and underline the double letters **gg** and **ll**. Talk about the need to ensure double letters are both the same height and size.
- Model writing the sets of double letters on the board.
- Point out the size and height of the letters; small letters are almost half the size of letters with ascenders.
- Remind the class that the double letters **tt** are not as tall as the double letters **ll**.
- Ask the children to practise writing and joining the double letters on their whiteboards.
- Read the words in section B. Tell the children to copy the double letters and the words into their books.

Extra

- Read the sentences, choosing the correct word to make sense in the context.
- Model writing the first sentence on the board.
- Ask the children to copy the sentences into their books.

Extension

- Tell the children to read and copy the passage.
- Ask them to underline all the words with double letters.
- Check that the double letters are the correct height and consistent in size.

Resources and Assessment

Focus

More practice ensuring double letters are correct size and height. Copying words with double letters and their synonyms.

unit 15 Focus Resource Book 4 Nelson Handwriting

Name ______ Date ______

possibly allow carry difficult different
annoy offer possess accident marvellous
feel look sunny little necessary

Choose a word from above that has a similar meaning to each word in this list. Write the words next to each other. The first one is done to help you.

perhaps perhaps possibly
permit
touch
astonishing
hold
own
gaze
mishap
essential
small
bright
vex
hard
unusual
bargain

Practising writing double letters.

Nelson Handwriting Resources and Assessment Book 3 and Book 4 © Anita Warwick, Nelson Thornes Ltd. 2003

Extension

Poem provides further practice in writing fluently and writing double letters within words. Copying poem on to plain paper, using guidelines underneath.

unit 15 Extension Resource Book 4 Nelson Handwriting

Name ______ Date ______

A Copy this poem in the space provided. Make sure your letters are the correct height and size.

BURIED TREASURE
In the heart of the forest
Where feet rarely tread,
A treasure lies buried
In a soft earthy bed.

No jewels of a princess,
No coins of gold;
No silver once hoarded
By pirates of old.

What is this treasure?
One day we may see;
Till then it lies hidden –
The seed of a tree!

by Ronald Kay

B Underline the words in the poem that contain double letters, such as feet.

Practising writing double letters.

Nelson Handwriting Resources and Assessment Book 3 and Book 4 © Anita Warwick, Nelson Thornes Ltd. 2003

Assessment

- All double letters are the correct height and size.
- The double letters are consistently sized.
- All ascenders are as tall as capital letters except for **t**.

UNIT 16

Objectives

- To write quickly, neatly and fluently.
- To use abbreviations to help you write quickly.

Nelson theme – cliffs and treasure

UNIT 16

Practising speedwriting.

Quick! Write this down!

FOCUS

When speedwriting, it can be quicker to use a shorter word in place of the original word. These words are different ways of saying 'dig', 'buried' and 'box'. Copy them into your book as fast as you can.

(dig)	excavate	tunnel	investigate	probe
(buried)	entombed	hidden	immersed	covered
(box)	case	trunk	container	chest

EXTRA

These are quickly written notes about the location of some treasure. Write the directions out in full into your book. Make sure your handwriting is neat.

Wlk 6 stps nth of lghthse.
Tke 10 stps est.
Go cave.
Fllow undgrd tnnl.
X mrks spot.

EXTENSION

Copy these sentences into your book in speedwriting.

1 There is a steep cliff around the cove.
2 The treasure chest is under the rock.
3 There are gold coins in the box.
4 The pirates land on the beach.
5 They excavate beneath the rock
6 They find the treasure and carry it up the cliff.

Use the shortened forms of words (there's) and some different, shorter words (box, dig) if you think it will help you to write quickly.

Developing Skills

Focus

- Explain the lesson objectives to the class.
- Point out that when writing quickly, and when making notes, abbreviations can be used, as long as it is clear what they mean.
- Advise the children also to use shorter words, e.g. **dig** instead of **excavate**, for the sake of speed.
- Remind them to slant their writing slightly to the right, join their letters and leave a consistent space between letters and words.
- Sitting correctly, with the paper in the correct position, is also helpful.
- A good pen will also help writing to glide over the paper.
- Ask the children to practise writing the words as quickly as they can, making sure they are still neat and legible.

Extra

- Read the notes about the location of some treasure.
- Try to work out what the notes mean.
- Write the directions out neatly, using best handwriting.
- Remind the children that we use our best handwriting when we know someone else is going to read what we have written.

Extension

- Tell the class to read and then copy the sentences as quickly as they can.
- As no one else is going to read their notes, tell the children they can use abbreviations and they do not need to use their best handwriting. It must still be neat and legible though.

Resources and Assessment

Focus

Copying patterns and sentences quickly but legibly. Formula to find writing speed.

16 Focus Resource Book 4 Nelson Handwriting

Name ______ Date ______

A Practise writing these patterns on plain paper. Gradually increase your speed.

B Copy this sentence. Try to improve the smoothness of your writing as well as the speed.

Writing quickly helps me keep up with the teacher!

C Copy this sentence. Remember to move your hand at a steady speed with no jerky movements.

No matter how fast I write I must keep my writing steady!

D Find your writing speed. Divide the number of letters written by the number of minutes taken, like this:

$$\frac{\text{Number of letters written}}{\text{Number of minutes taken}} = \text{writing speed (in letters per minute)}$$

Record your score here.
My writing speed is ☐ letters per minute.

Practising speedwriting.

Nelson Handwriting Resources and Assessment Book 3 and Book 4 © Anita Warwick, Nelson Thomes Ltd, 2003

Extension

Further practise of patterns. Copying a list of words about treasure quickly but legibly.

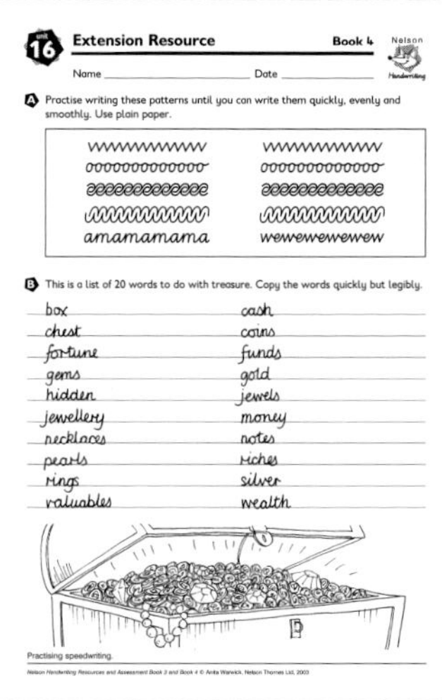

16 Extension Resource Book 4 Nelson Handwriting

Name ______ Date ______

A Practise writing these patterns until you can write them quickly, evenly and smoothly. Use plain paper.

amamamama wewewewewew

B This is a list of 20 words to do with treasure. Copy the words quickly but legibly.

box	cash
chest	coins
fortune	funds
gems	gold
hidden	jewels
jewellery	money
necklaces	notes
pearls	riches
rings	silver
valuables	wealth

Practising speedwriting.

Nelson Handwriting Resources and Assessment Book 3 and Book 4 © Anita Warwick, Nelson Thomes Ltd, 2003

Assessment

- The writing slopes slightly to the right.
- The letters are joined at, or near, the top of the next letter.
- Best handwriting is used for the final draft.

UNIT 17

Objectives

- To form letters the correct shape, height and size.
- To ensure tall letters are in correct proportion to small letters.

Nelson theme – cats

UNIT 17 Ensuring letters are in the correct proportion.

The cat was as quiet as a mouse.

FOCUS

Copy these similes into your book.

as quiet as a mouse
as hungry as a wolf
as fresh as a daisy
as brave as a lion

Remember, a descender, or tail, on a letter always falls below the line, like this: f g j p q y

EXTRA

Choose the correct word to finish these similes. Copy the similes into your book.

as steady as a... book/rock/jelly
as slow as a... hare/mouse/tortoise
as cold as... ice/custard/pasta
as green as... milk/a horse/grass

EXTENSION

Think of a simile to finish each sentence. Copy the sentences into your book. Make sure your letters are in the correct proportion to each other.

1 The cat was as quick as .
2 The dog was as cool as a
as the cat leapt towards him.
3 The cat's eyes sparkled like .
4 Mrs Smith's hat was as flat as
a after Tom sat on it!

Remember, the letter t is not as tall as other letters with an ascender.

38 39

Developing Skills

Focus

- Begin by reminding the class that letters need to be in correct proportion to each other.
- Write the whole class sentence on the board, explaining how capital letters and letters with ascenders (except **t**) are almost twice the height of small letters. Letters with descenders are the same size as letters with ascenders, but their descenders go below the baseline.
- Study and discuss the examples of similes.
- Model writing the similes on the board.
- Discuss the relative height of the letters, e.g. the letter **t** is not as tall as the other letters with ascenders; the letters **b**, **l**, **d**, **h** and **f** are all the same height.
- Ask the children to copy the similes into their books, making sure letters are in the correct proportion. (Use lined paper for lower-attaining groups and unlined for higher-attaining children.)

Extra

- Read the sentences, choosing a suitable word to complete each simile.
- Remind the children to keep their letters in proportion.
- Tell them to copy the sentences into their books.

Extension

- Read the sentences and decide on a suitable word to complete each similie.
- Ask the children to copy the sentences, ensuring letters are the correct shape, size and height.

Resources and Assessment

Focus

Choosing a word to complete each simile. Copying the completed similes neatly, ensuring letters are in correct proportion to each other.

17 Focus Resource Book 4 Nelson Handwriting

Name Date

lion bee snail mouse
owl ice rake peacock

Choose the correct word from above to complete each simile. Copy the completed similes neatly.

as slow as a
as thin as a
as wise as an
as proud as a
as busy as a
as cold as
as brave as a
as quiet as a

Ensuring letters are in the correct proportion

Extension

Copying similes, ensuring letters are in correct proportion. Matching sentences with similes.

17 Extension Resource Book 4 Nelson Handwriting

Name Date

A Copy these six similes neatly.

as cunning as a fox — as brown as a berry
as gentle as a lamb — as quick as lightning
as poor as a church mouse — as easy as winking

B Complete each of these sentences with a simile from above.

1 The beggar had no food and no money.
He was
2 I have never seen anyone move so fast.
She was
3 Sam is always playing clever tricks.
She is
4 The farmer works out in the sun all day.
He is
5 The sums we had to do were really simple.
They were
6 The nurse was very careful with my broken arm.
She was

Ensuring letters are in the correct proportion

Assessment

- Capital letters and letters with ascenders (except **t**) are the same height.
- The letter **t** is not as tall as other ascenders.
- Tall letters are almost twice the height of small letters.

UNIT 18

Objectives

- To take pride in presenting writing attractively.
- To use borders and/or a picture to decorate a poem.

Nelson theme – cats

UNIT 18

Practising presentation.

Presentation is Important

FOCUS

Copy this poem into your book. Make it look as attractive as you can.

MARMALADE
A ginger tom
name of Marmalade
shaved his whiskers
with a razor-blade

Last mistake
he ever made.

By *Roger McGough*

Remember,
it is easier to slope your letters to the right if you turn your paper at a slight angle and pull the pen strokes in the correct direction.

EXTRA

A kenning is a way of describing something without saying what it is.
This poem is a list of kennings. Copy it into your book.

A toe-nibbler
A dark-dreamer
A paw-padder
A floor-scratcher
A warm-sleeper
A night-creeper
A fur-cleaner
A flea-finder
A mouse-hunter
A house-minder
A secret-hoarder
A china-breaker
A four-foot-lander

'Cat' by *Rachel Myers*

Think about presentation. Plan where your poem will begin and end. Will you start your poem at the side of the page, or will you write it in the middle?

EXTENSION

Write your own poem about a kitten using kennings. Start by making some quick notes. Then write a first draft into your book. Use your best handwriting for the final copy.

Remember to add a border to decorate your poem.

Developing Skills

Focus

- This lesson will explore aspects of presentation.
- Study and discuss these suggestions:
  - writing on plain paper
  - leaving wide margins
  - adding flourishes
  - decorating the capitals
  - adding patterned borders
  - writing inside a shape
  - curving the lines of writing
- Explain that the emphasis of this unit is on the imaginative presentation of best handwriting.
- Read and discuss the poem. Ask for suggestions about how it might be presented. Where will you begin the poem? Will you begin at the side of the page?
- If you want to centre a poem, you need to work out where to begin writing; using a ruler can help.
- Encourage the children to copy and present this poem as attractively as they can in their best handwriting.

Extra

- Discuss what a kenning is (*a compound expression used in Old English and Norse poetry, which named something without using its name, e.g.* ***mouse catcher*** *=* ***cat****. A poem made of kennings would be a list of expressions about one subject.*)
- Read the kenning about a cat. Ask the children to think about how they would write this poem to make it look as attractive as possible. Would they place it in the middle of the page? Where will they start the writing? How far up/down the page? Will they add a border or illustration?
- Ask the children to copy the poem on plain paper, using guidelines underneath.

Extension

- Ask the children to write their own kennings poem.
- They will need to make some notes and then make a first draft of their poem.
- Next they will need to check spellings and edit their poem.
- Finally they will need to present their poem as attractively as possible on a piece of plain paper.
- The children should have a choice of writing tools for copying the poem.

Resources and Assessment

Focus

Copying an acrostic poem about cats, putting the lines in the correct order. Writing the poem on a piece of plain paper, setting it out as attractively as possible.

unit 18 **Focus Resource** **Book 4** Nelson Handwriting

Name ________________ Date ________

A Write the lines of this acrostic poem in the correct order.
The poem is called CATS.

Trying to catch mice,
Creeping about softly,
Scampering and squeaking.
Awake at night,

B Now write the poem neatly in the box below. Make it look as attractive as you can. Add a border.

Practising presentation.

Nelson Handwriting Resources and Assessment Book 3 and Book 4 © Anita Warwick, Nelson Thomes Ltd, 2003

Extension

Copying poem about cats, making it look as attractive as possible. Illustrating poem with a border and/ or picture.

unit 18 **Extension Resource** **Book 4** Nelson Handwriting

Name ________________ Date ________

Copy this poem on to plain paper. Make it look as attractive as you can.
Illustrate the poem with a picture or a border.

CATALOG
Cats sleep fat and walk thin.
Cats, when they sleep, slump;
When they wake, pull in –
And where the plump's been
There's skin.
Cats walk thin.

Cats wait in a lump,
Jump in a streak.
Cats, when they jump, are sleek
As a grape slipping its skin –
They have technique
Oh, cats don't creak,
They sneak.

By *Rosalie Moore*

Practising presentation.

Nelson Handwriting Resources and Assessment Book 3 and Book 4 © Anita Warwick, Nelson Thomes Ltd, 2003

Assessment

- A margin has been left around the poem.
- The writing is presented attractively.
- Best handwriting is used for the final draft.

UNIT 19

Objectives

- To revise the print letters.
- To use print letters when making a poster.

Spelling links

- short vowel words which double their final consonant before adding **ing**.

Nelson theme – travellers' tales

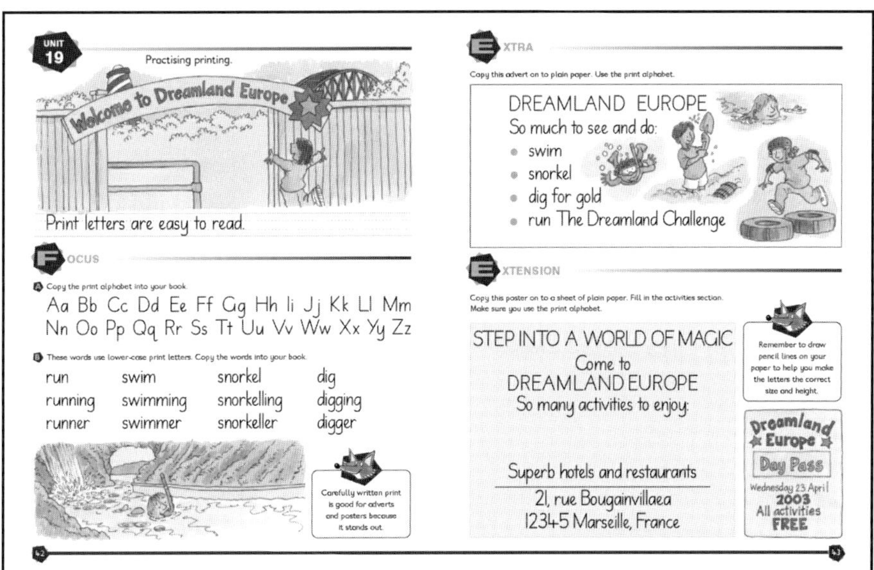

Unit 19

Practising printing.

Welcome to Dreamland Europe

Print letters are easy to read.

Focus

A Copy the print alphabet into your book.

Aa Bb Cc Dd Ee Ff Gg Hh Ii Jj Kk Ll Mm
Nn Oo Pp Qq Rr Ss Tt Uu Vv Ww Xx Yy Zz

B These words use lower-case print letters. Copy the words into your book.

run	swim	snorkel	dig
running	swimming	snorkelling	digging
runner	swimmer	snorkeller	digger

Carefully written print is good for adverts and posters because it stands out.

42

Extra

Copy this advert on to plain paper. Use the print alphabet.

DREAMLAND EUROPE
So much to see and do:
- swim
- snorkel
- dig for gold
- run The Dreamland Challenge

Extension

Copy this poster on to a sheet of plain paper. Fill in the activities section. Make sure you use the print alphabet.

STEP INTO A WORLD OF MAGIC
Come to
DREAMLAND EUROPE
So many activities to enjoy:

Superb hotels and restaurants
21, rue Bougainvillaea
12345 Marseille, France

Remember to draw pencil lines on your paper to help you make the letters the correct size and height.

Dreamland Europe
Day Pass
Wednesday 23 April 2003
All activities FREE

43

Developing Skills

Focus

- Explain that the lesson will focus on revising print letters.
- Remind the children that print letters are very plain, making them easy to read quickly.
- Model writing the lower-case print alphabet on the board.
- Ask the children to copy the lower-case print alphabet into their books.
- Discuss the words in section B. Can the class remember the spelling rule about final consonants?
- Point out that words ending in a single consonant preceded by a short vowel, double the final consonant before adding **ing**.
- Tell the children to copy the words into their books.

Extra

- Talk about the uses of print letters.
- Explain that carefully written print looks good on advertisements and posters.
- Ask the children to copy the advertisement onto plain paper.
- Point out that they will need to draw lines on plain paper to ensure letters are consistent in height and size.

Extension

- Ask the children to copy the poster using the print alphabet.

Resources and Assessment

Focus

Copying a fact sheet. Compiling new fact sheet based on information provided.

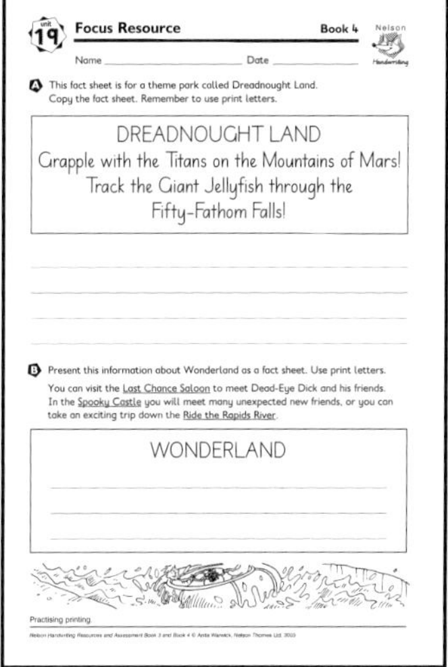

Unit 19 Focus Resource Book 4 Nelson Handwriting

Name ______ Date ______

A This fact sheet is for a theme park called Dreadnought Land. Copy the fact sheet. Remember to use print letters.

DREADNOUGHT LAND
Grapple with the Titans on the Mountains of Mars!
Track the Giant Jellyfish through the
Fifty-Fathom Falls!

B Present this information about Wonderland as a fact sheet. Use print letters.
You can visit the Last Chance Saloon to meet Dead-Eye Dick and his friends. In the Spooky Castle you will meet many unexpected new friends, or you can take an exciting trip down the Ride the Rapids River.

WONDERLAND

Practising printing

Extension

More practice printing letters, numerals and signs. Using print letters to copy a chart showing the prices of two-day breaks at Dreadnought theme park, in different hotels, in different months of the year. Completing and copying a sentence.

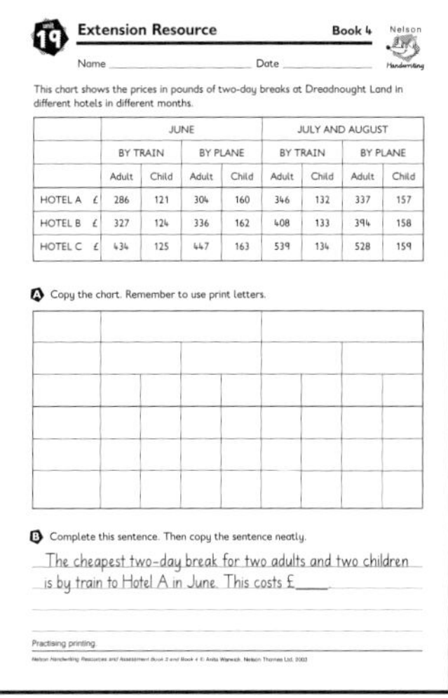

Unit 19 Extension Resource Book 4 Nelson Handwriting

Name ______ Date ______

This chart shows the prices in pounds of two-day breaks at Dreadnought Land in different hotels in different months.

	JUNE				JULY AND AUGUST			
	BY TRAIN		BY PLANE		BY TRAIN		BY PLANE	
	Adult	Child	Adult	Child	Adult	Child	Adult	Child
HOTEL A £	286	121	304	160	346	132	337	157
HOTEL B £	327	124	336	162	408	133	394	158
HOTEL C £	434	125	447	163	539	134	528	159

A Copy the chart. Remember to use print letters.

B Complete this sentence. Then copy the sentence neatly.

The cheapest two-day break for two adults and two children is by train to Hotel A in June. This costs £____

Practising printing

Assessment

- Lines drawn on plain paper to help write letters to the correct size.
- Print alphabet used correctly.
- Capital letters and small letters consistent in height and size.

NIT 20

Objectives

- To develop a personal writing style.
- To practise loops to speed up writing.

Nelson theme – travellers' tales

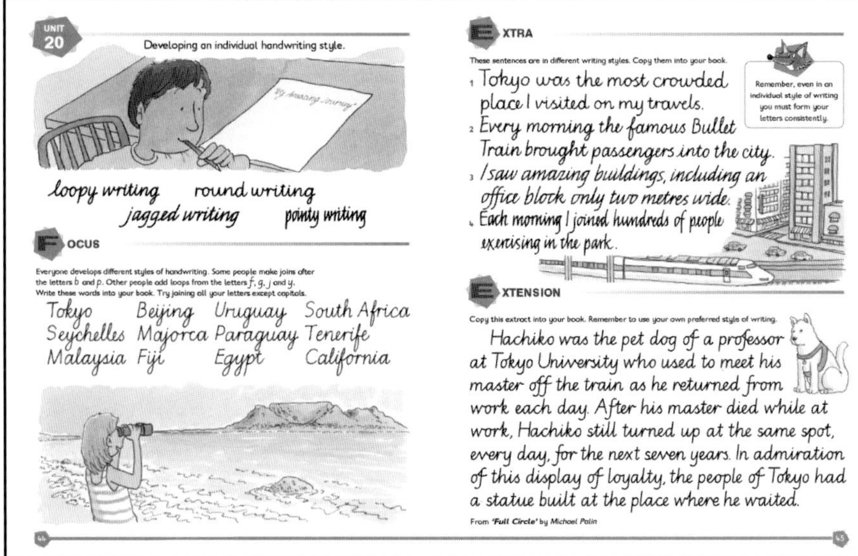

UNIT 20

Developing an individual handwriting style.

loopy writing round writing

jagged writing pointy writing

FOCUS

Everyone develops different styles of handwriting. Some people make joins after the letters b and p. Other people add loops from the letters f, g, j and y.
Write these words into your book. Try joining all your letters except capitals.

Tokyo Beijing Uruguay South Africa
Seychelles Majorca Paraguay Tenerife
Malaysia Fiji Egypt California

EXTRA

These sentences are in different writing styles. Copy them into your book.

1 Tokyo was the most crowded place I visited on my travels.
2 Every morning the famous Bullet Train brought passengers into the city.
3 I saw amazing buildings, including an office block only two metres wide.
4 Each morning I joined hundreds of people exercising in the park.

Remember, even in an individual style of writing you must form your letters consistently.

EXTENSION

Copy this extract into your book. Remember to use your own preferred style of writing.

Hachiko was the pet dog of a professor at Tokyo University who used to meet his master off the train as he returned from work each day. After his master died while at work, Hachiko still turned up at the same spot, every day, for the next seven years. In admiration of this display of loyalty, the people of Tokyo had a statue built at the place where he waited.

From *'Full Circle'* by *Michael Palin*

Developing Skills

Focus

- Explain to the children that the objective of this lesson is to build on all that has been learned using *Nelson Handwriting* to develop a personal style of writing.
- Point out that legibility and fluency are very important when writing in a personal style.
- Explain that although you have practised **b**, **g**, **j**, **p** and **y** as break letters, you can join them.
- Model joining the letters **b** and **p**, and looping **f**, **g**, **j** and **y**.
- Point out that adding loops to your writing can help you write even more quickly as you do not have to lift your pen off the page.
- Demonstrate by writing some of the words on the board.
- Show where you loop the **y** (near the base of the x-height of the letter, *not* at the bottom of the descender).
- There is more than one way of adding a loop to the letter **f**. Demonstrate to the children and encourage them to practise on their whiteboards.
- Tell the children to copy the words into their books

Extra

- Ask the class to copy the sentences using different handwriting styles.
- In one sentence they may just want to join the letters **b** and **p**, and write the remaining letters in Nelson Script. In another, they may want to loop letters like **f** and **g**, etc.
- Finally they may want to write one sentence joining all the letters. Ask them which style of writing they prefer, and why.
- Point out that to develop an individual style takes practice. Whichever style is chosen, it is very important that letters are formed and joined using a consistent approach, i.e. letters are consistent in height, shape, size and the way they are joined.

Extension

- Tell the children to copy the extract using their preferred style of writing.

Resources and Assessment

Focus

More practice developing an individual style. Practising writing poem using looped joins.

20 Focus Resource Book 4 Nelson Handwriting

Name ______ Date ______

Some people develop their handwriting style by adding loops to **f**, **g**, **j** and **y** and joining **b**, **p** and **q**, like this:

f g j y b p q

Copy this poem. Make a join after **b** and **p** and a loop from **f**, **g**, and **j**.

LOST
In a terrible fog I once lost my way,
Where I had wandered I could not say,
I found a signpost just by a fence,
But I could not read it, the fog was so dense.
Slowly but surely, frightened to roam,
I climbed up the post for my nearest way home,
Striking a match, I turned cold and faint,
These were the words on it: 'Mind the wet paint'.

By *James Godden*

Developing an individual handwriting style.

Extension

Further practice with joins after **p** and **b**, as well as words with looped joins.

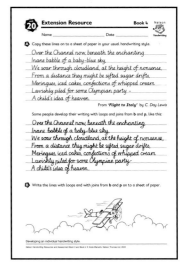

20 Extension Resource Book 4 Nelson Handwriting

Name ______ Date ______

A Copy these lines on to a sheet of paper in your usual handwriting style.

Over the Channel now, beneath the enchanting
Inane babble of a baby-blue sky,
We soar through cloudland, at the height of nonsense,
From a distance they might be sifted sugar drifts,
Meringues, iced cakes, confections of whipped cream
Lavishly piled for some Olympian party –
A child's idea of heaven.

From **'Flight to Italy'** by C. Day Lewis

Some people develop their writing with loops and joins from **b** and **p**, like this:

Over the Channel now, beneath the enchanting
Inane babble of a baby-blue sky,
We soar through cloudland, at the height of nonsense,
From a distance they might be sifted sugar drifts,
Meringues, iced cakes, confections of whipped cream
Lavishly piled for some Olympian party –
A child's idea of heaven.

B Write the lines with loops and with joins from **b** and **p** on to a sheet of paper.

Developing an individual handwriting style.

Assessment

- All loops are formed correctly.
- The letters are of consistent height and size..
- All joins are made consistently.

HECK-UP

Objectives

Explain to the pupils that this exercise is an assessment activity. The objective is to assess what the pupils can do and where they need extra practice. This exercise will help assess each pupil's ability to form and use the four handwriting joins, and their handwriting speed. Ask pupils to look at the checklist on the back of the flap to remind themselves of the important points.

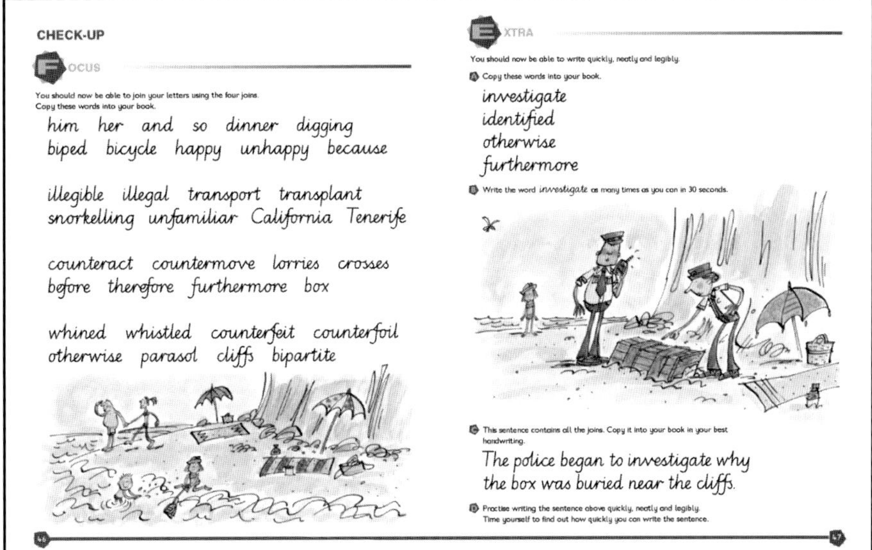

CHECK-UP

FOCUS

You should now be able to join your letters using the four joins.
Copy these words into your book.

him her and so dinner digging
biped bicycle happy unhappy because

illegible illegal transport transplant
snorkelling unfamiliar California Tenerife

counteract countermove lorries crosses
before therefore furthermore box

whined whistled counterfeit counterfoil
otherwise parasol cliffs bipartite

46

EXTRA

You should now be able to write quickly, neatly and legibly.

A Copy these words into your book.

investigate
identified
otherwise
furthermore

B Write the word *investigate* as many times as you can in 30 seconds.

C This sentence contains all the joins. Copy it into your book in your best handwriting.

The police began to investigate why
the box was buried near the cliffs.

D Practise writing the sentence above quickly, neatly and legibly.
Time yourself to find out how quickly you can write the sentence.

47

EXTENSION

Copy this poem on to plain paper. Use guidelines underneath.
Set the poem out carefully and neatly, remembering all you have learnt about presenting your work.

Marbles in my pocket,
Blue and green and red,
And some are yellow-golden,
And some are brown instead.

Marbles in the playground,
Big and little ring –
Oh, I like playing marbles,
But that's a different thing.

Marbles in my pocket,
Smooth within my hand,
That's the part that's nicest;
Do you understand?

Marbles in my pocket
To rattle when I run!
For winter days are here again,
And marble-time's begun!

From '**Marbles in my Pocket**' by *Lydia Pender*

48

Focus

Ask the pupils to copy the words into their books. The letter shapes should be the correct height, and there should be consistent spacing between the letters and words. The handwriting should also have a consistent slope.

Extra

Ask the pupils to copy the words and sentence into their books. The sentence contains all four handwriting joins. Ask the pupils to follow the instructions about timing their handwriting to develop speed while maintaining legibility.

Extension

Ask the pupils to copy the poem into their book. The poem contains a mixture of capital and lowercase letters and a variety of punctuation marks.

Assessment

- Do all letters join apart from break and capital letters?
- Are the correct joins used?
- Are the letters well shaped and clear?
- Are letters consistent in size and proportion?
- Are any letters too tall or too short?
- Does the handwriting have a consistent slope?
- Are the capital letters the correct height and size?

- For more Assessment see *Resources and Assessment Book 3 and Book 4*